Reflections on 1989 in Eastern Europe

This book presents a selection of recent research on the events and developments of 1989 in Eastern Europe. It offers a mix of detailed examinations of the events of 1989 in Eastern Europe, thoughtful and considered appraisals of developments, and 'middle-range' theoretical discussions of patterns of cause and effect. The authors range in their approaches from detailed examinations of government and ruling-party papers from the archives, some of it originally labelled top secret, to personal observations and oral history based on interviews with participants, to analysis of survey data and official statistics. In their chosen focus the essays range from explorations of the emerging crisis in the communist regimes that led to the events of 1989, reflections and insights into the events and changing mood during 1989 itself, and examinations of some of the consequences and legacies of 1989.

This book was published as a special issue of *Europe-Asia Studies.*

Terry Cox is Professor of Central and East European Studies at the University of Glasgow, and Editor of the journal *Europe-Asia Studies*. His recent research has focused on the politics and sociology of post-communist transformations in East Central Europe, including work on civil society and the politics of interest representation.

Routledge Europe-Asia Studies Series
A series edited by Terry Cox, University of Glasgow

The **Routledge Europe-Asia Studies Series** focuses on the history and current political, social and economic affairs of the countries of the former 'communist bloc' of the Soviet Union, Eastern Europe and Asia. As well as providing contemporary analyses it explores the economic, political and social transformation of these countries and the changing character of their relationships with the rest of Europe and Asia.

Challenging Communism in Eastern Europe
1956 and its Legacy
Edited by Terry Cox

Globalisation, Freedom and the Media after Communism
The Past as Future
Edited by Birgit Beumers, Stephen Hutchings and Natalia Rulyova

Power and Policy in Putin's Russia
Edited by Richard Sakwa

1948 and 1968 – Dramatic Milestones in Czech and Slovak History
Edited by Laura Cashman

Perceptions of the European Union in New Member States
A Comparative Perspective
Edited by Gabriella Ilonszki

Symbolism and Power in Central Asia
Politics of the Spectacular
Edited by Sally N. Cummings

The European Union, Russia and the Shared Neighbourhood
Edited by Jackie Gower and Graham Timmins

Russian Regional Politics under Putin and Medvedev
Edited by Cameron Ross

Russia's Authoritarian Elections
Edited by Stephen White

Elites and Identities in Post-Soviet Space
Edited by David Lane

EU Conditionality in the Western Balkans
Edited by Florian Bieber

Reflections on 1989 in Eastern Europe
Edited by Terry Cox

Reflections on 1989 in Eastern Europe

Edited by
Terry Cox

Routledge
Taylor & Francis Group
LONDON AND NEW YORK

University of Glasgow

First published 2013
by Routledge
2 Park Square, Milton Park, Abingdon, Oxfordshire OX14 4RN

Simultaneously published in the USA and Canada
by Routledge
711 Third Avenue, New York, NY 10017

First issued in paperback 2015

Routledge is an imprint of the Taylor & Francis Group, an informa business

This book is a reproduction of *Europe-Asia Studies*, vol. 63, issue 9. The Publisher requests to those authors who may be citing this book to state, also, the bibliographical details of the special issue on which the book was based.

British Library Cataloguing in Publication Data
A catalogue record for this book is available from the British Library

ISBN 13: 978-1-138-94573-9 (pbk)
ISBN 13: 978-0-415-63603-2 (hbk)

Typeset in Times New Roman
by Taylor & Francis Books

Publisher's Note
The publisher would like to make readers aware that the chapters in this book may be referred to as articles as they are identical to the articles published in the special issue. The publisher accepts responsibility for any inconsistencies that may have arisen in the course of preparing this volume for print.

Contents

Citation Information

The chapters in this book were originally published in *Europe-Asia Studies*, volume 63, issue 9 (November 2011). When citing this material, please use the original page numbering for each article, as follows:

Chapter 1
1989 and the Transformations in Eastern Europe
Terry Cox
Europe-Asia Studies, volume 63, issue 9 (November 2011) pp. 1529-1534

Chapter 2
The Demise of the Soviet Bloc
Mark Kramer
Europe-Asia Studies, volume 63, issue 9 (November 2011) pp. 1535-1590

Chapter 3
Welfare Dictatorship, the Working Class and the Change of Regimes in East Germany and Hungary
Eszter Bartha
Europe-Asia Studies, volume 63, issue 9 (November 2011) pp. 1591-1610

Chapter 4
New Life: The Poetics of Transition
George Szirtes
Europe-Asia Studies, volume 63, issue 9 (November 2011) pp. 1611-1626

Chapter 5
The Picnic on the Border: An Interview with László Vass
Terry Cox
Europe-Asia Studies, volume 63, issue 9 (November 2011) pp. 1627-1638

Chapter 6
Three Days in Bucharest: Making Sense of Romania's Transitional Violence, 20 Years On
John Gledhill
Europe-Asia Studies, volume 63, issue 9 (November 2011) pp. 1639-1670

Chapter 7
A Post-Socialist Capitalism
Nigel Swain
Europe-Asia Studies, volume 63, issue 9 (November 2011) pp. 1671-1696

Chapter 8
After the Party, the After-Parties? The Effects of Communist Successor Parties on Economic Reform in Central and Eastern Europe
Aleksandra Sznajder Lee
Europe-Asia Studies, volume 63, issue 9 (November 2011) pp. 1697-1718

Chapter 9
Satisfied, Sceptical or Simply Indifferent? Current Public Opinion towards the Fall of Communism in the Czech Republic
Pat Lyons & Alžběta Bernardyová
Europe-Asia Studies, volume 63, issue 9 (November 2011) pp. 1719-1744

Chapter 10
Evaluating Transitions: Human Rights and Qualitative Democracy in Central and Eastern Europe
Brad K. Blitz
Europe-Asia Studies, volume 63, issue 9 (November 2011) pp. 1745-1770

List of Contributors

Eszter Bartha is an Assistant Professor in the Department of Eastern European History at the Eotvos Lorand University in Budapest. She received her PhD in the Comparative History of Central, Southeastern and Eastern Europe from the Central European University in Budapest in 2007. With research interests focusing primarily on the history of communism, her current work examines and re-evaluates social changes in Europe in the 20th century, socialist dictatorships and the causes and consequences of changes of systems in Central and Eastern Europe from 1989–1990. Her forthcoming book, *Alienating Labor: Workers on the Road from Socialism to Capitalism in East Germany and Hungary* examines the relationship between the party and the working class in the last, declining phase of state socialism.

Alžběta Bernardyova holds degrees in American Studies and Security Policy from Charles University, Prague. Her main areas of research are US domestic security and intelligence post-9/11. She currently works as a programme coordinator with Radio Free Europe/ Radio Liberty (RFE/RL) in Prague.

Brad K. Blitz received his PhD from Stanford University and is currently Professor of Human and Political Geography at Kingston University London. A former Jean Monnet Chair and Research Associate in the Department of International Development, University of Oxford, he has published widely on issues of transition in East Central Europe. Recent publications include *Statelessness in the European Union: Displaced, Undocumented and Unwanted* (with Caroline Sawyer, Cambridge University Press, 2011) and *Statelessness and Citizenship: A Comparative Study on the Benefits of Nationality* (with Maureen Lynch, Edward Elgar Publishing, 2011). He is currently completing a four-country US State Department funded project 'Measuring the Costs of Statelessness'.

Terry Cox is Professor of Central and East European Studies at the University of Glasgow. His research interests are in the general area of the political sociology of post-communist transformations. His recent publications include: *Challenging Communism in Eastern Europe: 1956 and its Legacy* (Routledge, 2008); and *Reinventing Poland: Economic and Political Transformation and Changing National Identity* (with Martin Myant, Routledge, 2008).

John Gledhill is a Departmental Lecturer in the Department of International Development, University of Oxford. He was previously an LSE Fellow in Global Politics at the London School of Economics and has taught at Georgetown and George

Washington Universities. His works on issues of regime transition, conflict and transitional justice in Central and Eastern Europe have appeared in journals such as *Nationalities Papers, East European Politics & Societies* and *Sfera Politicii*, as well as several edited volumes.

Mark Kramer is Director of the Cold War Studies Program at Harvard University and a Senior Fellow of Harvard's Davis Center for Russian and Eurasian Studies. His latest book, *Crisis, Compromise, and Coercion in the Communist World, 1956: The Soviet Union, the Warsaw Pact, and Upheavals in Poland and Hungary,* will be published in 2012.

Pat Lyons holds degrees in history, sociology and European integration and has a PhD in Political Science from Trinity College, Dublin. He is currently a Senior Researcher at the Department of Political Sociology, Institute of Sociology, Czech Academy of Sciences. His main areas of research are public opinion, political attitudes, electoral and legislative behaviour and party politics. He has published two books and a number of articles.

Nigel Swain is a Lecturer in History in the School of Histories, Languages and Cultures at the University of Liverpool. He is author of *Collective Farms Which Work?* (Cambridge University Press, 1985), *Hungary: theRise and Fall of Feasible Socialism* (Verso, 1992), and, with Geoffrey Swain, *Eastern Europe since 1945* (Palgrave Macmillan, 1993, 1998, 2003, 2009). He has recently completed a study of the decollectivisation of agriculture in the 1990s in post-socialist Central Europe and the Balkans and is currently working on a study of the origins of Hungary's restitution and co-operative transformation legislation.

George Szirtes is a Hungarian-born poet. He moved to England at the age of eight in 1956 as a refugee from the uprising of 1956 and is the author or translator of some thirty books. Best known for his poetry, he won the Faber memorial prize with his first book of poems in 1979 and the T. S. Eliot Prize with his twelfth, *Reel* (Bloodaxe, 2004). His *New and Collected Poems* (Bloodaxe) appeared in 2008 and he was shortlisted again for the T. S. Eliot Prize with *The Burning of the Books* (Full Circle Editions) in 2009. He teaches at the University of East Anglia.

Aleksandra Sznajder Lee is Assistant Professor of Political Science at the University of Richmond. Her research interests pertain to the political economy of post-communist transitions, including industrial restructuring, state capacity and industrial relations. Her work appears in *American Journal of Sociology, Studies in Comparative International Development, Industrielle Beziehungen* (*German Journal of Industrial Relations*), among others. She received her PhD in political science from Yale University and was a postdoctoral fellow at the Harriman Institute at Columbia University.

László Vass is Professor and Rector at the Budapest College of Communication and Business. He has also been Associate Professor at the Political Science Institute of Budapest Corvinus University, where he was Vice Dean of the Faculty of Social Sciences. His research interests are in interest group politics, public policy and public management. He was president of the Network of Institutes and Schools of Public Administration and Public Policy in Central and Eastern Europe (NISPAcee) in 2004–2006. He is a member of the Accreditation Committee of the European Association for Public Administration Accreditation.

1989 and the Transformations in Eastern Europe

TERRY COX

IN THE FIRST DECADE AFTER THE REGIME CHANGES that brought an end to communist rule in Eastern Europe, a central focus of academic writing on the events of 1989 was a theoretical debate on the significance and character of the changes. Among the issues raised were the question of whether they should be understood as revolutions, or as a hybrid of reforms and revolutions, whether they marked a shift from traditional to modern society, or a transition from state socialism to capitalism, or from totalitarianism to liberal democracy, or some more nuanced form of transformation. On the whole, the debate made a significant contribution to our understanding of the complexity of the issues involved in the changes taking place in Eastern Europe and helped to bring a focus on the region into the mainstream of comparative social and political research.

In contrast, much of the academic work on 1989 that has been produced in the period around its 20th anniversary has adopted a more cautious attitude to the big issues and a more detailed focus on empirical enquiry. This shift in focus is reflected in the essays collected here, which provide detailed examinations, thoughtful and considered appraisals of developments, and 'middle-range' theoretical discussions of patterns of cause and effect. The authors range in their approaches from detailed examinations of government and ruling-party papers from the archives, some of it originally labelled top secret, to oral history based on interviews with participants, to analysis of survey data and official statistics. In their chosen focus the essays range from explorations of the emerging crisis in the communist regimes that led to the events of 1989, reflections and insights into the events and changing mood during 1989 itself, and examinations of some of the consequences and legacies of 1989.

The period between the establishment of the communist regimes in Eastern Europe in the late 1940s and their demise in 1989 can be seen as a long struggle by communist ruling elites to create the conditions for social stability and popular legitimacy in increasingly unfavourable circumstances.[1] Communist rule depended initially on three conditions: the external power and influence of the Soviet Union; the use by East

[1]For deeper discussion and detailed accounts of the issues mentioned in this essay, see, for example, Batt (1991), Berend (1996), Cox and Mason (1999), Pittaway (2004), Swain and Swain (2003), Tismaneanu (1999) and Verdery (1996).

European communist leaderships of coercion and surveillance against the population and even members of their own communist movements; and the social and economic exhaustion of their societies after the ravages of World War II. After a period of severe repression and grim austerity in the late 1940s and early 1950s, the foundations of the regimes were threatened by deep social unrest, reflected most overtly in protests and demonstrations in East Germany in 1953, in Poland in 1956, and culminating in the Hungarian Revolution of 1956. All of these challenges were overcome only by repressive measures with the backing and intervention of the Soviet Union.

Thereafter, from the late 1950s, communist leaderships attempted to establish a greater degree of legitimacy by improving living standards, at least for the 'core' skilled industrial workforce. However, the accommodation between regime and population remained fragile, especially since it was based on a contradiction between consumer demands and the inherent biases of the 'planned' economy that gave priority to investment for growth at the expense of domestic consumption. Increasingly, living standards could only be maintained by tacit acceptance of an informal and semi-legal (or sometimes illegal) economy of favours, or as in the case of Hungary after 1968, limited encouragement of market relations on a small scale outside the planned economy.

From the late 1960s or early 1970s in different countries in the region, the implicit 'deal' became more unstable as the planned economy reached the limits of extensive expansion and both labour productivity and the rate of innovation declined. Increasingly governments in the region turned to an accommodation with the West that involved taking out Western loans to boost the economy. This rested on an assumption that the resulting investment would generate expanded production of goods for export which would, in turn, produce income for the repayment of the loans. However, by the end of the 1970s, this strategy foundered on the downturn of the Western economies and increasing international energy prices.

Although the growing indebtedness of their economies was hidden from the people in the 1980s they became increasingly discontented nevertheless with the continuing problems of shortages of consumer goods and poor public services, and varying in degree between different countries, further austerity measures as the economies weakened further. In some countries, Poland and Romania in particular, although in different ways, there was an upsurge of working-class protest, to be met in turn by repression. In other countries the regimes were able to keep discontent in check by a mixture of repression and further tolerance of the shadow economy based on an economy of favours. In Hungary the response of the Kádár regime was to extend official tolerance of elements of a market economy and private ownership, and from the mid-1980s, limited democratising reforms that in some ways foreshadowed Gorbachev's political reforms in the Soviet Union a few years later.

Also, in the 1980s, alongside the growing economic and political problems faced by the communist regimes, significant changes in political culture were also becoming apparent. While working-class protests in Poland and Romania were indicative of a loss of legitimacy by the regimes among their core support group, attitudes among the intelligentsia throughout Eastern Europe were shifting away from ideas of a third way based on reforms of the state socialist system. While economists were becoming attracted to Friedmanite ideas and Reaganite or Thatcherite economic policies, attention more generally turned towards ways of promoting civil society beyond the scope of the regime, towards environmental politics, and also in a wide range of different ways towards nationalism. While in most countries nationalism found common cause with the emerging democratic opposition movements, in Serbia, and to some extent in Romania and Bulgaria, it became a tool to establish a new basis of legitimacy for the regime.

Into this increasingly fragile situation for the East European regimes came Mikhail Gorbachev and a new Soviet foreign policy that removed the constraints on change that had been enforced by previous Soviet regimes. Soviet acceptance of reforms that entailed the dilution or even collapse of the East European communist regimes was itself a key factor contributing to the changes of 1989. However, as events developed during that year it was not clear to the leading participants quite how far they could pursue an independent path. This lent a very distinctive atmosphere to the way developments were experienced during 1989 as government leaders experimented with new initiatives and opposition leaders tested the boundaries of what might be permitted. There was a mixture of emotions as participants experienced surprise and joy as new opportunities opened up, mixed with anxiety and concern over whether their actions would provoke a negative reaction. In this way, while the changes in each country had their own specific national characteristics, their pace and scale were largely shaped by the gradual discovery of what was becoming possible.

With surprising rapidity, by 1989 'capitalism' and 'democracy' had become the new slogans of most policy makers and the opposition. On the one hand these slogans reflected the defeat of the old ruling communist parties and the breakup of the old institutional framework within which their rule was conducted; on the other hand they signalled the broad social aims of new ruling elites as they pursued their projects to construct new institutional frameworks. However, the new frameworks could not simply be created within a social vacuum. They had to be negotiated through a process of transformation that reflected the constraints created by the different paths of development each society had followed since the 1940s. The different sources of power and influence, and the range of different social interests that had developed within each society during the communist period, would survive in modified form into the period of the new regimes. In each country therefore, the period of transformation in the 1990s continued to be concerned not only with questions of finding the right policies to restructure the economy, but with the competition between different interests and with ways in which elites would attempt to accommodate or deflect them.

During the first half of the 1990s, the economies of all the countries of Central and Eastern Europe shared similar experiences of a 'transition recession' that resulted from the development of a market economy. However, the duration and depth of that crisis varied considerably from country to country, with differing consequences for changing social patterns. While the Central European economies experienced shorter recessions and began to recover in the mid-1990s, the decline continued in Eastern Europe until later in the decade. The decline in output had severe consequences for the income of the population. Following the end of communist rule, the new political leaders hoped to introduce economic reforms while avoiding any significant decrease in the standard of living and social security of the industrial working class or the majority of the population in general. In general, governments were concerned, at the very least, to try and avoid alienating any substantial proportion of the population through the creation of high levels of poverty and unemployment. In practice, however, economic transformation resulted in both a decline in national income and the growth of income inequalities. While some sections of the old regime *nomenklatura* sought to transform their previous power and authority into the ownership of wealth, and new market economies allowed new economic classes of entrepreneurs and private sector managers to emerge, at the other end of the scale increasing numbers of people slipped into poverty.

Thus, transformation has taken a range of different forms and has posed serious political dilemmas for governments in Central and Eastern Europe in balancing the need to implement effective economic reforms against the problems of increasing inequalities, unemployment and poverty, and the increased popular discontent such problems could provoke. Governments in each country in the region have had very difficult balancing acts to perform. On the one hand, in the eyes of liberal reformers and business interests, the continuing extension of economic transition could not be delayed. Even after a significant amount of the ownership of capital had been formally transferred to private interests, it was argued that it was still necessary to further limit the role of the state in economic management and to reduce state expenditure on social welfare and pensions. The conditions of EU membership also required further liberalisation of the economy. On the other hand, although the economic policy agenda created pressures for austerity measures and cuts in the provision of social services, successive governments were afraid to fully implement these for fear of losing electoral support. Furthermore such conflicting views of economic policy have become interwoven with the basic post-socialist cleavage between, on the one hand, the reformed socialist parties that have developed out of the reform wings of the former ruling communist parties, and on the other hand, parties that have emerged from opposition movements that emerged in the last years of the old regime. While the former are often referred to as the 'left' and the latter as the 'right', in practice it is often the left that pursues more of a neoliberal political agenda than the 'right'.

A number of the key aspects of this complex story are explored by the essays collected here. The first two pieces deal with different aspects of the developments leading up to the momentous events of 1989. In the first contribution, Mark Kramer offers important insights, drawing in meticulous detail on a wealth of recently released archival material, into how the events of 1989 resulted in part from sweeping changes in Soviet policy, in part from the courageous actions of Eastern European citizens, and in part from the loss of will among East European communist leaders as they realised that the USSR would no longer come to their aid. He also shows how the rapidly improving state of East–West relations was an important backdrop. Kramer examines each of these sources of change in Eastern Europe, highlighting the interaction between them.

This is followed by an essay by Eszter Bartha which focuses on the experience of 1989 from the perspective of the industrial working class in the German Democratic Republic and Hungary. It argues that an examination of the communist parties' policy towards the working class helps to provide an important key to the understanding of the collapse of the regimes. The socialist regimes, she argues, turned into 'welfare dictatorships' that sought to win over the 'masses' with the promise of providing for ever-increasing levels of consumption. This policy—although successful at the beginning—in the long run proved to be detrimental for the regime because it shifted working-class political consciousness to the right while it effectively excluded leftist alternatives from the public sphere. By 1989 this meant that any influential constituency representing a socialist alternative to the adoption of liberal capitalism had effectively disappeared.

In the next two contributions attention turns to aspects of the atmosphere and events of 1989 itself. The first essay, by George Szirtes, offers an appreciation, through the lens of poetry, of the complex moods and experiences of living through 1989 in Budapest, and the complex encounters with new ideas and new relationships that emerged in conjunction with the political changes. The essay reflects the first-hand experiences of the author who was living in Budapest during that year. The essay was first delivered to an enraptured audience as the keynote lecture of the 2009 annual conference of the British Association of Slavonic and East European Studies.

A first-hand experience of a different kind is presented in the following piece in the form of an interview by the editor with László Vass who was a leading participant in the 'Picnic on the Border' in August 1989. Predating the fall of the Berlin Wall by a few months, the Picnic was the first occasion on which citizens of East Germany were able to pass through the Iron Curtain into the West. Vass's reminiscences provide an insight into the tentative and exploratory nature of the tactics adopted by a leading reformer such as Imre Pozsgay during 1989, and the unanticipated and often confused character of the events that occurred.

This is followed by an essay in which John Gledhill provides a detailed examination of the events that constituted the crucial phase in Romania's very distinctive political transition from communist rule. Beginning at the very end of 1989 with the violent overthrow of Nicolae Ceauşescu, initial pressure for further democratisation was frustrated by sections of the old elite who formed the National Salvation Front and won power in the elections of June 1990. The essay revisits the violent events that took place in Bucharest in June 1990 just after the elections. Drawing on newly available documents and interviews with key actors, the author argues that the violence was a by-product of competition between state security services (police, military and secret police) for power and resources in the emerging regime. That competition underwrote the outbreak of violence in Bucharest on 13 June, the mobilisation of miners for a descent on the capital, and the secret services' subsequent co-optation of the miners for attacks on those who had expressed opposition to Ion Iliescu's post-revolution political order.

The final group of contributions then explore different aspects of the impact, consequences and legacies of 1989 in post-communist Eastern Europe. First in this group, Nigel Swain provides an overview and discussion of some of the main political, social and economic developments across the region in the two decades following 1989. Both the economic and the political transformations, he argues, were distinctly radical and without precedent: creating capitalism 'out of a developed, highly articulated socio-economic entity dominated by political structures that had challenged the West with some success for a number decades ... was a step into the unknown'. Swain attempts to identify the development and key characteristics of the emerging post-socialist capitalism that have taken shape so far and to explore some of their implications for comparative social science.

This is followed by an investigation by Aleksandra Sznajder Lee of the economic reform effects of ex-communist parties in Central and Eastern Europe, using quantitative analysis of panel data collected for 10 new EU member states over the period 1991–2007. Testing hypotheses focusing on concepts of power conversion, partial reform and path dependence, the essay examines the impact of the communist successor parties on liberal economic reform in Central and Eastern Europe when they were in power. Offering insights into the complex patterns of political cleavages around the making of economic policy, the essay distinguishes communist successor parties that underwent substantial internal restructuring in a social-democratic direction early in the transition period, and those that did not.

The next essay by Pat Lyons and Alžbeta Bernardyová contributes to the theme of the politics of memory of 1989. Specifically, it explores contemporary public opinion in the Czech Republic toward the Velvet Revolution. A model of public opinion toward the events of 1989 is used to explore three key questions: who do the public think provided the lead in the fall of communism? What were the primary motivations? And why did this event occur? The evidence presented demonstrates first, that there is no single opinion toward the Velvet Revolution, and second, that differences among Czech citizens towards the fall of communism may be explained in terms of economic, political and informational criteria.

Finally, Brad Blitz contributes to debates about the character and quality of democratic consolidation in the years since 1989. While the countries of East Central Europe are generally seen in the literature as the clearest examples of full and effective democratic consolidation among the formerly communist-ruled countries, Blitz argues for a more nuanced view. Procedural accounts of democratic consolidation, he suggests, underestimate the degree to which normative developments are institutionalised in domestic human-rights enforcing bodies, including courts and the police. To examine the degree to which human rights have been institutionalised in Slovakia and Slovenia, he introduces the notion of 'qualitative democracy', which is examined in the context of the judiciary's capacity to address complaints in Slovenia, and the degree to which the authorities have been able to protect the rights of Roma minorities in Slovakia. The observed lack of effective enforcement of human rights, he concludes, undermines claims of consolidation and supports calls for more qualitative assessment of state practices.

University of Glasgow

References

Batt, J. (1991) *East Central Europe from Reform to Transformation* (London, Pinter).
Berend, I. (1996) *Central and Eastern Europe 1944–1993* (Cambridge, Cambridge University Press).
Cox, T. & Mason, B. (1999) *Social and Economic Transformation in East Central Europe: Institutions, Property Relations and Social Interests* (London & Geneva, Edward Elgar & UNRISD).
Pittaway, M. (2004) *Eastern Europe 1939–2000* (London, Arnold).
Swain, G. & Swain, N. (2003) *Eastern Europe Since 1945* (Basingstoke, Palgrave Macmillan).
Tismaneanu, V. (ed.) (1999) *The Revolutions of 1989* (London, Routledge).
Verdery, K. (1996) *What Was Socialism and What Comes Next?* (Princeton, NJ, Princeton University Press).

The Demise of the Soviet Bloc

MARK KRAMER

IN THE MID-1980s, JUST BEFORE MIKHAIL GORBACHEV became General Secretary of the Communist Party of the Soviet Union (CPSU), the East–West divide in Europe seemed as stark as ever. Both the Warsaw Pact and the North Atlantic Treaty Organization (NATO) had deployed new nuclear missiles against each other, and tensions between the two sides were acute. Certainly no one expected that, before the decade was out, the communist regimes in East–Central Europe would collapse peacefully (apart from violence in Romania) and that the Berlin Wall—the symbolic divide in Europe for nearly 30 years—would be opened.

The momentous events of 1989 led to drastic changes in the political complexion of Eastern Europe and the end of the Cold War. In the mid-to-late 1940s, communist governments had taken power throughout the region under Soviet auspices. For more than 40 years, those governments dominated political and economic life in Eastern Europe. The sudden downfall of the communist regimes in 1989 and the opening of the Berlin Wall are sometimes depicted as the inevitable result of a lengthy process of systemic decay, but in fact there was nothing inevitable about the outcome. Popular opposition to the communist regimes had long been intense almost everywhere in Eastern Europe, as demonstrated by the uprisings in Czechoslovakia and the German Democratic Republic (GDR) in June 1953, the rebellions in Poland and Hungary in June and October 1956, the public acclaim for the Prague Spring in 1968, and the rise of Solidarity (*Solidarność*), which was both a free trade union and a social movement, in Poland in 1980–1981. What changed in 1989, compared to earlier crises in Eastern Europe, was not the depth of popular opposition to the Soviet-backed regimes, but the whole thrust of Soviet policy in the region. The largely peaceful collapse of East European communism in 1989 was due as much to the fundamental reorientation of Soviet foreign policy under Mikhail Gorbachev as to the courage and restraint of protesters in Eastern Europe. Admirable as the protesters were, none of what they achieved would have been possible without the drastic changes in Moscow that allowed the events to occur.

Even though Gorbachev's reorientation of Soviet policy was a prerequisite for the events of 1989, it was hardly sufficient. In retrospect we know that leeway for radical change was available in 1989, but at the time no one outside the CPSU Politburo could be fully sure of that. At Gorbachev's behest, the Politburo had secretly decided in the spring of 1989 to refrain from any military intervention in Eastern Europe, no matter what happened to the communist regimes there, but the Politburo also decided that it would not publicly disclose this decision and would not even confidentially inform the East European communist leaders about it, for fear of demoralising them. Hence, as events unfolded in the late spring, summer and early autumn of 1989, a good deal of uncertainty persisted at all levels in Eastern Europe about how the Soviet Union would respond in an emergency. Memories of past Soviet military interventions in Eastern Europe, especially in 1953, 1956 and 1968, were still vivid for most people in the region. Amid this uncertainty, drastic change in the Soviet bloc could not just occur on its own. Instead, millions of ordinary people had to overcome lingering concerns and fears to make it happen. The vast number of Poles who voted for *Solidarność* in Poland's June 1989 legislative elections, the hundreds of thousands of Hungarians who gathered for the ceremonial reburial of Imre Nagy in Budapest less than two weeks later, the huge crowds of East Germans who took part in protest demonstrations in cities throughout the GDR in October and November 1989, and the millions of Czechs and Slovaks who participated in the Velvet Revolution against the hardline Czechoslovak communist regime in November 1989 all played crucial roles.

The events of 1989 resulted in part from sweeping changes in Soviet policy, in part from the courageous actions of individuals and groups in Eastern Europe, and in part from the loss of will among hardline East European communist leaders as they realised, to their horror, that the Soviet Union would no longer come to their aid with military force. The rapidly improving state of East–West relations was an important backdrop for the process, giving Soviet leaders greater confidence that Western governments would not seek to foment anti-Soviet uprisings or exploit changes in Eastern Europe against the USSR. In addition, an element of chance and contingency contributed to the auspicious outcome in the autumn of 1989, especially to the opening of the Berlin Wall, which occurred as much through inadvertence as through design. Paradoxically, the Chinese authorities' brutal crackdown on peaceful demonstrators in Beijing in June 1989 helped to spur the reorientation of Soviet policy toward Eastern Europe, providing as it did a stark example of the violence that Gorbachev desperately wanted to avoid in the Warsaw Pact countries.

This essay looks at each of these sources of change in Eastern Europe, highlighting the interaction between them. The essay then briefly recounts how the Berlin Wall was finally opened in November 1989 and concludes by explaining why Gorbachev, who had sought both to strengthen the socialist camp and to end the Cold War, achieved the latter objective but not the former. The analysis here underscores the importance of individual agency as well as larger social forces in revolutionary upheavals, but it also reveals how uncertain, confusing, and unpredictable such events can seem as they are under way. Although the key participants in the 1989 crises did not foresee the full cumulative impact of their actions, the effects were ultimately global in scope. The demise of communist regimes in the Warsaw Pact countries not only eliminated the Cold War divide in Europe but also had a transformative spillover in the Third World—particularly Mongolia, Latin America and southern Africa—in 1989 and after.

Initial continuity

Until the rise of Gorbachev, Soviet leaders after World War II regarded Eastern Europe as an extension of their own country's frontiers. Threats to the security of an East European communist regime, whether external or internal, were seen as threats to Soviet security as well. This sentiment took its most explicit form in the so-called Brezhnev Doctrine, the term coined in the West after August 1968 to refer to a series of authoritative statements by Leonid Brezhnev and other Soviet officials justifying the invasion of Czechoslovakia. The Doctrine linked the fate of every communist country with the fate of all other communist countries, required Soviet-bloc governments to abide by the norms of Marxism–Leninism as interpreted in Moscow, and subordinated the 'abstract sovereignty' of socialist states to the 'laws of class struggle' (Kramer 2010, pp. 276–362).

After Gorbachev came to power in March 1985, the Soviet–East European relationship initially underwent little change. In the mid-1990s, after the Soviet Union collapsed, Gorbachev claimed that he had informed the East European governments as early as 1985 that the Soviet Union would no longer come to their aid under any circumstances.[1] That claim has been repeated by a few of Gorbachev's former advisers.[2] Their retrospective assertions, however, have been undermined by a plethora of contemporaneous archival evidence that has emerged over the past decade-and-a-half in Russia and other former Warsaw Pact countries. Far from intending to let go of the Soviet bloc, Gorbachev arrived in office wanting to strengthen the military, political, economic and ideological institutions that linked the Soviet Union with the communist regimes in Eastern Europe. On 6 March 1985, five days before Gorbachev became CPSU General Secretary and when he was still serving as CPSU Secretary for Ideology, he met in Moscow with all the East European Communist Party secretaries for ideology. He called on them to 'intensify [their] ideological vigilance' and to strive for 'much tighter cohesion in all spheres of the socialist commonwealth'. He concluded his presentation by declaring that every Party and state official in the Soviet Union and Eastern Europe 'must be imbued with the spirit of constant readiness to defend socialist gains—the utmost task of all propaganda activity'.[3] The phrase 'defend socialist gains' was a core element of the Brezhnev Doctrine, as everyone at the meeting would have been aware.

[1]See, for example, Gorbachev's comments in Gorbachev and Mlýnář (2002, pp. 84–85) (originally published in Prague in 1995 under the title *Reformátoři nebývají šťastni: Dialog o 'perestrojce', Pražském jaru a socialismu*). Gorbachev refers here to a meeting he convened shortly after becoming General Secretary. The full transcripts of that meeting, which were declassified in December 2010 after my repeated requests, contradict Gorbachev's recollection of what he said there, as shown below. Evidently, Gorbachev was projecting back to 1985 a view that in fact he did not come to embrace until a few years later.

[2]See, for example, the comments by Anatolii Chernyaev and Vadim Medvedev reported in Garthoff (1994, pp. 571–72); and in Archie Brown (1996, p. 249). One of the problems in relying on Chernyaev's and Medvedev's *post-hoc* testimony about this matter is that neither of them became an adviser to Gorbachev until 1986. Hence, they were not in a position to know what Gorbachev said (or did not say) to the leaders of the other Warsaw Pact countries in March–April 1985.

[3]'Stenogramma pervogo (utrennego) zasedaniya vstupitel'noe slova chlena Politbyuro, sekretarya TsK KPSS M. S. Gorbacheva pri otkrytii vstrechi, utverzhdenie poryadka predsedatel'stvovaniya na

In subsequent months, after taking over as the CPSU General Secretary, Gorbachev promoted greater economic integration within the Council for Mutual Economic Assistance (CMEA) and an expansion of political–military cooperation among the members of the Warsaw Pact. In both respects, his early policies displayed strong continuity with the policies of his predecessors. Gorbachev's manner of presentation may have been more dynamic, but at no time during his initial years in office did he disavow the Brezhnev Doctrine or display the slightest inclination to accept the collapse of communism in Eastern Europe. In a secret memorandum to the CPSU Politburo, Gorbachev emphasised that 'although the countries of socialism have endured serious internal and external challenges, not a single one of [these countries] has suffered a return to the old order'—a record he clearly took great pride in and aspired to uphold.[4]

The declassified transcripts from Gorbachev's meetings and communications with East European officials belie the notion that the new Soviet leader at any point in 1985–1988 told the Warsaw Pact governments—or even hinted—that the Soviet Union would no longer take action to counter dire threats to communist rule in Eastern Europe. He never said anything remotely like that to his East European counterparts during his first few years as CPSU General Secretary, and indeed the records show that he frequently said the opposite, especially in his first year as he consolidated power. Immediately after Gorbachev took office, he pledged that his 'first priority' in foreign policy would be 'to protect and strengthen as much as possible the fraternal friendship with our closest comrades-in-arms and allies, the countries of the great socialist commonwealth'.[5] In early bilateral meetings with the East European party leaders, Gorbachev urged them to step up their 'fight against the encroachments of imperialism' and to 'do everything possible to undermine the aggressive attempts ... made by class enemies [who] are nowadays seeking to achieve the ideological dissolution of socialism from within'.[6] At an important plenum of the CPSU Central Committee in April 1985, Gorbachev called for

> the improvement and enrichment of cooperation among the fraternal socialist countries in every possible way, the development of comprehensive ties, the assurance of close collaboration in the political, economic, ideological, military, and other spheres, and the

zasedaniyakh, poryadka i reglamenta raboty, obmen maneniyami po obsuzhdaemym voprosam', Verbatim Stenogram with corrections marked by hand (Top Secret), 6 March 1985, in Rossiiskii Gosudarstvennyi Arkhiv Noveishei Istorii (RGANI), Fond (F.) 10, Opis' (Op.) 1, Delo (D.) 548, List (Ll.) 1–148. See also the subsequent discussion, 'Stenogramma vtorogo (vechernego) zasedaniya prodolzhenie obmena mneniyami po obsuzhdaemym voprosam, prinyatie teksta kratkogo soobshcheniya dlya pechati, zaklyuchitel'noe slovo sekretarya TsK KPSS M. V. Zimyanina pri zakrytii Vstrechi', Verbatim Stenogram with corrections marked by hand (Top Secret), 6 March 1985, in RGANI, F. 10, Op. 1, D. 549, Ll. 1–81. Vadim Zagladin, the CPSU official overseeing international information and propaganda activities, drafted Gorbachev's speech for this gathering. See 'Vystuplenie—proekt', Draft Text, 18 February 1985, in Arkhiv Gorbachev-Fonda (AGF), F. 3, Dokument (Dok.) 4487, Ll. 1–10.

[4] 'V Politbyuro TsK KPSS: O nekotorykh aktual'nykh voprosakh sotrudnichestva s sotsstranami', Memorandum from M. S. Gorbachev to the CPSU Politburo, 25 June 1986 (Secret), supplement to Point 1 of Politburo Protocol No. 18, in Arkhiv Prezidenta Rossiiskoi Federatsii (APRF), F. 3, Op. 102, D. 218, Ll. 4, 5.

[5] 'Rech' General'nogo sekretarya TsK KPSS tovarishcha M.S. Gorbacheva na Plenume TsK KPSS 11 marta 1985 goda', *Pravda*, 12 March 1985, p. 3.

[6] See, for example, the notes of Gorbachev's meeting with the Polish leader Wojciech Jaruzelski, 7 April 1985, in AGF, F. 3, Dok. 4380, Ll. 5–8.

> organic merger of the national and international interests of all members of the great [socialist] commonwealth.[7]

The official Soviet TASS and *Novosti* press agencies prominently highlighted all of these comments in their wire dispatches about Gorbachev's speech at the plenum.

A few days later, on 26 April, when Gorbachev and the other East-bloc leaders gathered in Moscow to extend the Warsaw Pact for an additional 30 years, the participants issued a joint communiqué vowing to 'increase their close cooperation in international affairs' and 'reinforce their efforts to strengthen the combat cohesion of the alliance'.[8] Nothing more about the proceedings was released at the time, but the declassified records show that Gorbachev, in his keynote speech at the meeting, praised the 'unity of action' that had 'thwarted the attempts by imperialism to subvert or "destroy" the socialist order in any of the fraternal countries', a clear reference to the events of 1968 and 1980–1981 when challenges to communist regimes in Eastern Europe were forcibly suppressed.[9] Gorbachev also lauded 'our joint efforts in accomplishing a task of historic importance—we have reached military–strategic parity with NATO. This was not at all easy to do'. He made clear that the Warsaw Pact must never fall behind in its ability to 'wage an active fight against the military threat' from NATO:

> Military–strategic parity is a vital prerequisite for the security of the socialist states. Understandably, safeguarding the military balance has required—and, if the situation does not improve, will continue to require—a great deal of resources and effort. But without this it will be impossible to defend socialist gains. This is our common affair, the success of which will depend on contributions from every socialist state.[10]

Far from displaying any inclination to relax Soviet military–political ties with the East European states, Gorbachev demanded 'a unified line' and 'stricter coordination of efforts' to 'consolidate the position of socialism'.[11] His insistence that the Warsaw

[7]'Plenum Tsentral'nogo Komiteta TsK KPSS, 22–23 aprelya 1985 goda', 22–23 April 1985 (Top Secret), in RGANI, F. 2, Op. 3, D. 347, L. 12. Gorbachev's speech was published the next day as 'O sozyve ocherednogo XXVII S'ezda KPSS i zadachakh svyazannykh s ego podgotovkoi i provedeniem: Doklad General'nogo sekretarya TsK KPSS M. S. Gorbacheva', *Pravda*, 23 April 1985, p. 2.

[8]'Kommyunike o vstreche vysshikh partiinykh i gosudarstvennykh deyatelei stran-uchastnits Varshavskogo Dogovora', *Krasnaya zvezda*, 27 April 1985, pp. 1–2.

[9]The passages quoted here are from the verbatim text of Gorbachev's speech, with corrections marked in by hand, 'Vystuplenie General'nogo sekretarya TsK KPSS M. S. Gorbacheva na vstreche 26 aprelya 1985 goda: Teksty okonchateln'yi i s redaktsionnymi pravkami', Stenogram (Top Secret), in RGANI, F. 10, Op. 3, D. 149, Ll. 1–44. For a Czech version of Gorbachev's speech, translated from the original Russian, see 'Vystoupení generálního tajemníka ÚV Komunistické strany Sovětského svazu soudruha M. S. Gorbačova: Příloha IV/d', 26 April 1985, 8696/24, in Český Národní Archiv (ČNA), Archiv Ústředního výboru Komunistické strany Československa (Arch. ÚV KSČ), PÚV 47/85, Listí (Ll.) 1–11. A reading of the Czech translation indicates that no passages were omitted from the Russian text after Gorbachev gave it. The translated version is a useful cross-check.

[10]"Vystuplenie General'nogo sekretarya TsK KPSS M. S. Gorbacheva na vstreche 26 aprelya 1985 goda: Teksty okonchateln'yi i s redaktsionnymi pravkami', Stenogram (Top Secret), in RGANI, F. 10, Op. 3, D. 149, L. 2.

[11]'Vystuplenie General'nogo sekretarya TsK KPSS M. S. Gorbacheva na vstreche 26 aprelya 1985 goda: Teksty okonchateln'yi i s redaktsionnymi pravkami', Stenogram (Top Secret), in RGANI, F. 10, Op. 3, D. 149, L. 8.

Treaty be extended by 30 years rather than a much shorter period (of perhaps between five and ten years) as some East European officials had wanted, and his determination to prevent any changes in the basic text of the treaty (or in the top-secret supplementary Provisions on the Unified Command of the Armed Forces of the member states of the Warsaw Pact), underscored his desire to push for greater cohesion and integration between the Soviet Union and its East European allies.

This same approach, with its echoes of the policies adopted by previous Soviet leaders toward Eastern Europe, was evident during other high-level deliberations in Moscow in 1985 and 1986. At meetings of the CPSU Politburo and CPSU Secretariat, Gorbachev called for an expansion of political and military ties within the Warsaw Pact and promised to safeguard the 'underlying path of development of our cooperation with the other socialist countries'.[12] The recently declassified transcripts and notes from these meetings and from other secret high-level discussions in 1985 and 1986 further contravene the notion that Gorbachev decided at an early stage to leave the East European states to their own devices.[13] The archival evidence shows that although Gorbachev was critical of some of the policies of his predecessors (including their failure to develop much greater economic and political integration within the bloc), he was certainly not proposing that the Soviet Union should or could stand by if communist rule in Eastern Europe were in danger of collapsing.[14] On the contrary, he believed that fortifying Soviet ties with the Warsaw Pact countries would help to avert potential crises akin to those in the past. He vowed that the USSR would establish 'greater [communist] party control' over Soviet–East European relations and 'strengthen the unity of the socialist countries and counter any centrifugal tendencies' in the Warsaw Pact.[15] Although he said it would be pointless to treat the East European states like 'little children who need to be brought to kindergarten', he was convinced that the Soviet Union's 'objective interests demand unity and cohesion

[12]'Zasedanie Politbyuro TsK KPSS 26 iyunya 1986 goda: Zapiska tov. Gorbacheva M. S. o nekotorykh aktual'nykh voprosakh sotrudnichestva s sotsialisticheskimi stranami', Politburo Protocol No. 18 (Top Secret), 26 June 1986, in RGANI, F. 89, Op. 36, D. 19, L. 1.

[13]Notes from CPSU Politburo meetings and many other high-level discussions from 1985 to 1991 were gathered in 2003–2004 by the Gorbachev Foundation for transcription in a planned six-volume document collection titled *Kak 'delalas'' politika perestroiki* (henceforth referred to as 'KDPP') that originally was scheduled to appear in 2004. Unfortunately, Gorbachev decided not to publish the volumes, which would have come to more than 3,500 pages in total. Later on, he did permit a much abridged single volume to appear (Chernyaev *et al.* 2006), as well as a collection of documents pertaining to Soviet policy in Germany (Galkin & Chernyaev 2006). In 2010, another thick volume was published with notes and materials (including some already publicly available) from Gorbachev's meetings and conversations with foreign leaders (Chernyaev & Veber 2010), but the other documents planned for KDPP have not yet been made generally available. Fortunately, Anatolii Chernyaev, who oversaw the project and would have preferred to release all of the materials, agreed to give me (and other researchers) access to the unpublished volumes when I was in Moscow numerous times from 2005 to 2009. I am grateful to Chernyaev for the opportunity to examine all of the documents.

[14]See, for example, 'V Politbyuro TsK KPSS: O nekotorykh aktual'nykh voprosakh sotrudnichestva s sotsstranami', and 'Zasedanie Politbyuro TsK KPSS 26 iyunya 1986 goda', in APRF, F. 3, Op. 102, D. 218, Ll. 1–6; and 'Politbyuro, 3 iyulya 1986: Rabochaya zapis'', Notes from CPSU Politburo meeting (Secret), 3 July 1986, in KDPP, vol. 1, pp. 152–56.

[15]'V Politbyuro TsK KPSS: O nekotorykh aktual'nykh voprosakh sotrudnichestva s sotsstranami', APRF, F. 3, Op. 102, D. 218, Ll. 4, 5.

among the countries of socialism' as well as 'comprehensive coordination of all foreign policy actions'. The East European governments, he argued in mid-1986, 'know that any initiative they put forth must enjoy our support and must be coordinated with us, or else it will never get anywhere and will be doomed from the start'.[16] Gorbachev assured his colleagues on the CPSU Politburo that the Soviet Union would continue to be, as it had been under his predecessors, 'the leader of the socialist world and the [military] guarantor of the security and socialist gains of the fraternal countries'.[17]

Gorbachev expressed similar views whenever he spoke with East European leaders during his first few years in office. In a series of bilateral and multilateral meetings with high-ranking East European officials in 1985 and early 1986, Gorbachev urged them to pursue closer military, political and economic integration with the Soviet Union. In 1985 alone, five separate gatherings of Warsaw Pact leaders were convened, including two in March and one in November shortly after Gorbachev returned from his first summit meeting with Ronald Reagan in Geneva. Gorbachev assured the East European leaders that the Soviet Union would show 'respect for [their countries'] experience and understanding of [their] national specifics' and would support their 'quest to follow national paths' to socialism, but he made these pledges in the expectation that the Warsaw Pact leaders would facilitate, rather than impede, the 'strengthening of our cooperation, cohesion, and unity'. Gorbachev left no doubt that his main aim in Eastern Europe was to 'develop comprehensive cooperation on all matters with countries of the socialist commonwealth'.[18] The new CPSU programme that was adopted at the 27th Soviet Party Congress in March 1986 spoke explicitly about the need for 'mutual assistance' in 'defending socialist gains' and about the paramount importance of 'socialist internationalism' for the Soviet bloc—the essence of the Brezhnev Doctrine.[19]

In the months following the 27th Soviet Party Congress, Gorbachev continued to stress the need for increased discipline and cohesion in the Soviet bloc, a theme he voiced both at a meeting of the Warsaw Pact's Political Consultative Committee (PCC) in June 1986 and at the 10th Congress of the Polish United Workers' Party (PZPR) a few weeks later. At the PCC meeting, he called for 'increasingly close cooperation among the socialist countries' and highlighted the 'great need for an increase in common action'.[20] At the PZPR congress, Gorbachev argued that the development of 'cooperative links among the socialist countries' should be given 'absolute priority' and should extend to all areas—'political, economic, cultural, and

[16]The quoted passages here and in the previous sentence are from Gorbachev's keynote speech to a closed meeting of the Soviet Foreign Ministry Collegium, 28 May 1986, declassified and published in Gorbachev (1993, pp. 46–55).

[17]'V Politbyuro TsK KPSS: O nekotorykh aktual'nykh voprosakh sotrudnichestva s sotsstranami', APRF, F. 3, Op. 102, D. 218, L. 5.

[18]'Niederschrift über das Treffen der Generalsekretäre und Ersten Sekretäre der Zentralkomitees der Bruderparteien der Teilnehmerstaaten des Warschauer Vertrages am 23. Oktober 1985 in Sofia', 23 October 1985 (Top Secret), in Stiftung Archiv der Parteien und Massenorganisationen der DDR im Bundesarchiv (SAPMO), Zentrales Parteiarchiv (ZPA), IV 2/1/638.

[19]'Programma Kommunisticheskoi partii Sovetskogo Soyuza', *Pravda*, 7 March 1986, p. 7.

[20]'Niederschrift über die interne Beratung der Generalsekretäre und Ersten Sekretäre der Bruderparteien der Mitgliedsstaaten des Warschauer Vertrages am 11.6.1986 in Budapest', 11 June 1986, in SAPMO, DY/30/2353, Blatt (Bl.) 11.

military'.[21] In a thinly veiled reaffirmation of the Brezhnev Doctrine, he declared that 'socialist gains are irreversible' and that any attempt by internal or external forces to 'wrench a country away from the socialist commonwealth would mean encroaching not only on the will of the people [in that country], but also on the entire postwar order and, in the final analysis, on peace'. His lengthy comments supporting the Polish regime's martial-law crackdown in December 1981 on the Solidarity movement (which he characterised as the 'internal enemies of socialist Poland') reinforced the point.

On the other hand, some seemingly modest steps that went largely unnoticed laid the groundwork for more sweeping changes in the years ahead. Gorbachev's decision in February 1986 to hire Anatolii Chernyaev as a foreign policy adviser augured a fresh approach to Soviet foreign policy generally. Chernyaev, a long-time official at the CPSU International Department, was known as a sharp, innovative thinker, and he soon became one of Gorbachev's close aides. The appointment in March 1986 of Vadim Medvedev as the CPSU Secretary responsible for intra-bloc affairs, replacing Konstantin Rusakov (who had held the post since 1977), brought in another official on whom Gorbachev could rely to instil greater flexibility into the CPSU Department for Ties with Communist and Workers' Parties of Socialist Countries, the body most directly responsible for policy toward Eastern Europe.[22] In September 1986 Medvedev designated the long-time deputy head of that CPSU department, Georgii Shakhnazarov, to become first deputy head in place of Oleg Rakhmanin. Shakhnazarov at the time was already known as a reform-minded official, and he subsequently (from 1988) proved to be one of the chief advisers to Gorbachev on Soviet policy toward Eastern Europe, often working with Chernyaev. (A comparison of Shakhnazarov's and Chernyaev's memoranda for Gorbachev shows that the two advisers were in broad agreement about the need for far-reaching change in foreign policy but that Chernyaev tended to be bolder than Shakhnazarov, whose somewhat more cautious inclinations were closer to Gorbachev's own outlook.)

More importantly, the official whom Shakhnazarov replaced, Rakhmanin, was a notorious hardliner who had published an article in *Pravda* in June 1985 that cast a pall on Soviet–East European relations.[23] The article warned the East European governments not to adopt any market-oriented economic reforms or political measures that would 'compromise Marxism–Leninism as the basis of the fraternal states' unity' and 'distort the general laws of socialist construction'. The article also repeatedly stressed the 'common responsibility of all the socialist countries for the fate of world socialism' and declared that 'on all major international issues the foreign policy of the USSR and of the Marxist–Leninist core of world socialism is identical'. Chernyaev later wrote that Gorbachev was deeply irritated by the unexpected appearance of Rakhmanin's article, which apparently was published without sufficient authorisation from the highest levels.[24] At a CPSU Politburo meeting a week after the article appeared, Gorbachev voiced his displeasure and rebuked Rakhmanin's

[21]'X Zjazd Polskiej Zjednoczonej Partii Robotniczej—wystąpienie tow. Gorbaczowa M. S.', *Trybuna Ludu*, 1 July 1986, p. 1.

[22]See Medvedev (1994) for his own first-hand account.

[23]The article was published pseudonymously under the name of O. Vladimirov (1985, pp. 3–4).

[24]Chernyaev (1993, pp. 49–51). Chernyaev's account contains two minor mistakes, giving Rakhmanin's surname as Rakhmaninov and referring to July instead of June.

superiors.[25] Although Gorbachev decided not to remove Rakhmanin immediately, the eventual appointment of Shakhnazarov as the department's new first deputy chief was a sign that concrete changes in Soviet policy toward the bloc might finally be coming.

Nevertheless, despite these glimmers of movement, Soviet policy toward Eastern Europe during Gorbachev's early years continued to reflect much of the residue of the past. When the Warsaw Pact's Military Council met in November 1986, the commander-in-chief of the alliance's joint armed forces, Marshal Viktor Kulikov, told the East European participants that the 'growing danger of war' with NATO 'compels us to adopt measures that will bolster the security of our countries and our peoples and to increase the combat readiness of the armed forces of the Warsaw Pact member-states'.[26] The following month, at a meeting of the Pact's Council of Defence Ministers, a Soviet deputy defence minister, Army-General Evgenii Ivanovskii, reported that the Soviet Union planned to 'deploy airborne assault forces on a wide scale in order to give a more dynamic character to [the Warsaw Pact's joint] offensive operations'.[27] In subsequent months, the Soviet defence minister, Marshal Sergei Sokolov, repeatedly vowed both publicly and privately that the Warsaw Pact countries would 'never under any circumstances permit [NATO] to gain military superiority' over them. Sokolov emphasised that the USSR and its allies would have to maintain a 'high level of combat readiness' for the indefinite future, and he called on the East European governments to contribute more to the Warsaw Pact's joint defence efforts.[28]

Gorbachev himself remained cautious in his statements and actions *vis-à-vis* the Soviet bloc during the first several months of 1987, both publicly and privately. He held out hopes of change, but not change of a fundamental nature. When he met with senior East European officials in a closed session in mid-February 1987, he assured them that the Soviet Union 'will not impose its own policy on anyone and will not call on you to act like us. We will, however, hope for solidarity and for understanding'.[29] He echoed these basic sentiments two months later during a long-awaited visit to Czechoslovakia. In his main public speech in Prague, Gorbachev declared that the Soviet Union was not 'calling on anyone to imitate us. Every socialist country has its

[25] 'Rabochaya zapis' zasedaniya Politbyuro TsK KPSS, 29 iyunya 1985 goda', Notes from CPSU Politburo meeting (Top Secret), in KDPP, vol. 1, pp. 21–25.

[26] 'Wesentlicher Inhalt der Ausführungen des Oberkommandierenden der Vereinten Streitkräfte zu den Ergebnissen und Schlußfolgerungen, die sich aus dem Treffen in Reykjavik ergeben', GVS No. A-470 410 (Top Secret), 10 November 1986, in Militärarchiv-Bundesarchiv (MA-BA), VA-01/32647, Bl. 2.

[27] Thesen zum Vortrag des Oberbefehlshabers der Landstreitkräfte und Stellvertreters des Ministers für Verteidigung der UdSSR, Armeegeneral J. F. Iwanowski, auf der 19. Sitzung des Komitees der Verteidigungsminister der Teilnehmerstaaten des Warschauer Vertrages zum dritten Tagesordnung-spunkt 'Schaffung und Gefechtseinsatz der Luftsturmtruppen under der Marineinfanterie in den verbündeten Armeen und Flotten', VVS-No. A 470 389 (Top Secret), 1–3 December 1986, in MA-BA, DVW 1/7 1046, Bl. 2.

[28] See, for example, 'Wesentlicher Inhalt der Ausführungen des Ministers für Verteidigung der UdSSR, Genossen Marschall der Sowjetunion Sokolow, am 18 Mai 1987', Notes from Sokolov's remarks to Warsaw Pact Defense Ministers, No. 1c\021\87 (Top Secret), 18 May 1987, in MA-BA, VA-01/40373, Bl. 124–28.

[29] 'Vstrecha Gorbacheva s sekretaryami TsK bratskikh partii po sel'skomu khozyaistvu, 11 fevryalya 1987 goda', Transcript of Discussion (Top Secret), 11 February 1987, transcribed in KDPP, vol. 2, pp. 89–91.

own specific features, and the fraternal [communist] parties determine their own political line with an eye to national conditions'. He insisted that 'the entire system of political relations between the socialist countries can and must be based unswervingly on a foundation of equality and mutual responsibility', and he pledged that the Soviet Union would not 'lay claim to a special status in the socialist world' or infringe on the 'independence of every [communist] party, its responsibility to its people, and its right to resolve problems of its country's development in a sovereign way'.[30]

Even though this rhetoric sounded a little different from that of past Soviet leaders, Gorbachev qualified each of these assertions with language distinctly reminiscent of the Brezhnev Doctrine. After stating that the USSR would not seek to impose its ideas and policies on other communist countries, he added: 'At the same time, we do not conceal our conviction that *perestroika* in the Soviet Union is in accordance with the very essence of socialism and the justified needs of social progress'. A short while later, after referring to the right of every Communist Party to resolve its own country's problems in its own way, Gorbachev immediately qualified this with the stricture that each member of the socialist commonwealth must show 'obligatory consideration not only for its own interests but also for the common interests' of the whole socialist camp, a phrase taken more or less verbatim from the Brezhnev Doctrine.[31]

Gorbachev's continued ambivalence about Soviet–East European relations was also reflected in his attempt during his visit to Czechoslovakia not to mention, either favourably or unfavourably, the August 1968 invasion and the repressive 'normalisation' that followed it. When confronted unexpectedly about the issue during a tour of Bratislava, he first tried to avoid a direct answer, describing the Prague Spring and ensuing crisis as a 'stern school' and a 'difficult period' that the Soviet Union and Czechoslovakia had 'experienced together with dignity and honour'; but then he suddenly added a blunt endorsement of the Soviet invasion: 'We [in Moscow and Prague] have bravely thought about what happened. ... We came to the right conclusions then. Look how far Czechoslovakia has advanced since 1968'.[32]

Events in subsequent months also suggested that Gorbachev had not yet decided how boldly he was willing to act in recasting Soviet–East European relations. In his keynote speech in November 1987 marking the 70th anniversary of the Bolshevik seizure of power, he spoke briefly about Eastern Europe, declaring that 'all [communist] parties are fully and irreversibly independent. We said this as far back as the 20th [Soviet Party] Congress. True, it took time to free ourselves from old habits. Now, however, it is an immutable reality';[33] but a few minutes later Gorbachev

[30]'Miting Chekhoslovatsko–sovetskoi druzhby: Rech' tovarishcha Gorbacheva M. S.', *Pravda*, 11 April 1987, p. 2.

[31]'Miting Chekhoslovatsko–sovetskoi druzhby: Rech' tovarishcha Gorbacheva M. S.', *Pravda*, 11 April 1987, p. 2.

[32]'Obshchie tseli, edinyi kurs: Prebyvanie M. S. Gorbacheva v Slovakii', *Pravda*, 12 April 1987, p. 1. These remarks later inspired Zdeněk Mlýnář to offer a caustic assessment of Gorbachev's 1987 visit, transcribed in Gorbachev and Mlýnář (2002, pp. 86–89).

[33]'Oktyabr' i perestroika: Revolyutsiya prodolzhaetsya—Doklad General'nogo sekretarya TsK KPSS M. S. Gorbacheva', *Pravda*, 3 November 1987, p. 5. In the weeks prior to Gorbachev's speech, the CPSU Politburo discussed various drafts in great detail, but the often heated debate focused almost exclusively on how to reassess and present the darker periods of Soviet history. The sections on foreign policy, including Eastern Europe, did not spark any controversy.

sharply narrowed this mandate by stipulating that intra-bloc relations must be based on 'the practice of socialist internationalism', including a 'concern for the general cause of socialism'. He then added an even more explicit restatement of key elements of the Brezhnev Doctrine: 'We know what damage can be caused by weakening the internationalist principle in mutual relations between socialist states, by deviating from the principles of mutual benefit and mutual assistance, and by failing to heed the common interests of socialism in action on the world scene'.[34]

A similar message was conveyed in Gorbachev's book *Perestroika*, which was published in dozens of countries just after the 70th anniversary celebrations. (Gorbachev had worked extensively on it during a break in the late summer, assisted by a few key aides.) The book acknowledged certain shortcomings in Soviet relations with other Warsaw Pact countries in the past, and it pledged that every socialist state would have full independence to proceed along its own path of development. The brief section on Eastern Europe, however, went no further than Gorbachev's earlier statements, and it contained a passage that linked the domestic complexion of each member of the socialist commonwealth with the interests of all others:

> The socialist community will be successful only if every party and state cares for both its own interests and common interests, if it respects its friends and allies, heeds their interests, and pays attention to the experience of others. Awareness of this relationship between domestic issues and the interests of world socialism is typical of the countries of the socialist community. We are united, in unity resides our strength. (Gorbachev 1987, p. 165)

For East European readers of the book, this assertion of a 'relationship between domestic issues and the interests of world socialism' was bound to be evocative of the Brezhnev Doctrine. In no respect did the book imply that drastic change in the political complexion of Eastern Europe would ever be tolerated in Moscow.

Sources and signs of change in Soviet policy

The year 1988 proved to be a turning point for the USSR on many key issues, both domestic and foreign. The Soviet–East European relationship was no exception. Soviet policy toward Warsaw Pact countries finally began to loosen in early 1988, adumbrating a fundamental reorientation of Gorbachev's approach. When the Soviet leader was confronted by stark choices and tradeoffs in relations with Eastern Europe, he opted to proceed more boldly, spawning events that soon went far beyond anything he had foreseen at the start.

The context of policymaking

One of the reasons that Gorbachev was able to move ahead more decisively in 1988 is that by this point he had steadily expanded his power within the CPSU and had made many personnel changes that gave him greater leeway to act. His latitude was reinforced in the summer and autumn of 1988 when he replaced numerous other long-time

[34]'Oktyabr' i perestroika: Revolyutsiya prodolzhaetsya—Doklad General'nogo sekretarya TsK KPSS M. S. Gorbacheva', *Pravda*, 3 November 1987, p. 5.

members of the CPSU Politburo and Central Committee who had become alarmed by the increasingly unorthodox nature of developments in the USSR and Eastern Europe.[35] Although Gorbachev's consolidation of political power was not a sufficient condition for a drastic change of course *vis-à-vis* Eastern Europe, it clearly was a necessary condition. The new foreign policy that Gorbachev pursued in 1988 and especially 1989 would have been infeasible in the domestic environment of 1985 and 1986, even if he had been inclined to embrace a radical agenda during those early years (which he was not). By the time Gorbachev truly did want to make sweeping changes in Soviet policy toward Eastern Europe, he had amassed sufficient power to do so without fear of being ousted by hardline forces.

Gorbachev's inclination in 1988 to begin restructuring Soviet relations with Eastern Europe was spurred in part by the disappointing results of his early economic policies of *uskorenie* (acceleration). By mid-1988 he had come to believe that economic revitalisation for both the Soviet Union and Eastern Europe would be impossible in the absence of thoroughgoing political reform. When Gorbachev first took office in 1985, he assumed that an overhaul of the economy would not require far-reaching political liberalisation. He had hoped that a combination of administrative reshuffling, personnel changes and increased discipline and order would be sufficient to bring about sustained economic improvements;[36] but as the magnitude of Soviet economic problems became more apparent, Gorbachev increasingly emphasised political reforms to help mobilise popular support for his programmes, to expose corrupt and incompetent officials, to undercut bureaucratic resistance to economic decentralisation, and to yield more accurate economic and social data. This gradual shift in domestic priorities convinced Gorbachev that he also needed to scale back Soviet foreign and military policies that were financially burdensome and were apt to divert resources from urgent domestic needs. In particular, he wanted to ensure that he would not be forced to undertake the sorts of costly actions in Eastern Europe that had been deemed necessary in the past.

Gorbachev's decision to move ahead with far-reaching changes in Soviet–East European relations was also facilitated by the significant easing of East–West relations since 1985, reflected above all in the Intermediate-Range Nuclear Forces Treaty of December 1987, which had been achieved thanks to major Soviet concessions. Not only did Gorbachev believe that the improved international climate would allow him 'to focus on constructive endeavours at home' and obtain much needed technology from the West; he also was confident that NATO governments would not try to

[35]On Gorbachev's consolidation of power, see Brown (1996), Evangelista (2001, pp. 5–35), Hough (1997), Breslauer (2002) and Gill (1994). See also US Director of Central Intelligence, 'Whither Gorbachev: Soviet Policy and Politics in the 1990s', NIE-18-87 (Top Secret), November 1987; US Central Intelligence Agency (CIA), 'Gorbachev's Reorganization of the Party: Breaking the Stranglehold of the Apparatus', Research Paper No. SOV 89-10052X (Secret), June 1989; and CIA, 'Gorbachev's Reform of the State Institutions: Toward a Parliamentary System?', Research Paper SOV 89-10024X, March 1989, all in CIA Records Search Tool (CREST), US National Archives and Records Administration (NARA), College Park, MD.

[36]For example, the declassified notes from CPSU Politburo meetings in KDPP, vols 1 and 2. See also CIA, 'Rejuvenating the Soviet Party Apparatus', Intelligence Assessment No. SOV 86-10011 (Secret), February 1986, in CREST/NARA.

undercut the Soviet Union.[37] Unlike in the past, when Soviet leaders feared that NATO would do everything it could to manipulate events in Eastern Europe against the USSR, Gorbachev was hopeful that the amelioration of East–West ties had created an opportunity for him to restructure Soviet policy towards Eastern Europe without endangering Soviet vital interests.

Signs of change

The first notable indicator of a shift in Gorbachev's policy came during his visit to Yugoslavia in March 1988, when the two sides issued a joint communiqué pledging 'unconditional' respect for 'the principles of equality and non-interference' and for 'the independence of [communist] parties and socialist countries to define, for themselves, the path of their own development'. Although most of the communiqué applied strictly to Soviet–Yugoslav relations, the phrases about independence, equality and non-interference were described as applying to relations among all socialist countries. In subsequent months the Soviet Union made good on these pledges by providing the East European governments with much greater latitude for internal political liberalisation and market-oriented economic reforms—latitude that Hungary and Poland (though not the four other Warsaw Pact member states) were quick to exploit.

Moreover, for the first time, Soviet analysts began to re-evaluate and criticise the whole postwar history of Soviet–East European relations. As early as May 1988 a lengthy article in the weekly publication *Literaturnaya gazeta* by the prominent 'new thinker' Vyacheslav Dashichev stressed that the Soviet Union's 'hegemonic policies and great-power mentality' in Eastern Europe after 1945, as reflected in 'the spread of Stalinist socialism wherever possible and its standardisation in all countries regardless of their national features', had been directly responsible for the cycle of 'sharp confrontations' between the Soviet Union and its supposed 'fraternal allies' in Eastern Europe.[38] Dashichev condemned 'the expulsion of Yugoslavia from the socialist system in 1948 and the attribution of all deadly sins to its leaders for the simple reason that they had refused to submit to Stalin and obey his dictates'. The article also suggested that 'hegemonism' and a domineering attitude toward Eastern Europe had continued under Stalin's successors, leading in time to 'armed clashes between socialist countries'. After berating the 'stereotyped and cliché-ridden thinking and mentality of leading [Soviet] cadres who effectively became prisoners of their own propaganda', Dashichev called for the 'total surmounting of Stalinism in foreign policy' and for the rectification of 'the mistakes and incompetent approach of the Brezhnevite leadership toward the resolution of foreign policy problems' (Dashichev 1988, p. 14). By the summer of 1988, criticisms of this sort were appearing regularly in the Soviet press, generating a spirited and intense public debate.

The main elements of Dashichev's critique were incorporated into a 'discussion paper' compiled in mid-1988 by a team of analysts at the Institute of Economics of the

[37]'Za bez'yadernyi mir, za gumanizm mezhdunarodnykh otnoshenii: Rech' M.S. Gorbacheva', *Pravda*, 17 February 1987, p. 1.

[38]Dashichev (1988, p. 14). In December 1988, Dashichev's article was voted one of the best to have appeared in *Literaturnaya gazeta* in 1988.

World Socialist System (IEMSS), the only research institute in the Soviet Academy of Sciences that dealt primarily with Eastern Europe and intra-bloc ties. The authors of the paper called for drastic changes in Soviet–East European relations to overcome the 'stagnant neo-Stalinism' bred by the 'hegemonic aspirations' of earlier Soviet leaders.[39] Although the IEMSS did not have a direct role in the policymaking process, the institute was an important source of advice and information for senior officials in the CPSU and the Soviet government. The IEMSS director, Oleg Bogomolov, conferred with several of Gorbachev's most trusted aides, including Shakhnazarov and Aleksandr Yakovlev. By disseminating the paper to policymakers and by publishing it in Moscow and abroad, the IEMSS specialists helped to make Soviet officials aware of the volatile conditions in Eastern Europe.

Gorbachev himself received a draft of the IEMSS paper from Shakhnazarov in June 1988 amid preparations for important meetings of CPSU organs and Warsaw Pact military–political bodies.[40] A cover note from Shakhnazarov summarising the document was marked by Gorbachev in various places, indicating that he had read it (and presumably had also read the full draft). When the Soviet leader delivered his keynote speech at the CPSU's 19th Party Conference in late June 1988, he echoed many points in the IEMSS document. Eschewing the platitudes used at earlier Party gatherings, he condemned 'the sediment that has accumulated on our relations' with the East European countries and promised that the Soviet Union in the future would adhere to a much different policy: 'The external imposition of a social system, of a way of life, or of policies by any means, let alone military, is a dangerous trapping of the past'.[41] In subsequent months, Gorbachev returned to this theme many times, both publicly and privately. In February 1989, for example, when he met with senior Party and state officials in Soviet Ukraine, he told them that the Soviet Union was 'restructuring its relations with the socialist countries' and would henceforth emphasise 'unconditional independence, full equality, strict non-interference in internal affairs, and rectification of deformities and mistakes linked with earlier periods in the history of socialism'.[42]

The increasing boldness of Gorbachev's pronouncements about Eastern Europe, combined with the publication of harsh reappraisals of earlier Soviet policies in the region (including condemnations of the Brezhnev Doctrine by name), fuelled the ongoing political spillover from the Soviet Union into the other Warsaw Pact countries. As the pace of *perestroika* and *glasnost'* accelerated in the USSR in the wake of the 19th Party Conference, the 'winds of change' gradually filtered throughout the communist bloc, bringing long-submerged grievances and social discontent to the surface. Under mounting popular pressure, the authorities in Hungary and Poland embarked on a wide array of ambitious reforms—more ambitious than what Gorbachev himself was pursuing. Rather than seeking to discourage or roll back the

[39]The paper was published in both Moscow and the West; see IEMSS (1988, pp. 60–67).

[40]Memorandum from Shakhnazarov to Gorbachev, 18 May 1988, with draft of IEMSS paper attached, in AGF, F. 1, Op. 1, Dok. 11731.

[41]'Doklad General'nogo sekretarya TsK KPSS M. S. Gorbacheva na XIX Vsesoyuznoi konferentsii KPSS 28 iyunya 1988 goda', *Pravda*, 29 June 1988, p. 3.

[42]'Rech' M. S. Gorbacheva na vstreche s trudyashchimisya v g. Kieve', *Krasnaya zvezda*, 24 February 1989, p. 3.

radical changes in Poland and Hungary, Gorbachev did just the opposite by praising developments in both countries.

The sweeping reorientation of Soviet–East European ties was symbolised in the latter half of 1988 by Gorbachev's bid to restructure and scale back the CPSU's role in political life. The crucial changes Gorbachev secured at the 19th Soviet Party Conference in July 1988, which were formally adopted at a landmark CPSU Central Committee plenum three months later, had the effect of eliminating or reducing the Party's ability to perform certain key tasks.[43] In particular, Gorbachev abolished many of the CPSU Central Committee departments, including the Department for Ties with Communist and Workers' Parties of Socialist Countries, whose functions were merged with an expanded International Department (ID) (Kramer 1990, pp. 429–46). The reconfigured ID, in turn, was placed under the jurisdiction of the new CPSU Commission on International Policy, headed by Gorbachev's close ally, Aleksandr Yakovlev, whose advocacy of 'new political thinking' in Soviet foreign policy had taken an increasingly radical turn.[44] During the first few years under Gorbachev, Yakovlev had focused mostly on improving the 'image' and packaging of Soviet foreign policy and on 'thwarting Western counterpropaganda against the new thinking',[45] but by the latter half of 1988, as events in the USSR gathered pace, Yakovlev was urging 'concrete changes' of a 'fundamental nature' that would 'reshape [Soviet] relations with all of the socialist countries' in ways 'consistent with the new directions in [Soviet] foreign policy'.[46] The elimination of the old CPSU department that had long coordinated intra-bloc affairs, the diffusion of the erstwhile department's responsibilities, and the supervisory role given to Yakovlev over Soviet ties with Eastern Europe could not help but mitigate the CPSU's entrenched

[43]'Stenogramma Plenuma TsK KPSS 30 sentyabrya 1988 goda', Plenum Verbatim and Corrected Transcript (Secret), 30 September 1988, in RGANI, F. 2, Op. 5, Ll. 163–76. For Gorbachev's rationale for the changes, see his memorandum transcribed in *Izvestiya TsK KPSS*, 1, 1, January 1989, pp. 81–86.

[44]'Postanovlenie Plenuma TsK KPSS: O Komissiyakh Tsentral'nogo Komiteta KPSS', *Pravda*, 29 November 1988, pp. 1–2. For an overview of Gorbachev's restructuring of the CPSU and Party–state relations, see Gill (1994).

[45]'O protivodeistvii Zapada politike perestroika po kanalam propagandy', o perestroike kak faktore neozhidannosti dlya Zapada, o politicheskom razmezhevanii na Zapade v otnoshenii k perestroike v SSSR', Memorandum from A. N. Yakovlev to M. S. Gorbachev (Top Secret), 4 July 1987, in Gosudarstvennyi Arkhiv Rossiiskoi Federatsii (GARF), F. 10063, Op. 1, D. 387, Ll. 1–12; 'O kurse na aktivizatsiyu vneshnepoliticheskoi deyatel'nosti SSSR', Memorandum from A. N. Yakovlev to the CPSU Politburo (Top Secret), 11 November 1986, in GARF, F. 10063, Op. 2, D. 69, Ll. 1–18; 'Tekst vystupleniya A. N. Yakovleva na Politbyuro TsK KPSS v svyazi s proektom Postanovleniya TsK KPSS, vnesennym na rassmotrenie Politbyuro TsK KPSS o perspektivnykh zadachakh vneshnepoliticheskoi propagandy', Text of speech (Secret), 6 January 1987, in GARF, F. 10063, Op. 1, D. 243, Ll. 1–7; and 'Stenogramma soveshchaniya, provedennogo A. N. Yakovlevym v TsK KPSS s rukovoditelyami informatsionnykh agentstv pechati stran sotssodruzhestva i stran sotsialisticheskoi orientatsii', Transcript of meeting with East-bloc press officials (Top Secret), 26 November 1987, in GARF, F. 10063, Op. 1, D. 171, Ll. 1–19.

[46]'Tezisy vystupleniya A. N. Yakovleva na Politbyuro TsK KPSS o 'novom politicheskom myshlenii': Kontseptsiyakh prodvizheniya vpered po ryadu napravlenii postanovke konkretnykh dolgovremennykh tselei takovogo prodvizheniya, prakticheskikh sdvigakh i samykh pervykh poka eshche rezul'tatakh' (Teoreticheskii aspect)', Revised text of speech to CPSU Politburo Session (Secret), 27 December 1988, in GARF, F. 10063, Op. 1, D. 190, Ll. 1–7.

habit of interfering in the activities of East European communist parties and governments.[47] Thus, from an institutional standpoint, the reorganisation of the Soviet central Party apparatus in 1988 both contributed to and heralded the looser Soviet policy in Eastern Europe.

Genesis and impact of unilateral force reductions

Another dramatic sign of the reorientation of Gorbachev's policy toward the Warsaw Pact countries came in December 1988 when he announced, in a landmark speech before the United Nations (UN) General Assembly, that the Soviet Union would unilaterally reduce its military forces in Eastern Europe by 50,000 troops, 5,300 tanks and 24 tactical nuclear weapons within two years.[48] This shift to major unilateral reductions of Soviet forces in Eastern Europe, an approach long dreaded by Soviet military officers, was particularly significant in light of the far-reaching political changes under way in the USSR, Hungary and Poland.

The decision to reduce Soviet troops and weapons unilaterally, and the related decision about precisely which forces to eliminate, were made exclusively in Moscow. Initially, at the end of October 1988, Gorbachev met with a small group of foreign policy advisers, including Eduard Shevardnadze, Aleksandr Yakovlev, Anatolii Chernyaev, Anatolii Dobrynin and Valentin Falin, to determine how the initiative should be conceived and presented.[49] The proposal was then fleshed out with specific numbers and discussed by the full CPSU Politburo on 10 and 24 November and 2 December.[50] The USSR Defence Council, which Gorbachev also chaired, met on 11 November to determine which Soviet forces should be weeded out and how quickly they should be withdrawn. In none of these deliberations did the East European leaders have any say or play even the slightest role. Last-minute 'consultations' with the East European governments about the matter were purely *pro forma*. The East German leader Erich Honecker, whose country was the most heavily affected by the reductions, was informed of Gorbachev's intentions only three days before the Soviet leader spoke at the UN.[51] According to Honecker's former associates, he was 'stunned

[47]See the illuminating account by Vadim Medvedev, a close ally of Gorbachev who headed the CPSU intra-bloc department until it was abolished and then became a CPSU Politburo member (1994, esp. pp. 117–23, 248–51).

[48]'Vystuplenie M. S. Gorbacheva v Organizatsii Ob'edinennykh Natsii', *Pravda*, 8 December 1988, p. 2. In early 1989 the US intelligence community prepared a classified assessment of the impact of these cuts. The document—US Central Intelligence Agency (CIA), 'Trends and Development in Warsaw Pact Theater Forces and Doctrine Through the 1990s', National Intelligence Estimate (NIE) 11-14-89, February 1989 (Top Secret)—is available in slightly redacted form in CIA (1999, Doc. 16); see also Odom (1998, pp. 146–47).

[49]'Soveshchanie po podgotovke kontseptsii vystupleniya Gorbacheva v OON', Notes taken by Anatolii Chernyaev, 31 October 1988, in KDPP, vol. 3, pp. 491–94.

[50]'Zasedanie Politbyuro TsK KPSS 10 noyabrya 1988 goda', 10 November 1988 (Top Secret), in KDPP, vol. 3, pp. 498–509; 'Zasedanie Politbyuro TsK KPSS 24 noyabrya 1988 goda', 24 November 1988 (Top Secret), in KDPP, vol. 3, pp. 509–22; and 'Zasedanie Politbyuro TsK KPSS 10 dekabrya 1988 goda', 2 December 1988 (Top Secret), in KDPP, vol. 3, pp. 524–29.

[51]'Wesentlicher Inhalt des Gesprächs des Generalsekretärs des ZK der SED und Vorsitzenden des Nationalen Verteiddigungsrates der DDR, Genossen Erich Honecker, mit dem Mitglied des Politbüros des ZK der SED und Minister für Nationale Verteidigung, Genossen Armeegeneral Kessler, am

and dismayed' by the news, but he had little choice other than to express his perfunctory endorsement.[52]

The aim of the reductions, according to the resolution adopted by the CPSU Politburo, was to 'accentuate the defensive character' of the Warsaw Pact, to 'give new and strong impetus to the process of lowering the military–strategic balance in Europe', and to 'improve relations between East and West and facilitate the process of disarmament'.[53] This last point was especially important for Gorbachev, who viewed the unilateral cuts as the best way to achieve economic savings in the near to medium term. At a CPSU Politburo meeting a few weeks after the speech, he claimed that unless the Soviet Union curbed its military forces and defence spending, it would 'never be able to sustain a long-term economic and social policy'.[54]

In both military and political terms, the reductions amply fulfilled Gorbachev's objectives. The US intelligence community, which carefully tracked the implementation of Gorbachev's projected cuts, reported in September 1989 that the withdrawals were leading to 'a very significant reduction in the offensive combat power of Soviet forces in Europe' and would result in 'the most significant changes in Soviet general purpose forces opposite NATO since Khrushchev's drastic force reductions of the late 1950s and early 1960s'. US intelligence analysts concluded that even if the Soviet Army added infantry fighting vehicles to its units in Eastern Europe to help offset the cuts, 'the loss of half the [Soviet] tanks previously stationed in Eastern Europe will significantly degrade Pact offensive capabilities'.[55] In political terms as well, the impact of the reductions was enormous. Gorbachev assured the CPSU Politburo that the cuts would 'show that our new political thinking is more than just words' and would signal a new Soviet approach to relations with Eastern Europe. Some members of the Soviet Politburo warned that the withdrawals would strengthen the impression that the Soviet Union would no longer provide 'fraternal assistance' to the East European regimes, thus causing 'undesirable consequences for the entire socialist commonwealth',[56] but Gorbachev was willing to accept that risk as he pressed ahead with his efforts to revive and restructure the Soviet economy, to recast Soviet foreign relations in accordance with 'new political thinking', and to transform the Warsaw Pact into a defensive alliance.

The decision to embrace unilateral reductions provoked consternation within the Soviet High Command. The very thing that Soviet marshals and generals had long

Sonntag, dem or. 12. 1988', GVS-Nr. A 613 225 (Top Secret), 4 December 1988, in MA-BA, VA-01/32665, Bl. 154–60.

[52]See, for example, the comments of Kessler (1996, pp. 240–41), Modrow (1991, p. 131; 2007, p. 181) and Krenz (1999, p. 107; 1990, pp. 23–24).

[53]'Wesentlicher Inhalt des Gesprächs des Generalsekretärs des ZK der SED und Vorsitzenden des Nationalen Verteiddigungsrates der DDR, Genossen Erich Honecker, mit dem Mitglied des Politbüros des ZK der SED und Minister für Nationale Verteidigung, Genossen Armeegeneral Kessler', Bl. 158.

[54]'Zasedanie Politbyuro TsK KPSS 27–28 dekabrya 1988 goda: O prakticheskoi realizatsii i prakticheskom obespechenii itogov vizita t. Gorbacheva M. S. v OON', 27–28 December 1988 (Top Secret), in RGANI, F. 89, Op. 42, D. 24, Ll. 1–34.

[55]US National Intelligence Council, 'Status of Soviet Unilateral Withdrawals', Memorandum NIC M 89 10003 (Secret), October 1989, pp. 2, 8, in CIA (1999, Doc. 18).

[56]'Zasedanie Politbyuro TsK KPSS 27–28 dekabrya 1988 goda', in RGANI, F. 89, Op. 42, D. 24, L. 31.

been denouncing as a 'dangerous', 'misguided' and 'completely unacceptable' option was now enshrined as state policy. The chief of the Soviet General Staff, Marshal Sergei Akhromeev, resigned five days before Gorbachev's speech. Although Akhromeev at the time did not publicly disclose why he stepped down, and although he agreed to stay on temporarily as a personal military adviser to Gorbachev, he later revealed that he had been 'distraught' about Gorbachev's willingness to act without gaining reciprocity by NATO.[57] In Akhromeev's view, the Soviet leader's failure to insist on corresponding Western reductions was 'incomprehensible' and a 'betrayal' (Akhromeev & Kornienko 1992, pp. 187–88). In subsequent weeks, many other high-ranking Soviet officers were dismissed, climaxing with the removal of Marshal Viktor Kulikov, the commander-in-chief of the Warsaw Pact, and his main deputy, Army-General Anatolii Gribkov, in early February 1989. The ouster of Kulikov and Gribkov, who together had been commanding the Warsaw Pact's joint military forces since 1977 and had publicly opposed any unilateral reductions, brought a symbolic end to the Soviet military's attempts to preserve the Pact as a cohesive, effective alliance. From then on, Soviet officers were hoping mainly that they could salvage at least something of the organisation and stave off outright collapse.

The challenge of coping with drastic change

All these developments left little doubt by the end of 1988 that Gorbachev had implicitly renounced the Brezhnev Doctrine and opened the way for far-reaching internal change in Eastern Europe. The real issue for the Soviet leader from that point on was no longer whether he should uphold the Brezhnev Doctrine, but whether he could avoid the 'Khrushchev Dilemma'. That is, the problem was not whether to accept peaceful domestic change, as in Czechoslovakia in 1968, but how to prevent widespread anti-Soviet violence from breaking out, as in Hungary in 1956. Gorbachev would have found himself in an intractable situation if he had been confronted by a large-scale, violent uprising in Poland, East Germany, Czechoslovakia or Hungary. On the two previous occasions when violent rebellions threatened Soviet control over those four countries—in East Germany in 1953 and Hungary in 1956—Gorbachev's predecessors responded by sending large numbers of Soviet troops to crack down. If a comparable crisis had erupted in the late-1980s, the pressure for Soviet military intervention would have been enormous, just as it was on Khrushchev in 1956. No matter how Gorbachev might have responded, he would have suffered grave damage. On the one hand, if he had declined to reassert military control in the face of widespread anti-Soviet violence, his opponents within the CPSU undoubtedly would have accused him of recklessness and betrayal and would have done their best to remove him from office. On the other hand, if he had proceeded with a full-fledged invasion, the adverse effects on Soviet domestic reform and on East–West relations would have been immense, just as they were after previous Soviet crackdowns in the region.[58]

[57]Interview with Akhromeev, transcribed in 'Deutschland, das neue Europa, und die Perestroika: Exklusivinterview mit Marschall Achromejev', *Neues Deutschland*, 4 October 1990, p. 8.

[58]The adverse domestic repercussions of Soviet military intervention in Eastern Europe were candidly assessed by Yurii Levada (1989, p. 7).

Hence, Gorbachev's overriding objective was to avoid the Khrushchev Dilemma altogether. He could not afford to be confronted by a violent uprising in one of the key East European countries. Only by forestalling such a disastrous turn of events would he have any hope of moving ahead with his reform programme. The problem, however, was that his very policies, by unleashing centrifugal forces within the Eastern bloc, had already made it more likely that a violent rebellion would occur. One of the main deterrents to popular anti-communist uprisings in Eastern Europe after 1956 was the local populations' awareness that, if necessary, Soviet troops would intervene to restore control. Because this perceived constraint had been steadily diminishing under Gorbachev, the risk of a violent upheaval had increased commensurately.

The possibility of a violent explosion in Eastern Europe had long been apparent to prominent Soviet specialists on the region, such as Bogomolov and Dashichev. Their forebodings shaped the outlook of Shakhnazarov, Aleksandr Yakovlev and Foreign Minister Eduard Shevardnadze, all of whom played crucial advisory roles on Eastern Europe. These senior officials—and eventually Gorbachev himself—came to realise that the longer the existing structures in Eastern Europe remained in place, the greater the danger would be for the Soviet Union. A secret memorandum prepared by Shakhnazarov for Gorbachev and the CPSU Politburo in October 1988 warned that 'social instability and crisis might well engulf the whole socialist world simultaneously'.[59] The memorandum offered a disconcerting appraisal of the situation:

> There are countless signs that all the fraternal countries are plagued by basically the same problems, which are rapidly growing and intensifying. The fact that the symptoms are alike in all these countries shows that the disease is caused not by some sort of noxious virus, … but by concrete factors rooted in the underlying economic and political model of socialism that was first developed in our country and that was then transferred, with essentially no modifications, to the countries that embarked on the socialist path in the postwar period. (Shakhnazarov 1993, p. 368)

Another of Gorbachev's key advisers on European affairs, Vitalii Zhurkin, later recalled that the Soviet authorities had finally 'faced up to the fact … that the authoritarian and totalitarian systems in the countries of Eastern Europe were artificial and would not last forever'. If those systems had been 'prolonged for another five or ten years', Zhurkin argued, the resulting 'explosions' would have been far more 'destructive' and would have caused greater 'destabilisation' and 'problems for everyone, not least for us'.[60]

Thus, both the record of previous crises in Eastern Europe and the prospect that new crises would emerge in the near future had convinced Gorbachev's advisers (and eventually Gorbachev himself) that, as Shevardnadze put it, 'if positive changes [in Eastern Europe] were suppressed or delayed, the whole situation would end in tragedy' (Shevardnadze 1990, p. 3). Far-reaching liberalisation, they believed, was the only way

[59]'K zasedaniyu Politbyuro 6/X-88 g.', 6 October 1988 (Secret), in AGF, F. 5, Op. 1, Dok. 15107. The text of the memorandum is featured as an appendix in Shakhnazarov (1993, pp. 367–69, quoted portion is from p. 367).

[60]Interview with Vitalii Zhurkin, adviser to Gorbachev on European affairs, transcribed in 'Evropa v menyayushchikhsya koordinatakh', *Izvestiya*, 26 May 1990, p. 5.

to forestall such crises, but Gorbachev was also aware that unless the 'positive changes' they were seeking in Eastern Europe occurred peacefully, his domestic reform programme—and his own political fate—would be in jeopardy.

Mindful of that dilemma, Gorbachev and his aides by late 1988 had established two basic goals for Soviet policy in Eastern Europe: first, they wanted to avoid direct Soviet military intervention at all costs. Shakhnazarov had emphasised in his memorandum to Gorbachev that 'in the future, the prospect of "extinguishing" crisis situations [in Eastern Europe] through military means must be completely ruled out'.[61] Second, they sought to achieve a peaceful but rapid transition to a new political order in Eastern Europe. By drastically modifying the region's political complexion, they could defuse the pressures that had given rise to violent internal crises in the past, but to ensure that the early stages of the process remained peaceful and that 'positive changes' would indeed occur, the Soviet Union itself had to play an active, initiating role. Shakhnazarov in his October 1988 memorandum stressed the need for an active policy:

> Some countries have followed our example or have even gone beyond us in undertaking profound reforms, but others, like the GDR, Romania, and Czechoslovakia, have still not acknowledged the need for reforms, primarily for political reasons and the current leaders' aversion to making changes in anything. In reality, all of these countries need fundamental changes, although we cannot speak about this publicly, lest they accuse us of trying to impose *perestroika* on our friends. But a fact remains a fact: The obvious signs of an impending crisis demand radical reforms everywhere in the socialist world. ... Those who stubbornly refuse to heed the pressures for change are just intensifying the ills they face and are greatly complicating matters for the future. This affects us in the most direct way. Even if we are not authorised to be an 'elder brother' in the socialist world, we cannot reject the role of a leader, a role that objectively belongs to the Soviet Union as the most powerful socialist country. If the situation were to reach a crisis point in one or more socialist countries, we would have to come to their rescue at the cost of enormous material, political, and even human losses.[62]

The basic problem, as Shakhnazarov indicated, was that if most of the East European communist parties had been left to their own devices, they would have sought to avoid reforms indefinitely and to crack down harshly on protests and discontent. In late 1988 and the first few months of 1989, Gorbachev and his aides considered how to escape this predicament. Their discussions paved the way for landmark decisions in March 1989 that prefigured the USSR's responses to mass unrest in Eastern Europe later that year.

The decision to abandon Soviet military hegemony in Eastern Europe

Gorbachev's efforts to decide how to forestall or at least cope with the Khrushchev Dilemma came to a head in the first few months of 1989 when, at his behest, the CPSU Politburo and Soviet Defence Council endorsed crucial guidelines about how the Soviet Union should respond to possible internal upheavals in Eastern Europe. In

[61] 'K zasedaniyu Politbyuro 6/X-88 g.', 6 October 1988 (Secret), in AGF, F. 5, Op. 1, Dok. 15107, L. 1.
[62] 'K zasedaniyu Politbyuro 6/X-88 g.', 6 October 1988 (Secret), in AGF, F. 5, Op. 1, Dok. 15107, Ll. 1–2.

effect, Gorbachev persuaded the Politburo and Defence Council to join with him in deciding well in advance that the Soviet Union would not take military action in Eastern Europe, even if the communist governments there collapsed. Gorbachev thus ensured that his colleagues on the Politburo and Defence Council—the only people who potentially could get rid of him—bore equal responsibility for this momentous decision and had no basis for moving against him if he declined to authorise a military crackdown in the face of widespread destabilising unrest in Eastern Europe. By forging a high-level consensus not to use military force, Gorbachev pre-emptively defused the Khrushchev Dilemma.

The process began on 24 January 1989 when Gorbachev received a memorandum from one of his top aides, Vadim Zagladin, who said he wanted to 'draw [the Soviet leader's] attention to a delicate and complicated matter that could take on immense significance for us'.[63] Zagladin averred that the Soviet Union's 'new military–political thinking' necessitated a 'painstaking review of our obligations regarding the provision of military assistance to foreign states in extreme circumstances'. The phrase 'extreme circumstances' (*chrezvychainye obstoyatel'stva*), which could also be translated as 'an emergency' in English, clearly referred not only to external military attack by NATO (which was deemed unlikely by this time), but also to a severe internal crisis, including the downfall of the communist regime. Zagladin warned that as long as the Soviet Union's existing obligations remained intact, 'extreme circumstances might compel us to take actions that could halt and even totally negate what we have achieved' through the embrace of 'new political thinking'. He argued that 'obligations undertaken amid the circumstances of the Cold War ... have sharply constrained [the Soviet Union's] freedom of action', and he expressed particular anxiety about 'unpublished and, for the most part, tightly held documents regarding certain understandings that could potentially create severe difficulties for us'. Zagladin said that in the future the Soviet Union must always 'approach this issue from the perspective of new military–political thinking', which presumably would bring the elimination of 'outdated commitments'. In his view, the best way to 'begin [is] by thoroughly analyzing *all* obligations we have undertaken that involve military assistance of any sort'.[64]

Gorbachev promptly authorised Zagladin to coordinate an in-depth, high-level review of the matter that would offer recommendations for the CPSU Politburo. On 27 January, Zagladin sent a note to senior officials responsible for foreign policy and national security, asking them to work together in compiling a critical appraisal of 'the USSR's current obligations to provide military assistance to foreign countries, including under extreme circumstances'.[65] Top experts from the Soviet Foreign Ministry and Defence Ministry, with input from a few other ministries and agencies, jointly produced a detailed study of major aspects of the issue that in effect repudiated

[63]'Dokladnaya zapiska o peresmotre obyazatel'stv po okazaniyu voennoi pomoshchi', Memorandum from V. Zagladin to Mikhail Gorbachev (Secret), 24 January 1989, in AGF, F. 3, Dok. 7179, Ll. 1–3.

[64]'Dokladnaya zapiska o peresmotre obyazatel'stv po okazaniyu voennoi pomoshchi', in AGF, F. 3, Dok. 7179, Ll. 2–3 (emphasis in original).

[65]'Zapiska', from V. Zagladin to E. Shevardnadze, D. Yazov and V. Kamentsev, 27 January 1989, in AGF, F. 3, Dok. 7179a., L. 1, with attachment.

the Soviet government's earlier interpretations of its multilateral obligations under the Warsaw Treaty and its bilateral obligations to each of the East European countries.

On 25 March 1989 Gorbachev received a 10-page memorandum from Foreign Minister Shevardnadze, Defence Minister Army-General Dmitrii Yazov, and State Foreign Economic Commission Chairman Vladimir Kamentsev summarising the findings of the review and laying out a series of far-reaching recommendations.[66] The memorandum noted that 'the extreme circumstances that might trigger the provision of military assistance [to a Warsaw Pact country] pertain only to foreign threats, that is, situations when the right to individual or collective self-defence is carried out in accordance with Article 51 of the UN Charter'. The document said that even 'in the case of an armed attack' from outside, the 'relevant provisions' in the Warsaw Treaty regarding collective defence were 'flexible and did not automatically require the provision of military assistance'. The Soviet Union's bilateral treaties with East European countries were 'more definite' in calling for 'the immediate provision of all manner of assistance, including military aid', but this was true only when 'needed to defend against external armed attack'.[67]

Shevardnadze, Yazov and Kamentsev stressed that 'internal situations in the [Warsaw Pact] countries ... do not fall into the category' of contingencies covered by the Warsaw Treaty or by the bilateral defence treaties linking the Soviet Union with individual Warsaw Pact states 'and therefore do not require us to take any sorts of measures in connection with our treaty obligations'. The memorandum noted that 'two of the [Soviet Union's bilateral] treaties—those with Czechoslovakia and the GDR—contain clauses about the defence of people's socialist gains', and the three Soviet officials acknowledged that these clauses 'are construed in the West as codifying a right to the collective defence of socialism, including the use of military force, against internal as well as external threats'. This was indeed the way Western observers had always interpreted those clauses in the two treaties, and it was also the way Soviet leaders had construed them prior to 1989. Shevardnadze, Yazov and Kamentsev argued that such interpretations were invalid and that 'the language in the [USSR's bilateral treaties with the GDR and Czechoslovakia] is in fact very general and does not in any way stipulate that military assistance must be provided'.[68]

The three officials argued that 'the phrasing of the Warsaw Treaty concerning the provision of military assistance is adequate for the current situation in the world and does not require any sorts of changes to be introduced'. They added that

> although the obligations contained in the USSR's bilateral treaties with allied states are formulated more strictly and could be construed in ways undesirable for us, it would not be

[66]'Tovarishchu Gorbachevu M. S.', Memorandum No. 242/OS (Top Secret) to M. S. Gorbachev from E. Shevardnadze, D. Yazov and V. Kamentsev, 25 March 1989, in Hoover Archives (Stanford University), Papers of Vitalii Leonidovich Kataev, Box 13, Folder 14, pp. 1–10. Vitalii Kataev was deputy head of the CPSU Defense Industry Department (renamed Defence Department in 1991) during the Gorbachev era and served as an adviser to the CPSU General Secretary on military issues, arms control and weapons production. Before he died in 2001, he and his daughter had arranged for copies of his papers to be transferred to the Hoover Institution, which acquired them in 2002. Five of the 20 boxes of papers have not yet been released, but all the rest are accessible.

[67]Papers of Vitalii Leonidovich Kataev, Box 13, Folder 14, pp. 1–2.

[68]Papers of Vitalii Leonidovich Kataev, Box 13, Folder 14, pp. 1–2.

> appropriate for us to take the initiative in suggesting modifications or a re-examination of the treaties, in light of the travails being experienced by these states and the complex processes under way in them. Such an initiative might result in a weakening of allied relations and exacerbate the centrifugal trends in the [socialist] community and facilitate the destabilisation of the situation in several of the countries.[69]

The memorandum went on to say that 'if the question of re-examining a bilateral treaty is raised by the allied state itself, as is now being done by Bulgaria, then of course we should pursue the task of clarifying the treaty's terms, albeit without detriment to the allied obligations laid out therein'. The three officials said that 'concretely what we have in mind is to include in a new bilateral treaty the phrasing that now appears in the Warsaw Treaty regarding the provision of [Soviet] military assistance' to a country under attack.[70]

Zagladin's original memorandum to Gorbachev on 24 January had proposed that 'after carrying out a review [of the USSR's military obligations] and taking account of the results of this review, we could consider raising this matter in strict confidence with the American side'.[71] Gorbachev did not reject the idea, and Zagladin subsequently recommended to Shevardnadze, Yazov and Kamentsev that the Soviet Union 'should discuss with the American side on a confidential basis [the USSR's] obligations concerning the provision of military assistance to allies'. The implication was that they should privately let US officials know that the Soviet Union would no longer be coming to the aid of East European regimes faced with severe internal crises. Shevardnadze, Yazov and Kamentsev said they found Zagladin's proposal to be of 'dubious merit', not only because 'the USA would promptly inform its allies about such discussions' but also because the confidential discussions 'inevitably would be leaked to the press and we would appear in the eyes of our allies to be conspiring behind their backs with the Americans regarding our obligations to our allies. The political effect of this [in Eastern Europe] would be extremely negative'. Although Shevardnadze, Yazov and Kamentsev expressed strong support for 'the further positive development of the Soviet–American dialogue', they warned against explicitly taking up such sensitive matters with the US government and argued that Soviet officials should instead discuss in a more general way with their American counterparts how the two sides could 'constructively approach the regulation of concrete problems that currently exist or could arise in different regions of the world'.[72]

Even though Zagladin's proposal was not ultimately adopted, the mere fact that he suggested it underscores the firmness of the Soviet Union's decision to avoid the use of military force in Eastern Europe and illustrates how much the international context of Soviet–East European relations had changed during the Gorbachev era. In the past, especially during the halcyon days of US 'rollback' and 'liberation' policies in the 1950s, the zero-sum nature of the Cold War rivalry would have caused Soviet leaders

[69]Papers of Vitalii Leonidovich Kataev, Box 13, Folder 14, p. 5.

[70]Papers of Vitalii Leonidovich Kataev, Box 13, Folder 14, p. 6.

[71]'Dokladnaya zapiska o peresmotre obyazatel'stv po okazaniyu voennoi pomoshchi', in AGF, F. 3, Dok. 7179, L. 3.

[72]Papers of Vitalii Leonidovich Kataev, Box 13, Folder 14, p. 9.

to fear that even the slightest relaxation of Soviet control in Eastern Europe would be exploited by the United States.[73] No Soviet official prior to the late-1980s would ever have suggested holding confidential discussions with the United States about Soviet intentions in Eastern Europe. Since 1985, however, the rapid improvement of US–Soviet relations had given Soviet leaders ample confidence that the United States was no longer trying to undermine Moscow's vital political–military interests in Eastern Europe.

Indeed, this very matter had come up explicitly in bilateral talks in mid-January 1989 (shortly before Zagladin sent his memorandum to Gorbachev) when former US Secretary of State Henry Kissinger travelled to Moscow unofficially on behalf of the Trilateral Commission with the knowledge and quiet blessing of the incoming administration of George H. W. Bush.[74] Kissinger's confidential discussions with Gorbachev and Yakovlev focused on, among other things, Soviet policy toward Eastern Europe in the context of US–Soviet relations. In a conversation with Yakovlev, Kissinger proposed that senior US and Soviet officials begin a secret 'political dialogue' that would help to promote 'political evolution' in Eastern Europe in an orderly way, eliminating the 'potential for instability'. The aim would be to defuse the 'dangerously volatile conditions' in the region and to avert any 'political explosions'. Kissinger reported that he had 'discussed this matter in detail with G. Bush's entourage', and that 'the incoming US administration would be ready to discuss these questions in a confidential format' while 'taking full account of [the USSR's] legitimate security interests' in Eastern Europe.[75] Gorbachev promptly surmised, as he later told the CPSU Politburo, that Kissinger was in effect advocating 'a US–Soviet condominium in Europe'—a largely accurate characterisation of Kissinger's intention (though not necessarily of any measures the incoming Bush administration would have been willing to embrace in public).[76]

Although Gorbachev clearly welcomed Kissinger's proposal, he expressed concern that it would give the impression of 'an attempt at collusion between the USSR and the USA at the expense of Europe'. When Shevardnadze, Yazov and Kamentsev turned down Zagladin's proposal, the reasons they cited were not that the United States was hell-bent on fomenting or taking advantage of turmoil in Eastern Europe. Instead, the problem, as they (and Gorbachev) saw it, was the opposite—namely, that relations between the United States and Soviet Union had warmed so much over the past few years that East European leaders would be inclined to suspect that US and Soviet officials were conniving behind the backs of the East European governments to promote the superpowers' common interest in the region's fate. The far-reaching

[73]See, for example, Khrushchev's comments in late October 1956 about the US government's malevolent designs *vis-à-vis* Hungary ('Rabochaya zapis' zasedaniya Prezidiyuma TsK KPSS, 31 oktyabrya 1956 g.', Transcript of CPSU Presidium Session (Strictly Secret), 31 October 1956, in TsKhSD, F. 3, Op. 12, D. 1006, Ll. 15–18ob).

[74]On the Kissinger–Gorbachev talks, see Matlock (1995, pp. 190–92).

[75]'Zapis' besedy A. N. Yakovleva s G. Kissindzherom (SShA) 16 yanvarya 1989 g. po mezhdunarodnym problemam', Summary Transcript of conversation (Secret), 17 January 1989, in GARF, F. 10063, Op. 1, D. 258, Ll. 1–5.

[76]'Zapis' zasedaniya Politbyuro TsK KPSS, 24 yanvarya 1989 goda', Transcript of CPSU Politburo Session (Top Secret), 24 January 1989, in AGF, F. 10, Op. 2, Ll. 198–99.

improvement of US–Soviet relations was thus conducive to bold Soviet actions *vis-à-vis* Eastern Europe—actions that would have been inconceivable at any previous stage of the Cold War.

The push for far-reaching change and the impact of Tiananmen

After forging a high-level consensus that the Soviet Union would not use military force to suppress internal upheavals in Eastern Europe, Gorbachev and his aides still faced the challenge of ensuring that what Shakhnazarov in October 1988 had described as the 'fundamental changes' and 'radical reforms needed everywhere' in the region would occur peacefully. This question took on particular urgency in the spring and summer of 1989 amid a surge of unrest in the USSR itself, including fighting between Azerbaijanis and Armenians over Nagorno-Karabakh and mass demonstrations in Tbilisi that were crushed by the Soviet Army in April 1989. The crackdown in Tbilisi, killing 19 people and wounding nearly 300, was implemented locally without Gorbachev's authorisation and against his expressed wishes. Both Gorbachev and Shevardnadze promptly disavowed and condemned the operation, vowing that 'this sort of tragedy will never be allowed to happen again'.[77] Moreover, even though Gorbachev was increasingly preoccupied by instability at home and other pressing domestic issues, the growing restiveness in several Soviet republics reinforced his desire to prevent violent turmoil from erupting along the USSR's western flank.

Because far-reaching liberalisation was already under way in Hungary and Poland, the main task for Soviet officials in those two countries was to encourage continued progress and to dispel any doubt that the Soviet Union would stand in the way of drastic change there. Even when the Hungarian government moved well ahead of the USSR itself in reassessing the 1956 Hungarian revolution and other sensitive issues in bilateral Soviet–Hungarian relations, Soviet leaders refrained from hindering the process.[78] The ceremonial reburial in June 1989 of Imre Nagy, the reformist Prime Minister of Hungary in 1956, was the culmination of a series of key events in 1989 linked with Hungary's efforts to come to terms with the 1956 revolution and the forceful suppression of it by Soviet troops (Kramer 1989–1990, pp. 44–45).

On 15 June, the day before the re-interment of Nagy, a small demonstration occurred in front of the Soviet embassy in Budapest. The next day, more than 250,000 people turned out for the ceremony, which featured emotional and often fiery speeches (including some with a distinctly anti-Soviet tinge), marking a turning point in Hungary's democratisation. Official Soviet commentary on the reburial referred to it as a 'humane act' undertaken 'in the spirit of national reconciliation'—a striking

[77]For a full account and evidence from declassified sources, see Kramer (2004, pp. 27–32).

[78]Until October 1991, by which time the Soviet regime was in its terminal phase, Gorbachev never criticised the Soviet invasion of Hungary in 1956 or reassessed the Hungarian revolution. As late as March 1989, in a private conversation with Hungarian Prime Minister Miklós Németh, Gorbachev argued that the unrest in Hungary in October 1956 had 'deteriorated into counterrevolution and bloodshed', and he expressed disapproval of attempts in Hungary to characterise the revolution as a 'popular uprising' ('Zapis' besedy M. S. Gorbacheva s chlenom TsK VSRP, Predsedatelem Soveta Ministrov VNR Mikloshem Nemetom, 3 marta 1989', Notes of conversation (Top Secret), 3 March 1989, in AGF, F. 1, Op. 1, Dok. 8325, L. 3).

contrast to the furious reaction that such an event (or anything remotely like it) would have provoked in Moscow under previous Soviet leaders (Kusin 1989). Soviet officials were even willing to forgo any criticism of the anti-Soviet comments voiced by some orators at the reburial, describing these as merely Hungary's 'internal affair'.

In Poland from late 1988 on, Gorbachev and his aides had to take a more active role than in Hungary as they nudged along the process of change and ensured that the Polish regime headed by Wojciech Jaruzelski would not try to backtrack and end the liberalising reforms.[79] Soviet leaders encouraged the re-legalisation of Solidarity, the convocation of Round Table talks between Solidarity and the communist regime, and the arrangement to hold partly free elections for a new Polish legislature. As far back as September 1988, Gorbachev had told a senior PZPR official, Józef Czyrek, that the Polish communists would lose out in the Round Table talks unless they finally 'took account of realities [in Polish society] that cannot be ignored' and stopped 'acting out of fear'. Gorbachev sensed that because the PZPR had 'wasted so much time', the Party would find it hard to 'cope with the prominence and broad popularity of the opposition'.[80] Whenever Jaruzelski or other senior Polish communist officials expected (or hoped) that the Soviet Union might try to curtail the liberalisation, Soviet leaders did just the opposite, pushing the authorities to compromise with Solidarity and signalling approval of any outcome that might emerge.

In the four other Warsaw Pact countries—Czechoslovakia, East Germany, Bulgaria and Romania—the communist regimes had staunchly eschewed any hint of liberalisation and had, if anything, become increasingly repressive and intransigent as the internal and external pressures for reform grew. Leading officials in those countries were heartened in early June 1989 when the Politburo of the Chinese Communist Party (CCP) ordered a brutal attack by army troops and security forces against a vast crowd of unarmed people around Tiananmen Square in Beijing, bringing an end to several weeks of protests.

The crisis in Beijing had begun in mid-April 1989 when a fledgling 'pro-democracy' movement coalesced in Tiananmen Square, inspired in part by the death of the ousted CCP leader Hu Yaobang (who had been removed in 1987 after seeking to move ahead with political liberalisation) and also by the rapid changes under way in the Soviet Union, Hungary and Poland. Mass demonstrations spread to Shanghai, Harbin, Chengdu, Nanjin and other cities in China, but the primary focus both for the Chinese regime and for the international community was the unrest in Beijing. Several weeks of peaceful if boisterous protests ensued by vast throngs of students, young workers, peasants and other people in and around Tiananmen Square.[81] Hunger strikes by students starting in mid-May drew particularly wide notice both at home and abroad. The CCP General Secretary, Zhao Ziyang, wanted to pursue a genuine compromise with the demonstrators and to introduce broad political reforms, but he was unable to win support from his

[79]For a detailed discussion of the Soviet Union's role *vis-à-vis* the changes in Poland, see Kramer (2003, pp. 178–256).

[80]'Zapis' besedy M. S. Gorbacheva s Sekretarem TsK PORP Yu. Chirekom', Notes from conversation (Secret), 23 September 1988, in AGF, F. 10, Op. 2, Dok. 0097.

[81]For varying perspectives on the Tiananmen Square crisis, see Brook (1998), Zhao (2001), Galenovich (1995), Reichenbach (1994) and Tokaev (1994); and the useful compendium of essays and documents edited by Ruth Cremerius, Doris Fischer and Peter Schier (1990).

colleagues on the CCP Politburo.[82] Although one senior official, Hu Qili, did side with Zhao, they were outflanked by eight Party elders led by Deng Xiaoping, who warned that 'if things continue this way, we could even end up under house arrest'.[83] Other Politburo members expressed strong support of Deng's views, arguing that any 'retreat' in the face of such an audacious challenge would lead to the 'destruction of the People's Republic' and the 'overthrow of our party and government'.[84] Loudest of all in calling for a massive crackdown was Wang Zhen, a staunch hardliner on the CCP Politburo, who described the protesters as 'goddamn bastards' and declared that the army should 'show them no mercy'. At Deng's behest, the CCP Politburo approved 'decisive measures to put down the counterrevolutionary riot' in Beijing and authorised the 'use of any means necessary to remove people who interfere with this mission'.[85]

On the evening of 3–4 June, cordons of troops from the 27th Group Army Unit and special-purpose security forces moved into the centre of Beijing and clashed with demonstrators at numerous points around Tiananmen Square. The troops then surrounded the area and repeatedly opened fire on serried crowds of protesters, killing more than 1,000 and wounding at least several thousand.[86] Tens of thousands of other

[82]Zhao Ziyang's invaluable memoir (2009, pp. 3–49) offers a fascinating perspective on the events of 1989 in China. His memoir amply corroborates the collection of notes from the deliberations of Chinese Communist leaders in April–June 1989 published by Andrew Nathan and Perry Link (2001). Although the exact provenance of these notes is still uncertain, Zhao Ziyang's memoir dispels lingering doubts about their authenticity. The notes, like Zhao's memoir, show that Zhao spoke strongly in favour of a political compromise at sessions of the CCP Politburo's Standing Committee on 13, 16 and 17 May 1989, but Deng Xiaoping left no doubt that he fundamentally disagreed with Zhao (see Nathan & Link 2001, pp. 147–52, 177–81, 184–89). From then on, Zhao's ouster was only a matter of time. (He was demoted on 20 May and then replaced altogether by Jiang Zemin shortly after the crackdown.) When reading Zhao's comments nowadays about the need to 'use the methods of democracy and law' in accommodating the protesters, one cannot help but be struck by the similarity to the policies advocated in the late 1980s and early 1990s by leading Soviet 'new thinkers' such as Yakovlev and Shakhnazarov. By contrast, the staunch hardliners on the Chinese Politburo in 1989, particularly Wang Zhen and Li Peng, were similar in their outlooks to the ultra-hardliners in Moscow, such as Oleg Baklanov and General Valentin Varennikov, both of whom were instrumental in the attempted coup in August 1991.

[83]Comments by Deng at meeting of the CCP Politburo's Standing Committee on 17 May 1989, in Nathan and Link (2001, p. 189); see also Zhao (2009, pp. 43–45).

[84]Comments by Deng Yingchao, Chen Yun and Wang Zhen at an enlarged meeting of the CCP Politburo's Standing Committee on 18 May 1989, in Nathan and Link (2001, pp. 204–11).

[85]Transcript of an enlarged session of the CCP Politburo's Standing Committee on 2 June 1989 (Nathan & Link, 2001, pp. 355–62).

[86]The precise number killed and wounded is as yet unknown and may never be known. Based on a canvass of major hospitals in Beijing, the Chinese Red Cross concluded that 2,600 civilians and troops were killed and more than 7,000 were wounded. In a secret cable to US Secretary of State James Baker on 22 June 1989, the US embassy in Beijing described the Chinese Red Cross's figures as 'not an unreasonable estimate' but noted that the totals 'do not include [unrecorded] deaths on the streets'. See 'What Happened on the Night of June 3/4?', Cable No. 1411 (Confidential), 22 June 1989, in George Bush Presidential Library, Texas A&M University, College Station, TX, Subject File: China Documents, FOIA Documents Collection 2000-0950-F, Doc. E44. Other estimates—some lower, some higher—have also been proposed, but no firm corroboration is yet available. Apparently no one was killed in Tiananmen Square itself because President Yang Shangkun (on behalf of Deng Xiaoping) had ordered the troops not to open fire there. The crackdown occurred at many key sites around the square, ranging up to a kilometre away.

protesters were arrested over the next few days on charges of 'counterrevolutionary rioting'.

The sweeping crackdown in the Chinese capital offered mixed lessons for Communist Party leaders in Eastern Europe and the Soviet Union. On the one hand, the crisis illustrated the potential efficacy of all-out force against internal unrest. The massacre and systematic arrests of 'lawless elements and counterrevolutionary ringleaders' in Beijing put an abrupt end to the escalating protests in China and allowed the Chinese Communist authorities to re-establish tight control. The decisive crackdown was seen by some hardliners in Moscow—and, even more, by orthodox communist leaders in Eastern Europe, who spoke appreciatively of the 'Chinese solution'—as a model for the sort of large-scale repressive actions that might soon be needed in most of the Warsaw Pact countries if mass unrest there continued to grow.[87]

On the other hand, the repression in China had a jarring effect on many high-ranking Soviet officials, including Gorbachev, who by all accounts was taken aback and dismayed by the scale of the bloodshed.[88] The massacre came less than three weeks after Gorbachev had made a landmark visit to China, the first such visit by a Soviet leader in 30 years. When the protests began in Beijing in April 1989, the Chinese authorities had hoped that they would soon peter out and that the demonstrators would be gone from Tiananmen Square by the time Gorbachev arrived on 15 May.[89] Far from diminishing, however, the protests—and foreign press coverage of them—increased sharply in the lead-up to Gorbachev's visit, which itself attracted even greater publicity to the demonstrations. Although Chinese officials who coordinated the Soviet delegation's itinerary tried to keep Gorbachev away from Tiananmen Square, the overflowing crowds there rapturously welcomed his presence in Beijing, believing that he shared their aims and would be able to convince the Chinese authorities to negotiate with them. The demonstrators held up large photographs of Gorbachev alongside placards exclaiming 'We salute the messenger of democracy!'[90] Gorbachev's statement during a public appearance that economic reform would work

[87]East German and Romanian communist leaders were especially enthusiastic about the 'Chinese solution'. See, for example, the text of a secret speech delivered on 9 June by East German State Security Minister Erich Mielke, reproduced in 'Krenz und Mielke vereinbarten auf Geheimkonferenz chinesische Lösung', *Die Welt,* 21 May 1990, p. 6. See also the secret deliberations recorded in '"Chinesische Lösung": Wollten Stasi-Leute ein Blutbad unter Demonstranten provozieren?', *Der Spiegel*, 51, 18 December 1989, pp. 42–44; König (1989, p. 4); and the two-part article by Cordt Schnibben (1990a, pp. 72–90; 1990b, pp. 78–98).

[88]The jarring effect that the Tiananmen crackdown had in Moscow in 1989 was emphasised by Shakhnazarov, Yakovlev and Chernyaev in several interviews with the author in Moscow, 14 March and 7 May 1998 (Shakhnazarov), 10 June 2001 (Chernyaev), and 21–22 January 2003 (Yakovlev).

[89]Zhao Ziyang's memoir and the records of CCP Politburo meetings published by Nathan and Link (2001) bear out much of the analysis in a secret, 16-page report issued by the CIA three months after the crackdown, *The Road to the Tiananmen Crackdown: An Analytic Chronology of Chinese Leadership Decision Making,* EA 89-10030 (Confidential/No Foreign Distribution), September 1989, declassified in March 2000, available in NARA/CREST. Some of the dates and details in the CIA report are inaccurate but the thrust of the report and many specific details hold up surprisingly well against the newly released evidence.

[90]The account here is drawn from *Novosti* television evening news broadcasts on 15, 16 and 17 May 1989 (programme videotapes stored at Davis Center for Russian Eurasian Studies, Harvard University) as well as from descriptions of Gorbachev's trip in *Ekho planety*, 22, 61, 25 May 1989,

only if accompanied by broad democratisation (a view championed by Zhao Ziyang, whom Gorbachev regarded as a like-minded leader in Beijing), struck a particular chord of approval among the protesters.[91]

Two days after arriving in Beijing, Gorbachev was asked at a news conference what he would do if confronted by large-scale demonstrations in Moscow comparable to those taking place in the Chinese capital. He replied that 'if problems of this sort or of a similar nature were to occur in the Soviet Union, we would analyse their specific features and seek political methods of resolving them'. He praised the efforts that Chinese leaders (or at least Zhao Ziyang individually) were making to initiate a 'constructive dialogue' with the demonstrators.[92] Although Gorbachev stressed that his comments were not intended as 'advice to the Chinese people about how they should act in this specific situation', and although he believed that the Chinese authorities were justified in trying to restore order and tranquillity in the capital, he made clear throughout his visit that he supported 'political processes and political solutions', not mass bloodshed.[93]

After Gorbachev returned to Moscow on 18 May, he had to focus on important sessions of the Soviet parliament and the CPSU Central Committee. Nonetheless, his trip to China continued to reverberate in both China and the USSR. On 21 May, tens of thousands of pro-democracy activists in Moscow held a rally calling for bolder reforms and expressing fervent admiration of the protesters in China. Cries of 'Long live the demonstrators on the streets of Beijing!' earned thunderous applause at the rally. By this point, however, Gorbachev's foreign policy advisers sensed that the situation in China was taking a turn for the worse.[94] On 20 May, Prime Minister Li Peng had declared martial law and brought armed soldiers into central Beijing, and this was soon followed by indications that Zhao Ziyang had been stripped of all his functions. In the light of the growing uncertainty about events in China, the official Soviet media featured restrained (though generally favourable) coverage of the protests in Tiananmen Square in the final week of May and first few days of June.[95] To the extent that Soviet leaders were monitoring events abroad, their attention was focused mostly on Poland, where partly free legislative elections were to be held on 4 June.

As it turned out, 4 June was also the day of the massacre in Beijing. Shakhnazarov, Yakovlev and Chernyaev later recalled that when Gorbachev learned about the harshness of the crackdown in China and the high death toll, coming so soon after his

pp. 21–22, and press coverage in *The New York Times*, *The Washington Post*, the *Los Angeles Times*, the *Financial Times* (London) and *Le Monde* (Paris).

[91]On Gorbachev's highly favorable assessment of Zhao Ziyang, as well as other interesting details about the Soviet delegation's arrival, see 'Informatsiya M. S. Gorbacheva o poezdke v Kitai', Report to the CPSU Politburo (Top Secret), 20 May 1989, and 'Razgovor Gorbacheva (po telefonu iz Pekina) s Medvedevym, 15 maya 1989 goda', Notes from telephone conversation, 15 May 1989, both in KDPP, vol. 4, pp. 392–93 and 391–92, respectively.

[92]'Press-konferentsiya M. S. Gorbacheva v Pekine', *Pravda*, 18 May 1989, p. 3. The dilemma facing Gorbachev during the trip is well captured in Palazhchenko (1997, pp. 134–38).

[93]On the Chinese leaders' reaction to Gorbachev's visit, see especially the comments at meetings of the Chinese Politburo on 16 and 17 May 1989, transcribed in Nathan and Link (2001, pp. 180–98).

[94]See the diary entry for 21 May 1989 in Chernyaev (2008, pp. 795–98).

[95]For a very useful analysis, see Lukin (1991, pp. 119–36).

visit, he was 'shocked', 'nearly speechless' and 'shaken'.[96] Yakovlev remembered being 'appalled' at the violence and said that he and Gorbachev 'realised right away that the methods they used in China were exactly what we [in Moscow] had to avoid'.[97] Gorbachev's interpreter, Pavel Palazhchenko, likewise recalled that both Gorbachev and Shevardnadze found the massacre 'abhorrent' but were in a 'real quandary' about how to respond (Palazhchenko 1997, pp. 137–38). Gorbachev had concurred with the Chinese leaders' goal of restoring order in Beijing and avoiding 'chaos and social upheaval', but in his view the price they paid in achieving it was so onerous that it would be wholly unacceptable if replicated in Eastern Europe or the Soviet Union itself. The number killed in Beijing was at least 50–100 times greater than in Tbilisi in April 1989, an event that had caused weeks of intense controversy and anguish in the USSR and recriminations against the Soviet Army.

Televised images of the carnage in China in early June, juxtaposed with news from Poland that Solidarity had won an overwhelming victory in the parliamentary elections (gaining all but one of the 261 seats it was allowed to contest), reinforced the widespread belief in Moscow that urgent steps were needed to forestall a cycle of violent unrest and repression in Eastern Europe that might escalate and lead to a Tiananmen-style crackdown. The broadcasts from China also coincided with live television coverage of the newly opened session of the Soviet parliament. Gorbachev did not want strong criticism of China to be voiced in public at the parliament, and he turned off the microphone when Andrei Sakharov started giving a speech denouncing the massacre and calling for the Soviet ambassador in Beijing to be withdrawn in protest.[98] Sakharov also organised a group of parliamentary deputies to issue a statement publicly condemning the mass killing in China and 'urging the Chinese government to stop the bloodshed now'.[99] In Hungary, too, senior officials expressed 'great shock and indignation' at the 'massacre' and 'deeply condemned the use of military force and terror against unarmed crowds'. Thousands of ordinary Hungarians took part in a protest rally in front of the Chinese embassy in Budapest, with the Hungarian government's tacit consent. The demonstrators voiced 'outrage' at the 'bloodbath' perpetrated by 'mass murderers' (Reisch 1989, pp. 1–6).

Although Gorbachev and his advisers did not join in the public criticism of the Chinese regime in the immediate aftermath of the Tiananmen Square crackdown, the Soviet leader did soon afterwards address the Soviet parliament in public about 'our reaction to the well-known events in Beijing'. He tactfully but firmly rejected the approach used by the Chinese authorities and the consequences that ensued:

> We have expressed our attitude to the tragedy that happened in Beijing [on 4 June]. We deplore that it turned out that way. We are in favour of having the most acute problems

[96]See the interviews adduced in note 88.

[97]Interview by the author with Yakovlev, 21–22 January 2003, Moscow.

[98]Sakharov's speech on 7 June was excluded from the proceedings published in *Izvestiya* the next day, but the full text was put out as a brochure by the Inter-Regional Group in mid-June 1989. Soon thereafter, the American lawyer Edward Kline, a long-time champion of Sakharov's defence of human rights, translated the full text of the speech and published it as 'A Speech to the People's Congress' in *The New York Review of Books* (Sakharov 1989, pp. 30–31).

[99]'Obrashchenie Mezhregional'noi gruppoi narodynkh deputatov (iyunya 1989 g.)', 9 June 1989, reproduced in Sakharov (1996, p. 574).

> solved solely through political dialogue between the authorities and the people. This is what we believe. Such is the method we have chosen for ourselves. Each people solves its problems in its own way, but [reliance on dialogue] is our principled and, I believe, irreversible position.[100]

Even though Gorbachev's public criticism of the Tiananmen Square massacre was not as strong as the speech delivered by Sakharov, the Soviet leader's comments left no doubt that he viewed the bloodshed as a 'tragic' blunder. Far from seeing the Tiananmen Square crackdown as a model for what should be done in the Soviet bloc, Gorbachev and other high-ranking Soviet officials, especially Shevardnadze, Yakovlev and Shakhnazarov, regarded it as something to avoid in Eastern Europe (and the USSR) at all costs.

The Tiananmen Square crackdown thus accelerated the trends that had been shaping Soviet policy toward Eastern Europe since late 1988. The brutal repression in China, and the widespread condemnation it evoked around the world, reinforced the decision the CPSU Politburo had taken a few months earlier to eschew any Soviet military responses to internal crises in Eastern Europe. Equally important, the traumatic example of the mass unrest and violent reaction in Beijing impelled Gorbachev to strive more actively in the latter half of 1989 to promote peaceful, far-reaching liberalisation in Eastern Europe.

Contending with hardline regimes

Even if Gorbachev and other senior officials in Moscow saw the massacre in China as a reason to push ahead with democratising reforms in Eastern Europe and the USSR, the 'lesson' drawn by the leaders of East Germany, Czechoslovakia and Romania was just the opposite—namely, that any move toward political liberalisation would be dangerous and that large-scale violent repression, as in China, would enable them to crush any opposition that might emerge. But even the most hardline officials in those countries were aware that any attempt they might make in the future to emulate the Tiananmen Square crackdown—if the need should arise—would require at least tacit Soviet approval and probably direct backing.

Gorbachev was well aware that communist leaders in East Berlin, Prague and Bucharest were alarmed by what was going on in Hungary, Poland and the USSR and were determined to avoid any movement in that direction themselves. Shakhnazarov had argued in his October 1988 memorandum that the East German, Czechoslovak and Romanian authorities were 'averse to making changes in anything' and were 'stubbornly refusing to heed the pressures for change'—sentiments that became even more pronounced as 1989 wore on. Hence, the challenge Soviet officials faced was to push, discreetly but meaningfully, for liberalisation in the four countries that were holding out. At a minimum, Soviet leaders wanted to convey the message through all possible channels that the Soviet Union would oppose the use of violent repression.

[100] 'Vystuplenie M. S. Gorbacheva na pervoi sessii Verkhovnogo Soveta SSSR po itogam vizitov v Velikobritaniyu, Federativnuyu Respubliku Germanii i vo Frantsiyu i ob uchastii v soveshchanii PKK gosudarstv-uchastnikov Varshavskogo Dogovora', *Pravda*, 2 August 1989, p. 2.

To this end, Gorbachev's public comments about Eastern Europe grew bolder. In a speech before the Council of Europe in July 1989, he expressed support for the maintenance of socialism in Europe, but then indicated a willingness to accept whatever result might come:

> The social and political orders of certain countries [in Europe] changed in the past, and could change again in the future. However, this is exclusively a matter for the peoples themselves to decide; it is their choice. Any interference in internal affairs, or any attempts to limit the sovereignty of states—including friends and allies, or anyone else—are impermissible.[101]

The speech, coming at a time when Solidarity seemed poised to form a non-communist government in Poland and when 'Round Table' talks were moving briskly ahead in Hungary, dispelled any lingering hopes the hardline East European regimes might have had that Gorbachev would try to rein in the forces he had unleashed. The morale of the East German, Czechoslovak and Romanian leaders, which had been eroding for at least a year, plummeted further, and a sense of desperation crept in during the latter half of 1989.

The quickening pace of events throughout the Soviet bloc in the late summer of 1989 culminated in two developments that together marked a point of no return in the political complexion of Eastern Europe and also in Soviet policy towards the region: the formation of a Solidarity-led government in Poland in late August, and the Hungarian government's announcement on 10 September that it would open Hungary's border with Austria to let out thousands of East German citizens who had been pouring into Hungary over the previous few months, hoping to make their way from there to the Federal Republic of Germany (FRG). A year or two earlier, neither of these developments would have seemed plausible, but by August–September 1989 they not only were occurring but were occurring with the Soviet Union's consent.

Ascendance of Mazowiecki's government

On 27 May 1989, a week before the elections in Poland, the CPSU Politburo received a memorandum from the deputy head of the CPSU International Department, Rafail Fedorov, reporting that 'the election campaign [in Poland] has not unfolded in the PZPR's favour' and that 'the authority of the PZPR has continued to fall'. Fedorov expressed concern that 'results that are very unfavorable for the PZPR will be dangerous [for the Soviet Union] both at this point and in the future'. He warned that although 'the PZPR leadership has belatedly come to appreciate the danger of the situation', the Party's 'efforts to halt all the negative trends' might not be enough to turn the situation around.[102] Sobering as Fedorov's report may have been, it actually underestimated the humiliation that was about to be inflicted on the PZPR. On 4 June the Polish communists suffered a resounding defeat, which left the leaders of the Party in stunned disbelief.

[101] 'Rech' M. S. Gorbacheva', *Izvestiya*, 7 July 1989, p. 2.

[102] 'TsK KPSS: O predvybornoi kampanii v Pol'she', Memorandum No. 17-382 (Top Secret) from R. Fedorov, first deputy head of the CPSU International Department, to the CPSU Politburo, 27 May 1989, in RGANI, F. 5, Op. 102, D. 762, Ll. 123–26.

Despite this unwelcome setback, Gorbachev and his advisers publicly and privately expressed acceptance of the results, giving the Polish communist authorities no choice but to go along with their party's defeat, if only reluctantly. Plans devised by the Polish Ministry of Internal Affairs for the possible imposition of martial law in the event of an undesired outcome had to be shelved.[103] Gorbachev's speech at the Council of Europe declaring that the Soviet Union would 'respect the absolute right of every nation to choose its own social system as it sees fit' provided a further boost to Solidarity in Poland's post-election manoeuvring. To dispel any ambiguity about this phrasing, Gorbachev instructed one of his top aides, Vadim Zagladin, to make clear that Poland, like every other nation, had the 'absolute right to choose its own social system', including the option of a non-communist government. When Zagladin was asked, on the eve of Gorbachev's visit to Strasbourg, whether the Soviet Union would be willing to tolerate a Solidarity-led government in Warsaw, he replied: 'We will maintain ties with any Polish government that emerges after the recent elections. This is purely a Polish internal affair. Any solution adopted by our Polish friends will be acceptable to us'.[104]

By indicating that the question of whether Poland would remain a communist state was 'purely a Polish internal affair', Zagladin sent a powerful message to the Polish authorities (and, indirectly, to all the other leaders in Eastern Europe). Certainly no one in the PZPR could any longer hope that the Soviet Union would, *in extremis*, come to the rescue—militarily or otherwise—of the decaying communist regime in Warsaw.

The Soviet Union's role in the process remained vital in late July 1989, when pressure mounted in Poland for the establishment of a non-communist government headed by Solidarity. Jaruzelski tried to stave off this development by publicly warning that 'adjoining states', especially the Soviet Union, would 'look at this askance'.[105] The Polish leader was hoping that the Soviet government would back him up, but his hopes proved in vain. After consulting with Gorbachev, Aleksandr Yakovlev discreetly sought assurances from Solidarity that it would uphold Poland's obligations in the Warsaw Pact and under bilateral treaties with the USSR. Having obtained these assurances, Yakovlev declared that 'political arrangements in Poland are solely for the Poles themselves to decide, without interference from outside'. The Soviet Union, he added, would accept any government that emerged, 'no matter who is in charge'.[106]

With that, the PZPR's last hope of preserving its 'leading role', its hegemonic political position in Polish society, disappeared. By the third week in August the Polish communist authorities were forced to give Solidarity an opportunity to form its own government under Tadeusz Mazowiecki. Before Mazowiecki's government could actually take office, however, Soviet intervention was required again. The PZPR First

[103]For details on these plans, see Kramer (2003, pp. 195–97).

[104]'Każdy rząd będzie dla nas partnerem', *Gazeta wyborcza*, 4 July 1989, p. 1; see also the commentary by Adam Michnik (1989, p. 5).

[105]'Przed utworzeniem rządu—mówią uczestnicy konsultacji', *Trybuna Ludu*, 27 July 1989, p. 2.

[106]TASS, 29 July 1989, Item 1127/203. See also 'Predlozheniya o razgovore s pol'skimi deyatelyami', Memorandum from A. N. Yakovlev to M. S. Gorbachev (Secret), 18 August 1989, in GARF, F. 10063, Op. 2, D. 187, Ll. 1–5.

Secretary, Mieczysław Rakowski, made a last-ditch effort to undercut the new government by declaring that he would not go along with Mazowiecki's appointment unless the PZPR was given additional ministerial slots beyond the two already promised. Lech Wałęsa and Mazowiecki warned Rakowski to 'stop rocking the boat' with 'threats and blackmail', and a deadlock ensued.[107] For a brief while the whole arrangement in Poland seemed on the verge of collapse, but Gorbachev stepped in to salvage it. He brought the matter before the CPSU Politburo and gained unanimous support for a direct admonition to Rakowski.[108] The Soviet leader then made a 40-minute telephone call to Rakowski as the process reached its most delicate stage. Although Gorbachev assured him that the PZPR would continue to enjoy staunch Soviet backing, he 'recommended' that the Polish communists avoid a costly and prolonged confrontation with Solidarity—a striking reversal of the situation in 1980–1981 when the Soviet Politburo had vehemently demanded that the leaders of the PZPR crack down harshly on Solidarity as soon as possible.[109] Right after the phone call, Rakowski announced that he would seek 'partner-like cooperation' between the PZPR and Solidarity and would no longer insist on receiving extra portfolios. Shortly thereafter, a PZPR press official hailed Solidarity for its 'realistic approach', and the outgoing communist prime minister, Czesław Kiszczak, lauded Mazowiecki as 'an outstanding personality' and 'a wise man'.[110]

The prospect of a non-communist government in Poland provoked alarm among the anti-reformist East European states, which openly expressed consternation at 'the destruction of socialist gains in Poland'. The Romanian authorities publicly denounced the pending changes in Poland, arguing that they would benefit 'imperialist, reactionary forces' and 'jeopardise the interests of socialism, including the Warsaw Pact'.[111] In an ironic reversal of Romania's position in 1968, leaders in Bucharest secretly urged the other Warsaw Pact states to join in sending troops to Poland to prevent Solidarity from coming to power:

> As a Communist Party and socialist country, [we] cannot consider this to be solely a Polish internal affair. [We] believe it concerns all socialist countries. ... The communist and workers' parties of the socialist countries, representing the members of the Warsaw Pact, should adopt a stance and demand that Solidarity not be entrusted with the mission of forming a government. [We] have decided to appeal to ... the leaders of the parties in the Warsaw Pact countries and other socialist countries to express serious concern and to ask for joint [military] action to avert the grave situation in Poland and to defend socialism and the Polish people.[112]

[107] 'Więcej rozumu, mniej serca', *Gazeta wyborcza*, 23 August 1989, p. 1; and 'Nowy premier, nowy rząd: Czego się po nich spodziewać', *Gazeta wyborcza*, 24 August 1989, p. 1.

[108] 'Postanovlenie Politbyuro TsK KPSS No. 164/133 21 avgusta 1989 g.', CPSU Politburo Resolution (Top Secret), 21 August 1989, in RGANI, F. 3, Op. 103, D. 180, L. 63.

[109] 'Konferencja prasowa rzecznika KC: Wtorek wydarzen i rozmów', *Trybuna Ludu*, 23 August 1989, pp. 1–2.

[110] 'Rząd—kiddy, jaki, czyj?', *Gazeta wyborcza*, 23 August 1989, p. 3; and 'Murem za sprawami wsi', *Gazeta wyborcza*, 24 August 1989, p. 1.

[111] 'De la Varşovia', *Scînteia*, 20 August 1989, p. 1.

[112] The full text of Romania's appeal, dated 19 August 1989 (the same day that Mazowiecki was officially invited to form a government), is reproduced in 'Dokumenty: Polska–Rumunia', *Gazeta*

Soviet leaders immediately dismissed any such notion and lodged a stern protest with the Romanian leader Nicolae Ceauşescu, whose relationship with Gorbachev had long been uneasy and strained.[113] Ceauşescu had sought to gain the PZPR's backing for joint Warsaw Pact action against Solidarity, but Polish communist leaders had swiftly rejected the 'invitation' and openly criticised it. The CPSU Politburo thereupon told Ceauşescu that 'the PZPR is better qualified than anyone to judge whether such action would be worthwhile', and that the Romanians should 'heed the PZPR's advice' and drop the matter.[114] The Soviet Politburo emphasised to Ceauşescu that the USSR would refuse to 'take any steps that would vitiate Poland's sovereignty', a position that Ceauşescu himself had championed until August 1989.

In subsequent days, the Soviet press went out of its way to commend Mazowiecki for being a 'calm, equable politician' (Toporkov 1989, p. 4) who during 'his many years of experience' had 'never sought to promote himself' (Starukhin 1989, p. 7). Coverage of Solidarity also turned distinctly favourable. High-ranking Soviet officials stressed that 'the Poles have chosen their own path of development' and 'are able to decide their fate for themselves'.[115] Mazowiecki's government was able to take office without further ado, and the Soviet Union transmitted a message of congratulations pledging continued 'friendship and cooperation' with Poland.[116]

Gorbachev reaffirmed his willingness to accept and even welcome the new Polish government when he sent the head of the Soviet State Security Committee (KGB), Vladimir Kryuchkov, who was also a CPSU Politburo member, to Warsaw shortly after Mazowiecki took office. Kryuchkov conveyed Gorbachev's 'wishes of great success' and praised Mazowiecki as 'a solid man' who 'knows what his country needs'.[117] In a separate meeting with senior PZPR officials, Kryuchkov warned that

Wyborcza, 29 September–1 October 1989, p. 6. This bizarre episode was reported at length in the same issue of *Gazeta Wyborcza*.

[113]'Postanovlenie Politbyuro Tsentral'nogo Komiteta KPSS No. P164/132: Ob obrashchenii t. N. Chaushesku', CPSU Politburo Resolution No. 164/132 (Top Secret), 21 August 1989, in RGANI, F. 5, Op. 102, D. 180, Ll. 2, 6–7, 63; 'Postanovlenie Politbyuro Tsentral'nogo Komiteta KPSS No. P164/169: Ob otvete rumynskomu rukovodstvu na predlozhenie o provedenii vstrechi rukovoditelei bratskikh partii sotsialisticheskikh po voprosu o polozhenii v Pol'she', CPSU Politburo Resolution No. P164/169 (Top Secret), 21 August 1989, in RGANI, F. 5, Op. 102, D. 180, Ll. 2, 7, 76; and 'Otvet rumynskomu rukovodstvu na predlozhenie o provedenii vstrechi dlya obsuzhdeniya o polozhenii v Pol'she', Draft Letter (Top Secret) from CPSU Politburo to Nicolae Ceauşescu, 21 August 1989, in RGANI, F. 5, Op. 102, D. 181, Ll. 140–41.

[114]'Otvet rumynskomu rukovodstvu na predlozhenie', in RGANI, F. 5, Op. 102, D. 181, L. 140. In Hungary the authorities expressed even sharper criticism of the Romanian proposal. See "Jegyzőkönyv az Elnökség 1989. augusztus 21-én megtartott üléséről: 7. A Román Kommunista Párt és Nicolae Ceauşescu üzenete a magyar vezetéshez a lengyelorszagli eseményekkel kapcsolatban," MSZMP Elnökség 1989/141 (Top Secret), 21 August 1989, in Imre Pozsgay Papers, Box 45, Folder MSZMP Elnöksége, 1989, Group 5.

[115]Comments by Evgenii Primakov, chairman of the Council of the Union of the USSR Supreme Soviet, transcribed in 'Press-konferentsiya v Londone Predsedatelya Soveta soyuza Verkhovnogo soveta SSSR E. M. Primakova', TASS, 5 September 1989, item 3. (Two weeks later, Primakov was elevated to candidate membership on the CPSU Politburo.) See also the interview with Nikolai Shishlin, in *Libération*, 22 September 1989, p. 4.

[116]'Predsedatelyu Soveta Ministrov Pol'skoi Narodnoi Respubliki Tadeushu Mazovetskomu', *Izvestiya*, 25 August 1989, p. 4.

[117]'Vstrechi v Varshave', *Izvestiya*, 27 August 1989, p. 3.

the Polish communists must help, rather than hinder, the new prime minister. Rakowski heeded this message by promptly ordering all PZPR members in the state administration to work loyally for Mazowiecki and his ministers.[118]

Even though Gorbachev undoubtedly would have preferred to see the Polish government come under the control of reform-minded communists rather than Solidarity, he and his advisers on Eastern Europe increasingly sensed that no communist leader in Poland could win sufficient popular support to guarantee political stability. Only a government led by Solidarity could take the steps needed to forestall political turmoil and dangerous crises in Poland and the unpalatable dilemmas that would follow. Faced with a choice of promoting the formation of a stable, non-communist government in Poland or upholding orthodox communist rule by any means necessary, Gorbachev—unlike his predecessors—opted for the former.

The opening of the Hungarian border

Barely two weeks after Mazowiecki took charge of the Polish government, an equally momentous development rocked the GDR. On 10 September the Hungarian government announced that it would allow free passage from Hungary into Austria for many thousands of East German citizens ensconced on Hungarian territory. Because Austria was contiguous with both Hungary and West Germany, the East German squatters viewed it as their most viable route of entry into the FRG, where they knew they would be granted citizenship automatically. Thus began the largest exodus of East Germans to the West since August 1961, when the building of the Berlin Wall had essentially halted the flight of GDR citizens to the FRG.

The Hungarian announcement did not come out of the blue. Pressure for it had been building since early May 1989, when the Hungarian government sought to burnish its liberal, pro-Western credentials by 'dismantling the Iron Curtain' along the border with Austria, the only Western country adjoining Hungary.[119] The decision to take this symbolically important step had been adopted by Hungarian leaders at the end of February 1989 with the consent of Gorbachev, who met in Moscow a few days later with Hungarian Prime Minister Miklós Németh and said approvingly that both Hungary and the Soviet Union were 'becoming more open'.[120] The Hungarian authorities' gesture of removing electronic barriers and barbed wire at border points with Austria (and also with Yugoslavia) did aptly convey a new spirit of openness, but it also had the unintended effect of spurring tens of thousands of East Germans to travel to Hungary, a country they were allowed to visit with minimal restrictions. Once

[118]Information about Kryuchkov's visit was supplied by Georgii Shakhnazarov when I interviewed him in Moscow on 21 March and 7 May 1998. Kryuchkov himself offered essentially the same account when I interviewed him in Moscow, 2 July 1999; see also Dudek (2002, p. 205).

[119]For brief but perceptive accounts of this episode in the larger context of Hungary's relations with the two German states, see Kurz (1991, pp. 123–63) and Horváth and Németh (1999, pp. 329–33). For additional context, see Horváth (2009, pp. 131–34).

[120]'Zapis' besedy M. S. Gorbacheva s chlenom TsK VSRP, Predsedatelem Soveta Ministrov VNR Mikoshem Nemetom, 3 marta 1989', Notes of conversation (Top Secret), 3 March 1989, in AGF, F. 1, Op. 1, Dok. 10325.

in Hungary, the East Germans moved *en masse* to the western border area, hoping to be granted permission to cross into Austria.

After Hungarian officials did little to prevent a few hundred East Germans from entering Austria, leaders in the GDR angrily demanded that Hungary abide by a 20-year-old bilateral treaty, which required that individuals attempting to cross a border illegally, without proper authorisation from their own country, be returned to their country of origin. To forestall a bitter confrontation with the GDR, the Hungarian government temporarily blocked any border crossings until a satisfactory arrangement could be worked out between East Germany and West Germany. In the meantime, the Hungarian government declined to return any of the East Germans to the GDR and instead set up makeshift refugee camps for them, much to the irritation of authorities in East Berlin, who insisted that 'citizens of the GDR who are illegally present on Hungarian territory are not "refugees" and must be returned immediately'. As several more weeks dragged by and the dispute remained at an impasse, conditions in the camps deteriorated with the onset of summer rains and mud. Hungarian commentators and members of parliament increasingly urged the government to settle the matter 'in accordance with Hungary's humanitarian commitments and goals' (Horváth & Németh 1990, p. 331).

By late August the situation in the camps was becoming untenable to maintain for much longer. On 25 August, Hungarian leaders met in the FRG with their West German counterparts to resolve the matter irrespective of what the GDR wanted. In discussions with West German Chancellor Helmut Kohl and Foreign Minister Hans-Dietrich Genscher at Gymnich Castle outside Erfstadt, Hungarian Prime Minister Miklós Németh and Foreign Minister Gyula Horn agreed to allow the East Germans in the camps to leave for Austria *en route* to the FRG. In tacit exchange for this step, the West German leaders promised to give Hungary financial support for its democratisation and market reforms and to encourage other major Western countries to do the same.[121] This bargain was struck before the Hungarians had consulted with Soviet leaders (though some Soviet diplomats in Bonn and Budapest had heard about the arrangement by this point). Subsequently, Foreign Minister Horn spoke to Shevardnadze, who agreed with the Hungarian position that the East German refugees 'must not be returned by force' and should be allowed to go. Chancellor Kohl, for his part, contacted Gorbachev to gauge his reaction to the plan. The Soviet leader replied laconically that 'the Hungarians are good people', a phrase he intended as a green light (Kohl 1996, pp. 71–75).

Over the next two weeks, Hungarian leaders made a last-ditch attempt to resolve the matter with the GDR's consent, but these efforts, too, proved futile. East German officials continued to insist that the refugees first had to return to the GDR, where 'with legal assistance they could pursue their individual exit visas'. In response, Horn emphasised that the East Germans on Hungarian territory had 'no desire to return to the GDR'. He told his East German counterparts that their proposal to coerce people

[121]Horn (1991, pp. 317–20) and Genscher (1995, pp. 639–40). Declassified German transcripts of the negotiations held on 25 August, 'Vermerk des Bundesministers Genscher über das Gespräch des Bundeskanzlers Kohl mit Ministerpräsident Nemeth und Außenminister Horn auf Schloß Gymnich' and 'Gespräch des Bundeskanzlers Kohl und des Bundesministers Genscher mit Ministerpräsident Nemeth und Außenminister Horn wahrend des Mittagessens auf Schloß Gymnich', are reproduced in Küsters and Hofmann (1998, pp. 377–83).

into going back 'was simply out of the question'. Horn expressed great scepticism when East German Foreign Minister Oskar Fischer claimed that his government did 'not intend to restrict travel to Hungary from the GDR'.[122]

The leaders of the East German Socialist Unity Party (SED) tried to convene an emergency session of the Warsaw Pact's Committee of Foreign Ministers that would compel the Hungarians to return East German refugees to the GDR. Soviet, Hungarian and Polish officials demurred, arguing that such a gathering would be an inappropriate venue for dealing with the situation. When the SED Politbüro met on 5 September, the assembled officials had no doubt that 'Hungary will be yielding to pressure from the FRG' and 'will not play its cards openly'.[123] The SED Secretary for ideological affairs, Kurt Hager, complained that Hungary was 'behaving hypocritically' and 'doing the bidding of Bonn' at the expense of 'hitherto normal relations with [the GDR]'. Others at the meeting expressed confidence that by 'strengthening allied ties [in the Warsaw Pact], especially with the Soviet Union', East Germany could weather the worst of the storm.[124] Soviet diplomats in the region had indeed shown distinct sympathy for the East German regime's plight and had tried to persuade the Hungarians to avert any exodus,[125] but the SED Politbüro's hopes that the highest Soviet leaders, including Gorbachev, would begin pressuring Hungary to reverse its policy were quickly dashed. Gorbachev by this point had no intention of cracking down.

Most revealing of all at the SED Politbüro meeting was Erich Mielke's comment that 'Hungary is betraying socialism' (*Ungarn verrät den Sozialismus*)—a sentiment that reflected East German leaders' dismay at the whole course of events in the Soviet bloc over the past year-and-a-half.[126] Mielke, Erich Honecker, and other senior East German officials had long feared that far-reaching internal liberalisation in Hungary, including sweeping reassessments of the 1956 revolution, would erode Hungary's loyalty to Warsaw Pact allies, especially the GDR. The East German hardliners were alarmed by what they saw as Hungary's steady 'movement out of the community of socialist states', reflected in public discussion in Budapest of the possibility of 'abandoning Marxism–Leninism, doing away with democratic centralism, and abolishing the centrally planned economy in favour of private ownership'.[127] Even though Gorbachev by late 1988 had

[122]These exchanges are recounted on the basis of a conversation between West German and Hungarian Foreign Ministry officials, the latter of whom described Horn's meeting with Fischer, transcribed in 'Fernschreiben des Staatssekretars Bertele an den Chef des Bundeskanzleramtes Ausreisewillige DDR-Burger; Lage in Ungarn und in der Standigen Vertretung', 1 September 1989 (Küsters & Hofmann 1998, p. 391).

[123]'Verlauf der SED-Politbürositzung am 5. September 1989', Stenographic Summary of SED Politbüro meeting (Top Secret), 5 September 1989, in SAPMO, ZPA, J IV 212/039/77.

[124]'Verlauf der SED-Politbürositzung am 5. September 1989', Stenographic Summary of SED Politbüro meeting (Top Secret), 5 September 1989, in SAPMO, ZPA, J IV 212/039/77, Blatt (Bl.) 3.

[125]'Vermerk über das Gespräch des Ministers für Auswärtige Angelegenheiten der DDR, Oskar Fischer, mit dem Außerordentlichen und Bevollmächtigten Botschafter der UdSSR in der DDR, Wjatscheslaw Kotschemassow, am 7.9.1989', Notes from conversation (Secret), 7 September 1989, in SAPMO, ZPA, J IV 212/AI3/239.

[126]'Vermerk über das Gespräch . . .', in SAPMO, ZPA, J IV 212/AI3/239 Bl. 4.

[127]'Jegyzőkönyv a Politikai Bizottság 1989 szeptember 19-i üléséről', Verbatim Transcript of MSZMP Political Executive Committee Session (Secret), 19 September 1989, in Magyar Országos Levéltár, M-KS 288, F. 5/1068. ő. e.

jettisoned the Brezhnev Doctrine, the members of the SED Politbüro clearly had not. They were averse to deviations from orthodox communism anywhere in the Soviet bloc, and they were especially worried now that the USSR, far from trying to block and undo the democratic changes under way in Hungary and Poland, was itself embracing similar policies and encouraging liberalisation in other countries.

The East German authorities' fears of being isolated in the Warsaw Pact came to a head on 10 September when Horn publicly announced that Hungary would allow some 20,000 East German refugees to cross freely into Austria, from where they could make their way to the FRG. Hungary, he declared, did not want to 'become a country of refugee camps' and was determined to 'resolve the situation on humanitarian grounds' (Horn 1991, pp. 327–28). Hungarian Foreign Minister Ferenc Somogyi told journalists that in taking the decision, the Hungarian government was seeking 'to open up and diversify relations with Western Europe and the West in general' and to 'keep [Hungary] from losing prestige and respect in the international community' (Kamm 1989, p. A10). He stressed that Hungary was now giving 'absolute primacy to universal humanitarian values' and was thereby moving much 'closer to the West in humanitarian concerns' and away from the GDR.

Honecker and his colleagues had been expecting the announcement but still reacted with fury. They had received a scathing report on 11 September from the East German ambassador to Hungary, Gerd Vehres, who insisted that 'discussions with the GDR' regarding the refugees had amounted to nothing more than 'stonewalling and deliberately misleading the GDR'. Hungarian officials, Vehres claimed, had 'made no serious attempts' to persuade the East German citizens to return to the GDR and had obstructed efforts by East German embassy officials to 'contact GDR citizens in the camps to explain the GDR's point of view'. The ambassador blamed the Hungarian media for 'stirring up and promoting a campaign directed against the GDR' that had 'encouraged GDR citizens to stay' in Hungary.[128] Similar complaints were voiced by high-ranking communist officials in Bucharest and Prague, who feared that the destabilisation of the GDR would endanger their own hardline regimes.

In Moscow, however, the Hungarian decision generated only a low-key response and no protest at all from the Soviet government. The Soviet Foreign Ministry spokesman, Gennadii Gerasimov, merely said that the step was 'unusual' and then added—in a statement that must have stunned East German leaders—that 'it does not affect us [in the USSR] directly'.[129] Official Soviet television coverage of Hungary's decision was surprisingly sympathetic, pointing out, for example, that 'The situation on the Austro-Hungarian border had become tense, and there were a growing number of illegal border crossings and various crimes. It was in this context that the

[128]'Schreiben von DDR Botschafter in Ungarn, Gerd Vehres, an den Außenminister Oskar Fischer vom 10. September 1989', Cable (Top Secret) from Vehres to Foreign Minister Fischer, 10 September 1989, in SAPMO, ZPA, J IV 2I2/A13/239, Bl. 1–2. Annotations indicate that copies were distributed to all SED Politbüro members on 11 September 1989. On this point, see also "Jegyzőkönyv az Elnökség 1989. szeptember 11-én megtartott üléséről: 4. Nyers Rezső elvtárs szóbeli bejelentése alapján," MSZMP Elnökség 1989 (Top Secret), 11 September 1989, in Hoover Archives, Imre Pozsgay Papers, Box 45, Folder MSZMP Elnöksége, 1989, Group 8, pp. 4–6.

[129]'V Press-tsentre MID SSSR', 12 September 1989, TASS newswire, Item 2–12.

Hungarian government was forced to take its decision' (Obrman 1989, p. 2). The Soviet news broadcast also pointed out that Hungarian leaders had spent a great deal of time 'consulting with the appropriate agencies' and had acted only after 'talks between the GDR and the FRG on this matter had produced no results'.

The Soviet Union's willingness to go along with the Hungarian decision, and Gerasimov's comment separating the USSR from the GDR, were bound to deal a further blow to the morale of the East German regime. Even though Honecker still hoped that, ultimately, the Soviet Union would never allow the SED to be ousted from power, he had finally started to worry that a scenario he once thought would never happen—namely, that his regime would be abandoned by the Soviet Union—was coming true. Honecker conveyed his deep unease to a sympathetic CPSU Politburo member, Egor Ligachev, who happened to be visiting the GDR at the time.[130] Ligachev himself had become increasingly disaffected with the changes under way in the Soviet Union as well as in Hungary and Poland, and he did his best to stiffen Honecker's resolve and reassure him that the USSR fully supported its East German ally. Ligachev promised that Gorbachev would be attending the celebrations in October 1989 marking the 40th anniversary of the founding of the GDR, as a demonstration of Moscow's support. At a meeting with Gorbachev in Moscow on 28 July 1989, Honecker had invited—indeed urged—him to attend the 40th-anniversary celebrations, and the Soviet leader had initially agreed to take part,[131] but by early September Gorbachev had tentatively changed his mind about going to East Berlin, lest he be seen as trying to strengthen Honecker's position against more reform-minded communists in East Germany. Thus, Ligachev's comments to Honecker at the time were not strictly accurate. Only after considerable hesitation and further discussions with advisers did Gorbachev finally decide to travel to the GDR (Falin 1993, p. 484).

Honecker welcomed the news that Gorbachev would be coming, evidently hoping that it would stabilise the situation in the GDR, but in the meantime the departure of East German citizens to the FRG—mostly from Austria via Hungary but also some via Czechoslovakia and other transit countries—continued at a brisk pace, reaching a total of more than 230,000 within several weeks.[132] The East German government tried to stem the outflow by imposing severe restrictions on travel to Hungary, including a strict visa requirement, but many people were still able to cross into Hungary. The exodus helped to fuel political unrest and mass demonstrations in

[130]On Ligachev's discussions with SED leaders, see 'Niederschrift über das Gespräch von Günter Mittag mit KPdSU-Sekretär Jegor Ligatschow am 14. September 1989', Notes from conversation (Top Secret), September 1989, in SAPMO, ZPA, J IV 2/2A/3241.

[131]'Postanovlenie Politbyuro TsK KPSS 30 iyulya 1989 goda: VII. Ob itogakh besdey t. Gorbacheva M. S. s General'nym sekretarem TsK SEPG, Predsedatelem Gosudarstvennogo soveta GDR t. E. Khonekkerom', CPSU Politburo Resolution No. 152/VII (Top Secret), 30 July 1989, in RGANI, F. 3, Op. 103, D. 177, Ll. 6–7.

[132]The figure of 230,000 comes from 'Telefongespräch des Bundeskanzlers Kohl mit Generalsekretär Gorbatschow 11. November 1989', Transcript of telephone conversation (Secret), 11 November 1989, with notation 'zdA T[eltschik] 16/11', in Küsters and Hofmann (1998, pp. 165–69); see also Kurz (1991, pp. 159–60).

the GDR itself, and by early October 1989 the very survival of the East German regime, not to mention Honecker's hold on power, was increasingly in doubt.

Change and upheaval in Eastern Europe

If Gorbachev had been determined to prevent Hungary from allowing the East German refugees to depart for the FRG, he certainly could have done so. Even though Hungarian leaders were acting with greater independence by the summer of 1989, they would not have defied the Soviet Union if Soviet political and military officials had applied strong pressure and engaged in threats. Far from exerting pressure, however, Gorbachev did the opposite when he indicated to Hungarian and West German leaders that the Soviet government would not object if Hungary permitted the East Germans to enter Austria. Soviet policy on this matter in 1989 amounted to a fundamental rejection of the principles and assumptions that had guided Soviet policy until the late 1980s. No Soviet leader prior to Gorbachev would have even contemplated allowing an event to happen that would cast doubt on the legitimacy and *raison d'être* of the GDR.

Gorbachev's determination to avoid violent repression against peaceful protests in Eastern Europe, no matter how turbulent the situation became, was a remarkably bold posture to adopt in circumstances that would have induced all previous Soviet leaders to crack down. The pressure of events can often force undesirable actions, but Gorbachev sedulously resisted it. Moreover, by siding with the Hungarian and Polish governments as they undertook far-reaching liberalisation and democratisation, Gorbachev signalled his endorsement of their domestic policies. By the same token, even though he claimed that the Soviet Union would not be imposing reforms on other socialist countries, he left no doubt in his public and private comments that he believed all the East European governments must sooner or later enact major changes at home—changes that no previous Soviet leader would have tolerated, much less encouraged. The growing radicalisation of Gorbachev's own political agenda, combined with his approbation of the sweeping political programmes in Hungary and Poland, was bound to provoke a good deal of restiveness in the four East European countries that had tried to eschew any loosening of political control.

This surge of ferment was reinforced by the increasing perception in Eastern Europe that the Soviet Union would not defend hardline regimes against internal challenges—a perception that not only emboldened protesters but also demoralised the communist leaders who were the targets of the protests. The full magnitude of the forces unleashed by Gorbachev's policies and by the 'winds of change' that spread from the Soviet Union (and Hungary and Poland) to other Warsaw Pact countries became apparent in the last few months of 1989, when millions of people in Eastern Europe—most of whom until 1989 would never have dared to join mass protests against communist rule—seized the opportunity to push, both collectively and individually, for sweeping political change and democratisation. Events that would have been unthinkable even a year or two earlier suddenly happened in rapid succession: a peaceful revolution from below in East Germany, the opening and gradual dismantling of the Berlin Wall, popular unrest and the downfall of Todor Zhivkov in Bulgaria, the Velvet Revolution in Czechoslovakia, and violent upheaval and the execution of Nicolae and Elena Ceauşescu in Romania. Change from below in East Germany and Czechoslovakia had been made possible by change at the top in the Soviet Union and had accelerated once the morale of hardline elites in Eastern Europe began collapsing as they increasingly realised that the Soviet Union would not be intervening on their behalf. None of these factors on its own, however, would have been enough to transform the political complexion of the region. Only through the interaction of these sources of change, along with some degree of luck, could the Soviet bloc have fallen apart.

The crucial test case in all this, at least for Soviet policy, was the GDR, which for historical, geographic and strategic reasons was the keystone of the Warsaw Pact. Demonstrations that had begun there in September 1989 escalated in early October, spreading to many cities.[133] Although the protesters still worried that the East German regime might crack down with deadly force, fears of a Tiananmen-style onslaught steadily waned in the light of the stance taken by Soviet leaders, notably during Gorbachev's visit to the GDR in early October 1989, which Honecker mistakenly had assumed would help shore up his position in the SED. Gorbachev's presence at the 40th anniversary celebration did give a dose of support to the GDR, but the impact of his visit on Honecker personally was much less auspicious. Gorbachev had told his aides beforehand that he had 'no desire to go' to the GDR, and he vowed 'not to say a single word in support of Honecker'.[134] Gorbachev's initial meeting with Honecker on 7 October took place after the two leaders had walked by crowds of East Germans who conspicuously ignored Honecker and joyfully chanted 'Gorby! Gorby!' and held up signs in Russian exclaiming 'Gorbachev, you are our only hope!'

During the initial discussions with Honecker, Gorbachev implied that the East German leader was 'deeply confused' about the political changes under way in the Soviet Union. Honecker, for his part, stuck to old dogmas, claiming that the only people 'pressuring the GDR to adopt reforms' were the state's 'opponents', especially the 'chauvinists' in West Germany, who 'are seeking to dictate rules of behaviour to us'.[135] Honecker insisted that 'the working class and especially the peasants [in the GDR] are in a good mood now. The workers support the party's line'. Years later, Gorbachev recalled that Honecker's dulcet characterisation of the social mood in the GDR was particularly 'bewildering'. The East German leader's comments, Gorbachev said, 'had nothing to do with reality' and were '100 percent rubbish'.[136]

At a follow-on meeting later in the day with Honecker and other SED Politbüro members, Gorbachev was blunter than usual in indicating that it was time for Honecker to go. The Soviet leader began by warning that 'when the party lags behind

[133]See, for example, Maier (1997, pp. 108–67), Apelt (2009, pp. 145–72) and relevant essays in Conze *et al.* (2009).

[134]Diary Entry for 5 October 1989, in Chernyaev (2008, pp. 805–6).

[135]'Zapis' besedy M. S. Gorbacheva s E. Khonekkerom', Notes from conversation (Secret), 7 October 1989, in AGF, F. 1, Op. 1, Dok. 10205. For the German transcript, see 'Niederschrift über das Gespräch des Generalsekretärs des Zentralkomitees der SED und Vorsitzenden des Staatsrates der DDR, Erich Honecker mit Generalsekretär des ZK der UdSSR, Michail Gorbatschow, am 7.10.1989, mit handschriftlichen Korrekturen von Honecker', Marked-up Transcript (Top Secret), 7 October 1989, in SAPMO, ZPA, J IV 2/2035/60.

[136]Interview with Gorbachev, in Moscow, 15 March 2007.

in a theoretical and practical sense, there will be bitter fruit to harvest'.[137] He then stressed that the SED had been lagging behind under Honecker and that an overhaul was needed:

> Adopting a decision to carry out political changes is definitely not an easy matter. The time awaits you when you will have to make courageous decisions. ... People are demanding a new social atmosphere and more oxygen in the society, especially because this pertains to a socialist order. ... I am referring here to the need to create not only a material but also a social-spiritual atmosphere for the development of society. It seems to me this is a lesson for us. It is important that you do not miss your chance. Life punishes us when we are late. ... On the basis of our own experience and the experience of Poland and Hungary in particular, we can say with great confidence to you that if your party pretends that nothing special is going on and does not react to the demands of life, it will be doomed. ... You and we have only one choice—to move decisively forward or to be defeated. ... We often see that someone among the leaders cannot pull his weight any longer, but we do not decide to replace him, as though we are afraid of offending him. In the meantime, problems fester and become extremely acute. On the whole, there are many 'warning bells' for your party.[138]

Separately, Gorbachev spoke with Egon Krenz, a leading figure in the SED who was 25 years younger than Honecker and was widely seen as the likely successor, about the need to replace Honecker as soon as possible.[139]

On 11 October, a few days after Gorbachev had returned to Moscow, he received word from the Soviet ambassador in the GDR that Krenz would be pushing for a leadership change at the next session of the SED Politbüro.[140] The news came as an obvious relief to Gorbachev, who, upon returning from the GDR, had told his aides that Honecker was a 'jackass' (*mudak*) who wanted to stay in power indefinitely and who kept on muttering the same empty shibboleths. Gorbachev felt that Honecker would have done a service to everyone, including himself, if he had resigned voluntarily rather than waiting until he was forced out:

> He could say to his people that he has had four surgical operations and is now 78, and a lot of strength is required for such a turbulent period, and could you please release me from my duties now that I have done my part. That way, he could keep his place in history.[141]

[137]'Zapis' besedy M. S. Gorbacheva s chlenami Politbyuro TsK SEPG', Notes from Gorbachev's meeting with SED leaders (Top Secret), 7 October 1989, in AGF, F. 1, Op. 1, Dok. 10174, Ll. 1–9. For the German version, see 'Treffen der Genossen des Politbüros des Zentralkomitees der SED mit dem Generalsekretär des ZK der KPdSU und Vorsitzenden des Obersten Sowjets der UdSSR, Genossen Michail Sergejewitsch Gorbatschow, am Sonnabend, den 7. Oktober 1989 in Berlin-Niederschönhausen: Stenografische Niederschrift', Transcript of Meeting (Top Secret), 7 October 1989, in SAPMO, ZPA, J IV 2/2035/60.

[138]'Zapis' besedy M. S. Gorbacheva s chlenami Politbyuro TsK SEPG', in AGF, F. 1, Op. 1, Dok. 10174, Ll. 1–3, 4–6, 9.

[139]Diary Entry for 8 October 1989, in Chernyaev (2008, p. 806); see also Krenz (1999, pp. 77–78, 80–83).

[140]Diary Entry for 11 October 1989, in Chernyaev (2008, pp. 808–9).

[141]Diary Entry for 11 October 1989, in Chernyaev (2008, pp. 808–9). Actually, Honecker at the time was 77, not 78.

Gorbachev's aides were more doubtful that Honecker would be remembered favourably even if he resigned right away. In their view, he was so 'reviled by his own people' that nothing he could do would improve his image.[142]

Even as Honecker was about to be removed, he and Mielke were still desperately hoping that Gorbachev would ultimately give them the go-ahead for a full-scale crackdown in the GDR. The East German ambassador in Moscow left no doubt about this later on in a private conversation with Aleksandr Yakovlev describing the 'extraordinary nervousness' at the highest levels of the SED.[143] Rather than providing a green light, however, Soviet officials went out of their way to stress that they wanted change in the GDR to move ahead without repression. This message was conveyed to the leaders of the SED through all available channels, and the 380,000 Soviet troops in the GDR received orders to stay in their barracks.[144]

Having failed to secure Moscow's approval for the violent quelling of protests, the leaders of the SED concluded that they could not deploy the East German State Security (*Stasi*) forces and National People's Army to crush internal unrest over Moscow's strong opposition. An operation of this sort, on the scale of China's brutal crackdown in June 1989, would have required at least Soviet acquiescence and more likely direct support, given the huge presence of Soviet troops on GDR territory and the KGB's extensive influence over the *Stasi*. Even though East German leaders were planning to subdue the demonstrations with their own security forces and troops rather than asking for Soviet military assistance, they knew that such action would be impractical if the Soviet Union vehemently objected to it (Andert & Herzberg 1991, pp. 182–83). Hence, Honecker and Mielke ultimately took no action against the protests, paving the way for Krenz's move against Honecker, who was ousted on 17 October, barely a week after Gorbachev visited and issued his injunction.

If Krenz had displaced Honecker a few months earlier, he might have been able to gain control of the situation and nip the wave of popular unrest in the bud. Krenz was by no means a dynamic or innovative leader, but if he had come to power in June or July he might have been able to forge viable compromises with church leaders and others who ended up playing key roles in the protest movement. The delay of a mere few months in such a fluid situation proved crucial. By the time Honecker was actually removed on 17 October, the situation was too far gone. Rather than diminishing, the protests waxed ever larger and spread to almost every part of the GDR. With remarkable celerity, the SED's erstwhile dominant position in East German society ebbed and disappeared. East German officials had spurned reforms earlier, and essentially what they found in October and early November 1989 was that drastic changes were forced on them, bearing out Gorbachev's warning that 'life punishes us when we are late'.

[142]Diary Entry for 11 October 1989, in Chernyaev (2008, pp. 808–9).

[143]'TsK KPSS: Zapis' besedy s poslom GDR v SSSR G. Kenigom 20 oktyabrya 1989 g.,' Memorandum of conversation from A. N. Yakovlev to the CPSU Politburo (Secret), 21 October 1989, in GARF, F. 10063, Op. 2, D. 185, Ll. 1–13.

[144]See, for example, Kochemasov (1994, pp. 168–69).

The opening of the Berlin Wall

As events unfolded in the last few months of 1989, the role of chance and contingency became crucial. Nothing illustrated this better than the opening of the Berlin Wall, which occurred on 9 November largely by chance.[145] By the time the Wall opened, the GDR had been in political turmoil for nearly two months, Honecker's regime was long gone, and throngs of East Germans were continuing to try to flee to the West via Hungary or Czechoslovakia. Thus, the sudden opening of the Wall did not seem as startling as it would have a few months earlier, but the precise timing was unexpected, driven by a series of fortuitous events.

On 9 November, after considerable work had been done by officials from relevant government agencies to codify new travel guidelines for East German citizens, the SED Central Committee approved draft guidelines permitting East Germans to pass through checkpoints along the border between the GDR and West Germany and between East Berlin and West Berlin, starting the following week.[146] The East German government later in the day expanded the measure to cover private travel for people with appropriate documents.[147] The main impact of the document was on people seeking to leave the GDR permanently, but the distinction between this category and temporary travellers was lost when a senior SED Politbüro member, Günter Schabowski, who had just returned to East Berlin and had not yet seen the directive or taken part in any discussions about it, was given the task of announcing it on East German television.

In response to questions from journalists, Schabowski mistakenly claimed that the measure was effective immediately, and when asked by reporters whether it applied to checkpoints along the Berlin Wall, he responded affirmatively. In response to other questions, he erroneously stated that the regulations applied to everyone, and he characterised the guidelines in an open-ended way, implying that all trips were covered and that access through border points was essentially unrestricted. Both of these assertions were erroneous, but Schabowski apparently was unaware of the significance of what he was saying.

Schabowski's announcement spurred subsequent broadcasts on West German and East German television and radio claiming that the Wall had already opened. The reports were incorrect, and initially almost no one was even present at the border checkpoints, which were still closed with no one passing through; but as the broadcasts continued, many Germans on both sides of the border assumed that they were true and that free passage was now allowed.[148] Large numbers of people began streaming

[145]This event has been recounted and reassessed in many works about the events of October–November 1989 in the GDR. See, for example, Hertle and Elsner (1999), Hertle (1999, 1996), Funken (2009) and von Schwan and Steininger (2009).

[146]'10. Tagung des ZK der SED im Plenarsaal des ZK-Gebäudes in Berlin, 8. November 1989', Record of SED Central Committee plenum (Secret), 8 November 1989, full transcript in SAPMO, ZPA, Ton YI/TD738, reproduced in Hertle and Stephan (1997, pp. 135–439).

[147]Ministerrat der DDR, 'Beschluß: Zur Veränderung der Situation der ständigen Ausreise von DDR-Bürgern nach der BRD über die ČSSR', 9 November 1989.

[148]For an interesting compendium of younger people's reactions in impromptu letters and notes, see Jung (2009).

toward the Berlin Wall from both sides, gradually forming an immense crowd. East German border guards, who were still technically under orders to prevent any crossings, had no idea what they should do and tried to ease the crush by letting out a small number of people. Far from helping matters, those crossings caused greater confusion and restiveness. The border guards tried repeatedly to call the authorities to obtain up-to-date instructions, but most of the highest officials were taking part in an SED Central Committee meeting and could not be reached. No one else at upper levels was willing to give orders to enforce the existing rules. Hence, the erroneous broadcasts triggered actions that ultimately converted the error into reality.

Without any clear instructions to follow, the border guards started to let more people through, at first in a trickle and then in an overwhelming wave. When the SED meeting ended, Party leaders were startled to learn what was going on, but they realised it was too late to defuse the situation or to return to the *status quo ante* (Krenz 1999, pp. 236–50). Germans gathered along the wall, crossed over it, danced on it, hacked away at it, hugged, drank euphoric toasts, and savoured a moment that, until very recently, many had felt they might never experience. The sheer exuberance of that magical night was unforgettable for those who witnessed it.

The response in Moscow to the opening of the Wall was low-key overall.[149] Even as leaders in Warsaw, London, Paris and one or two other capitals privately expressed great unease and even alarm about what they saw as 'the excessively rapid pace of events in the GDR' (to use the words of Lech Wałęsa, the leader of Solidarity in Poland), officials in Moscow avoided any shrill reactions to the unexpected turn of events.[150] Although the Soviet ambassador to the FRG, Yulii Kvitsinskii, was unnerved by the events and hoped that a four-power meeting would be convened, senior officials in Moscow were far more restrained. Because of the two-hour time difference in Moscow, Gorbachev was already in bed when the crowds were gathering along the Wall. The next day he learned what had happened from the Soviet ambassador to East Germany, Vyacheslav Kochemasov, who was surprised by the equanimity of Gorbachev's reaction (Kochemasov 1994, pp. 199–201). In a telephone conversation on 11 November with West German Chancellor Helmut Kohl, Gorbachev was upbeat about Soviet–FRG relations and said that 'events in the GDR' marked a 'historic turning point toward new relations and indeed a new world'.[151] Although Gorbachev worried that some people in the GDR or FRG might be tempted to 'force the situation' and create 'chaos', he was confident that he and Kohl could ensure that 'profound changes' would unfold in a 'stable' and 'balanced' way. Gorbachev's comments reflected a certain degree of unease, but overall he

[149]In *Germany Unified and Europe Transformed: A Study in Statecraft* (1995, pp. 105–7), Philip Zelikow and Condoleezza Rice mistakenly claim that the opening of the Wall sparked 'euphoria' in London and Paris but 'barely disguised panic' in Moscow. Their characterisations of the reactions in all three of these capitals are inaccurate. Declassified documents make clear that in both London and Paris leaders were deeply uneasy about the situation, whereas in Moscow the reaction was far short of panic.

[150]'Gespräch des Bundeskanzlers Kohl mit dem Vorsitzenden der Gewerkschaft "Solidarität", L. Wałęsa', Transcript of conversation, 9 November 1989, in Küsters and Hofmann (1998, pp. 492–96).

[151]'Zapis' telefonnogo razgovora M. S. Gorbacheva s G. Kolem, 11 noyabrya 1989 goda', Transcript of conversation (Secret), 11 November 1989, in AGF, F. 1, Op. 1, Dok. 8841.

seemed relieved that the situation had not spun out of control and that everything had remained peaceful. An even greater sense of relief was expressed by his adviser Anatolii Chernyaev, who wrote in his diary on 10 November that by having facilitated the opening of the Wall, Gorbachev 'has proven to be a great figure' who 'has sensed the pace of history and has helped it reach its "natural turn"'.[152]

The Wall did not fully open until several weeks later, but the breach of it on 9 November signalled the rapid end of communism in the GDR and the growing movement toward German reunification. It also marked the death knell of East European communism and the end of the Cold War. Less than 24 hours after the Wall opened, the long-time communist dictator in Bulgaria, Todor Zhivkov, who had been in power for 35 years, was forced to step down. A week later, the Velvet Revolution began in Czechoslovakia, escalating within a few days to demonstrations in Prague involving more than a million people. By the end of the month, communist rule in Czechoslovakia was fatally weakened and soon disappeared altogether. So drastically did the situation change in Czechoslovakia that the renowned dissident writer Václav Havel, who as recently as January 1989 had been imprisoned after criticising the harshness of the Czechoslovak regime, was elected president on 29 December 1989. At the start of November 1989, a modicum of uncertainty had still existed about the duration of communism in Eastern Europe, but by the end of the month there was no longer any doubt that the Soviet bloc was irrevocably in tatters. Never before had political change of such colossal magnitude occurred so quickly with almost no bloodshed.

In January 1989, at a commemoration of the 500th anniversary of the birth of the theologian and rebel leader Thomas Müntzer, Erich Honecker had declared that 'the [Berlin] Wall will be standing in 50 and even in 100 years, if the reasons for it are not yet removed'.[153] What Honecker (and others) did not foresee is that the 'reasons for it' would be 'removed' before the year was out.

Aftermath

By presiding over the demise of the communist bloc, Gorbachev vastly improved the climate for East–West relations (including East–West trade) and eliminated the perceived burden that Eastern Europe had long imposed on Soviet economic and military resources.[154] He also removed a major impediment to his programme of domestic reform. Whereas previous Soviet leaders were wont to invoke the concepts of 'socialist internationalism' and a 'socialist commonwealth' to confer 'legitimacy' on the traditional Marxist–Leninist model, Gorbachev and his aides could point to the

[152]Diary Entry for 10 November 1989, in Chernyaev (2008, pp. 816–17).

[153]'Erklärung von Erich Honecker über den Fortbestand der Berliner Mauer, 19.1.1989', audio recording of Honecker's speech, 19 January 1989, in the superb audio collection, *Die Mauer fällt: Die Wende in Deutschland vom Januar 1989 bis zum 3. Oktober 1990*, assembled by Walter Roller for the Deutsches Historisches Museum, Deutsches Rundfunkarchiv, Frankfurt am Main.

[154]The impact on East–West relations is highlighted in memoirs by former key Western officials: Bush and Scowcroft (1998), Baker (1995), Gates (1996), Matlock (1995), Kohl (1996), Genscher (1995) and Thatcher (1993). See also the memoir by the Soviet ambassador in Washington from 1986 to 1990, Yurii Dubinin (2003).

developments in Eastern Europe as evidence of the model's bankruptcy. Yakovlev, for example, argued in November 1989 that the upheavals in Hungary, Poland, East Germany and Bulgaria 'pose a threat to no one, except, perhaps, to the countries that have not yet gone through the process of democratisation'.[155] Another of Gorbachev's aides, Sergei Karaganov, stressed in early 1990 that 'the changes in the German Democratic Republic, Czechoslovakia, and Romania have provided a potent push for *perestroika*. ... They have strengthened its irreversibility and showed that there is no reasonable alternative to the democratisation of the political system and the marketisation of the economy' (Karaganov 1990, p. 122). The upheavals in the Eastern-bloc countries thereby negated a key external prop on which Gorbachev's opponents in Moscow might have relied. In all these respects, the dissolution of Soviet hegemony over Eastern Europe was highly beneficial for the Soviet leader.

At the same time, Gorbachev's policy, for all its positive aspects, was fraught with severe costs. The historian Vyacheslav Dashichev has rightly observed that 'no one in the Soviet Union—neither Gorbachev nor the ruling political elite nor the wider Soviet society—was ready, either psychologically or conceptually, for the fundamental turnaround that occurred' (Dashichev 1999, p. 119). By late 1990, the Soviet Union was unable to salvage what little remained of its political and military leverage in Eastern Europe. Even before the Warsaw Pact was formally abolished in July 1991, the erstwhile effectiveness of the alliance had disappeared. The fundamental political changes that occurred in Eastern Europe in 1989 and 1990—changes that the Warsaw Pact in earlier decades was supposed to prevent, especially in the GDR—deprived the alliance of its main *raison d'être*. Soviet officials themselves privately acknowledged in early 1990 that the collapse of communist regimes throughout Eastern Europe had 'shifted the military balance on the European continent in favour of the West'.[156] Some in Moscow concluded at an early stage that the shift in the military balance was 'fundamental' and 'decisive', especially with the prospect of a unified Germany in NATO. Other Soviet officials initially hoped that the Soviet Union could 'minimise [its] "losses"' by 'promoting the formation of an all-European security system' that would supplant both NATO and the Warsaw Pact.[157] It soon became clear, however, that no such system would ever actually materialise.

Instead, the Warsaw Pact rapidly disintegrated, leaving NATO as the only security organisation in Europe. The elaborate command-and-control infrastructure that Soviet leaders had worked so long to develop for the Pact became defunct, and pressures quickly mounted for the withdrawal of all Soviet troops and weapons from the region (Akhromeev & Kornienko 1992, p. 295). In February 1990 the Soviet Union agreed to remove its entire Central and Southern Groups of Forces from Czechoslovakia and Hungary by July 1991, a schedule that many Soviet military officers believed was too compressed.[158] Marshal Viktor Kulikov, who had served as

[155]TASS, 16 November 1989.

[156]'Voenno-politicheskie aspekty obstanovki v Evrope (Analiticheskaya zapiska)', prepared by the Soviet Foreign Ministry's Directorate on Arms Control and Disarmament, n.d. (c. early March 1990), in AGF, F. 2, Op. 2, D. 12, Ll. 1–16.

[157]'Voenno-politicheskie aspekty ...', in AGF, F. 2, Op. 2, D. 12, Ll. 1, 2.

[158]'Soglashenie mezhdu Pravitel'stvom Soyuza Sovetskikh Sotsialisticheskikh Respublik i Pravitel'stvom Chekhoslovatskoi Sotsialisticheskoi Respubliki o vyvode sovetskikh voisk s territorii

commander-in-chief of the Warsaw Pact until February 1989, later recalled the bitterness that he and other military commanders had felt about the pace of the withdrawals:

> To call it a give-away is putting it far too mildly. I would say it bordered on criminality. The decision to pull troops so quickly out of Hungary, Czechoslovakia, and especially Germany was rash and ill-conceived. The officer corps was left in a disastrous state, bereft of housing, material support, and the right to a new job. Everything was done in a slapdash manner. . . . I have to acknowledge that [we in] the military leadership were too docile; we were not perseverant enough and failed to insist that our troops should be pulled out in an orderly manner, with adequate support for our armed forces, the officer corps, and their families.[159]

Despite these sentiments (which some Soviet military officers voiced in public), the withdrawals from Hungary and Czechoslovakia proceeded with great alacrity over the next 16 months, finishing slightly ahead of schedule. A provisional agreement regarding the Soviet Union's Northern Group of Forces was concluded with the Polish government in October 1991, and it was then reaffirmed in a formal Russian–Polish treaty in May 1992. Under that treaty, all combat soldiers from the ex-Soviet Army were taken out of Poland by the end of October 1992, and the small number of remaining logistical troops departed by September 1993 (Henzler & Kalski 1993, pp. 12–13). The withdrawal of several hundred thousand Soviet and Russian troops and support personnel from eastern Germany was completed in September 1994, four months ahead of the timetable laid out in treaties signed by the Soviet and German governments a few weeks before German reunification in the autumn of 1990.[160] The final pullout of forces from German territory put an end to the presence of the former Soviet Army in Eastern Europe, thus completing the disintegration of the Warsaw Pact.

The fate of the Council for Mutual Economic Assistance (CMEA) was no better. Although most of the East European states after 1989 still relied heavily on the Soviet Union for trade and energy supplies (both natural gas and oil) and many raw materials, the inexorable trend in the region was toward much greater economic contact with the West. The new East European governments looked upon CMEA as a cumbersome, antiquated organisation that should be abolished, and they drafted formal proposals to that effect. Soviet leaders, too, soon acknowledged that the organisation had never come close to living up to its stated aims and that its erstwhile functions had been overtaken by events.[161] Even if the Soviet government had tried—very belatedly—to implement drastic reforms in CMEA, the organisation was doomed

Chekhoslovatskoi Sotsialisticheskoi Respubliki', *Vestnik Ministerstva inostrannykh del SSSR,* 6, 31 March 1990, pp. 4–5; and 'Soglashenie mezhdu Pravitsl'stvom Soyuza Sovetskikh Sotsialisticheskikh Respublik i Pravitel'stvom Vengerskoi Respubliki o vyvode sovetskikh voisk, vremenno nakhodyashchikhsya na territorii Vengrii', 9 March 1990, supplement to 'Postanovlenie TsK KPSS: O vyvode sovetskikh voisk iz Vengrii', K-227/OS (Secret), 9 March 1990, pp. 10–13, in RGANI, F. 89, Per. 8, D. 21, Ll. 1–8. The Hungarian and Czechoslovak governments initially had pressed for the withdrawals to be completed by the end of 1990. Only with reluctance did they settle for the mid-1991 deadline.

[159]Interview with Kulikov in Labetskaya (1999, p. 2).

[160]'Dogovor ob okonchatel'nom uregulirovanii v otnoshenii Germanii', *Izvestiya* (Moscow), 13 September 1990, p. 4.

[161]See, for example, Shabalin (1990, pp. 8–9).

by the upheavals of 1989–1990. Hence, like the Warsaw Pact, it was formally disbanded in mid-1991.

In all these ways, events in Eastern Europe moved so far and so fast, and the Soviet Union's influence in the region declined so precipitously, that the fate of the whole continent eluded Soviet control. The very notion of a 'socialist commonwealth' lost its meaning once Gorbachev not only permitted, but actually facilitated, the collapse of communist rule in Eastern Europe. Hopes of 'reforming' or 'adapting' the structures that had undergirded Soviet hegemony in Eastern Europe, or of replacing them with an 'all-European security system', proved illusory. Despite gaining certain benefits from the disintegration of the bloc, Gorbachev found that the steady elimination of all remnants of Soviet influence in Eastern Europe undercut his political fortunes and cast doubt on the long-term viability of the USSR.

Conclusion

Gorbachev did not come to office intending to abandon the Soviet bloc in Eastern Europe, nor did he foresee that the changes he initiated both domestically and externally would lead to the demise of communism in Eastern Europe. He had never anticipated that communist rule in Eastern Europe would simply dissolve. On the contrary, he believed that his programme would strengthen rather than undermine the socialist camp, placing it on a much sounder footing than in the past. He hoped to preserve the integrity of the Warsaw Pact and other multilateral institutions and to create favourable conditions in Eastern Europe for a liberalised form of communism ('socialism with a human face') that would enable the socialist commonwealth to overcome the destabilising political crises that had plagued it so often in the past.

The problem for Gorbachev, however, was that his approach to Eastern Europe was based on conflicting objectives. Even though he wanted to buttress Soviet ties with the other Warsaw Pact countries and to encourage movement toward reformist communism, his paramount goal by 1989 was to avoid the use of military force in Eastern Europe if internal crises arose there. Well into 1989, considerable uncertainty persisted in Eastern Europe about Soviet intentions and the bounds of Soviet tolerance, but when 'life itself' (to use one of Gorbachev's pet phrases) increasingly showed that the Soviet Union in fact had no intention of intervening militarily in any of the Warsaw Pact countries no matter what the provocation, pro-democracy elites and millions of ordinary people in Eastern Europe took matters into their own hands. Even when the process of change in the region developed a revolutionary momentum, Gorbachev declined to interrupt it or even to try to slow it down. He consistently stuck to his policy of avoiding the use of military force in Eastern Europe. Hardline communist leaders in the Soviet-bloc countries, who would have been perfectly willing to rely on violent repression to quell mass unrest as the Chinese regime did, lost their will to do so when they finally concluded that the Soviet Union would not be backing them up.

These converging trends—from above, from below and from outside—produced an outcome in Eastern Europe that Gorbachev had neither desired nor anticipated. The upheavals of 1989 transformed the region so completely that they eliminated Soviet influence. The Warsaw Pact and other Soviet-led organisations ceased to function in any meaningful way after 1989 and were soon abolished, a fate that rarely happens to an international organisation even after it becomes dysfunctional. Gorbachev's foreign policy adviser Anatolii Chernyaev was not quite right when he wrote in his diary in early October 1989 that events in Eastern Europe were leading to 'the total dismantling of socialism as a world phenomenon'.[162] In fact, communist regimes in China, North Korea, Vietnam, Laos and Cuba survived the distant upheavals of 1989 and subsequently fended off all pressure for political liberalisation. Nonetheless, even though a handful of communist regimes outside Europe proved resilient, Chernyaev's point was fully apt about Eastern Europe and later the USSR (and also Mongolia). Chernyaev in his diary contended that the dissolution of communist regimes in Eastern Europe was, 'truth be told, an inevitable and good' process that would return 'humanity to foundations of common sense'.[163] Gorbachev himself clearly did not view things in as positive a light, but he accepted the outcome and tried to make the best of it.

Even though Gorbachev prior to 1989 did not anticipate that communist rule would disintegrate in Eastern Europe or that the reunification of Germany would suddenly loom large on the East–West agenda, his basic approach to Soviet–East European relations proved remarkably successful in averting mass violent turmoil. Had it been left to the East German or Czechoslovak authorities in the autumn of 1989, Tiananmen-style repression would have resulted and would have severely complicated the situation for the Soviet Union. The lack of violence was attributable in part to the remarkable discipline shown by East European protesters, in part to the eroding will of East European leaders who in earlier years would have forcibly crushed unrest, and in part to the deliberate policies adopted by Moscow. Throughout the latter half of 1989 (and even earlier in Poland and Hungary), the Soviet Union took timely and effective action to forestall violence and promote liberalisation in the Warsaw Pact countries. At each of the many points when the Soviet Union could have stepped in to halt or reverse the process of fundamental change in Eastern Europe, Gorbachev instead expedited it, sometimes deliberately and on other occasions inadvertently. By eliminating any prospect that the Soviet Union would use military force in Eastern Europe, he effectively deprived the hardline East European communist leaders of the option of violent repression.

The one notable exception of Romania, with its bloody and chaotic revolution cum *coup d'état*, merely proves the rule.[164] From the mid-1960s on, Soviet influence in Romania had always been much weaker than in the other Warsaw Pact countries. If the Soviet Union had been able to maintain the same degree of influence in Romania that it enjoyed elsewhere in Eastern Europe, the violent rebellion of December 1989 might not have occurred. The Romanian crisis was illuminating in its own right, however, insofar as it underscored the lengths Gorbachev was willing to go to avoid Soviet military intervention in Eastern Europe. Despite serious provocations by the forces loyal to Nicolae Ceauşescu, including the firing of shots at the Soviet embassy in Bucharest and threats by the Romanian *Securitate* to blow up nuclear power stations

[162]Diary Entry for 5 October 1989, in Chernyaev (2008, p. 806).

[163]Diary Entry for 5 October 1989, in Chernyaev (2008, p. 806).

[164]For a solidly researched, perspicuous account of the Romanian crisis, see Siani-Davies (2007).

near the Soviet border, and despite explicit statements by the US and other Western governments that they would welcome Soviet intervention in Romania, Soviet leaders refrained from sending in any troops (Friedman 1989, p. 6; Greenhouse 1989, p. 6). Indeed, newly declassified documents confirm that Gorbachev was so determined to avoid the use of military force in Eastern Europe that he did not even seriously broach such a step when the CPSU Politburo gathered at the height of the Romanian crisis to discuss what to do.[165]

Gorbachev's fundamental reorientation of Soviet policy toward Eastern Europe encompassed not only his success in getting the CPSU Politburo to decide in March 1989 to eschew any use of military pressure and force in the region, but also his role in promoting far-reaching liberalisation. In addition to tolerating drastic changes in the Warsaw Pact countries, Gorbachev helped to bring about those changes, indirectly in some cases and directly in others, as when he pushed for a new direction and change of Party leadership in the GDR in October 1989. Gorbachev had pledged in mid-1988 that the Soviet Union 'would not impose [its] methods of development', including *perestroika* and *glasnost',* 'on anyone else', but the situation in Eastern Europe was so volatile and was changing so rapidly by early to mid-1989 that it necessitated greater Soviet involvement than he initially anticipated.[166] Valentin Falin, who as head of the CPSU International Department oversaw Soviet relations with Eastern Europe during this crucial period, later acknowledged:

> The CPSU Central Committee was aware of the unsavoury processes under way in the [East European] countries and therefore—to the extent permitted by the principle of non-interference in internal affairs and respect of the right of peoples to choose—we tried to influence the situation.[167]

Unlike in the past, when Gorbachev's predecessors relied on military force to 'defend socialist gains' in Eastern Europe, the Soviet Union in 1989 tried to do what it could to counteract the 'unsavoury processes' that might eventually have triggered widespread violent upheavals in one or more of the Warsaw Pact countries.

The dissolution of the Soviet bloc and the opening of the Berlin Wall were by no means inevitable. Momentous historical phenomena often seem inevitable in retrospect, but the reality is bound to be more complex. Gorbachev did have choices to make in 1989; nothing was preordained. If he had been determined to uphold orthodox communist rule in Eastern Europe, as his predecessors were, he undoubtedly could have succeeded. The Soviet Army in the late-1980s was still fully capable of enforcing the Brezhnev Doctrine, provided that Soviet political leaders were willing to shed blood. If the top post in the CPSU in March 1985 had gone to a hardline

[165] 'Vypiska iz protokola No. 175 zasedaniya Politbyuro TsK KPSS ot 23 dekabrya 1989 goda: O pervoocherednykh merakh v svyazi s obstanovkoi v Rumynii', CPSU Politburo Discussion No. P175/50 (Top Secret), 23 December 1989, in RGANI, F. 89, Op. 8, D. 77, Ll. 1–3. See also 'Postanovlenie Politbyuro TsK KPSS No. P175/61 "O napravlenii pozdravlenii novym rukovoditelyam Rumynii"', CPSU Politburo Resolution No. P175/61 (Top Secret), in RGANI, F. 3, Op. 103, D. 192, Ll. 2, 26–27, 144–45.

[166] 'Otvety M. S. Gorbacheva na voprosy gazety "Vashington post" i zhurnala "N'yusuik"', *Pravda*, 23 May 1988, p. 2.

[167] 'XXVIII S'ezd Kommunisticheskoi Partii Sovetskogo Soyuza', *Pravda*, 9 July 1990, p. 5.

Politburo member such as Viktor Grishin, Grigorii Romanov or Nikolai Tikhonov instead of Gorbachev, the Brezhnev Doctrine undoubtedly would have remained in full force. It is inconceivable that Grishin, Romanov or Tikhonov—all of whom nearly outflanked Gorbachev in 1985—would have even contemplated a drastic change of policy *vis-à-vis* Eastern Europe or would have refrained from using military force if necessary to keep the Soviet bloc intact.

The peaceful disintegration of the bloc was the unintended consequence of Gorbachev's reorientation of Soviet domestic priorities—a reorientation aimed at 'laying to rest all remnants of Stalinism and starting the Soviet Union on its way to the twentieth century'. This was the phrasing used by Adam Ulam in an interview for Radio Free Europe in May 1975, 10 years before Gorbachev became General Secretary of the CPSU. Ulam was speculating about what would happen if 'ten years from now, some individual or group in the [Soviet] Politburo emerges with the avowed intent' of doing away with the Stalinist legacy in the USSR:

> Modernization, rationalization, economic reform, political relaxation, and the proper observance of the Soviet Constitution would follow. In the political and cultural climate created by such a change, I cannot see how Romanian, Polish, Czechoslovak, and Hungarian claims for independence could be resisted.[168]

To be sure, in 1975 neither Ulam nor anyone else expected a figure like Gorbachev to come to power in Moscow 10 years later, but what Ulam did correctly foresee is that any Soviet leader who was truly intent on extirpating the Stalinist residue at home would have to be willing to implement drastic changes in policy toward Eastern Europe. Far-reaching political liberalisation and much greater openness within the USSR would have been incompatible with, and eventually would have been undermined by, a policy requiring military intervention on behalf of communist dictatorships in Eastern Europe. As Ulam rightly predicted, a fundamental reorientation of Soviet domestic priorities toward democratisation, public accountability and a relatively free press necessitated the relinquishment of Soviet hegemony in Eastern Europe.

By the end of 1989, the pace and scope of events in Eastern Europe had greatly outstripped Gorbachev's expectations. Millions of people in the region had decided that the opportunity for drastic political change was finally at hand, and they took full advantage of it. Two years later, the USSR ceased to exist, and over the next decade-and-a-half all of the East European countries except for a few of the former Yugoslav states (and excluding the former Soviet republics other than the three Baltic countries) were integrated into NATO and the European Union. Numerous problems persisted in the region, both economic and political, but the upheavals of 1989 brought lasting improvements, above all the spread of democratic polities and free-market economies. The combination in 1989 of reform from above, pressure from below and sheer luck produced some of the most propitious and memorable events of the twentieth century.

Harvard University

[168]Interview with Adam B. Ulam, May 1975, RFE/RL Research Institute, verbatim transcript in Open Society Archives (Budapest), F. 8, Subfond 200, Series 8, Subject File, Interview—Ulam, Adam B.

References

Akhromeev, S. F. & Kornienko, G. M. (1992) *Glazami marshala i diplomata* (Moscow, Mezhdunarodnye otnosheniya).

Andert, R. & Herzberg, W. (1991) *Der Sturz: Honecker im Kreuzverhör* (Berlin, Aufbau-Verlag), pp. 182–83.

Apelt, A. (2009) *Die Opposition in der DDR und die deutsche Frage 1989/90* (Berlin, Ch. Links), pp. 145–72.

Baker III, J. A. (1995) *The Politics of Diplomacy: Revolution, War, and Peace, 1989–1992* (New York, G. P. Putnam's Sons).

Breslauer, G. W. (2002) *Gorbachev and Yeltsin as Leaders* (New York, Cambridge University Press).

Brook, T. (1998) *Quelling the People: The Military Suppression of the Beijing Democracy Movement* (Stanford, CA, Stanford University Press).

Brown, A. (1996) *The Gorbachev Factor* (New York, Oxford University Press), p.249.

Bush, G. H. W. & Scowcroft, B. (1998) *A World Transformed* (New York, Knopf).

Central Intelligence Agency (CIA), Center for the Study of Intelligence (CSI) (1999) *At Cold War's End: US Intelligence on the Soviet Union and Eastern Europe, 1989–1991* (Washington, DC, CIA), Doc. 16.

Chernyaev, A. (2008) *Sovmestnyi iskhod: Dnevnik dvukh epokh, 1972–1991 gody* (Moscow, ROSSPEN), pp. 795–98.

Chernyaev, A., Veber, A. & Medvedev, V. (eds) (2006) *V Politbyuro TsK KPSS: Po zapisyam Anatoliya Chernyaeva, Vadima Medvedeva, Georgiya Shakhnazarova* (Moscow, Al'pina Biznes-Buks).

Chernyaev, A. S. (1993) *Shest' let s Gorbachevym: Po dnevnikovym zapisyam* (Moscow, Progress-Kul'tura), pp. 49–51.

Chernyaev, A. S. & Veber, A. B. (eds) (2010) *Otvechaya na vyzov vremeni: Vneshnya politika perestroiki—Dokumental'nye svidetel'stva* (Moscow, Ves' mir).

Conze, E., Gajdukowa, K. & Koch-Baumgarteneds, S. (eds) (2009) *Die demokratische Revolution in der DDR 1989* (Cologne, Böhlau Verlag).

Cremerius, R., Fischer, D. & Schier, P. (eds) (1990) *Studentenprotest und Repression in China, April–Juni 1989: Analyse, Chronologie, Dokumente* (Hamburg, Institut für Asienkunde).

Dashichev, V. (1988) 'Vostok-zapad: poisk novykh otnoshenii—O prioritetakh vneshnei politiki Sovetskogo gosudarstva', *Literaturnaya gazeta*, 20, 18 May, p. 14.

Dashichev, V. (1999) 'Edinaya Germaniya v edinoi Evrope', *Svobodnaya mysl'*, 7, July, p. 119.

Dubinin, Y. (2003) *Vremya peremen: Zapiski posla SShA* (Moscow, Aviarus-XXI).

Dudek, A. (2002) 'Kalendarium, 1986–1989: Polska droga do demokracji', in Machcewics, P. (ed.) (2002) *Polska 1986–1989: Koniec systemu—Materialy miëdzynarodowej konferencji*, Vol. 1. (Warsaw, Wydawnictwo Trio).

Evangelista, M. (2001) 'Norms, Heresthetics, and the End of the Cold War', *Journal of Cold War Studies*, 3, 1, Winter, pp. 5–35.

Falin, F. (1993) *Politische Erinnerungen* (Munich, Droemer Knaur), p. 484.

Friedman, T. L. (1989) 'Baker Gives US Approval if Soviets Act on Rumania', *The New York Times*, 25 December, p. 6.

Funken, M. (2009) *Das Jahr der Deutschen: Die glückliche Geschichte von Mauerfall und deutscher Einheit* (Munich, Pendo).

Galenovich, Yu. M. (1995) *Protivostoyanie: Pekin, Tyan'an'men', 1989 god*, 3 Vols. (Moscow, Institut Dal'nego Vostoka).

Galkin, A. & Chernyaev, A. (eds) (2006) *Mikhail Gorbachev i germanskii vopros: Sbornik dokumentov, 1986–1991* (Moscow, Ves' mir).

Garthoff, R. L. (1994) *The Great Transition: American–Soviet Relations and the End of the Cold War* (Washington, DC, Brookings Institution Press), pp. 571–72.

Gates, R. M. (1996) *From the Shadows: The Ultimate Insider's Story of Five Presidents and How They Won the Cold War* (New York, Simon and Schuster).

Genscher, H.-D. (1995) *Erinnerungen* (Berlin, Siedler).

Gill, G. J. (1994) *The Collapse of a Single Party System: The Disintegration of the Communist Party of the Soviet Union* (New York, Cambridge University Press).

Gorbachev, M. (1987) *Perestroika: New Thinking for Our Country and the World* (New York, Harper and Row), p. 165.

Gorbachev, M. (1993) *Gody trudnykh reshenii* (Moscow, Al'fa-print), pp. 46–55.

Gorbachev, M. & Mlýnář, Z. (2002) *Conversations with Gorbachev: On Perestroika, the Prague Spring and the Crossroads of Socialism* [translated by George Shriver] (New York, Columbia University Press), pp. 84–85.

Greenhouse, S. (1989) 'France Offers Aid to Ceausescu Foes', *The New York Times*, 25 December, p. 6.
Henzler, M. & Kalski, W. (1993) 'Wyechali: Armia Radziecka z nami od dziecka', *Polityka*, 39, 25 September, pp. 12–13.
Hertle, H.-H. (1996) *Chronik des Mauerfalls: Die dramatischen Ereignisse um den 9. November 1989* (Berlin, Ch. Links).
Hertle, H.-H. (1999) *Der Fall der Mauer: Die unbeabsichtigte Selbstauflösung des SED-Staates*, 2nd edn (Opladen, Westdeutscher Verlag).
Hertle, H.-H. & Elsner, K. (1999) *Mein. 9. November: Der Tag, an dem die Mauer fiel* (Berlin, Nicolai).
Hertle, H.-H. & Stephan, G.-R. (eds) (1997) *Das Ende der SED: die letzten Tage des Zentralkomitees* (Berlin, Ch. Links), pp. 135–439.
Horn, G. (1991) *Freiheit, die ich meine: Erinnerungen des ungarischen Außenministers, der den eisernen Vorhang öffnete* (Hamburg, Hoffmann and Campe Verlag), pp. 317–20.
Horváth, I. (2009) *Az elszalasztott lehetőség: A mahyar-német kapcsolatok 1980–1991* (Budapest, Corvina), pp. 131–34.
Horváth, I. & Németh, I. (1990) *És a falak leomlanak: Magyarország és a német egység (1945–1990)* (Budapest, Magvető), pp. 329–33.
Hough, J. F. (1997) *Democratization and Revolution in the USSR, 1985–1991* (Washington, DC, Brookings Institution Press).
Institute of Economics of the World Socialist System (IEMSS) (1988) 'East–West Relations and Eastern Europe: The Soviet Perspective', *Problems of Communism*, 37, 3, May–August, pp. 60–67.
Jung, P. (ed.) (2009) *AufBRUCH, 9. November '89: Leserbriefe aus der DDR* (Cologne, PapyRossa).
Kamm, H. (1989) 'Hungary's Motive: Earning Western Good Will', *The New York Times*, 15 September, p. A10.
Karaganov, S. A. (1990) 'The Year of Europe: A Soviet View', *Survival*, 32, 1, Spring, p. 122.
Kessler, H. (1996) *Zur Sache und zur Person: Erinnerungen* (Berlin, Edition Ost.), pp. 240–41.
Kochemasov, V. (1994) *Meine letzte Mission: Fakten, Erinnerungen, Überlegungen* (Berlin, Dietz), pp. 168–69.
Kohl, H. (1996) *Ich wollte Deutschlands Einheit* [edited by Kai Diekmann & Ralf Georg Reuth] (Berlin, Propyläen), pp. 71–75.
König, E. (1989) 'Der Honecker-Befehl zum Blutbad war am 9. Oktober schön unter schrieben', *Die Presse*, 24 November, p. 4.
Kramer, M. (1989–1990) 'Beyond the Brezhnev Doctrine: A New Era in Soviet–East European Relations', *International Security*, 14, 3, Winter, pp. 44–45.
Kramer, M. (1990) 'The Role of the CPSU International Department in Soviet Foreign Relations and National Security Policy', *Soviet Studies*, 42, 3, July, pp. 429–46.
Kramer, M. (1998) 'The Soviet Union and the 1956 Crises in Hungary and Poland: Reassessments and New Findings', *Journal of Contemporary History*, 33, 2, April, p. 191.
Kramer, M. (2003) 'The Collapse of East European Communism and the Repercussions within the Soviet Union (Part 1)', *Journal of Cold War Studies*, 5, 4, Fall, pp. 195–97.
Kramer, M. (2004) 'The Collapse of East European Communism and the Repercussions within the Soviet Union (Part 2)', *Journal of Cold War Studies*, 6, 4, Fall, pp. 27–32.
Kramer, M. (2010) 'The Kremlin, the Prague Spring, and the Brezhnev Doctrine', in Tismaneanu, V. (ed.) (2010) *Promises of 1968: Crisis, Illusion, and Utopia* (Budapest, Central European University Press), pp. 276–362.
Krenz, E. (1990) *Wenn Mauern fallen: Die friedliche Revolution—Vorgeschichte, Ablauf-Auswirkungen* (Vienna, Paul Neff), pp. 23–24.
Krenz, E. (1999) *Herbst '89* (Berlin, Neues Leben), p. 107.
Kurz, F. (1991) 'Ungarn 89', in Grosser, D., Bierling, S. & Kurz, F. (eds) (1991) *Die sieben Mythen der Wiedervereinigung: Fakten und Analysen zu einem Prozeß ohne Alternativen* (Munich, Ehrenwirth), pp. 123–63.
Kusin, V. V. (1989) 'Hard-Line Response to Imre Nagy Reburial and Intensification of Hungarian Reforms', *RAD Background Report*, No. 115 (Eastern Europe), *Radio Free Europe Research*, 29 June.
Küsters, H. J. & Hofmann, D. (eds) (1998) *Dokumente zur Deutschlandolitik: Deutsche Einheit Sonderedition aus den Akten des Bundeskanleramtes 1989/90* (Munich, R. Oldenbourg Verlag), pp. 377–83.
Labetskaya, E. (1999) 'Marshal Kulikov: "Voennye byli slishkom poslushnymi"', *Vremya MN*, 6 September, p. 2.
Levada, Y. (1989) 'Reaktivnaya otdacha', *Moskovskie novosti*, 34, 20 August, p. 7.
Lukin, A. (1991) 'The Initial Soviet Reaction to the Events in China in 1989 and the Prospects for Sino-Soviet Relations', *The China Quarterly*, 125, March, pp. 119–36.

Maier, C. S. (1997) *Dissolution: The Crisis of Communism and the End of East Germany* (Princeton, NJ, Princeton University Press), pp. 108–67.
Matlock, Jr, J. F. (1995) *Autopsy on an Empire: The American Ambassador's Account of the Collapse of the Soviet Union* (New York, Random House), pp. 190–92.
Medvedev, V. (1994) *Raspad: Kak on nazreval v 'mirovoi sisteme sotsializma'* (Moscow, Mezhdunarodnye otnosheniya).
Michnik, A. (1989) 'Pożegnanie doktryny Breżniewa', *Gazeta wyborcza*, 4 July, p. 5.
Modrow, H. (1991) *Aufbruch und Ende* (Hamburg, Konkret Literatur), p. 131.
Modrow, H. (2007) *In historischer Mission: als deutscher Politiker unterwegs* (Berlin, Edition Ost), p. 181.
Nathan, A. & Link, P. (eds) (2001) *The Tiananmen Papers: The Chinese Leadership's Decision to Use Force Against Their Own People* (New York, Public Affairs).
Obrman, J. (1989) 'East European Reaction to Hungary's Decision on East Germany Refugees', *RAD Background Report*, No. 174 (Eastern Europe), *Radio Free Europe Research*, 15 September, p. 2.
Odom, W. E. (1998) *The Collapse of the Soviet Military* (New Haven, CT, Yale University Press), pp. 146–47.
Palazhchenko, P. (1997) *My Years with Gorbachev and Shevardnadze: The Memoir of a Soviet Interpreter* (University Park, PA, Pennsylvania State University Press), pp. 137–38.
Reichenbach, T. (1994) *Die Demokratiebewegung in China 1989: Die Mobilisierung durch Studentenorganisationen in Beijing* (Hamburg, Institut für Asienkunde).
Reisch, A. (1989) 'Hungarian Government and Party Condemn Use of Military Force in China', *RAD Background Report*, No. 119 (Hungary), *Radio Free Europe Research*, 30 June, pp. 1–6.
Sakharov, A. (1989) 'A Speech to the People's Congress', *The New York Review of Books*, 36, 13, 17 August, pp. 30–31.
Sakharov, A. D. (1996) *Vospominaniya: V dvukh tomakh*, Vol. 2 (Moscow, Prava cheloveka), p. 574.
Schnibben, C. (1990a) '"Ich bin das Volk": Wie Erich Honecker und sein Politburo die Konterrevolution erlebten (I)', *Der Spiegel*, 16, 16 April, pp. 72–90.
Schnibben, C. (1990b) '"Makkaroni mit Schinken, bitte": Wie Erich Honecker und sein Politbüro die Konterrevolution erlebten (II)', *Der Spiegel*, 17, 23 April, pp. 78–98.
Shabalin, A. (1990) 'Ekonomika vostochnoevropeiskikh stran: Mify i real'nost", *Pravitel'stvennyi vestnik*, 14, April, pp. 8–9.
Shakhnazarov, G. Kh. (1993) *Tsena svobody: Reformatsiya Gorbacheva glazami ego pomoshchnika* (Moscow, Rossika-Zevs), pp. 367–69.
Shevardnadze, E. (1990) 'O vneshnei politike', *Pravda*, 26 June, p. 3.
Siani-Davies, P. (2007) *The Romanian Revolution of 1989* (Ithaca, NY, Cornell University Press).
Starukhin, A. (1989) 'Reshenie seima PNR', *Pravda*, 25 August, p. 7.
Thatcher, M. (1993) *The Downing Street Years* (New York, HarperCollins).
Tokaev, K. (1994) *Kak eto bylo: Khronika volnenii v Pekine, aprel'-iyun' 1989* (Almaty, SP 'Diana').
Toporkov, L. (1989) 'Trudnyi vybor: V Pol'she skladyvaetsya novaya rasstanovka politicheskikh sil', *Izvestiya*, 23 August, p. 4.
Vladimirov, O. (1985) 'Vedushchii faktor mirovogo revolyutsionnogo protsessa', *Pravda*, 21 June, pp. 3–4.
von Schwan, H. & Steininger, R. (eds) (2009) *Mein 9. November 1989* (Düsseldorf, Artemis & Winkler).
Zelikow, P. & Rice, C. (1995) *Germany Unified and Europe Transformed: A Study in Statecraft* (Cambridge, MA, Harvard University Press), pp. 105–7.
Zhao, D. (2001) *The Power of Tiananmen: State–Society Relations and the 1989 Beijing Student Movement* (Chicago, IL, University of Chicago Press).
Ziyang, Z. (2009) *Prisoner of the State: The Secret Journal of Zhao Ziyang* [translated and edited by Bao Pu, Renee Chiang & Adi Ignatius] (New York, Simon & Schuster).

Welfare Dictatorship, the Working Class and the Change of Regimes in East Germany and Hungary

ESZTER BARTHA

IN THE HUNGARIAN 'HOT' SUMMER OF 1989 A COUNTY party conference was held in the Congress Hall of the Rába Hungarian Wagon and Machine Factory (*Rába Magyar Vagon-és Gépgyár*, Rába MVG), the largest factory in the county of Győr-Sopron. The purpose of the conference was to discuss a radical reform programme put forward by the Hungarian Socialist Workers' Party (*Magyar Szocialista Munkáspárt*, MSZMP).[1] At this time the economic programme of the reformist wing of MSZMP did not differ much from that of the democratic opposition: both sides called for marketisation and privatisation—although the concept of mixed (state, private and co-operative) property forms had not yet been abandoned by either the old or the new political forces.[2] With respect to internal Party politics, the reformers advocated democratisation from below and the revitalisation of grassroots activity. The purpose of this programme was two-fold: first, the reformers sought to win over the 'masses', who were becoming alienated from the Party; and secondly, and perhaps more importantly, the reformist Party leaders and ideologists—or at least the idealists among them—hoped that if they could mobilise creative energies from below, among the rank and file, this popular support would serve as a basis for the establishment of a new, more liveable and likeable socialism.[3]

The essay was completed with the support of Bolyai János Kutatási Ösztöndíj. I would also like to express my thanks to the two anonymous referees, whose comments helped me to improve the essay.

[1]Rába employed more than 20,000 people in Győr, the seat of the County of Győr-Sopron (now the County of Győr-Moson-Sopron).

[2]In 1987 the Hungarian democratic opposition published a manifesto entitled *Társadalmi Szerződés* (*Social Contract*), in which they outlined the conditions of a democratic reform. With respect to the economy, they urged the legal recognition of mixed (state and private) ownership, the expansion of the private sector and the decentralisation of enterprise management to so-called enterprise councils elected from below.

[3]Unique among the literature offering Party programmes in this period was one book that sought to outline a social programme for the MSZMP and to explore the question of how the Party could revitalise its movement and gain wider support for its reforms (Földes 1989). The book also gives valuable insights into the internal politics of MSZMP in the Kádár era.

It is uncertain, of course, how far these ideas, which were debated amongst the top Party leadership, were communicated to the county Party members, or how far the target group, the grassroots membership, were receptive to the democratising call of the MSZMP. The grassroots members had many reasons to feel alienated from the Party, which was at best associated with the failed promises and the hasty and misconceived reforms of the 1980s. There is much evidence from county reports of the Party, which were collected by Party functionaries on a regular basis to monitor the political mood of the population, that discontent with the government and the ruling regime was widespread among the Party membership at the time. Also, membership of the League of Communist Youth (*Kommunista Ifjúsági Szövetség*, KISZ) fell dramatically in many large factories.[4]

Discontent with the national Party leadership was also voiced by many delegates at the Győr-Sopron county conference. Nonetheless, the call for democratisation and the social programme that was outlined by the reformist wing of MSZMP did receive some consideration, perhaps surprisingly, from the delegate of the factory Party organisation of Rába, who chose to speak not only on behalf of the largest factory in the county but also on behalf of the working class:

> Today in this country uninvited speakers agitate, act and demand in the name of the working class and the nation. I am a worker. No-one should make declarations, let alone demands, on my behalf. It would be good if people understood that in the past 40 years we have learnt to think and work for ourselves, and that it is not robots but thinking people who stand by the machines. What kind of society do we want? Democratic and socialist. I think that we want a society where people receive a fair share of the reward from what they produce. We want a society where workers receive the real share of political power that they deserve on the basis of their work. For us the socialist direction means a development built on communal democracy. It is incomprehensible to me that some smart, nationally recognised politicians, who declare themselves to be reformers, do not even dare to speak of socialism as a possible way forward. We, however, think that this is the real reform task.[5]

Within the ruling Party however, this was very much a minority view. While, in 1989, there were some Eastern European intellectuals who still argued for a democratic socialism based on workers' control, other groups, including many of the MSZMP reformers, were calling for a 'third way' between capitalism and socialism, and some for the creation of a social democracy based on a mixed economy and strong trade unions, even though it was also widely expected that the working

[4]*Győr Megyei Jogú Város Levéltára* (GYML, Archive of the City of Győr), X. 415/234/3, MSZMP Győr-Sopron Megyei Bizottsága. Apparátus iratai. A lakossági közhangulatot jellemző főbb tendenciák, September 1988. In the Rába Mosonmagyaróvár Tractor Factory (*Rába Mosonmagyaróvári Mezőgazdasági Gépgyár*) KISZ lost half of its members in the second half of the 1980s (GYML, X. 415/529/14/3, MSZMP Magyar Vagon-és Gépgyári Bizottságának anyagai. Pártbizottsági ülés jegyzőkönyve. Jelentés a gyár ifjúsága társadalmi helyzetének javítására tett intézkedésekről, 19 November 1987). However, this factory may not have been typical since the population of the County of Győr-Sopron had already come under capitalist influences because of the proximity of the Austro-Hungarian border.

[5]GyML, X. 415/226/1, MSZMP Győr-Sopron Megyei Bizottsága iratai. Megyei Pártértekezlet anyaga, 6–7, 10 June 1989.

class would either resist any attempt to restore capitalism or even support a reformist collectivist alternative.[6] Of course, this expectation proved to be wrong, and there was little effective working-class resistance to the introduction of a capitalist economy. There was no country in Eastern Europe where workers supported any kind of democratic socialist alternative to the existing system.[7]

Nevertheless, in other respects, there were important differences in the political activities of workers during the change of regimes between the Eastern European countries. In the German Democratic Republic (GDR) and Czechoslovakia large demonstrations paved the way for the collapse of the communist regimes, while in Hungary the transition to a parliamentary democracy and market economy was negotiated by the MSZMP and a number of newly formed parties.[8]

This essay focuses on the experience of 1989 from the perspective of the industrial working class in the German Democratic Republic and Hungary. It argues that an examination of the policies of the ruling communist parties towards the working class in the years before 1989 can provide the key to an understanding of the collapse of the regimes. It is argued that, after the protests and demonstrations in the GDR in 1953, and even more notably after the Hungarian Revolution of 1956,[9] the communist regimes abandoned the harshness of the Stalinist strategy of modernisation and turned themselves into 'welfare dictatorships' that sought to win over the 'masses' with the promise of providing for ever increasing levels of consumption. This strategy achieved working-class acquiescence, but in the long run it proved to be detrimental for the regime because it shifted working-class political consciousness to the right and effectively excluded leftist alternatives from the public sphere. The essay seeks to rethink the relationship between the working class and the 'workers' state' in order to explain the apparent contradiction that while, on the surface, the rule of the communist parties seemed consolidated in Eastern Europe, and that outside Poland there were no visible signs in the 1980s of significant working-class resistance to the socialist regime, in 1989 the working class essentially refused to commit itself to any left-wing alternative, and readily accepted the restoration of capitalism.

Thus the main thesis of this essay is that the remarkable absence of independent working-class action at the time of the collapse of the authority of the communist

[6]In Hungary the idea of democratic socialism without the MSZMP was represented most completely by the Leftist Alternative Union (*Baloldali Alternatíva Egyesület*). After the political failure of its project, the intellectual heritage of this school was continued by the journal *Eszmélet* (*Consciousness*) launched in 1989.

[7]This concept had particularly strong theoretical roots in Hungary because of the work of George Lukács. Disappointed with Stalinist society and refusing to accept a capitalist restoration, Lukács wrote a famous essay ('Demokratisierung heute und morgen') in the 1960s in which he sought to outline a third road. There is a sad irony in the fact that by the time this book was published in Hungary (1985), the reformers pressed for more, rather than less capitalism.

[8]The change of regime in Hungary has been referred to as 'negotiated revolution' or 'constitutional revolution'. On the political history of the roundtable discussions (the negotiations among MSZMP and the new parties) see Bozóki (2000). For a study of the historical roots of the peaceful transition see Tőkés (1996).

[9]For an illuminating study of the social history of the revolution see Pittaway (2007). The study is all the more important because it explores how mounting working-class discontent shaped the course of the revolution.

parties can be explained through major contradictions between the economic and social policy of the government on the one hand, and the communist ideology that they propagated on the other hand. The essay draws its evidence from two factory case studies: Carl Zeiss Jena in the GDR and Rába MVG in Győr. Both were large factories, located in the most developed regions of the two countries; both had a pre-socialist past; both were regarded nationally as model factories.[10]

I chose the two factories as examples because both had workforces that the regime considered to be part of its main social base: members of the skilled working class employed in large-scale industry. I attempt to reconstruct workers' responses to the 'welfare dictatorships' from local archival sources and oral history interviews that I conducted with workers of the two factories between 2002 and 2004. I seek to illustrate that since the Party in both countries saw an increase in consumption levels as the chief goal of the government and the main guarantor of social peace, workers also regarded emancipatory measures and projects as part of 'communist propaganda', which they refused to believe. The consumerist turn of the Party therefore paved the way for the eclipse of left-wing alternatives in 1989.

My main archival sources are all documents produced either by the Party organisation of the factory or by other Party-controlled organs such as the trade union or women's committees working under the umbrella of the Party. In addition to the reports documenting the everyday functioning of the Party organisation, the production campaigns, brigade diaries and other reports about the number and conduct of Party members, information reports were collected on a regular basis in accordance with the wish of the high Party leadership to monitor the public mood of the population. It can be argued that these documents are biased, and pay lip service to the leadership's view of reality. However, they can be very informative, in particular when they are negative because—as we can see from the Hungarian example—they frequently expressed discontent within the Party organisation, and especially the discontent of low-level functionaries with the high Party leadership. I also conducted 40 life-history interviews with workers in each factory. My interview partners mainly belonged to the 40–60 age group so that they had work experience in both regimes. The majority of them were production workers but I also interviewed foremen and former Party functionaries, who benefited from the educational opportunities that the regime offered to them, and who held or had retired from white-collar jobs. Memory of the socialist past can be biased, too; nonetheless, when I contrasted archival evidence with the interviews conducted 15 years after the collapse of socialism in Eastern Europe, I found remarkable similarities in the Hungarian case. The East German documents in the Honecker era were far less reliable, which reflects the differences in the political climate and the use of disciplinary and coercive methods in

[10]Rába was the focus of sociological research as a model factory under socialism. Csaba Makó and Lajos Héthy conducted a pioneering study of the plant in the early 1970s, which led to official discussions on the informal bargaining power of groups of workers who were highly skilled or occupied other key positions in production. Makó and Héthy published their first report of the research in English in 1972 (Héthy & Makó 1972a, 1972b). Héthy later studied other groups of workers in the construction industry to prove the thesis that workers who were indispensable for production because of their skills or their advantageous position in the production process could successfully represent their interests in wage disputes even against the enterprise management (Héthy 1977).

the two countries. In the Hungarian case, the memories of the low-level functionaries supported the evidence collected from the archival sources; critical as they were of the new, capitalist regime, they all reported a deeply rooted disillusion with 'actually existing socialism'.

The policies of the ruling communist parties towards the working class contained a number of contradictions. It can be argued that some elements of their policies actually did correspond to the project of building a socialist society that would offer an alternative model to capitalism. One example of such an element was the promotion of female emancipation and the establishment of full female employment, which was facilitated through a wide range of centrally provided child-care institutions such as nurseries, kindergartens, afternoon schools, organised holidays and summer camps for children.[11] These facilities were available at very low prices. Further examples include state investment in schools and teaching with the aim of levelling differences in the educational and social background of parents and of providing equal educational opportunities; and community building at the workplace, supported in the form of the socialist brigade movement, which was supposed to be the basis for working-class education and cultivated entertainment.

However, while the above-listed elements could, indeed, be reconciled with the concept of a society based on workers' communities, there was a crucial contradiction between this programme and the reality of the power structure of the one-party state: namely, the Party had no intention of renouncing its monopoly of power and transferring at least some of its decision-making power to working-class communities. Therefore, the promotion of ideas of community within the workplace was not meant to prepare the workers for taking control of the means of production. Documentary evidence from brigade diaries, and the records of Party meetings where the brigade leaders discussed their problems, as well as evidence from interviews I conducted with workers, shows that the members of the brigades did indeed participate in an intensive community life. They went to theatres, cinemas and pubs together, they celebrated state festivals (in the GDR these were particularly numerous), they held common family parties, they helped each other with the repair of cars, renovating flats, and resolving personal problems such as an alcoholic partner or a divorce; but this sphere of social interaction was firmly separated from the sphere of power. It is telling that, in my interviews with former brigade leaders, when I asked if they were members of the Party, most would answer no. For example, one respondent said:

> No, the Party was not for me ... I was always a social-minded person, I liked being in company, organising things ... of course, they [party members] tried to convince me to join, but I always said no ... not because I fundamentally disagreed with them, no ... the Party was simply not for me.[12]

[11]It is a very much debated question, of course, to what extent the policy towards women that was followed in the socialist countries was eventually successful in emancipating women. For a challenging analysis of the GDR see Harsch (2007); for Hungary see Tóth (2007).

[12]Information from an interview conducted with Edith (54), an East German production worker in her house in Jena in 2003. In Hungary I also met similar opinions among production workers. Since I promised anonymity to all of the interview partners, I use pseudonyms.

Some (even those who were in the Party) openly admitted that fellow workers considered Party members to be careerists, and this held back those who were indeed community-minded people.

Therefore, it would seem that, since the ruling parties had no real programme to extend political power to the working class, both Party functionaries and ordinary people came to believe that the legitimacy of the regime rested on the satisfaction of consumer needs. Authors such as Földes (1995) for Hungary and Kopstein (1997) and Steiner (2004) for the GDR have analysed the political history of indebtedness, which largely contributed to the collapse of the two regimes. While both the MSZMP and *Sozialistische Einheitspartei Deutschlands* (SED, United Socialist Party of Germany) can be justly criticised for a series of economic policy mistakes that increased the indebtedness of their countries over the 1970s, it can be argued that the factors that prevented them from pursuing an alternative course were structural. The Party was reluctant to give up 'the standard-of-living policy', as it was aptly called in Hungary, precisely because of the political pressure by the working class. In both the GDR under Honecker and in Hungary under Kádár, one can apply the term 'welfare dictatorship' to describe these policies, even though the political climate was much freer in Hungary than in the ideologically rigid and oppressive GDR.

It is not accidental that the new policy towards the working class was first advocated and implemented in János Kádár's Hungary in an attempt to pacify the workers and win them—or at least part of them—over to the MSZMP, the re-organised Communist Party.[13] The new policy towards the working class recognised that working-class needs and demands were not much different in the capitalist and socialist systems. The Kádár government made significant efforts to provide for the material welfare of the working class by means of wage increases, support for the building of housing, education and the training of working-class managers. The 'workers' state' was therefore not a true workers' state in the sense of the working class acting as a ruling class and neither did the workers exercise control over the means of production. Nonetheless, the working class could exert significant political pressure on the government, as is well demonstrated by the Hungarian case, and it was in a good bargaining position because the Party could not allow itself to alienate its declared social base.

The recognition that working-class demands did not differ substantially under capitalism and socialism triggered a consumerist turn in the Party's policy towards the working class. Hungary was in a specific situation because of the legacy of the 1956 Revolution. Nonetheless, a similar orientation towards consumerism can be observed in the GDR, which experienced the rivalry with capitalism very directly because of its situation as one part of a divided Germany. While Walter Ulbricht built a wall to prevent the escape of the population to the Western 'consumer paradise', his successor Erich Honecker implemented the East German variant of the Hungarian policy regarding the standard of living in order to convince the people of the superiority of socialism. A social compromise was thus established between the Party and the

[13]After the change of regimes it was no longer fashionable to admit that MSZMP did have a policy towards the working class. Földes (1989) gives a very good summary of the roots and impact of the 1958 resolution on the new policy towards the working class; see also Pető (1992).

working class: people gave up their political demands, or at least refrained from open protest, in exchange for the state providing an uninterrupted and reasonable increase in the standard of living of the working people. I chose to investigate these two countries because, for political and economic reasons, they are the best examples of this historical attempt to tie the workers to the workers' state, something which resulted in the political system's transformation into a 'welfare dictatorship' in each case.[14]

The GDR: squaring the circle? From revolutionary agents to dissatisfied consumers

In 1977 the first secretary of the factory Party organisation of Carl Zeiss sent the following information in a report to the Party secretary of the District of Gera to which the Zeiss factory belonged:[15]

> Our economic policy is not yet fully comprehended by all of the employees. There is criticism of the Exquisit shops and Intershops,[16] and workers even ask why the government tolerates this. We reported that some of the employees—among them even Party members—argue that in the GDR there are three classes: 1. those who have relatives in West Germany; 2. those who have incomes above the average and they can buy in the special shops; 3. 'normal' consumers. They would add that the latter are in the worst situation because they cannot buy what they want in the normal shops and they have to wait eight weeks or even longer for the repair of their cars.

This kind of criticism of the new inequalities—symbolised by the Exquisit shops and Intershops—was a frequent cause for Party disciplinary actions, which could lead to expulsion from the Party. Nonetheless, such criticism was by no means uncommon among the East German workers, and it must have been fairly general given the fact that Zeiss was nationally recognised as a factory that rewarded its workers well. A report in 1977 mentioned the case of a skilled worker who commented that

> the theory of Marxism–Leninism is good but the practice of the Party and the government is not in line with the theory. The high functionaries have been detached from the people and in the GDR there are differences between the classes; look at the Intershop, Exquisit and Delikat shops. People are not correctly informed about the economic situation, and those who tell the truth are silenced.[17]

The report continued that these comments were made at a Party meeting and 'some comrades nodded because he referred to existing holes in the supply of goods. He had

[14]In Czechoslovakia also, a form of 'welfare dictatorship' ensured the quiescence of workers after the suppression of the Prague Spring in 1968; in Romania the regime introduced a national Stalinism and a neo-Stalinist export-oriented economic model in the 1980s that depressed workers' standards of living; and in Poland the Party lost the trust of both the intelligentsia and the working class, which effectively prevented the creation of a compromise.

[15]Large factories such as Zeiss and Rába had their own Party organisations.

[16]Intershops sold goods for Western currency and Exquisit shops sold goods at prices which were considerably higher than in the normal shops. Many of the goods which were subject to shortages in the GDR could be bought in the Exquisit shops.

[17]*Thüringisches Staatsarchiv* (ThStA, State Archive of Thüringen), Rudolstadt, Bezirksparteiarchiv der SED Gera, IV D-4/13/76, Informationsbericht von IKL Zeiss, 10 November 1977.

authority in his Party group, because he had been a member of the Party since 1945, and he had held leading Party functions until 1960'—so the investigators concluded.[18]

What was the economic policy that the Zeiss employees failed to 'fully comprehend'? Under Ulbricht, all efforts had been concentrated on the strategic sectors and there were not enough consumer goods in the shops. The first task for Honecker, on succeeding Ulbricht as Party leader in 1971, was to strengthen the alliance between the working class and the Party. The government immediately took steps to increase the availability of consumer goods and cut back on strategic investments. In response to the anxiety of Party functionaries about the shortage of goods, and the anger of the workers who could not buy what they wanted in the shops, the GDR Party leadership were now driven by their perceived need to increase the production of consumer goods. According to Kurt Hager, a member of the *Politbüro*, in a speech to the district Party leadership, there was an 'actually existing' shortage of several consumer goods, which were, in fact, daily necessities:

> We cannot provide the population with a regular supply of drinks, bakery products and various industrial goods such as electrical products, household goods, furniture, heaters, sewing machines, prams, and tableware. We cannot satisfy the demand for these articles. I won't even mention shoes now; the problem came up yesterday during a conversation and I think that you know much more about the topic in this district than I do. This means that the struggle to fulfil the plan targets for consumer goods' industries and services, so that we can provide the population with a continuous supply of consumer goods, is the fundamental and decisive question of our work today. We have to provide people with a stable and continuous supply of basic food products, fruit, greengroceries, everyday consumer goods, children's clothes and spare parts; in short, we have to satisfy the needs of population; that is the main question and task that we have to face today. And, comrades, I consciously declare here, in front of the district Party leadership that the success of the Eighth Party Congress depends on how we can realise this task.[19]

Party functionaries and the national leadership believed that if they could continuously improve the standard of living of the workers, this would establish a lasting social consensus, and people would leave politics to the Party as long as their need for a higher level of consumption was satisfied. The crucial question was how these consumption needs were defined—and as we shall see, this was precisely where the Party leaders miscalculated.

From the moment when they decided to base their legitimacy and popularity on increasing consumption, the Party leaders severely limited their political room for manoeuvre. In 1976 Honecker felt confident enough to announce *die Einheit von Wirtschafts- und Sozialpolitik* (the unity of economic and social policy), which aimed

[18]ThStA, Rudolstadt, Bezirksparteiarchiv der SED Gera. Nr. IV-D/2/4/242, Bezirksparteikontrollkommission, 4 January 1978. The same skilled worker who made this criticism of the new inequalities was expelled from the Party—in spite of his past history of political activism.

[19]ThStA, Rudolstadt, Bezirksparteiarchiv der SED Gera. Nr. IV B-2/1/20, Protokoll der Bezirksleitungssitzung, Die sich aus den Beschlüssen de VIII. Parteitages ergebenden Schlussfolgerungen für die Arbeit der Bezirksparteiorganisationen, 19 July 1971. This is a remarkably open acknowledgement that the success of the Party depended on the increase of the consumption levels of the population.

to implement a socialist welfare programme to compete with the GDR's West German rival on living standards. He promised a constant improvement of working and living conditions to his people, which, according to his later critics, largely contributed to the growing indebtedness of the GDR.[20] The most important elements of this programme were a wages policy, state housing construction and support for families with a special emphasis on the improvement of the situation of working women.[21] Wages increased while prices were kept relatively stable. In 1971 the minimum wage was increased from 300 to 350 Ostmarks, and in 1976 to 400 Ostmarks. Even according to Western analysts, the real incomes of the population significantly increased in the period up to 1978 (Cornelsen 1988).[22]

Nonetheless, the Party's goal to provide for satisfied consumers met with the 'objective difficulties' of a planned economy, which was ill-prepared to satisfy ever changing and ever growing consumer needs, and even less suitable for a successful competition with one of the most developed capitalist economies. East German Party functionaries could not afford to be 'liberal' under Honecker: in public at least, they were expected to follow the line of the Party. Nonetheless, even in the local Party documents we find a number of complaints about shortages of consumer goods that were in high demand such as coffee, automobile components and even cars. Although the Party sought to satisfy the needs of all consumers equally, in practice there was a hierarchy among them, depending on the means and contacts that they had.[23] Visible material hierarchies increasingly undermined the egalitarian ideology of the Party and discredited its social message. From the Zeiss factory it was reported repeatedly that 'most of our comrades and employees believe that the spread of Exquisit shops only nourishes social differences and renders them more visible'.[24]

In contrast, while the shortage of consumer goods was relatively often mentioned in Party documents, there was no discussion of whether housing policy worked, or of people's satisfaction with their new homes. However, at factory level, complaints were made in relation to the factory's policy for allocating flats. In accordance with this new, consumption-oriented policy, a grandiose housing project was started with the purpose of building, renovating or modernising 3.5 million flats and providing every adult GDR citizen with comfortable and spacious housing, centred on the promise of

[20]Even in the 1980s when the GDR faced a deteriorating balance of foreign trade, Honecker consistently refused to increase the prices of consumer goods, arguing that the counter-revolutionary attempts in the other socialist countries such as Poland all started with increases in prices (Steiner 2004, p. 190).

[21]On Honecker's social policy see Bouvier (2002).

[22]Hübner (1995, pp. 86–88) also shows that workers' wages increased during the reform era although the Party was determined to resist the wage demands of the workers. In 1967 the government made significant concessions to lower-income groups: the minimum wage was increased from 220 to 300 Marks and, as a result, the ratio between the minimum and average wages decreased from 1:2.8 in 1964 to 1:2.2.

[23]Zeiss, as a nationally important factory, also enjoyed certain privileges. One woman worker recalled that when there was a shortage of women's underwear, the managing director of Zeiss, Wolfgang Biermann, ordered a truck of women's underwear, which was reserved only for the Zeiss employees.

[24]ThStA Rudolstadt, Bezirksparteiarchiv der SED Gera, IV C-2/3/721, Informationsbericht des 1. Sekretärs der IKL Zeiss, 24 October 1977.

an individual room for each adult family member.[25] In this context, every year Zeiss received a consignment of flats which were allocated to employees according to various criteria including family size, level of expertise, involvement in shift work and social need. In 1976, Zeiss provided 11,321 flats and 3,342 places in workers' hostels in Jena.[26] However, supply continued to be insufficient because, particularly in the 1970s, there was a massive influx of workers into Jena as a result of the rapid expansion of the Zeiss enterprise which created a very high demand for extra workers. State housing construction could not keep pace with the demands of the new settlers and the problem of a shortage of housing continued into the 1980s. This prompted a number of angry letters of complaint addressed to the managing director, who was in charge of the allocation of the flats, accusing the flat committees of cronyism, dishonesty and social insensitivity. The following letter illustrates the level of frustration that many workers felt, who had to wait for years in the workers' hostel with their families until they could move to their new homes:

> I have lived for five years in an AWU [*Arbeiterwohnunterkunft*, workers' hostel] of the VEB [*Volkseigener Betrieb*, state-owned enterprise] Carl Zeiss. My daughter was born last year and since then three of us have been living in a room of $12m^2$. I think our situation needs no further description. Since we were on the priority list of our plant, we were supposed to get a new flat in 1980. To our great disappointment, instead of the promised new flat we received an offer of a totally miserable, dirty old, damp flat without a bath, a toilet or functioning wiring. Under no circumstances would I move to this flat with a small baby. What has happened to the flats that our plant received? I was told that out of the 84 flats, 59 were allocated according to the decisions of the management, not by the flat distribution committee. Why do they make priority lists then if the managers allocate the flats anyway and it is connections that matter, not the situation of the family concerned? I cannot understand at all why there are couples without babies who have only been in the AWU for a few weeks and then immediately get a flat. Where is justice here?[27]

After he received the flat allocation list of his plant, the same man turned to the manager with a new complaint:

> I do not accept the reply to my last letter because my questions have been answered only partly or not at all. The list that I got confirms my main argument: flats are not allocated according to the social situation of people. Otherwise how can childless couples receive two-room flats while families with a child have to wait for years in the AWU? When I inquired about specific cases, the flat distribution committee was unable to justify these decisions. They referred to the 'summary of criteria' but they could not be concrete about them. I was told that the age of the child was not important. For us who are concerned, it is, however, a crucial question: how long do we have to live with our child under these miserable conditions? I expect a concrete answer to my question![28]

[25]For a critique of this programme see Bouvier (2002). However, Kopstein (1997) showed how the success of this programme in one Berlin district contributed to the higher level of satisfaction of the workers with the socialist system after the collapse of the regime.

[26]*Unternehmensarchiv der Carl Zeiss Jena GmbH, Jena* (UACZ, Enterprise Archive of Carl Zeiss Jena), VA Nr. 1583, Unterlagen zur Direktion Kultur und Sozialwesen, 20 May 1976.

[27]UACZ, VA Nr. 3741, Eingabe, 1 April 1980.

[28]UACZ, VA Nr. 3741, Eingabe, 24 April 1980.

The reply was characteristic of the authoritarian leadership style of the managing director, even though it was most probably written by one of his administrators:

> In my answer to your repeated complaint I take the opportunity to explain to you once more the policy of the factory on flats. According to the regulations of 1973 the factory has full responsibility for its employees with respect to housing. I have decided the following: first, every plant will receive a consignment of flats in each year; second, the managers of the plants are fully responsible to me in this question; third, there is a special consignment at my disposal so that I can personally solve special cadre problems or urgent social problems during the year. I am fully aware of my responsibility, and my decisions are in line with the social political requirements of the Ninth Party Congress. I do not tolerate any deviation in this respect. My colleagues told you about the tense situation of the town regarding housing. That is why it is all the more incomprehensible to me that you have refused two offers of old flats (a three-room flat in Mühlenstr. 41 and a two-room flat in Dornburger St. 131) because of the external toilet and the lack of a bath. I once again inform you that according to the urgency of your case your name will appear on the list for next year. That said, I regard your complaint to be once and for all settled.[29]

The correspondence between the desperate family man and the chief manager does, in fact, prove the opposite of his argument: his social situation was, after all, taken into consideration. The managing director of Zeiss was feared as an authoritarian leader—nonetheless, the petitioner had the courage to demand an explanation from him, which he eventually received. Such harsh letters of complaint display not only the strong emotions that arose from the system of central allocation but they also testify to the fact that while the GDR was undoubtedly a dictatorship, and moreover, a much harsher dictatorship than Kádár's Hungary, Party functionaries—especially in very high posts—both had to take into consideration, and respect the social rights of the working class.[30]

The following letter provides a further example of the problems that workers experienced in receiving adequate housing.

> I have read the article about our social policy in the 30 January 1987 issue of *Volkswacht* with interest. The report states that two thirds of working-class families received new flats between 1971 and 1986 and that adult people have at least 26m^2 at their disposal. Further, 76% of the flats are equipped with baths or showers and 68% have internal toilets. Between 42% and 45% of new houses are to be given to working-class people. I have to say that the living conditions of my family (four people) are very different. We live in a flat of 48m^2 in an old building. We cannot use the largest room (11m^2) in winter because it is damp and cold and it has heating. So my eight-year old daughter and my two-year old son have to share a bedroom (10m^2). The flat has neither a bath nor a shower and the toilet is in the common stairwell. There is no drying room so we have to dry our washing in the flat. The building is in a very bad state (the gutters are broken, the plaster is falling off, and the windows can't be closed properly). I accepted this flat in 1978 because I lived with my baby in half a room in my parents' house. After my second marriage and the birth of my son, four of us lived in a flat that I received for two people. My husband and I are both blue-collar workers and my

[29]UACZ, VA Nr. 3741, Ihre erneute Eingabe vom 24 April 1980 and 8 May1980.

[30]For good analyses of the nature of the SED dictatorship see Fulbrook (1995), Lindenberger (1999) and Maier (1997). Klessmann (2007) gives valuable insights into the social history of labour.

> husband works on two shifts. I applied for a co-operative flat in 1971 but after 16 years of waiting I was told to file a new application. I have the impression that the flat distribution committee consciously deceived me, so I just don't trust them anymore. Because of the circumstances that I described above, I consider this complaint as my only opportunity to improve my living conditions. I would like to ask for your support in this matter.[31]

The answer of the chief manager has not survived but the letter reinforces the picture of a tense relationship between the workers and management in which authoritarianism and social justice were often paradoxically combined.

Hungary: co-opting the market?

Economic reform in Hungary differed from that in the GDR. Beginning in 1968 with the introduction of the New Economic Mechanism (NEM), it involved a reorganisation of enterprise management,[32] but equally importantly, it extended the legal basis of the private sector into agriculture. Then, as the economic decline of the system became manifest at the end of the 1970s, the government responded to the problems that emerged in the state sector with the extension of the second or private economy: while the state could no longer offer substantial wage increases, it gave workers the opportunity to earn extra money in the private sector.[33] The sacrifice of free time for a higher income, of course, further 'pushed' working-class consciousness towards an acceptance of consumerism as the sole measure of the good life.[34]

The Party itself was divided over Hungary's new economic mechanism with hardline communists warning of the danger of alienating the industrial working class from the Party. Indeed there were signs that this would happen. After 1968, Party reports provided examples of considerable working-class criticism.[35] Workers complained about the high wages of managers and the high income of the peasantry; they felt that although they were asked to make the greatest sacrifices, their wages lagged behind those of other social classes who, according to the Party's ideology, were claimed to be less important for the building of socialism.[36] Widespread anger was also provoked by the allocation of large numbers of newly built flats, which were supposed to be

[31]UACZ, VA Nr. 5170, Eingabe, 30 March 1987.

[32]For an analysis of the Hungarian enterprise structure see Schweitzer (1982). According to Szalai (1989) the interests of the great enterprises, which dominated state industry, effectively prevented any further reform.

[33]Swain (1992) offers a thought-provoking analysis of the Hungarian attempt to integrate the private sector into the structure of the planned economy.

[34]Many economists believed at the time that the second economy contained the seeds of a new, capitalistic society and the small businesses that were set up in Hungary after 1982 could function well in a 'proper' market economy. Nonetheless, this assumption was much debated in the literature. See, for instance, Róna-Tas (1997) and Gábor (1994).

[35]GYML, X. 415/124/12, MSZMP Győr-Sopron Megyei Bizottsága. Pártbizottsági ülés jegyzőkönyve, napirendi anyagai. A munkásosztály helyzetéről szóló KB. és megyei pártszervek határozatai végrehajtásának főbb tapasztalatai, 5. 25 February 1972; GYML, X. 415/122/5, MSZMP Győr-Sopron Megyei Bizottsága. Apparátus iratai. Összesítő jelentés a PB levelével és a KEB állásfoglalásával foglalkozó május havi taggyűlések főbb tapasztalatairól, 6 June 1972.

[36]I analyse this period at length in Bartha (2009).

distributed among workers, to members of other social groups such as administrators, the intelligentsia and Party functionaries.[37] A further problem, as shown by leading sociologists such as Zsuzsa Ferge (1976), was that educational inequalities continued to exist because of large differences in the levels of teaching between regions and different types of settlement. Ferge also found that schools were ill-equipped to level the differences in the knowledge and preparedness of children, and therefore, the Hungarian school system remained highly selective and elitist.

Prompted by the workers' criticisms, the hardliners in the Party suggested a return to the policy pursued by the Party before 1968 and, in response, the Party made significant concessions to hardliners by halting the reform, and refocusing its policy towards the working class, which it aptly called its standard-of-living policy. While no changes were made affecting relations in agriculture, workers' wages were increased throughout the 1970s. According to national statistics, the real wage increase was the greatest from 1970 to 1975; in the second half of the 1970s real wages still increased but at a lower rate because of rapidly increasing prices.[38] The government also decided to introduce new checks into the system of the allocation of state flats; it initiated new administrative measures to increase the proportion of working-class managers and leaders; and it decided to introduce special courses only for working-class children to prepare them for higher education.[39]

As in the East German case however, although such policies towards the working class in Hungary combined the goal of working-class material prosperity with more emancipatory objectives in terms of improving working-class life chances, there is also evidence that Hungarian workers were more receptive to the Party's promise of higher levels of consumption than to the watchwords of socialism. Again, as in the GDR, the government promised to raise the standard of living of the working class but it refused to change the established power structure. Thus, workers essentially measured the popularity of the government against their standard of living.

A survey, conducted in 1976 among the Party members in machine-manufacturing enterprises across the county of Győr-Sopron, gives us illuminating information in this respect.[40] In six enterprises 1,013 people (almost half of them, 471, were from Rába MVG) were asked to evaluate their material circumstances. Of those surveyed, 35% were skilled workers, 13% were semi-skilled and 3% were unskilled workers, while the remaining 49% were described as 'other'. Blue-collar workers amounted to 53% of the Party membership in the machine-manufacturing sector. The survey confirmed that

[37]This was one of the conclusions of an inquiry conducted by Szelényi and Konrád (1969). It was this study of the system of flat distribution that initially inspired the famous work of the two authors (Konrád & Szelényi 1979), in which they argue that under 'mature' socialism the intellectuals were developing into a new ruling class.

[38]*Statisztikai évkönyv 1980* (Budapest, Központi Statisztikai Hivatal), p. 355. The index of real wages increased by 17% between 1970 and 1975 (100% = 1970) while it increased only by 4% between 1975 and 1980 (100% = 1970). In 1980 the real wage index was lower than in 1979 and the net nominal wage index increased less than consumer prices.

[39]Parents could, of course, always find a loophole in the system, and send their children to these courses even if they were not of working-class origin.

[40]GYML, X. 415/7/14, MSZMP Győr-Sopron Megyei Bizottsága. Pártbizottsági ülés jegyzőkönyve, napirendianyagai. Az életszínvonal-politikánk értelmezése a gépipari nagyüzemek párttagsága körében, 27 April 1976.

workers in this sector were in a better financial situation than the working-class average. In the county as a whole only about 40% of the industrial workforce earned more than 3,000 Ft while in the sample this proportion was 66%. In the sample 16.5% earned between 4,100 Ft and5,000 Ft while in the industry of the county as a whole 9.3% fell into this category. In contrast, at the top of the scale, in the sample 0.7% earned more than 6,000 Ft while in the county as a whole the figure was 2.4%. The majority of the respondents were owner-occupiers: one third of the respondents (31%) lived in their own houses, one quarter (24%) in their own flats, while one third (30%) were life-long tenants of state or council flats, 11% lived at home with family members, and only 4% rented a room. No-one lived in workers' hostels. The households of the respondents were well equipped with durable consumer goods: 93% had a television, 94% a radio, 91% a washing machine, 69% a spin-drier, 87% a fridge and 83% a vacuum-cleaner. One quarter of the respondents (24%) owned a motorcycle, 26% had a car, and 22% of the households possessed a record player.

However, even though the material conditions of the respondents were 'objectively' good, their subjective evaluation of the standard-of-living policy was less positive. Although almost everybody (99%) agreed with the statement that the standard of living had improved, opinions differed as to the extent of the increase. Of the respondents surveyed, 21% thought that there had been a significant increase in the standard of living during the plan period 1971–1975, 64% described it as average and 14% said that the increase was insignificant. Two thirds of the sample (68%) described the supply of consumer goods as satisfactory, 31% as unsatisfactory and 1% as bad. On real wages, 33% said that income had increased more than prices, 28% thought that the increase in pay balanced price rises and 39% thought wages had not kept pace with inflation; in Rába MVG, 44% of the respondents agreed with this statement.[41] The 1976 survey showed that price increases were regarded more negatively than the evidence indicated; respondents 'disregarded the improvement of the technical standard of products and evaluated only the prices'.[42] People were only 'moderately' content with their wages: 75% of the respondents described their wages as average (even though in reality they were higher than the average industrial wages in the county); 19% thought that their wages were good and 6% said that they were paid badly. The majority of people (57%) were not content with the pace of growth of their earnings.

Overall, the survey showed that people evaluated their standard of living only according to wage increases, and they did not consider the improvement of the communal infrastructure, schools, health services, roads and parks. Since the main social message of the Party concerned its standard-of-living policy, Party members were unlikely to contradict assertions that the standard of living had increased, but the detailed answers showed a more contested picture: it seemed that people expected more from the standard-of-living policy than what it delivered. As noted by the representative of the Rába MVG in a meeting of the executive committee of the

[41]GYML, X. 415/7/14, MSZMP Győr-Sopron Megyei Bizottsága. Pártbizottsági ülés jegyzőkönyve, napirendianyagai. Az életszínvonal-politikánk értelmezése a gépipari nagyüzemek párttagsága körében, 27 April 1976.

[42]GYML, X. 415/7/14, MSZMP Győr-Sopron Megyei Bizottsága. Pártbizottsági ülés jegyzőkönyve, napirendi anyagai. Az életszínvonal-politikánk értelmezése a gépipari nagyüzemek párttagsága körében, 27 April 1976.

factory Party organisation, 'the majority of the workers measure the standard of living with their wages, cars and weekend plots'.[43]

In order to improve their standards of living people were willing to work more: nearly half of the respondents (48%) said that they worked in their free time. At the same time many people saw little relation between the work performed and their wages: according to 22% of the survey as a whole, and 25% of the Rába MVG sample, performance rarely or never determined wages, and only 19% thought that people were paid according to their work.[44]

Thus the survey showed that the standard-of-living policy in Hungary had failed to satisfy people sufficiently to convince them of the superiority of socialism, even when they had effectively received an increase in real wages. While East German citizens had only felt the economic crisis of the system in the last years of the Honecker regime, in the Hungarian case even relative prosperity lasted only until the end of the 1970s. Throughout the 1980s real wages stagnated and in 1988 they actually fell. The deteriorating economic conditions largely determined the political mood of the people and, as can be shown clearly in the Hungarian case, effectively undermined the legitimacy of the regime. Direct political criticism, which had once been a rare phenomenon, manifested itself more often throughout the 1980s. People openly started to express their doubts about the credibility of the socialist media, and low-level Party functionaries (who were often blue-collar workers in a factory Party organisation) often reported on their own discontent with the economic situation of the country, the increase in food prices and—a main concern—the increase in the price of petrol, in the regularly collected information reports. Some even expressed scepticism about the use of these reports, which they had to submit to the higher Party leadership. People refused to believe official explanations for the price rises, particularly when the media had previously declared that the oil crisis would not affect the socialist countries, but only their capitalist rivals. People also refused to believe that the economic problems were only temporary: 'In our opinion, our leaders, who declare even today that we can preserve the standard of living of the 1970s, themselves do not think it seriously'.[45]

An even stronger source of discontent was the perception that the failure of the standard-of-living policy mainly affected the industrial working class. Throughout the 1980s informants (who were often production workers) frequently stressed that the workers were the main losers from the state's failure to control private sector incomes and their attempt as a result to reduce expenditures elsewhere.[46] Growing material inequalities not only triggered envy but also made it clear that the 'building of

[43]GYML, X. 415/7/14, MSZMP Győr-Sopron Megyei Bizottsága. Pártbizottsági ülés jegyzőkönyve, napirendi anyagai. Az életszínvonal-politikánk értelmezése a gépipari nagyüzemek párttagsága körében, 27 April 1976.

[44]GYML, X. 415/7/14, MSZMP Győr-Sopron Megyei Bizottsága. Pártbizottsági ülés jegyzőkönyve, napirendi anyagai. Az életszínvonal-politikánk értelmezése a gépipari nagyüzemek párttagsága körében, 27 April 1976.

[45]GYML, X. 415/206/28, MSZMP Magyar Vagon-és Gépgyári Bizottságának anyagai. Információs jelentés az Új Acélöntödéből, March 1980.

[46]GYML, X. 415/206/28, MSZMP Magyar Vagon-és Gépgyári Bizottságának anyagai. Információs jelentés az Új Acélöntödéből, March 1980; GYML, X. 415/206/28, MSZMP Magyar Vagon-és Gépgyári Bizottságának anyagai. Információs jelentés az Új Acélöntödéből, July 1980; GYML, X. 415/211/38, MSZMP Magyar Vagon-és Gépgyári Bizottságának anyagai. Információs jelentés az Új

socialism' was a theme only of socialist ideology and not of social policy. As the regularly collected (monthly) information reports show, scepticism towards the regime was increasing among the workers.[47] They found it ever more impossible to believe that they were the beneficiaries of the state's economic policy when the real beneficiaries, in their eyes, were managers, high functionaries and those who worked in the private sector. Informants often consciously refused to write more informative reports: 'There is no positive change in the prices and transport so the people's opinions (which we have reported earlier) have not changed, either'.[48] One informant elaborated his position in another report:

> In the training courses we received many instructions concerning the structure of information reports. It is, however, difficult or impossible to satisfy these demands if people fail to react to events according to the given criteria. It is often remarked that information reports are limited to complaints about the provision of consumer goods and public transport. If we do not want to forge the reports (and we certainly don't), we can only write about the things that really concern people. These are the increase of prices, the provision of consumer goods, transport and the 'preservation' of the standard of living. We cannot write new things about them because the circumstances have not changed; or better to say, they have deteriorated after the increase of the price of fuel. I request the acceptance of our information report![49]

In the Industrial Tool Unit of Rába the workers also complained about the decline of the standard of living while other social classes prospered—at least this was how they saw it:

> Our statistical office always publishes data about the savings of the population, and then they can argue that people can afford to pay the higher prices. Our workers say that if someone investigated, who were the lucky ones, who had money in the bank, one would find very few Rába-workers among them.[50]

If we take into account that the reports were written by lower-ranking functionaries who were often foremen or skilled workers, then it is reasonable to argue that the social basis of the Party was crumbling.

In the second half of the 1980s the decline of the regime evidently accelerated; in the various reports both the economic and social problems received an ever greater emphasis. The reasons for the declining social support of the Party and the government were well summarised in the county report of 1986:

Acélöntödéből, April 1982; GYML, X. 415/528/2, MSZMP Magyar Vagon-és Gépgyári Bizottságának anyagai. Információs jelentés a Szerszámgépgyár Pártalapszervezetétől, March 1982.

[47]Information reports were collected from all base organisations of the Party. The reports were summarised and the summaries were sent to the high Party leadership in Budapest every month. Informants were often themselves production workers so the negative political mood for the Party that they reported expressed the discontent of the low-level Party functionaries.

[48]GYML, X. 415/211/38, MSZMP Magyar Vagon-és Gépgyári Bizottságának anyagai. Információs jelentés az Új Acélöntödéből, February 1982.

[49]GYML, X. 415/211/38, MSZMP Magyar Vagon-és Gépgyári Bizottságának anyagai. Információs jelentés az Új Acélöntödéből, April 1982.

[50]GYML, X. 415/528/2, MSZMP Magyar Vagon-és Gépgyári Bizottságának anyagai. Információs jelentés a Szerszámgépgyár Pártalapszervezetétől, March 1982.

> The decrease of the real wages of the workers and the employees increases the sensitivity of the population. They frequently mention social injustices, which seem to be known to everybody but still nothing happens. There are opinions that the dependence of the employees becomes stronger while the wishes of a narrow stratum (those with property) are met. Moral judgment does not correspond to the rules of law and private business, and incomes are uncontrollable. There is an ever decreasing number of people who have the moral right to call anybody to account.[51]

More and more people demanded the punishment of the country's leaders, which showed the declining authority of the Party. Informants were often themselves production workers so the negative political mood for the Party that they reported was based on personal experience. It is also important to stress that the reports also reflected the discontent of the low-level Party functionaries, who wrote the reports:

> Our economic problems should be discussed more frankly. People want to know who got the country into this situation. The leadership is largely to be blamed for this. Why don't they take responsibility? There is much cunning in this country, ever more people are making illegal profits. How long will it go on like this? People are waiting for the programme of the government but they would like to hear a clear speech; not that one leader says this and the other leader says that.[52]

The lack of confidence in the leadership manifested itself in many other information reports:

> Our employees are displeased with the fact that the leaders relieve themselves of the responsibility referring to the unpredictably and unfavourably changed circumstances. Comrade Gáspár [the chairperson of the trade union] admitted in his recent TV appearance that the leadership was not always truthful with the public. Many people ask how we can believe official declarations after this. The mood of our employees is not optimistic, to put it mildly. They do not see the beginning of real development and they say that they are afraid of the future. Neither can the leadership guarantee success.[53]

Among the workers of the Gear Unit of Rába there was doubt about whether the leadership, who had let conditions deteriorate to this point, would be able to make any tangible progress.[54] Indeed, these were not sporadic manifestations of social discontent; according to a county report of 1987, the process of disintegration irresistibly continued, and the Party possessed an ever decreasing authority while distrust in the government increased.

[51]GYML, X. 415/232/4, MSZMP Győr-Sopron Megyei Bizottsága. Apparátus iratai. A lakossági közhangulatot jellemző főbb tendenciák, November 1986.

[52]GYML, X. 415/538/1, MSZMP Magyar Vagon-és Gépgyári Bizottságának anyagai. Információs jelentés a Motor Pártalapszervezettől, April 1987.

[53]GYML, X. 415/538/3, MSZMP Magyar Vagon-és Gépgyári Bizottságának anyagai. Információs jelentés a Szerszámgépgyár Pártalapszervezetétől, September 1987.

[54]GYML, X. 415/538/6, MSZMP Magyar Vagon-és Gépgyári Bizottságának anyagai. Információs jelentés a Futómü Pártvezetőségétől, May 1987.

Conclusion

In both Hungary and the GDR the consumption-oriented policy towards the working class proved to be both a blessing and a curse for the Party. It was a blessing because it stabilised the regime, eliminated the threat of the formation of a strong opposition with working-class roots and, in the short term, it even increased the popularity of the government. In the long term, however, it undermined the communist regimes because it legitimised consumer demands that the planned economies were incapable of satisfying. Moreover, the Cold War forced regimes to compete economically with the capitalist countries in a way that was economically harmful because it put an extra burden on the poorly performing planned economies that they could not bear. It was also politically dangerous because workers measured the achievements of the socialist system solely and exclusively against the material conditions that it could offer to them.

The welfare dictatorships did their best to transform workers into consumers and, albeit unintentionally, they succeeded in effectively undermining the credibility of socialist ideology. In order to preserve the *status quo*, they were willing to give concessions to consumerism; and moreover, they were constantly worried that left-wing critics would destroy the consensus, which they held to be the basis of their political rule. There is evidence from both countries that repression was used against left-wing critics of the system, which was occasionally harsher than the retribution they handed out for 'Western revisionism'. In Hungary for example, Miklós Haraszti, the author of *A Worker in a Worker's State* (1977) was also held to be a left-wing dissident and prosecuted on that basis.[55] In the GDR there was the case of Matthias Domaschk, a young worker from Jena, who joined a commune at the beginning of the 1980s. Because of his alternative looks, dress and political views he was placed under police supervision. After travelling to Berlin by train to visit his friends at the time of a Party conference, he was arrested and subsequently committed suicide in custody. There is an archive in Jena, which bears his name (*Thüringer Archiv für Zeitgeschichte 'Matthias Domaschk'*).

As the above examples illustrate, the two regimes effectively prevented the propagation of any leftism other than the official legitimising ideology. 'Official socialism' was, however, increasingly undermined by the wide gap between the practice of welfare dictatorships and the egalitarian socialist project.[56] It well describes the extent to which people became disappointed with actually existing socialism in Hungary, in which many Rába workers believed that workers were not rewarded on the basis of the work that they performed and they would have a better life under capitalism. East German interviewees have also repeatedly told me that it was only after they started to live in capitalism that they believed the Marxist critique that they learnt at school. While welfare dictatorships did establish social peace, in the long run they paved the way for capitalism because they essentially failed to demonstrate a viable socialist alternative. After they could no longer increase the standard of living of the people, they lost popular support. As a result, by the time the authority of the

[55]A further example, of a trial of left dissidents as early as 1971, is provided Tütő (1993).
[56]The existence of this gap is confirmed by Burawoy and Lukács (1992) and Szalai (1986).

communist parties collapsed the majority of the workers did not see capitalism as a major enemy; and many expected that they would be better treated under capitalism than under socialism because they saw that the standard of living of the workers was higher in West Germany and Austria than in the GDR or Hungary. Western shops and supermarkets, which were full of goods, were better at convincing people of capitalism's apparent superiority over the bankrupt socialist economies.

The balance of 1989 is therefore, at best, ambiguous from the perspective of the working class. The kind of state socialism that existed in the GDR and Hungary was a welfare dictatorship that failed essentially because it based the legitimacy of the regime on consumption, and it sought to win over the working class with the promise of making them consumers like the workers of advanced capitalist countries. The spectacular failure of this project undermined the legitimacy of socialism and nourished illusions about the nature of capitalism and the level of egalitarianism in a market economy and effectively created the conditions for the introduction of capitalism after 1989 without any serious organised challenge from the working class.

Eötvös Loránd University of Budapest

References

Bartha, E. (2009) '"Would You Call Back the Capitalists?": Workers and the Beginning of Market Socialism in Hungary', *Social History*, 34, 2.

Bouvier, B. (2002) *Die DDR—ein Sozialstaat? Sozialpolitik in der Ära Honecker* (Bonn, Dietz).

Bozóki, A. (ed.) (2000) *A rendszerváltás forgatókönyve: kerekasztal-tárgyalások 1989-ben: alkotmányos forradalom: tanulmányok* (Budapest, Új Mandátum Könyvkiadó).

Burawoy, M. (1985) *The Politics of Production: Factory Regimes under Capitalism and Socialism* (London, Verso).

Burawoy, M. & Lukács, J. (1992) *The Radiant Past: Ideology and Reality in Hungary's Road to Capitalism* (Chicago, IL & London, The University of Chicago Press).

Cornelsen, D. (1988) 'Die Wirtschaft der DDR in der Honecker-Ära', in Glaessner, G. (ed.) (1988) *Die DDR in der Ära Honecker* (Opladen, Westdeutscher Verlag).

Ferge, Zs. (1976) *Az iskolarendszer és az iskolai tudás társadalmi meghatározottsága* (Budapest, Akadémiai Kiadó).

Ferge, Zs. (1979) *A Society in the Making: Hungarian Social and Societal Policy, 1945–1975* (Harmondsworth, Penguin).

Ferge, Zs. (2010) *Társadalmi áramlatok és egyéni szerepek* (Budapest, Napvilág Kiadó).

Földes, G. (1989) *Hatalom és mozgalom 1956–1989* (Budapest, Reform Könyvkiadó-Kossuth Könyvkiadó).

Földes, G. (1995) *Az eladósodás politikai története 1957–1986* (Budapest, Gondolat).

Fulbrook, M. (1995) *Anatomy of a Dictatorship: Inside the GDR, 1949–1989* (Oxford, Oxford University Press).

Gábor, R. I. (1994) 'Modernity or a New Kind of Duality? Second Thoughts about the Second Economy', in Kovács, M. J. (eds) (1994) *Transition to Capitalism? The Communist Legacy in Eastern Europe* (London, Transaction Publishers).

Haraszti, M. (1977) *A Worker in a Worker's State* (New York, Penguin).

Harsch, D. (2007) *Revenge of the Domestic: Women, the Family, and Communism in the German Democratic Republic* (Princeton, NJ, Princeton University Press).

Héthy, L. (1977) 'Bérvita az építkezésen (Az érdékérvényesítési képesség problémája)', *Valóság*, 20, 11.

Héthy, L & Makó, C. (1972a) 'Work Performance, Interests, Powers and Environment (The Case of Cyclical Slowdowns in a Hungarian Factory)', *The Sociological Review Monograph*, 17.

Héthy, L. & Makó, C. (1972b) 'Az automatizáció és az ipari munkások. Beszámoló egy nemzetközi kutatási program menetéről', *Szociológia*, 1, 2.

Hübner, P. (1995) *Konsens, Konflikt und Kompromiß: Soziale Arbeiterinteressen und Sozialpolitik in der SBZ/DDR 1945–1970* (Berlin, Akademie Verlag).

Kalb, D. (2009) 'Conversations with a Polish Populist: Tracing Hidden Histories of Globalization, Class, and Dispossession in Postsocialism (and Beyond)', *American Ethnologist*, 36, 2.

Keren, M. (1978) 'The Rise and Fall of the New Economic System', in Legters, L. H. (ed.) (1978) *The German Democratic Republic: A Developed Socialist Society* (Boulder, CO, Westview Press).

Klessmann, C. (2007) *Arbeiter im ‚Arbeiterstaat' DDR: Deutsche Traditionen, sowjetisches Modell, westdeutsches Magnetfeld (1945 bis 1971)* (Bonn, Dietz).

Konrád, G. & Szelényi, I. (1979) *The Intellectuals on the Road to Class Power* (New York, Harcourt Brace Jovanovich).

Kopstein, J. (1997) *The Politics of Economic Decline in East Germany, 1945–1989* (Chapel Hill, NC, University of North Carolina Press).

Krausz, T. (1991) *Pártviták és történettudomány: Viták 'az orosz fejlődés' sajátosságairól, különös tekintettel az 1920-as évekre* (Budapest, Akadémiai Kiadó).

Krausz, T. (2007) 'Perestroika and the Redistribution of Property in the Soviet Union: Political Perspectives and Historical Evidence', *Contemporary Politics*, 13, 1.

Krausz, T. & Márkus, P. (eds) (1995) *Önkormányzás vagy az elitek uralma?* (Budapest, Liberter).

Linden, M. (2007) *Western Marxism and the Soviet Union: A Survey of Critical Theory and Debates since 1917* (Leiden, Brill).

Lindenberger, T. (ed.) (1999) *Herrschaft und Eigensinn in der Diktatur. Studien zur Gesellschaftsgeschichte der DDR* (Cologne, Böhlau).

Lukács, G. (1985) *Demokratisierung heute und morgen* (Budapest, Akadémiai Kiadó).

Maier, C. (1997) *Dissolution: The Crisis of Communism and the End of East Germany* (Princeton, NJ, Princeton University Press).

Pető, A. (1992) *A munkások életkörülményei Magyarországon az 1950-es években*, PhD dissertation, Eötvös University, Budapest.

Pittaway, M. (2007) 'The Revolution and Industrial Workers: The Disintegration and Reconstruction of Socialism, 1953–1958', *Hungarian Studies Review*, 34, 1–2.

Pittaway, M. (2010) 'Workers and the Change of System', in *After Twenty Years*, Budapest, 15–16 January (Budapest, ELTE-Politikatörténeti Intézet).

Róna-Tas, Á. (1997) *The Great Surprise of the Small Transformation: The Demise of Communism and the Rise of the Private Sector in Hungary* (Ann Arbor, MI, The University of Michigan).

Schweitzer, I. (1982) *A vállalatnagyság* (Budapest, Közgazdasági és Jogi Könyvkiadó).

Steiner, A. (1999) *Die DDR-Wirtschaftsreform der sechziger Jahre: Konflikt zwischen Effizienz- und Machtkalkül* (Berlin, Akademie-Verlag).

Steiner, A. (2004) *Von Plan zu Plan: eine Wirtschaftsgeschichte der DDR* (Munich, Dt. Vrl.-Anst.).

Swain, N. (1992) *Hungary: The Rise and Fall of Feasible Socialism* (London & New York, Verso).

Szalai, E. (1986) *Beszélgetések a gazdasági reformról* (Budapest, Pénzügykutató Intézet).

Szalai, E. (1989) *Gazdasági mechanizmus, reformtörekvések és nagyvállalati érdekek* (Budapest, Közgazdasági és Jogi Könyvkiadó).

Szalai, E. (2003) *Baloldal—új kihívások előtt* (Budapest, Aula).

Szalai, E. (2004) 'Tulajdonviszonyok, társadalomszerkezet és munkásság', *Kritika*, 33, 9.

Szelényi, I. & Konrád, G. (1969) *Az új lakótelepek szociológiai problémái* (Budapest, Akadémiai Kiadó).

Tőkés, R. L. (1996) *Hungary's Negotiated Revolution: Economic Reform, Social Change, and Political Succession, 1957–1990* (New York, Cambridge University Press).

Tóth, E. Z. (2007) *Puszi Kádár Jánosnak* (Budapest, Napvilág).

Tütő, L. (1993) 'A szocialista ellenzékiség történetéből—Az 1971-es Kemény-per', *Eszmélet*, 5, 3.

New Life: The Poetics of Transition

GEORGE SZIRTES

> In that part of the book of my memory before which little can be read, there is a heading, which says: 'Incipit vita nova: Here begins the new life'. Under that heading I find written the words that it is my intention to copy into this little book: and if not all, at least their essence.[1]

DANTE'S COMBINATION OF POETRY AND COMMENTARY, a pattern I would like to follow, is a venture into Courtly Love as it leads into blessedness, and, eventually, in the great Commedia, to Paradise.

The 'New Life' I have more immediately in mind is, however, a poem by the Hungarian poet, Zsuzsa Rakovszky, one that appeared in a book titled *Fehér–Fekete* or *White Black*, written in the period 1987–1991 (Rakovszky 1994, p. 53). The poem's Hungarian title, *Új élet* means, literally, new life, and is about, among other things—most poems are about other things as well as the ostensible subject—changes in social circumstances. The poem, written in a modern fractured version of Dante's own *terza rima*, begins with a simple change of address to a new flat, looking around at what Philip Larkin calls, one's own specially chosen junk, noting that it will not be too different from that of the last occupants.

> For keeps this time? Why not? The flat, it's true
> is crammed to the hilt with others' history,
> but what if it is? Theirs will not be so
>
> different from yours. Some potted greenery
> brought in for winter ... three, four months swim by
> and you don't even notice the scenery:
>
> crash-helmet on the wardrobe, the pleated sky
> of a deep-blue fan pinned out against the wall
> like a dead bat, on which two pochards fly
>
> skeetering towards the shelf ....
>
> (Rakovszky 1994, p. 51)

[1]Dante Alighieri, *La Vita Nuova* (*The New Life*), translated by A. S. Kline, 2001, available at: http://www.poetryintranslation.com/PITBR/Italian/TheNewLifeI.htm, accessed 15 March 2009.

The ways in which things are the same soon become apparent. People around her are doing what they ever did. Someone is writing a book or a thesis, the musician comes home trailing his girlfriend's Pekinese dogs. Another acquaintance still possesses that dreadful old TV set . . .

> A couple of years, and you don't even think of moving
> or you might, but know it's just not on. Your friend
> D, will not move either, but will still be striving
>
> with vibrant Dostoevsky's soul, and spend
> the next five hundred years hunched over the screen
> of his word processor, nor will there be an end
>
> of J, the musician, trailing his scores between
> the ground floor and the third, not to mention the Pekes
> inherited from his girlfriend, trembling obscene
>
> up greasy wooden stairs. A's lousy TV freaks
> her out, with its constant humming, heads and busts
> of terrorists or commentators with El Greco physiques,
>
> grey skulls aflame in interstellar gusts . . . .
>
> (Rakovszky 1994, p. 51)

But the times they are a-changing, indeed have changed, and that needs getting used to. Suddenly there is choice, choice in consumer goods:

> Two, three years, there's no doubt now; unfazed
> By sheer excess, by eighteen kinds of mustard,
> I've found my favourite cereal, appraised
>
> The various brands of bathsalts, and adjusted [there being choice in self-image too]
> To being nun or nautch girl, jewel or jade.
>
> (Rakovszky 1994, p. 52)

And, while we are at it, a new choice in political engagements. What if:

> . . . the rain-blurred years' spry
>
> progress offered me a part more in the vernacular:
> teacher or housewife or—why ever not?—
> a leader in the struggle for gay rights, or the Popular
>
> Front for the Liberation of Animals, with a pot
> Of paint at the ready, and a razor in my hand
> To slash a bourgeois fur . . . .
>
> (Rakovszky 1994, p. 53)

All this rushes by us with a degree of bemusement, a dizzy not-quite-seriousness, that at bottom is, paradoxically, serious and deeply disorientated by the time the poem ends:

> ... To aband-
>
> on your life is a matter of sloughing skins:
> the check-out girl at the grocer's, an Albanian
> on the game, tries to recall her origins
>
> as a Friesian fisherman, or a lady in Japan
> with a little white dog at her heels .... Always
> there is something .... Something beyond the span
>
> of time or space, from which their combined rays
> are simply deflected, as from bullet-proof glass ...
> some tiny dense trapped particle, something one pays
>
> like an unreturnable deposit, like a compass
> pointing beyond endless dark ....
>
> (Rakovszky 1994, p. 53)

We could talk about a post-modern notion of shifting identity but something firm yet elusive remains behind, a tiny dense trapped particle, an unreturnable deposit, a compass pointing beyond endless dark ... the new flat, the new world, the new life.

In speaking of the poetics of transition I should admit that I am using the term *poetics* loosely. Aristotle begins his study of poetics by stating that he regards poetry as a mode of imitation, referring to variations in the poetic medium, to its objects and the manners of imitation. He talks about metre, rhythm and tune, about dancing, flute-playing and lyre-playing. He talks about the pleasure we get from imitating even those objects that cause us pain and about the instinct for harmony and rhythm that help bring about the sensation of pleasure. He talks also, importantly, about structure—plot, unity and universality—and tells us 'that it is not the poet's function to describe what has actually happened but the kinds of thing that might happen' (Aristotle *et al.* 1965, p. 43), in other words to be kind of a prophet.

We know that literary analysis can concern itself with more than the traditional categories of drama, prose fiction and poetry. We know that reading is a skill that can be applied across modes, that it may make not only perfectly good sense but prove positively enlightening to apply critical vocabularies across boundaries, employing terms adopted from film, for example, such as 'zoom' or 'pan' or 'dissolve' or 'jump cut' to a poem, or—*vice versa*—to apply 'rhyme', 'rhythm', 'alliteration' and '*caesura*' to film. Aristotle does, after all, mention harmony, rhythm and language as common to the arts.

It is in this loose spirit that I want to talk about the poetics of transition in Hungary. I mean political and cultural transition, as well as the actual poetry produced under conditions of political and cultural transition. I speak, of course, not as a native but as a visitor, albeit one with a special connection, being a returning child refugee of 1956, particularly one who spent most of 1989 in Budapest as a British Council Scholar, writing my own poems about the events of that year as a kind of poetic journal, and translating poetry and fiction from Hungarian into English.

Aristotle talks of tragedy, comedy, dithyramb, plot and epic, of beginning *in medias res*, in the middle of things: these are all patterns that, to some degree, imitate life. We all begin in the middle of something else. Nevertheless, I tend more and more to think that our first experiences in life offer us a set of psychological and aesthetic base notes: they tune us much like an instrument is tuned, to resound and reverberate with whatever follows, to give us our internal rhymes, resonances and key symbols. So the room that is the first room is the measure of all rooms; the street that is the first street is the measure of other streets; the space, light, noise and tone of all we first register in language tunes us and prepares us for the world as music.

It was Easter, Budapest 1984, the mid-1980s, the last four years of the administration of János Kádar who had been in power in Hungary for precisely as long as my family and I had been in England. Budapest in 1984 looked like a war-torn and revolution-torn city that had hoisted itself up by its own fancy bootstraps: it rang and resonated. The silent ringing courtyards with their wooden scaffolding; the elevations with their shell marks and their damaged decorative figures—figures that seemed to be leaping from walls or caught in the act of climbing through them just as a bullet had caught a shoulder or a head or an arm and blown it away; the falling stucco; the hopeless grandeur of imperial nineteenth century form as damaged architectural rhetoric with its post-Classical, post-Baroque, post-Eclectic, post-Romantic, post-Transylvanian hunting lodge, remnant-*Jugendstil*, remnant-Art Deco, remnant-*Bauhaus*, remnant-Soviet, remnant Fascist-monumental Babel of architectural tongues; the stairwells grandly spiralling with graffiti and blackened *putti*; the grand apartments edged with cheap oversized furniture, low-grade East-German white goods, between-the-wars kitsch, heated by tall ceramic stoves edged with tiny ceramic figurines; the social gaiety and jokes edged with caution, and even with a little fear . . . the whole fabric was nervous but equipped with a certain tentative self-confidence that impressed itself on me and produced three long poetic sequences.

Here are two sections from one of them, titled *Courtyards*, in which the central figure is a blind woman, a friend of my by then long dead mother, who we call on to visit. One section sees a tenement block from the outside, the next from the inside:

Outside, a rusticated, vermiform
ebullience; outside, a cluttering
of pediments, pilasters, pargeting,
embroidery; outside, the balconies
expand in their baroque epiphanies,
their splendid Biedermeyer uniforms;

outside, the casement windows under rolls
of stonework, rough or smooth or both; facades
with manners courtly as old playing cards;
outside, the straining figures stiffly bent

to hold up yet another pediment
disfigured by a web of bulletholes;

outside, the falling masonry, the hard
emphatic counter-patterns of collapse,
the shattered panes and almost hingeless flaps
that bang like toy guns to disturb the dust.
Inside, the ironwork, the lines of rust;
inside, the piles of rubble in the yard.

Inside, the caretaker; his wife; his cat;
a cage for small bikes; rows of potted plants
reaching for light; stuff that no one wants
left in the stairwell; little dingy signs
for manicurists, tailors; heavy lines
of washing stretched out tight from flat to flat;

inside, a sort of life. At one o'clock
the ringing feet of children up the stair,
the scrape of chalk where someone scrawls a bare
diagrammatic girl with breasts like bells
and leaves a message in rough capitals;
inside, the noisy opening of locks.

Inside, I think of someone else, a blind
and aged woman treading the fourth floor,
as if it were a jetty from a shore
suspended in a band of warming light.
She feels her way to the door opposite.
The hollow building trembles in her hand.
(Szirtes 2008, pp. 126–27)

The physical fabric of the city and its people seemed, as the poem says, to tremble in the hand. That seemed to be the nature of the place. It trembled with excitement and fear. Trembling, of a sort, is the movement that anticipates a poem. I do not mean a physical trembling, more a sense of expectation, as if language were at a peculiar tension. So, in the poem, the walls of Budapest act as the equivalent of a language seeking its echoes. That sense of tightening, en-tensioning in language, is, if I may put it that way, an element in the first half of a pair of rhymes, or the kind of rhythm or metre that constitutes a beginning, or at least an inkling of a beginning: a series of tensions to come.

Economically the city looked healthy, or at any rate, much healthier than it might have been, and certainly healthier than its equivalents in neighbouring states. The New Economic Policy that had been introduced in 1968, suspended in 1973 and revived between 1978 and 1980, had resulted in Hungary being regarded as 'Little America' by Russian visitors and as 'the happiest barracks in the communist camp' by Western journalists who attributed the jollity to the country's Goulash version of communism. I quickly understood that Goulash communism was the product of a black economy, that is to say of moonlighting, corruption and circulation of consumer goods through undeclared earnings and stashed cash, and that what gave it its edge of anxiety and excitement was the knowledge that this could not go on forever and that it was, moreover, morally sapping.

How morally sapping I could not tell. Instead of morality there was poetry. Some of the greatest poets of the second half of the century were still alive: Sándor Weöres, István Vas, Ágnes Nemes Nagy and Ferenc Juhász. Over the years I was to meet them all and become friend and translator to Vas and Nemes Nagy and even, to a lesser extent, to Weöres. All bar Juhász were to die by 1991. Their world became familiar to me and was already so through their writing. The works of these poets were all, to a large degree, though not equally, formed by the history of post-war Hungary. They were the kind of writers likely to be gathered together in Western anthologies of Eastern European poetry as political-literary exemplars, examples of what poetry could do under pressure: poetry as morality. The British *Penguin European Poets* list of the late 1960s and early 1970s, was a bringing together of this general world-view, starting as it did with Yevgenii Yevtushenko, and soon enough adding Czeslaw Miłosz, Zbigniew Herbert, Miroslav Holub, Vladimir Holan.

Nemes Nagy (1922–1991) and Vas (1910–1991) had both registered the forces acting on them, chiefly in the form of censorship between 1949 and 1953. For Vas this left him with translation, a period he remembers in a poem called *The Translator's Vote of Thanks*, which begins:

I render thanks to you, you gracious giants,
That although silenced I still wagged my tongue,
That my voice spoke through your voice in defiance,
In Moliere's epigram and Shakespeare's song,
In Goethe, Schiller; that I did not fill
My throat with pompous, lying hymns of praise,
But hid my thought in scattered several
Secret fragments, in foreign poems and plays.

. . .

The living lie; in our town only those
Considered to be mummies should be heard
But you are resurrected, verse or prose,
My will had charged the wire: the body stirred ....
(Vas 1989, p. 40)

Nemes Nagy's more ferocious assault[2] came in the form of brilliant epigrammatic verse, such as these from her poem *Journal*:

Revenge

He who cannot take revenge,
Nor yet forgive, must find redress
In burning for ever the low flame
Of his unquenchable bitterness.

[2]She was banned for longer than Vas and her career was stopped before it could start.

Sic Itur ad Astra

Compared with these I am a saint
no judge would dare try me;
if the world wags on like this
they will deify me ....
(Nemes Nagy 2004, p. 19)

Nemes Nagy's answer to censorship was to focus the repression inward and to work it through the intellect into precisely cut, passionate, philosophical shapes.

Perhaps the most striking poem of the heroic age of pre-1956 totalitarianism in Hungary was Gyula Illyés's (1902–1983) very long *One Sentence on Tyranny* written in 1950 but not published until the revolution itself, then suppressed again until after 1989. I myself was shown it first in a still banned, stapled-together copy, in 1985. This is how it begins:

One Sentence on Tyranny

Where tyranny exists
that tyranny exists
not only in the barrel of the gun
not only in the cells of a prison

not just in the interrogation block
or the small hours of the clock
the guard's bark and his fists
the tyranny exists

not just in the billowing black fetor
of the closing speech of the prosecutor,
in 'the justified use of force'
the prisoners' dull morse

not merely in the cool postscript
of the expected verdict
there's tyranny
not just in the crisp military

order to 'Stand!' and the numb
instruction 'Fire!', the roll of the drum,
in the last twitch
of the corpse in the ditch

not just in the door half-open
and the fearful omen,
the whispered tremor
of the secret rumour

the hand that grips,
the finger before the lips,

tyranny is in place
in the iron mask of the face

in the clench of the jaw
the wordless O . . . .
(Illyés 1996, p. 31)

This was a dangerous poem that had to be hidden away from anyone but the closest friends. It is not that the sense of danger necessarily guarantees the quality of art since the reverse can be the case, and at over 50 verses the poem might be thought to be too long, but its power is undeniable. It was the heroic age of totalitarian verse: the conditions poetry operated under and reflected were of the classic, oppressive type.

The world was no longer quite like this in 1984. Illyés himself had died the year before, and there was a subtler, more sophisticated form of state censorship in place, one that Miklós Haraszti describes in his book *The Velvet Prison* (1988). The generation after Vas, Illyés, Nemes Nagy and the rest—that is to say my own Hungarian generation, a generation that might include an older or younger brother or sister—was formed by the conditions of the velvet prison. The Hungarian version was one in which the writer was materially looked after with sinecures and positions; where his or her work was not examined too thoroughly for veiled or implied criticism; where no one style of writing was regarded as ideologically correct; where the old banned writers were allowed to publish books containing poems critical of the earlier state of affairs, and no-one was expected to produce works praising the party, its leaders or its programme. Optimism was no longer obligatory. In other words it was a relatively relaxed state of affairs—providing the state and its representatives were not actually criticised, that the memory of 1956 was not invoked, that the presence of poverty, of over-employment, of the black economy and of Russian troops was politely ignored. It was, as Haraszti explains in his book, essentially, self-censorship.

György Petri was born in Budapest in 1943, read Philosophy and Hungarian Literature at university and, after his first two books appeared in the early 1970s, was recognised to be one of the most original younger talents. In 1975 however, the year after the publication of his second book, *Körülírt zuhanás* (*Circumscribed Fall*), his poems became 'politically unacceptable' and he published his next three books in *samizdat* (and they remained only in *samizdat* for 13 years). At the same time he was one of the founder members of an unofficial and persecuted body, The Foundation for the Support of the Poor (*A Szegényeket Támogató Alap*, acronym SZETA in Hungarian). He was clearly and visibly of the underground opposition. His *samizdat* books were enormously popular. They were cyclostyled and stapled together and quickly bought whenever people could get hold of them.

Petri's poems began to appear in the English press, first in the *Times Literary Supplement* in 1982, then in *The Observer* in 1984, then in *Index on Censorship* in 1985, and in 1986 in *Encounter*. His first book in English, *Night Song of the Personal Shadow* appeared in 1991 (Petri 1991).

In his introduction to the book Clive Wilmer, introducing Petri as a satirist, wrote:

> To a dissident like György Petri, Kádár, 'this Aegisthus with his trainee barber's face' [as Petri puts it in one poem] was even more contemptible than the hard-line leaders of the other

Communist countries. The Hungarian dictatorship, he says, was 'more sophisticated ... more clever'; the control it exerted, therefore, went deeper, so the 'moral state of the people was more dangerously corrupted'. (Petri 1991, p. 10)

For Petri there were two important years, as he wrote in his poem *On the 24th Anniversary of the Little October Revolution*, remembering 1956 in 1980. The poem, in Gömöri and Wilmer's translation, is addressed to the party-state and ends:

... I say just two numbers:
56
68.
You can add them, subtract them,
divide or multiply.
Your innumerable doctrines, baseness is their basis,
have failed, are bankrupt.

(Petri 1991, p. 44)

Petri could write devastatingly directly, but a less direct form of criticism, and in my view a more effective one, came through his poems about love and sex. It was the work of a lyrical poet deliberately gone sour in an endeavour to match the times, as in the poem *Gratitude* (1981):

The idiotic silence of state holidays
is no different
from that of Catholic Sundays.
People in collective idleness
are even more repellent
than they are when purpose has harnessed them.

Today I will not
in my old ungrateful way
let gratuitous love decay in me.
In the vacuum of streets
what helps me to escape
is the memory of your face and thighs,
your warmth,
the fish-death smell of your groin.

You looked for a bathroom in vain.
The bed was uncomfortable
like a roof ridge.
The mattress smelt of insecticide,
the new scent of your body mingling with it.

I woke to a cannonade
(a round number of years ago
something happened). You were still asleep.
Your glasses, your patent leather bag
on the floor, your dress on the window-catch
hung inside out—so practical.

One strap of your black slip
had slithered off.
And a gentle light was wavering
on the downs of your neck, on your collar-bones,
as the cannon went on booming

and on a spring poking through
the armchair's cover
fine dust was trembling.

(Petri 1991, p. 33)

Clearly this is a different sensibility from the kind animating Vas, Nemes Nagy and the poets of their generation. It is predicated less on overt political forces as on politics completely internalised into style; politics, in other words, as a thorough soaking through, of the kind the Northern Irish poet and critic Tom Paulin was to talk about in his Introduction to the *Faber Book of Political Verse*, where he wrote: 'To consider Pasternak's career is to understand how completely the personal life can be saturated by political reality, for politics is like a rainstorm that catches us all in its wet noise' (Paulin 1986, p. 18). The soaking through, the wet noise and the trembling dust in Petri, like the hollow building trembling in the hand of the old blind woman in my own *Courtyards*, are all conditions, or rather forms of apprehension: a kind of pre-language.

For me the rediscovery of Budapest was, in the first place, a rediscovery of the city of my parents' generation. It was not so much the present that first interested me, but an earlier history made material. I returned in 1985 and 1986 and the next two years too. In 1988 a very long poem of mine called *Metro* appeared. It ran to almost 800 lines in ten sections of six 13-line curtailed sonnets each. In *Metro* the underground system of Budapest becomes a living metaphor, the underworld pressing close to the skin of the pavements. Here is a verse from it:

There are certain places healthy to have lived in,
Certain streets, hard cores of pleasure,
Their doorways are ripe fruit, stay soft and open,
Exhaling a fragrance of drains or tobacco,
Others are more proper, starched and sun-eaten,
Doorways where things happen
In a particularly fortunate way, which echo
To words of parting, or thrill to an exact measure
Recollected in the pleat of an arch;
Doorways which see military bands march
Across a square on a blazing hot afternoon,
Or catch a particular angle of the moon.
There are places to be happy in if only you can find them.

(Szirtes 2008, p. 153)

Underneath this lies the empire of the lost and dead.

The empire underground; the tunnelling
Begins. The earth gives up her worms and shards,

Old coins, components, ordnance, bone and glass,
Nails, muscle, hair, flesh, shrivelled bits of string,
Shoe leather, buttons, jewels, instruments.
And out of these come voices, words,
Stenches and scents,
And finally desire, pulled like a tooth.
It's that or constancy that leads us down
To find a history which feels like truth ….
(Szirtes 2008, p. 154)

In 1989 I received a longer British Council grant and the four of us, my wife and two children, came to live in Budapest for most of the year. That year marked an entirely different poetic, another kind of transition. We arrived in early January 1989. Our accommodation, as it turned out, was Miklós Haraszti's vacant flat—he was in the USA. I had never met him: it was a mutual friend who made the arrangements. The street was situated in the university quarter, close to the river and the city centre. As we arrived our neighbour was listening to the televised debates in parliament. That was in itself unusual. No-one listened to proceedings in parliament, but something had changed.

The change had begun with Mikhail Gorbachev, the import of his policies filtering down into practical Hungarian politics in 1988, leading in the May of that year to the removal from office of János Kádár. Since May, almost every week, there had been some perceptible shift in the landscape. Everything was on the move. Kádár's successor, Károly Grósz, was in the process of losing his footing. By the time we left in September 1989 one could see the man beginning to fall in slow motion.

Here I would like to rely on the text of a broadcast I made for the BBC at the end of 1989, a form of report or 'Letter from Budapest'.

What last year was strictly *samizdat* and passed conspiratorially from hand to hand is no longer forbidden. It lives in a no-man's-land, a dream-world which is itself in constant motion. Many of the authors appear to be in eternal transit. Some who left the country last year as dissidents have returned as members of the official opposition. It is disorientating, both for them and the public at large. All the more so as the original underground press has been joined in the Metro by new commercial publishers. The two worlds overlap so that the same vendor sometimes carries both the party programme of the Free Democrats Alliance [*Szabad Demokraták Szövetsége*] and pirated editions of books from the West. In a single station there may be three or four groups of paper vendors, often selling the same items. The revelations of a Romanian secret agent rub shoulders with the revelations of Ilona Staller, *La Cicciolina*.

But it's not only books and magazines that appear on the rugs but patriotic badges, cassette recordings of old speeches, neatly packaged pieces of the Iron Curtain and sachets of earth from Imre Nagy's grave. Martyrology and necrophilia collude with demand. History conducts an intense affair with nostalgia. It is appropriate that these brief encounters should take place at a railway station. The badges actually offer a choice: they bear the arms either of St Stephen's monarchic Hungary, with crown, or of liberal Hungary, vintage 1848, without. A transition period keeps its options open.

In the course of the summer a newer kind of magazine appears in the underground. At first it is aesthetically clad in poetry and psychological jargon but this veil is quickly stripped away. To describe it as not quite hard pornography is awkwardly accurate, though the sell itself is anything but soft. These are not imports but home brew. Young men display open copies and push them towards passers-by with an aggressive, almost patriotic, pride.

The unbearable lightness of being has infected authority itself. Used to the arbitrary exercise of a power that passed for substance the police drift through streets and stations somewhat at a loss. At the Western Rail Terminal groups of neglected looking adolescents hang about the television. Some of them are travellers from abroad, others simply have nowhere else to go. The police eye them suspiciously, inspect their ID cards, search them for drugs, then let them go. Soon the groups are back again, their eyes flickering between the television and the movement round them. At the Eastern Rail Terminal the black market money-changers, mainly foreigners, almost outnumber the passengers. Asked to move on, one of them takes three paces to his left. It is the policeman who moves on .... (Szirtes 1989)

The year produced its rhymes of course. The poetics of transition might be furnished out by events. The marches of 1989 started precisely where the marches of 1956 did. The cutting out of the centre of the flag along that march rhymed with the cutting out of the Soviet emblem in 1956. The reappearance of Imre Nagy's face was not just a rhyme but a repeated choric motif.

The classical ode is divided into three: the statement of the choric strophe, the counter-statement of the antistrophe and the resolution of the epode. It is a tantalising possibility that almost all lyric poems resolve into three parts in varying proportions. A first condition comprising a place or a figure, a second complicating factor sometimes indicated by a 'but' or a 'then', or a 'while', and a third stage, often signalled by an 'and' or 'so', which is not exactly a resolution, but an opening out onto some apprehended state of affairs, a state of affairs where language falls into the uncertain yet resonant space that constitutes a poem, and offers more possibilities than seemed feasible at the outset. If the ceremonial reburial of Imre Nagy was the strophe spoken by the chorus, so the burial of János Kádár a few weeks later was the antistrophe. The epode was as yet undecided.

The poet Ottó Orbán was a good friend. He was just developing Parkinson's Disease when we first met in the mid-1980s. Orbán was the closest thing to a daily chronicler of Hungary's social and political life, writing his unrhymed, loosely hexametric sonnets from what would turn out to be his deathbed. In 1989, just as the political situation was coming to a crisis where one side or the other would win, he wrote *A Roman Considers the Christians*:

May the gods forgive me but I really can't abide them.
Their idea is a great one, but look at them all:
a bunch of quarrelsome eggheads picking their noses,
who, under the spell of their thesis, would if they could
be hard-line dictators, all for the sake of tolerance naturally,
who'd not kill with weapons but with murderous disdain,
while breeding their own sloppy aristocracy,
along with other oppressive, life-hating state institutions ...
So, let me embellish this with a gesture—a fig for them all!
Just one little problem: the starved lion bawling in the arena ...
There are plenty with vision, but they are the ones prepared to be eaten,

in dust clouds of water-cannon where out of the screaming and bloodshed
something emerges ... the same thing? The worse? Or the better?
The gods only know, if they know, what lies in the future ....
(Orbán 1993, p. 92)

The gods here are keeping the epode to themselves, as indeed they must. I, for my part maintained my own poem journal that was to form the backbone of my 1991 book *Bridge Passages*. That journal formed a sequence of 18 poems in the same six-line stanza form, rhyming ABC ABC, two longer lines then a short third, twice for each stanza. 'National Anthem' is one of these (Szirtes 1991, p. 45). It is April. Nature is awakening, so are the streets. The meanings of things are changing before our very eyes: political meaning, psychological significance. Everything is opening out, struggling for meaning. Then, one day, a saxophonist wanders into the courtyard below and plays a slow, bluesy version of the national anthem.

National Anthem

The spring begins an age of festivals:
the outbreaks and foundations, liberations,
appointed days, appointed modes
of putting on. The flags hang from the walls.
The weather bustles by. The operations
of the state. The empty roads.

The corridors too are empty though the sun
has laid its fingers underneath each door
to beckon us out. It's quiet:
something bothers the sky. Something remains undone.
April now. But it could be May: Nature,
that great abstraction is set

before us: small green arguments of leaves,
the proclamations of blossom on each branch,
the flowers with their furious dance.
Meaning! Meaning! They jostle. Whoever believes
in us must give us meaning! An avalanche
of meaning! Let us have significance!
(Szirtes 2008, p. 209)

The poem then notices 'a statue always looking past/ the same old clump of trees/ winter and summer, the same look on its face', and asks 'How long can faces at the windows last?', and answers: 'They disappear by slow degrees ... '.

... each disappearance quick in its own terms.
Mother, father, child. They call out names
that no one understands but them.
They wear their universal forms,
their worn-out clothes. The sunlight frames
each figure like a theorem.

We're here, such as we are. We will be missed.
Some children gather opposite, look down
into the courtyard where
music's playing. A lone saxophonist
proffers the national anthem. The notes are blown
random, slow, into the air.
(Szirtes 2008, p. 210)

Several times in my last months there I saw the same vagrant couple. The first time was at a bus stop. The man was crouching on the pavement, peering through the woman's legs. He looked first from one side then the other. It was an extraordinary performance. I took him for a drunk but she seemed to be undisturbed. She stood with her back to us, making no gesture of appeal. When the bus arrived and he got on, she slowly turned and, with a glazed expression, followed him. Her face glowed as if bruised. Next time I saw them on the street near Liberation Square. He was just disappearing into an arcade, beckoning her to follow him. She did so mutely, as if she were his dog. Twice more I saw them, both times in Metro stations. It was on one of these occasions that I first heard him speak. They were coming down an escalator while I was riding up. His voice was thin, high, almost effeminate, but there was a mechanical and nagging quality in it. I suppose I must have heard five or six seconds of his conversation. I could not make much sense of it. When they reached the bottom they set off, she behind him, moving slowly as if in some rough dream. Thinking back to her now I seem to see a vision out of some downmarket *spiritus mundi*, like W.B. Yeats's rough beast slouching towards Bethlehem. Towards an epode, if you like.

The couple were rhyming, or counter-rhyming with the crowds marching, with the burials and reburials. Within a couple of months of returning everything else, everywhere else, was being buried and reburied. I want to end with two short *rondeaux*, the first titled *Unter Den Linden*, the second *Clumsy Music*. The first is clear enough. In the second, Hogmanay is the Scottish ceremony of New Year where the man with the darkest hair is sent out to bring in a piece of coal. The Berlin Wall fell officially on 9 November. At Christmas Eve I was outside the Romanian Embassy joining a vigil. The second poem mentions Christmas day and talks about guilt and ghosts.

Two Rondeaux

1. Unter den Linden

In Unter den Linden and Wenceslas Square
The candles wink their laissez-fair,
People are trampling over borders,
Packing their luggage. Cassette recorders
Hiss like steam in the cold air,

Cameras roll and spokesmen prepare
Brief noncommittal statements, tear
Pages from notebooks and wait for orders.
Prisons open: prisoners and warders
Mix in Unter den Linden.

In Prague and Budapest they wear
Rosettes, wave flags. A furious year
Gathers to a close. The wind disorders
Ships of state and fleets of boarders.
Men link hands, dance, and boldly stare
Across Unter den Linden.

2. Clumsy Music

A clumsy music: years lurch on
And fugitive clocks on the run
Must settle debts by Hogmanay.
At Christmas guilty parents pay
The devil who pays debts to none.

Important things remain undone,
The boxes open: one by one
Their ghosts are spirited away:
The piper stands by, set to play
His clumsy music,

Artificial, yet homespun,
A rondeau much like this, begun
In hope as much as fear, to lay
His fears and keep wild hopes at bay,
With dancing, linking hands, best done
To clumsy music.
(Szirtes 2008, p. 220)

Clumsy music is an aspect of the poetic. It gives us the rhythm and rhyme of things without perfecting itself because perfection would be stillness and poems have to be moving on. Poems are language in transition. The last part of a poem is not, as many would have it, a closure, a closing, but an opening. The reason we love poems, if we do love them, is because they open, as our lives do, onto apprehensions without firm conclusions. *New Life* is dramatic change. 'To be apprehensive' and 'to apprehend' come from the same root. To apprehend means to fear, to arrest, and to understand, and yet not quite to understand, not quite to comprehend. Apprehension is as good as it gets.

Wymondham, Norfolk

References

Aristotle, Horace & Longinus (1965) *Classical Literary Criticism* [translated with an Introduction by T. S. Dorsch] (Baltimore, MD, Penguin Books).

Haraszti, M. (1988) *The Velvet Prison: Artists Under State Socialism* (London, I.B. Tauris).

Illyés, G. (1996) 'A Sentence About Tyranny' [translated by George Szirtes], in Gömöri, G. & Szirtes, G. (eds) (1996) *The Colonnade of Teeth: Modern Hungarian Poetry* (Tarset, Bloodaxe).

Nemes Nagy, Á. (2004) *The Night of Akhenaton: Selected Poems* [translated by George Szirtes] (Tarset, Bloodaxe).

Orbán O. (1993) *The Blood of the Walsungs* [edited by George Szirtes] (Tarset, Bloodaxe & Budapest, Corvina).

Paulin, T. (1986) 'Introduction', in Paulin, T. (ed.) (1986) *The Faber Book of Political Verse* (London, Faber & Faber).
Petri, G. (1991) *Night Song of the Personal Shadow* [translated by Clive Wilmer & George Gömöri] (Tarset, Bloodaxe).
Rakovszky, Z. (1994) *New Life* [translated by George Szirtes] (Oxford & New York, Oxford University Press).
Szirtes, G. (1989) *The Underground in the Underground*, BBC Radio 3, 21 November, available at: http://www.georgeszirtes.co.uk/index.php?page=articles, accessed 25 July 2011.
Szirtes, G. (1991) *Bridge Passages* (Oxford & New York, Oxford University Press).
Szirtes, G. (2008) *New and Collected Poems* (Tarset, Bloodaxe).
Vas, I. (1989) 'The Translators Vote of Thanks' [translated by George Szirtes], in Vajda, M. (ed.) (1989) *Through the Smoke* (Budapest, Corvina).

The Picnic on the Border: An Interview with László Vass

TERRY COX

Introduction

ON 28 FEBRUARY 1989, THE LEADERSHIP OF THE Hungarian Socialist Workers' Party took a momentous decision to dismantle the high-security installations along its border with Austria. The National Headquarters of the Frontier Guards then worked out a programme, initially seen as lasting for two years, for the removal of the high wire fence and electric alarm system that had been installed all along the 350-kilometre border. It thus marked the beginning of the dismantling of the iron curtain across Europe and preceded the fall of the Berlin Wall by several months.

The new border policy was announced on 2 May at an international press conference at Hegyeshalom, and on the 27 June a ceremony was held in which some wire of the border fence was symbolically cut by Alois Mock and Gyula Horn, the Ministers of Foreign Affairs of Austria and Hungary. The decision, carried out with the approval of the Soviet leadership, was seen initially as a means of improving relations between Hungary and Austria and 'normalising' the movement of the citizens of each country across the common border. However, as Mark Kramer notes in his essay in this collection, it 'had the unintended effect of spurring tens of thousands of East Germans to travel to Hungary, a country they were allowed to visit with minimal restrictions', from where they planned to move '*en masse* to the western border area, hoping to be granted permission to cross into Austria'.

Meanwhile the relaxation of border controls attracted the interest of people in opposition circles in Hungary; an idea soon emerged to organise a symbolic meeting between Hungarians and Austrians from each side of the border, based on a picnic at which Austrians and Hungarians would move across the border to eat and drink with each other. The event, it was hoped, would give further impetus to the many other changes taking place in Hungary in 1989 in the direction of democratisation and greater openness. Perhaps surprisingly, the idea for the event came from the opposite end of Hungary, from Debrecen in the east. The idea originated with Ferenc Mészaros, along with Mária Filep and László Magas, members of the Debrecen Hungarian Democratic Forum (HDF, *Magyar Demokrata Fórum*) group following a dinner with Otto von Hapsburg on 20 June 1989. Hapsburg, a direct descendent of the last Hapsburg

Emperor of Austria and Hungary, and then a German MEP, was a frequent visitor to Hungary in the late 1980s. The Debrecen HDF group then contacted members of the Opposition Round Table of Sopron, in western Hungary near the Austrian border. The Sopron Round Table, following the example of the Budapest Opposition Round Table, was made up mainly of members of the newly emerging opposition political parties, the HDF, Free Democrats (*Szabad Demokraták Szövetsége—a Magyar Liberális Párt*), *FIDESZ* and Smallholders (*Független Kisgazda, Földmunkás és Polgári Párt*). Members formed an organising committee including primarily László Nagy[1] and László Magas of the HDF and Zsolt Szentkirályi of the Free Democrats.

The organisers invited Otto von Hapsburg and Imre Pozsgay to be co-sponsors of the Picnic. The leading reformer in the Hungarian ruling Party, Pozsgay held the position of Minister of State in the Hungarian government. As chairman of the Party's mass organisation, the Patriotic Front, he had pioneered links between the ruling Party and civic groups during the 1980s and, in 1989, was especially known as the first member of the Party leadership to label the 1956 Hungarian revolution not as a counter-revolution but as a popular uprising. He was to play an important role behind the scenes in facilitating the preparations for the Picnic.

The Picnic was planned to be held at Sopronpuszta, outside Sopron and near the border, on 19 August 1989. Permission was given by authorities on each side of the border for a previously disused wooden border gate to be opened that day from 3pm to 6pm to allow Austrian and Hungarian citizens to show their passports and cross the border. It was also agreed, in the spirit of informality of the occasion, that only a small number of border guards from each side would be on duty at the border. Also in the spirit of informality it was agreed the event would be opened by short speeches from the organisers and sponsors, and then the Picnic would take place in a relaxed atmosphere.

Although permission had been given for the Picnic on the Border by the Hungarian government, as an initiative of civic groups and nascent opposition parties it was still seen as an unusual event in the summer of 1989, and was met with some suspicion and hostility among more conservative circles in the government and ruling Party. There was also a concern to avoid aggravating the increasingly tense relations that were developing between Hungary and more conservative Warsaw Pact governments, and increasingly with the East German government in view of the increasingly large numbers of East Germans now gathering in Hungary. Perhaps with such tensions in mind, Hapsburg and Pozsgay decided not to participate in the Picnic themselves and to each send a representative instead; Hapsburg sent his daughter Walburga Hapsburg and Pozsgay sent his deputy, László Vass.[2]

In contrast to the organisers' original plans for a relatively small event involving people living each side of the border, the Picnic became more of a mass event involving several thousand people. Extensive leafleting by Hungarian opposition groups ensured a large attendance, not only by Hungarians but also by large numbers of East German 'tourists' who were staying in Hungary that summer seeking ways—legal and illegal—

[1]For Nagy's own memoir of the Picnic see László Nagy, 'The Pan-European Picnic, and the Opening of the Border', available at: www.hungarianhistory.com/lib/piknik.doc, last accessed 25 July 2011.

[2]At the time László Vass was head of Pozsgay's office and had the title of Deputy President of the Office of the Council of Ministers.

to cross the border to Austria and then make their way to West Germany. In the weeks preceding the Picnic there had been several attempts by East Germans to cross the border, a few of them successful, others resulting in their being turned back with a warning from the border guards.

On the day of the Picnic the schedule for the organisers and representatives of the two sponsors was to hold a press conference at a nearby hotel and then proceed in buses to the border for a brief opening ceremony. However, before they arrived some East Germans had already taken advantage of the low level of security and had pushed their way past the border guards, forced open the rather flimsy wooden gate, and crossed into Austria. Faced with orders that were not entirely clear, and which had not been issued with that particular situation in mind, the senior officer in command of the border guards, Árpád Bella, took the decision not to restrain the East Germans and to stick to their formal role of checking the papers of people coming into Hungary from Austria.[3] While Bella's decision was both realistic and humane, given the limited information he would have had about the direction of the political winds in the governing circle in Budapest, it was also rather courageous.

By the time the official Party arrived therefore, the situation was already rather chaotic and further waves of East Germans continued to cross the border during the next few hours. The organisers decided that the best policy was to accept what had happened and continue with the programme.

After 19 August the border was closed again to those without official papers and border guards were deployed to direct back all cars with DDR number plates. There were several attempts to cross the border on foot and, while some were successful, many of these were also intercepted. For the next few weeks, while the East German authorities called for the repatriation of their citizens, the Hungarian government attempted to negotiate terms with the DDR government to enable the East Germans in Hungary to exit to West Germany with official permission. Finally, in view of the increasingly desperate situation of the East Germans living in temporary camps in Budapest and elsewhere, the Hungarian government gave up on its attempts to persuade their East German counterparts and, on 11 September, opened the border to allow the East Germans to leave.

After 1989 László Vass left politics and followed an academic career. He is now one of Hungary's leading specialists in public policy and is currently Rector of Budapest College of Communication and Business, a university-level institution in Hungary. The following interview with him took place in Budapest on 9 February 2010.

The Picnic: the birth of an idea

Terry Cox (TC): Where did the idea of a Picnic on the Border first come from? As I understand it, from what I have read, the suggestion was raised initially at a dinner in Debrecen to which Otto von Hapsburg was invited, and at some point after that, those involved had the idea of asking Imre Pozsgay to be a sponsor of the Picnic, is that right?
Laszlo Vass (LV): As I remember, the idea originated with the local Hungarian

[3]For an interview with Árpád Bella by Nicholas Brautlecht, see www.goethe.de/ges/pok/dos/dos/mau/auf/en4236972.htm, last accessed 25 July 2011.

Democratic Forum (HDF) branch in Debrecen. I think it was also a good opportunity for Otto von Hapsburg who wanted to involve himself in East European politics. He appeared in Hungary many times in the late 1980s and was very popular here. And in Debrecen he took up the opportunity to support the Picnic initiative. As a politician promoting the idea of pan-European politics, the idea of opening borders was attractive to him. The HDF were keen to involve Pozsgay, partly because they already had some experience of cooperating with him and recognised he was a really committed democrat. They especially saw him as someone they could work with after he had arranged for the founding declaration of the Democratic Forum to be published in a newspaper. He had to do it in a very tricky way because at that time it was still very strictly forbidden.

Well, those two politicians, Hapsburg and Pozsgay, looked like a very attractive combination to promote the idea of relaxing controls over the border. Pozsgay was very happy when he was invited.

TC: Did Pozsgay have to consult his Party and government colleagues before accepting?

LV: Well, at that time he got many, many invitations and he never asked for permission to accept them, he just informed the government. He never asked the prime minister or others to agree. You see, he was not a really disciplined Party person. He was very open, very friendly, and very unorthodox. To those of us who worked with him, he gave us advice and guidelines if we needed them, but sometimes we were surprised by what he did because he did not inform us about some of his strange moves. He met hundreds of people and maybe sometimes, a month later, we learned that he already discussed this or that issue but it was not what was in his portfolio formally.

TC: Some people have called him the Hungarian Gorbachev, but probably he's a very different personality, and also in a very different situation—he had much less power than Gorbachev.

LV: Yes, Gorbachev wanted an orchestrated transition, and this was the idea also of some other Hungarian politicians, like Károly Grósz. Pozsgay was absolutely different; he was much more, well, not an administrator, and not a tricky politician. He wanted to make declarations, to show perspectives and strategies and values; so in some ways a typical East-Central European figure; he was not a pluralistic politician or a liberal in a Western sense.

TC: But, it seems to me he shared one thing in common with Western politicians, he knew the value of publicity and the public gesture, and I suppose if he didn't have so much organisational power behind him, this was his big weapon?

LV: Yes, yes. And also the language he used was very important. He did not use the Party language. He would speak in terms of rhetoric and it was very, very different from [the speech of] the average communist leader. They used very boring, ideological, fake-scientific language sometimes, without any meaning, just formal scientific sentences. But Pozsgay had a very wide knowledge of Hungarian literature and he knew lots of poems, lots of stories. So he could use the Marxist methodology if he wanted, but at the same time he was deeply rooted in the Hungarian popular culture; this gave him a new language which was very sympathetic for the people. He broke through, penetrated some taboos as well: [the official view of] 1956 at first, but not only '56; we were openly talking about a national interest, and this phrase 'national interest', this expression had been forbidden before then. So he was not a big administrator; he liked to be popular; he liked to be influential; and he wanted to open up discussion on things that had been taboo.

TC: And perhaps that puts the Picnic into context, in that it was an opportunity to stimulate the flow of events?

LV: Yes it was one issue among others that people wanted to hear his views on. During 1989 Pozsgay was much in demand, especially after the famous January speech when he declared that '56 was not a counter-revolution, but an uprising against the oppression. Before the Picnic he was giving four or five speeches every week around the country; he was very popular. He was invited by even local small communities and he liked to speak to the people and so he travelled a lot to give speeches. Pozsgay's approach was to try to push back the boundaries of current thinking and he had been doing this for some time; it was a normal process for him.

Prelude to the Picnic

TC: With Pozsgay's involvement, did the Picnic become an official event or was it a civil initiative, not a Party or a government initiative?

LV: Everything was done by the civil society groups, and by the local HDF groups, especially the Sopron HDF group. I remember the first stage in July; the first information came from them. When the Debrecen and the Sopron HDF groups had agreed on the details, we got the information from them, and then I had some telephone conversations with the Sopron organisers. They did not ask for much support, and not for advice from us at all.

TC: And when it came to the stage of the detailed organisation, was that still a civil initiative or did you or Pozsgay actually help with the arrangements?

LV: The main help we could give was to keep in touch behind the scenes with the Ministry of Interior; and it was very important looking back at the event. At that time it seemed quite natural to us but looking back I suppose it was quite significant. I think Pozsgay had quite serious discussions with the Minister of Interior, István Horváth, who was responsible for law and order. They were very good friends and I think that Pozsgay informed his friend regularly what was happening with regard to events on the border. He asked for his support and the minister gave it. So looking back from today, maybe he was much more important in that story than we thought [at] that time.

TC: Reading the memoir of the event written by László Nagy [the local HDF organiser of the Picnic], it seems that he and his colleagues had very good cooperation from all the local government people, police, fire service, ambulance, public transport and so on. Was this something spontaneous from those local people or did they receive guidance or even instructions from national level government or Party officials?

LV: Of course, the organisers had to conform to the regulations set out by the government, and these were quite detailed. But otherwise it was their job to make the arrangements. I am sure Pozsgay, supported by Horváth, sent some supporting messages, but they could not intervene directly at that level so I think most of the collaboration from the local government came spontaneously from the locals. It was quite risky for them because they could not see the broader political situation very clearly and the way the momentum for reform was changing day by day. The relative strengths of the different politicians were also changing gradually. So it could have been risky for the local people to support the Picnic organisers. But I think they probably asked the police, and maybe the police got some 'relaxing' message from the centre.

TC: Should we see Pozsgay's support for the Picnic in the same spirit as the symbolic cutting of the wire of the border fence by Gyula Horn and his Austrian opposite number which had taken place earlier? Was it a similar kind of gesture to cut the border?

LV: No. Well what Horn did was part of a very cautiously planned move towards changing foreign relations specifically between the two countries, between Hungary and Austria, and it was controlled by the government; it was a political act under the government's control. But, as I have mentioned, the Picnic was a civil initiative; it was not a government idea and not the idea of the Communist Party; because of that it had an absolutely different character.

And, of course, behind the scenes obviously, there was a kind of competition or jealousy between the politicians. Horn was not known as the leading reformist; the leading reformer was Pozsgay.

And one invitation Pozsgay received, I don't remember exactly when, in July or June, was to speak to officers of the western border guard. The officers had invited him to speak about the new policies [of the government] regarding the border. And Pozsgay told them then that the iron curtain was finished and we had to remove it. His speech caused some slight confusion among the border-guard officers; and it was also controversial because the border guards belonged to the army, not to the police, and among military officers there were some hardline communists who did not agree with Pozsgay's ideas. He was also criticised by other politicians, especially by Horn and from Grósz, both because the border issue was not part of his portfolio, and because he had made statements that were too definite on things which had not yet been decided by the government.

TC: When he received his invitation from the border guards did he regard this as a sign that they were sympathetic to his reform ideas?

LV: I suppose the border-guard officers were very, very curious. Maybe there were many who supported him, but it is very difficult to know what proportion were supportive or not; they were quite disciplined. But the border question was of immediate concern to them at that time because as at the beginning of that summer East German tourists started to gather in Hungary and day-by-day they tried to penetrate the western border. The number of attempts just increased and some of the border guards had a major dilemma because they had a valid command to open fire in the case of illegal actions ....

TC: When the border guards heard about the plans for the Picnic was there any opposition from them or were they told by their superiors that they should cooperate?

LV: What I knew was that some days before the Picnic there were some signs of concern, some worries from the local and the county border-guards' commanders. They asked for clear orders, an exact clear command from the centre on what they should do. But the orders they received were not very explicit. The law governing the border was in their written documents but during the previous two months they had experienced how difficult it was to decide on issues in practice on the border. If there was a small group of East Germans with small children trying to penetrate the border what they should do? They were also under permanent observation from the press and everybody was watching them. The local people in the border area were helping the East Germans and the border guards were able to feel the popular mood: that the people would not support them if they opened fire on people crossing the border.

You see, before the Picnic, for two months already before the Picnic they were building up experience and learning what a difficult situation they were facing. They knew this was not a clear situation and they would have to decide on their own, without clear commands. They were in a position where they could not refuse to take responsibility themselves, using a higher command as an excuse. They would have to decide if they should comply with the law on the border which gave them the right to shoot. According to the written law it was a very, very hard regime on the border. But of course, the actual situation had become very relative.

So, for these reasons, they were not very happy about the Picnic. They were afraid of the Picnic ... they were very nervous. And that was part of the reason for their invitation to Pozsgay. They wanted to hear from a leading politician directly about the leadership's thinking on the border question.

TC: And what was the leadership's thinking about the border question by then? Did Pozsgay receive any criticism from among the Party and government leadership for his support of the Picnic initiative?

LV: I don't remember that he was criticised ... there was some debate; people asked what was going on. But by June nobody in governing circles saw it as a serious problem; it was seen as an interesting symbolic event on the border, but not very risky politically. Of course, there was growing concern through the summer about the situation of the East Germans who had come to Hungary and whether the Hungarian government should help them. But, as far as I remember, in the weeks before the Picnic this was not linked directly to the Picnic, or at least not in open discussion.

TC: What was the feeling in governing circles about the situation regarding the East Germans?

LV: You can imagine how much confusion there was. There was a lot of sympathy for the East Germans in Hungary. I may say that every day you could feel on the streets that the people were supporting the East Germans and for the Hungarian government to release them. And I don't remember that there was any person in the government who was strictly against it. Maybe the Minister of Defence was a bit ... he was not so enthusiastic, but maybe he was the one who was most conscious of how many Soviet troops were in Hungary. There were 60,000 troops in Hungary at that time and we did not have any hard information about what they would do. The [Hungarian] army officers were openly discussing what happened in '56: how to begin with the Soviet troops had remained silent and did not move [against the uprising] and then one day they suddenly intervened. We knew Gorbachev and the people in Moscow had said that we were a sovereign state we could decide what we wanted—but we were a 'sovereign state' with 60,000 troops in occupation ....

It was a risk anyway, and we were advised also by Chancellor Kohl to be very, very cautious. We were told that he obviously wanted to see the East Germans in Western Germany and he would be very happy if the Hungarian government released them but this was the responsibility of the Hungarian government.

TC: And how about relations with the GDR leadership?

LV: I'm sure there was a lot of tension but I didn't have direct experience of that in my job. But I can give you an example of something that I witnessed that illustrates the situation. At the time of the Picnic I was on holiday at a government resort and the management there were due to receive a visit from some East German ministers. I remember, maybe two days before the Picnic was organised, we were standing at the main building and one East German Minister arrived with his family. He got out the car, and he was very, very upset. He told the director of the resort: 'Here in Hungary there is no order, you should make order. How can we relax here if there is no order?'

Then two days later I went to the place where the Picnic was being held. I had a speech to give on behalf of Imre Pozsgay ... .

TC: So you had to interrupt your holiday to give a speech at the Picnic. Did you know in advance you would be doing this instead of Pozsgay?

LV: Yes, I had the speech already before I went on holiday.

TC: Why did Pozsgay not attend in person?

LV: It was not very clear to me how they decided; I was just told that he and Hapsburg had agreed they would not go in person. They were a bit frightened; and they decided together that they did not want to elevate the event to government level; they wanted to leave it as a civic thing. So I represented Pozsgay and Hapsburg was represented by his daughter, Walburga Hapsburg.

TC: Was it Pozsgay's speech that you delivered? Did he write it or did you write it?

LV: As far as I remember, he told me some key thoughts; I then wrote the speech and he revised it. So the final version was his version. However, I remember one sentence which was mine; this was about ideological camps which are separated by the iron curtain, something like that. In Hungarian it sounded a bit 'strong' at that time ....

TC: Did Pozsgay cut this?

LV: No, he just smiled; he thought it was a good sentence. But 90% of the content was his. It was not too long a speech and it was a very, very straightforward speech supporting the event and making a commitment to freedom and democracy, and supporting the idea of breaking the iron curtain ... that we should remove the border.

The Picnic

TC: What were the formal arrangements for the way the Picnic event would be managed?

LV: Yes, finally there was an agreement between the Hungarian and Austrian authorities as well as between the local border guards. Remember the Picnic had been designed to be a symbolic event to show the border would become a normal international border, open for crossing by people on either side if they could show their passports. For that reason there was a decision on both sides, Austria and Hungary, to only have five border guards on the border at that particular crossing that was opened especially for the Picnic.

But what was very uncertain on the day was how many East Germans would come to the Picnic. The Picnic was not for the East Germans, but for a small number of local Hungarian and Austrian people living on each side of the border. The agreement was that there would only be a very few border guards, and there would be only one gate that would be open for some hours, and the people would move through the gate with a valid passport. And of course, the East Germans did not have valid passports. So formally, everything had been agreed clearly.

But in practice of course, the situation was very different. There was a lot of tension in the country during the two weeks before the Picnic. Nobody in official circles wanted the Picnic to be offered to the East Germans. No-one wanted to publicly say 'please come here and you can cross the border'. But some days before the Picnic the HDF started to advertise the time and the place of the Picnic publicly, and at the same time they started to distribute German-language leaflets among the East Germans with a small map. And I heard afterwards that the Hungarian secret service had reported that the West German secret service was also distributing such leaflets among the East Germans.

The problem was that the Sopron area border guards were not really prepared for such action. They knew clearly that they had not enough force, or manpower, or command to deal with the situation.

TC: What are your own main memories of the events of the Picnic?

LV: The official Party met first at a hotel nearby and then we travelled together on buses and we went to the gate in the border that had been chosen as the site of the Picnic. There were official speeches with a few words from the HDF guys and then they opened the gate. And there were some people with valid passports who crossed to the other side where the local Austrian mayor received them.

While the official Picnic event was going on I went over to the border gate to speak to the officer in charge of the border guards, Árpád Bella. I had already heard that East Germans were on the plot and had crossed the border. He was very annoyed. He didn't know what to do. If they had tried to use force to stop them it would have caused unnecessary panic and violence; so he let them through.

And while I was standing next to him we saw a group of 50, not more, East Germans, some with motorcycles, coming towards the crowd near the gate. People started to make way for them and pushed us a bit to the side and the Germans crossed the border. Bella became very angry and he shouted to me that it was not good, and we should do something about it. He was very nervous and said it was not fair on him and his men. I tried to persuade him to relax. I said that I was the highest ranking government official in the area now and so I took responsibility for what had happened. He was very angry though, and answered me that I was not his supervisor; and obviously it was true that I was not his supervisor. I tried to tell him not to worry. If there were any problems from his superiors, if he was blamed for letting the East Germans through, I had a phone number he could use. I think I said 'don't worry, come have a beer', but he didn't come.

TC: What specifically was he most angry about? That he was unable to stop people crossing the border?

LV: Well, the border guards had not got any very clear commands and the real situations on the border were very, very different. They had general orders to defend the border, following the regulations and only allow people through if they had the right papers. But there were grey areas in the orders. They got soft commands: 'don't shoot—you can use your weapon only if you are attacked', and 'if you are attacked defend yourself'. But these didn't cover the exact situations the guards found themselves in. So there was a gap in the orders, and this is why he was very anxious; it was not a nice situation at all; he was left alone in the situation and it was a political situation. But he behaved in a very correct and humane way.

TC: This raises an interesting question I think about how prepared the Hungarian authorities were for this breakthrough with the border. Was there any discussion in governing circles that it might be likely that the East Germans would cross the border that day, and it could lead to violence?

LV: I don't think it was considered as very likely at all. There were already incidents on the border that summer that resulted in East Germans being turned back from the border, but it was done in a low-key way, without violence.

The border-guard officers were politically confused but perhaps it could be said they had a typically Hungarian attitude. Well, it is not too easy to understand the atmosphere that time, and this is a main key question of the Hungarian transition. Psychologically, politically, anthropologically, Hungarians behaved so that within each person one part of them followed the law, and the other part challenged the law every time. Somehow people, and even the politicians, struck a balance between the law and their feelings of what was just. And hardliners in the military, in the police, even in the workers guard, they could not turn back history.

TC: But could clearer orders have been given to the border guards: 'You have to expect the East Germans to cross today and you must NOT shoot'? Could they have said that? Would that not have been possible?

LV: No.

TC: What would have stopped them? What would have prevented them from doing that?

LV: Well, they would have created immediately a political conflict between different political groups within the leadership. The border guard was under the Minister of Defence, and he had quite a few reservations about the Picnic and it was not possible to avoid him. And if he was challenged explicitly that could have undermined the whole Picnic initiative. But the biggest risk concerning the Picnic was international. It was the question of how the harder international partners of the Soviet Union would react.

The biggest fear was Soviet behaviour and the only thing that was really cautiously followed that day was the behaviour of the Soviet troops, all of their camps were under rigorous surveillance all day, to check whether they would move or not; and they did not move, and there was not any sign of any alarm.

TC: Was this a possibility that had been discussed?

LV: Yes, this was the only warning I received from Pozsgay before I left Budapest for my summer vacation some days before 19 August. He told me that if the Soviets move, no, there will be no Picnic, so this was the only message.

You see, regarding the Picnic, but also more generally regarding the changes taking place that year, there was not any plan fixed; it was an improvisation; there was no grand strategy day-by-day and everybody did his best or her best.

After the Picnic

TC: What was the situation like in your office when you returned after the Picnic? Was there a lot of political discussion about it?

LV: Well we only had a very small staff, and at that time we were busy with political negotiations and although the East German problem was very important, it was not the main priority. So we had no time to reflect on the Picnic or any recent events. We just had to finish the political negotiations and immediately after came the constitutional amendments and it was a very, very busy time. In the first part of September, if you remember, that was the time of the political negotiations, which were concluded on 14 September and we formally opened the border and released the East Germans on the 11th so it was very, very condensed time and all attention was absolutely drawn towards the democratic transition issues.

TC: And now, with hindsight, how do you see the significance of the Picnic?

LV: Well, looking back we can see it was quite a chaotic situation, and fortunately it did not end in any tragedy; but of course, there could not have been any complete guarantee—no guarantee for a safe outcome. Árpád Bella, László Nagy and all the others who were involved, I think they all did their best and what happened was all very confused and very worrying for Árpád Bella at the time, but I don't think it could have happened in any more orderly way.

There have been some suggestions in recent years that there was an agreement to use the Picnic as a convenient way to force the issue of the East Germans in Hungary. And of course I was delighted they were able to leave through Austria. And perhaps some people in HDF and others hoped they could use the event to let the East Germans through the border. But there was no real plan to release the East Germans that day, it was not planned. Later, on 10 September the government made the decision on releasing the East German refugees to Austria.

TC: One final question, and more of a more personal one perhaps; I feel that unlike some others who were involved that day, you have not wanted to be associated with the commemorations of the Picnic in the years since then.

LV: Absolutely … I decided to leave politics after 1989. And the commemoration of the Picnic became part of the politics of commemoration along with some other events. I felt aggrieved in 1990, on the first anniversary of the meeting, that I was not invited, and even Pozsgay was not invited; that seemed so awful to me. The HDF-led government just took over that event and they used it as an HDF celebration. After that I practically put the whole thing behind me. And in 1994 it was election year and the competition started between the politicians as to who organised it and who played the biggest role, and between 1994 and 1998, under the socialist government, Horn was presented as the key player and Pozsgay was not mentioned. As memories faded people started to mix-up the Picnic and the Horn business [when Horn cut the border wire]. And it continues to be a political game and I decided I did not want to participate in this game. *Budapest, February 2010.*

Three Days in Bucharest: Making Sense of Romania's Transitional Violence, 20 Years On

JOHN GLEDHILL

ON 13 JUNE 1990, JUST WEEKS AFTER ROMANIA'S FIRST post-revolution elections, hopes for a swift consolidation of democracy and institutionalisation of the rule of law in Romania were dealt a severe blow when riots broke out on the streets of Bucharest. The following day, around 16,000 miners and factory workers descended on the capital from all around the country. Upon arrival, compact groups of miners broke off into violent squads and then systematically moved about the town, attacking any and every political group that had expressed opposition to the transitional governing elite, the National Salvation Front (*Frontul Salvării Naţionale*, the 'Front'). By the time the miners had completed the tasks at hand, regrouped and headed home, the official casualty count for the three days of violence stood at six dead and 542 injured or wounded (Parlamentul României 1991, pp. 71, 74). Political groups opposed to the Front, however, estimated that the death count ran in excess of 130.[1]

The events of 13–15 June 1990, now known sardonically as the *mineriadă*,[2] had a defining influence on Romania's post-communist political trajectory. Specifically, internal and external fallout from the violence proved to be a key factor in delaying Romania's transition to, and consolidation of, liberal democracy. Despite the significance of the June 1990 events, however, they have received little rigorous scholarly attention. This has not been for want of contemporary interest; the events continue to receive almost constant media coverage in Romania. Rather, the lack of serious studies of the violence has largely been a function of data limitations. Political controversy and sensitivity surrounding the violence meant that, until recently, those

I would like to thank two anonymous referees for their comments on earlier drafts of this essay, as well as many friends and colleagues for their fruitful discussions on the topic over several years. Research for the project was supported by the Romanian Cultural Institute, the New Europe College, the American Consortium on European Studies, Georgetown University, and the London School of Economics. Of course, I alone am responsible for any errors, omissions or misrepresentations.

[1]See the website 'Civicnet—Piaţa Universităţii', available at: http://www.civicnet.info/Articol.asp?ID=4002, accessed 20 January 2011.

[2]The term '*mineriadă*' combines the noun '*miner*' with the suffix '*-iadă*'. The word is a parody term that is designed to invoke the idea of an honourable mission by mimicking the construction of words such as *cruciadă* (crusade) or *olimpiadă* (olympics).

implicated in the events were reluctant to speak of their experiences. It also meant that there were limits on the availability of relevant documents. Romania's belated accession to the European Union, however, has opened up new avenues for studying the June 1990 violence, since adoption of the *acquis communautaire* has been accompanied by the introduction of legislation that increases ease of access to state and government documents. This essay draws on newly available sources, and the increased willingness of implicated parties to discuss their experiences, in order to give a detailed, and novel, account of Romania's transitional violence.

The core argument is that the violence of 13–15 June 1990 was a by-product of competition between state security institutions for resources and responsibility in post-Ceauşescu Romania. That competition developed within, and as a function of, the particular institutional environment that emerged from Romania's bloody revolution of December 1989. While state institutions remained intact and largely unreformed across the change of regime, and one set of elites (the Front) enjoyed clear control over the levers of governmental power following Ceauşescu's fall, it was unclear how those governing elites intended to distribute funds and power among state organs in the new regime. Within that context of distributional uncertainty, Romania's state security services (the police, the military and the secret services) began to compete among one another for position in the emerging regime. More immediately, they began to compete for the favour of the Front's governing elites, who were set to enjoy control over the distribution of state resources in that regime. Inter-agency competition took various benign forms in early 1990. In June 1990, however, the competition turned malign when inter-agency jostling sparked the development and escalation of two waves of violence in Bucharest.

The first wave broke out on 13 June, following a set of incendiary actions that were taken by the Interior Ministry (police), within the context of its competition with the Ministry of National Defence (military) for position as Romania's pre-eminent overt security service. Specifically, in an apparent effort to demonstrate the relative institutional utility of the police in the new regime and, therefore, the need for the police to be well funded in that regime, Interior Minister Mihai Chiţac responded with zeal to Ion Iliescu's request for the evacuation of a handful of protestors from Bucharest's University Square. That zeal manifested itself in an exaggerated deployment of police troops and an excessive use of force by the police against protestors on the morning of 13 June. The police actions then prompted counter-demonstrations from an incensed public and, after crowds had gathered, low-level rioting broke out. The collective capacity of the state to control the riots, meanwhile, was weakened by the fact that the Interior Ministry and the Ministry of National Defence failed to cooperate with one another in the restoration of order. Violence then escalated across the course of the day and, although the army eventually managed to re-establish order on the evening of 13 June, provisional president Ion Iliescu chose to make an ill-considered call for civilians to come to Bucharest and defend the new regime with their own hands. That call actively dissolved the rule of law in the capital and, in so doing, opened up opportunities for the country's two main secret services—'UM 0215' and the Romanian Information Service—to use extra-constitutional methods in support of their own competition for the favour of Front elites. Those efforts saw the secret services support processes of civilian mobilisation that took place around the country on the night of 13 June, in wake of the president's call for vigilante support. The next day, secret service officers then co-opted groups of belligerent civilians as they arrived in Bucharest and guided them around the city, encouraging the most thuggish of the recruits to channel their aggression toward attacks on political groups that had expressed opposition to Iliescu and the National Salvation Front. The resulting violence constituted a political pogrom that was without parallel in the region.

In the sections that follow, I expand on this argument and give a micro-political account of the events of 13–15 June 1990, in three steps. I first examine the institutional context in which the June violence developed and describe how the Romanian revolution of December 1989 gave rise to clarity over the locus of political power, but also ambiguity over the distribution of resources among state institutions in the emerging regime. I then present an analytic narrative of the events that unfolded in June 1990 and describe ways in which intra-agency competition sparked, and then perpetuated, the events of 13–15 June. I conclude by arguing that recognition of the complex interactions between agency and structure that underwrote the production of Romania's transitional violence should not be seen to complicate assessments of where responsibility for these events lies. Rather, it should allow for an effective, apolitical identification of all responsible parties.

Post-revolution Romania: strong elites, intact state institutions, ambiguous regime

Political continuity and clarity of governmental power

Ironically, although Romania's bloody revolution was the most dramatic and violent of all Central and East European transformations in 1989, it gave rise to the least revolutionary outcome. Indeed, as the smoke cleared from the streets of Bucharest in late December 1989, it became clear that the street revolts had not given rise to a wholesale turnover of power. Rather, a set of second-level communist elites calling themselves the National Salvation Front had managed to move swiftly during the early, spontaneous phases of the revolution, wrest control of state institutions, and then appoint themselves as Romania's transitional governing authority (Siani-Davies 2005). Although a number of renowned dissidents lent their names to the Front during the early, heady moments of the revolution, none were given senior roles in the provisional government that was established. Instead, Front leader and provisional president, Ion Iliescu, argued that communist-era elites needed to retain governing roles in order to help avoid the danger of total anarchy in transitional Romania (Shafir 1990, p. 35). Consequently, six of the 11 appointees to the Front's executive bureau were top-ranking members of the communist *nomenklatura*, and the remaining members had close ties to the Party (Grosescu 2004, pp. 109–11).

Over the weeks and months that followed the revolution, Iliescu and senior Front activists were able to use their advantage as early movers to consolidate control over state organs and, in so doing, ensure that there was no uncertainty over the locus of governmental power in transitional Romania. The Front's consolidation of power was built on two foundations. The first was broad (albeit manipulated) popular support, which was rooted in Iliescu's ability to use his access to state media resources to generate an image of himself and his associates as 'emanation[s] of the revolution', who had risked life and limb to place themselves at the centre of efforts to topple Nicolae Ceauşescu (Gallagher 2005, p. 73). The second foundation was a series of nationwide clientelist networks, which Front leaders managed to consolidate within weeks of taking power and which ran directly up to the central Front leadership. These networks were not created by the Front *per se*. Rather, when the Front's executive committee claimed control over the resources and organisational structures of the Romanian Communist Party (RCP, *Partidul Comunist Român*) in the name of the state in January 1990 (Guvernul României 1990a), Iliescu and his associates simply inherited control over the vast network of patron–client relationships that had been established under Ceauşescu (Siani-Davies 2005, p. 191).

Shortly after adopting Communist Party organisational structures, the Front declared itself a political Party and announced its candidacy for the first set of elections, despite earlier promises from Iliescu that his organisation would only serve a limited mandate, as a provisional organ of governance. With a massive resource advantage over competing political factions, a national organisational structure, and experienced political actors, the Front's victory in the elections was never in doubt. Indeed, the Party's control over the levers of governance was formally confirmed when free, albeit not wholly fair, elections were held on 20 May 1990. The Party took 66% of the parliamentary vote and Iliescu won 85% of the presidential ballot.[3]

Continuity of state security institutions

Despite early declarations from Iliescu that the Front would fundamentally restructure and liberalise Romania's moribund state apparatus, including the country's heavily politicised state security services, the Front-led provisional government showed little interest in making those changes in the months that followed the revolution. Instead, the Party's early legislative measures suggested that Front leaders would leave state institutions largely unreformed in the short term, and then partially reconstruct the relationship between the ruling Party and state institutions that had existed under Ceauşescu over the longer term (Siani-Davies 2005, Chapter 5; Tismaneanu 2003, Epilogue). To that end, in February 1990 the Front's executive committee took control over the organisation of all 'industrial centres, companies, factories, manufacturing plants, mines and other similar state units' (Guvernul României 1990b). This co-optation of the productive resources of the state was then matched shortly thereafter by decrees which saw the Front award itself control over Romania's state-owned transportation services, media sources and, to a lesser extent, agricultural production.

The most controversial and, ultimately, most problematic domain in which Iliescu and the Front guaranteed state institutional continuity was the security sector. That continuity was not evident at first, however. Rather, since Ceauşescu's feared and loathed secret police—the *Securitate*—had been the key institutional prop for the outgoing dictator, the country's 'new' leaders needed to be seen to be taking some

[3]University of Aberdeen, 'Elections in Romania', available at: http://www.abdn.ac.uk/cspp/romelec.shtml, accessed 10 September 2009.

steps toward dismantling and restructuring the service if they wished to legitimate their claim to be 'revolutionaries'. Thus, just days after taking power, the Front's executive committee transferred the *Securitate*'s patrimony and personnel from the Interior Ministry to the Ministry of National Defence (Guvernul României 1989). Then, on 30 December 1989, the *Securitate* was formally dissolved and the Front's vice-president, Gelu Voican Voiculescu, was charged with demobilising the loathed service and its sibling organisations. These early signs of reform were, without doubt, popular. However, for Dennis Deletant, they were mere 'window dressing[s]' (Deletant 2001, p. 213), which were designed to distract the public's attention from the Front's interest in assuring a high level of institutional continuity in the intelligence sector.

Informal reconstruction of the *Securitate* began in January 1990, when Voiculescu took 260 officers that had served in the Bucharest branch of the *Securitate*, combined them with officers that had served in the *Securitate*'s notorious Directorate IV (Counterintelligence), and placed the combined forces in a new service, which was named 'UM 0215' (Oprea 2004, p. 100; Ionescu 1994, p. 28). Although the unit was put under the formal command structure of the Interior Ministry, UM 0215 managed its own budget and Voiculescu is said to have retained indirect control over the unit throughout 1990 (Oprea 2004, p. 100). Those arrangements afforded UM 0215 near complete autonomy as an institution—autonomy that would soon see it come into confrontation with the second *Securitate* legacy institution, the Romanian Information Service (*Serviciul Român de Informaţii*, SRI, by its common Romanian acronym), as the two jostled for position as the pre-eminent intelligence agency in post-revolution Romania. The SRI proved to be a formidable competitor for that title, since it was the primary inheritor of the *Securitate*'s mantle, both in terms of mandate and personnel. The service, which was placed under the leadership of former *Securitate* officer and academic Virgil Măgureanu, was somewhat stripped down in terms of numbers compared with its communist-era predecessor; however, with more than 60% of its initial officer corps coming directly from the *Securitate* (Watts 2003, p. 5), the SRI quickly became a safe haven for many communist-era officers.

In addition to assured continuity in Romania's covert services, Front leaders allowed for a high degree of institutional continuity in Romania's two overt security structures: the Ministry of the Interior and the Ministry of National Defence. No reforms of any sort were introduced to the policing structures of the Interior Ministry, which was placed under the control of Mihai Chiţac (a general who had become infamous in December 1989, following his involvement in the state's violent repression of civilians during the early stages of the revolution). Rather, under Chiţac's supervision, the police were 'named the [communist era] *Miliţiă* one day, renamed the *Poliţiă* the next morning, and then just got on with it'.[4] By contrast, some limited internal restructuring programmes were introduced to the military.[5] The impetus to reform efforts did not come from the Front leadership, however, which showed no particular interest in the internal workings of the military. Rather, mid-ranking army

[4]Virgil Măgureanu, SRI Chief 1990–1997, interview with Robert Turcescu, *Sută la sută*, Realitatea TV, 13 June 2005, author's personal archive.

[5]Comments made by a senior military officer from the period of transition, interview with the author, Bucharest, 6 August 2009.

officers took it upon themselves to initiate a 'depoliticisation' of the military from the inside (Niculae 2004). The full range of the officers' demands, which included lustration of communist-era officers and a new promotion system, was never fully met, but their activism did force the Minister of National Defence, Victor Atanasie Stănculescu, to create a level of institutional distance between the military and Front that other state organs did not enjoy. That distance, however, did not exclude the military from competing with the Interior Ministry for the favour of Front leaders, who held a tight grip over the levers of government and, therefore, over the distribution of resources among state institutions in the new regime.

An ambiguous regime and uncertain distribution of resources

By the middle of 1990, it was clear to the public and to holders of state office that Iliescu and the Front were set to control Romania's post-revolution government—at least over the short to medium term. There was simply no structured opposition movement that was in a position to challenge the Front effectively. Clarity over the distribution of governmental power, however, was not matched by clarity over the question of how the Front would institutionalise its power. That is, it was unclear what type of regime Iliescu and Front leaders intended to introduce in order to institutionalise and consolidate their control over governmental power. Such uncertainty seems to have been a function of the fact that Iliescu was, essentially, an opportunistic actor, who did not have a strong ideological position. Instead, his post-revolution strategising was more about assuring executive power and state security than about introducing a particular regime type.[6] Indeed, according to Petre Roman (then provisional prime minister), Iliescu did not have a fixed ideological 'vision' for post-revolution Romania.[7]

Iliescu's willingness to prioritise his Party's political interests over the introduction and consolidation of a particular type of regime was reflected in the inconsistency of his early statements concerning Romania's post-revolution institutional trajectory. In his first televised address, which was delivered only hours after Ceauşescu had fled on 22 December 1989, Iliescu refused to condemn communism (Siani-Davies 2005, pp. 108–9). Instead, he seemed to show an interest in introducing reformist or *perestroika* communism to Romania—a kind of 'socialism with a human face'. However, he was soon to realise that, as a result of the snowballing of democratisation across Europe, neither local counsel nor the international community would accept such an arrangement.[8] By early April 1990, Iliescu was publicly acknowledging the importance of democracy. Still, he continued to talk about a 'third way' between Western democracy and other forms of government (Grosescu 2007, pp. 206–7; Almond 1990, p. 489). Specifically, he maintained that the Front was a 'consensus' movement, whose 'saviour' act was the proposal of a 'political mechanism' that would somehow foster

[6]Comments made by a senior counsellor to Ion Iliescu, 1990, interview with the author, Bucharest, 14 April 2005.

[7]Roman suggested, instead, that 'the vision' for transition was his, while Iliescu 'had some ideological reflexes'. Petre Roman, Prime Minister of Romania, 1990–1991, interview with the author, Bucharest, 31 May 2005.

[8]Based on comments made by Petre Roman, interview with the author, Bucharest, 31 May 2005.

'dialogue among all the [political] forces, harmonization of the interests of the various social categories, and cooperation among them . . .'.[9] Although he provided few details of what such an 'original democracy' might look like in practice, his allusions to the concept suggested an interest in a kind of single-party or plebiscitary democracy (Verdery 1996, p. 112)—one akin to Mexico's system at the time.

Uncertainty over the institutional arrangements that Iliescu and Front leaders would introduce not only meant that democracy in post-revolution Romania was built on unstable foundations; it also meant that there was a high level of uncertainty among state organisations over the question of how power and funds would be distributed between them in the emerging political order. Different types of regime are, after all, associated with different understandings of how resources should be disbursed among state organs. Liberal democracies, for example, are likely to see a reduction in funding for the secret police services, but an increase in funding for the professional military; single party authoritarian regimes, by contrast, are likely to boost support for the secret services at the expense of backing for the military; and, in illiberal or delegative democracies, the executive's high level of discretion over policy and resources means that the distribution of state funds will partly depend on the whim of the president, and on which institution he or she feels will offer the most political support. Since Iliescu's prioritisation of power over ideology meant that all of the above regime outcomes were possible in 1990—at least to some extent—there was also a high level of uncertainty among state institutions about how resources and institutional power would be distributed in the new Romania.

Regime ambiguity and intra-state competition

Arguably, within the context of regime and resource ambiguity, each state organ had a simple institutional interest: to maximise its institutional funding and influence in the new regime. When concurrently held by diverse state organs, that interest would have become a source of competitive pressure, since funding and institutional power were both scarce and finite resources in transitional Romania, and so the distribution of those resources among state organs was, essentially, a zero-sum game. On the financial side, a sudden contraction of Romania's productive output in 1990 (Smith 2001, p. 129) had seen the state's purse shrink, which meant that the demand for state funding was set to far outstrip supply. Given that budgetary imbalance, it was likely that the Front government would be forced to make strategic decisions about where and how funds should be distributed among state actors. Institutional prominence in the new regime, meanwhile, was also necessarily a scarce and ordered resource, since a given state agency could only claim pre-eminence in a given domain (say, the provision of security) if it proved itself superior to any institutions that held overlapping mandates. Within this environment of scarcity, if any state agency wished to gain an edge in the race for power and resources, it needed to ensure that the demand for its services in the emerging regime outstripped demand for the services of any competing institutions. Such demand superiority could be achieved in two ways; a state institution could demonstrate that its unique set of skills and public services would be of greater use in

[9]Iliescu in FBIS (1990, p. 57).

post-revolution Romania than the services of competing organisations; or an institution could demonstrate to the Front leadership that, if given sufficient funds and power, it could best provide the new ruling elites with the kind of institutional support that they would need, if they wished to consolidate political power over the long term.

Competition between state actors to demonstrate institutional superiority on these two fronts manifested itself most clearly in the security sector, for two reasons. First, from the Front's perspective, there was more institutional overlap in security (between the military, police and secret services) than in other domains (Ursu 2008, p. 27). In particular, there was a complete overlap in the mandate and responsibilities of the two successor organisations to the *Securitate*: the SRI and UM 0215. That wholesale redundancy meant that it was unclear whether both services would be able to coexist in the emerging regime. Even if they did both survive, the budget and responsibilities of one of the two services was bound to be significantly reduced. The second reason for the particular intensity of inter-agency competition in the security sector was that new, transitional tensions were laid over existing mutual resentments between the Ministry of National Defence, the Interior Ministry and the secret services. That resentment was rooted in communist-era resource allocations in which Ceauşescu had transferred funds and responsibility away from the military and towards his personal security service, the *Securitate* (which was housed in the Interior Ministry at the time). When some of the *Securitate*'s material resources were then shifted back to the military immediately after the revolution, resentment merely shifted in the opposite direction.[10]

Over the course of the six months that followed the revolution, tensions between Romania's four primary security services seem to have congealed into two main competitive confrontations. The first was between Virgil Măgureanu's SRI and Gelu Voican Voiculescu's UM 0215. From Măgureanu's perspective, overlap in the core mandate of these two organisations meant that 'the birth of Romania's internal secret service was done on a basis of conflict' (Măgureanu & Stoenescu 2008, p. 155). By mid-1990, that conflict had grown into 'competition between the principal information services in Romania'.[11] Inter-agency competition manifested itself in competitive bidding between the SRI and UM 0215, as the two organisations formulated and operationalised their responses to security issues that arose in the early months of 1990. Most notably, the two agencies arguably sought to outdo one another when responding to a seven-week-long, anti-Front demonstration, which took place in Bucharest's central University Square between April and June 1990. The demonstration, which was the largest of its kind in Central and Eastern Europe, brought together diverse sets of actors, including students, academics, artists, centre-right political activists, self-declared revolutionaries and former political prisoners (Dumbrăveanu & Pîrvu 1992). The protestors had little in common beyond opposition to Iliescu, frustration over the Front's monopolisation of formal political institutions and a willingness to vent that frustration on the streets of the capital. The protestors showed no signs of aggression across the seven weeks that they occupied the square,

[10]Comments made by a state counsellor on national security, interview with the author, Bucharest, 10 April 2009.

[11]Comments made by a former senior SRI officer, interview with the author, Bucharest, 14 April 2009.

but they did constitute a visible challenge to the (Front-controlled) political order and, as such, the SRI saw the protest as an opportunity to demonstrate both its strength as an intelligence agency and its political loyalty to the Front by setting up a surveillance operation in and around the demonstration (Oprea 2004, p. 113). UM 0215 allegedly responded by setting up a clandestine operation in which its officers directly infiltrated the ranks of protestors and then sought to monitor the demonstration from within (Watts 2003, p. 23). Officers from both services profiled figures associated with the demonstration and, it can be assumed that former *Securitate* officers were associated with the intimidation of opposition figures through the provision of threatening letters and phone calls (Cesereanu 2003, p. 166).[12]

The second main point of institutional competition developed between Romania's two largest security services: the Ministry of National Defence and the Ministry of the Interior. Since the mandates of the military and the police were relatively distinct, there was, perhaps, less of an evident basis for confrontation between these two agencies than there was for the country's secret services. However, rivalry did develop between the military and the Interior Ministry in early 1990, over questions of resources and prestige. On both fronts, the Interior Ministry, which had held the advantage under communism (mainly because it had been home to the *Securitate*), suffered a decline after the revolution, relative to its competitor. In terms of resources, the Interior Ministry had watched its patrimony pass over to the formal control of the Ministry of Defence straight after the revolution, when the Front temporarily placed the police and *Securitate* under the military's command. The military then boosted its resources further, relative to the Interior Ministry, by successfully lobbying Front leaders for an increase in the military budget in February.[13] In terms of prestige and reputation, meanwhile, the Ministry of National Defence had succeeded in framing itself as something of the 'hero' of the revolution and it had passed blame for the civilian deaths over to the Interior Ministry's troops (which included the *Securitate* at the time) in a way that had seen the Interior Ministry become something of a black sheep of the security sector (see Ursu 2008, p. 43). That sidelining naturally generated strong resentment, and Interior Ministry officers became 'convinced that the Ministry of National Defence want[ed] to try to dominate, to coordinate everything'.[14] This sentiment, and broader tensions between the two ministries, intensified over the course of the pre-electoral period and likely peaked shortly thereafter, when the Front's elected government was taking shape and debates over the distribution of power and resources in post-revolution Romania were moving toward their end game. In June 1990, claims concerning the intensification of competitive tensions were recognised by the leaders of the two ministries (Stănculescu & Ursu 1990) and also from the outside

[12]The author was told of anonymous threats received by Doina Cornea, interview with the author, Cluj, 22 July 2005; Ana Blandiana, interview with the author, Bucharest, 8 August 2005; and Gabriel Liiceanu, interview with the author, Bucharest, 14 July 2005.

[13]Comments made by a senior military officer from the period of transition, interview with the author, Bucharest, 6 August 2009.

[14]Viorel Tache, counsellor to Gelu Voican Voiculescu and legal counsel in the Interior Ministry, 1990, testimony before the parliamentary commission, *Arhivele Camerei Deputaţilor*, d. 533/1990, p. 8. This comment was made despite Tache initially negating the proposal of a commissioner that there was a battle between the ranks of the police and the army.

by observers from the British Foreign Office.[15] Over the course of 13–15 June 1990, those competitive tensions, and tensions between the two secret services, arguably proved to be a catalyst to waves of transitional violence in Bucharest. Indeed, as Defence Minister Stănculescu suggested in the immediate wake of the June violence, 'competition between different sectors' of the 'old structures [of power]' that had taken up residence in the new security services led to political games being played out in obscurity over the course of those days.[16] Those games were violent.

The dynamics of violence: 13–15 June 1990

Although the intensity of inter-agency competition had gradually increased over the course of the first six months of 1990, there was a concurrent decrease in the number of security threats that demanded responses from the security services and, therefore, a decrease in the number of forums in which inter-agency competition for position in the new regime could play itself out. Ethnic tensions which had threatened to escalate following clashes between ethnic Hungarians and Romanians in March 1990 had receded; low-level violence that had developed in and around the election campaign had ended; and the opposition protest in Bucharest's University Square had all but come to a close after the 20 May elections. In fact, by early June, the only security issue that demanded any kind of response was the ongoing presence of a handful of protestors in University Square—hunger strikers who had remained after the dissolution of the large demonstration and who were demanding the establishment of an independent television station. Since there was a dearth of real security issues, Iliescu's call for security services to remove the strikers in mid-June was the one and only forum in which competing security agencies could try to demonstrate the relative need for their particular services in the new regime and/or their relative loyalty to Front elites. It was efforts to demonstrate utility on both those fronts that seem to have underwritten an exaggerated use of force by the Interior Ministry during the police effort to clear University Square on 13 June 1990. That unwarranted show of force sparked rioting on the streets of Bucharest. The dynamics of inter-agency competition then drove an escalation of the violence, until it peaked on 14 and 15 June, when secret service officers used miners to violently repress anti-Front opposition groups. In the sections that follow, I give an account of each of those two phases of violence and then detail ways in which political and state elites tried to articulate the causes of that violence, following its conclusion.

Phase I: the origins and escalation of violence on 13 June 1990

Competition and exaggeration. On the evening of 11 June 1990, Iliescu and his prime minister, Petre Roman, convened a meeting, with a view to arranging for security

[15]British Embassy Bucharest, 'From Bucharest to Immediate FCO', Report 161230Z (June 1990). These recognitions came in the immediate wake of the June violence.

[16]Victor Atanasie Stănculescu, Letter of resignation, 16 June 1990, and further testimony before the parliamentary commission, *Arhivele Camerei Deputaţilor*, d. 531/1990, pp. 3, 24; also cited in Ivan (1993, pp. 146–48). His resignation was not accepted by Iliescu.

forces to clear the remaining protestors from University Square over the following days. The meeting was attended by Front leaders and heads of the four major security organs—the Interior Ministry, the Ministry of National Defence, the SRI and UM 0215.[17] After a short introductory discussion, Interior Minister Chiţac seized on the opportunity to use the operation as a means for demonstrating the relative utility of his institution, by actively requesting that the evacuation be coordinated by the Interior Ministry (rather than by any of the services whose mandates overlapped with those of the Ministry of the Interior).[18] Chiţac's eagerness was, no doubt, unsurprising to Iliescu; the president later claimed that Chiţac had long wanted to lead his troops in an evacuation of the square and, to that end, had actually requested (but been denied) approval for such an operation on several previous occasions.[19] Since, on paper, matters of internal security were the domain of the Interior Ministry, Chiţac's proposal was accepted and approved by Roman and Iliescu (Pleşu *et al.* 2002, p. 67). Details of the evacuation plan were then finalised the following day by Chiţac and the police inspector general, Corneliu Diamandescu.

The nature of the plan of action that was put together by Chiţac and Diamandescu suggests, in two ways, that the interior minister partly intended to use the evacuation operation as a mechanism for demonstrating the need for a strong, well-funded Interior Ministry in post-Ceauşescu Romania. First, a decision was taken to use a hugely exaggerated number of troops. In theory, the evacuation should have been a relatively small operation, involving some tens of police, since there were fewer than 20 protestors camping overnight in University Square by early June 1990.[20] However, Chiţac and Diamandescu chose to significantly upgrade the nature of the action, by arranging for the mobilisation of more than 1,400 Interior Ministry troops.[21] That decision can be understood as an attempt by the ministry's leaders to foment and feed a perception that there were serious internal threats to the stability of the new regime. Where such an impression could indeed be created, the Ministry of the Interior stood to benefit, since the existence of strong internal threats would have demanded the resourcing of a strong Interior Ministry, rather than a strong Defence Ministry (whose primary mandate was to address external threats). Second, Chiţac chose to arrange for the mobilisation of 5,000 local factory workers, who were to be brought into University Square immediately after the initial police operation and encouraged to

[17]There are mixed reports about exactly who was in attendance at this meeting. However, the basic makeup of the meeting seems to be clear. See the testimony of Mihai Chiţac before the parliamentary commission, *Arhivele Camerei Deputaţilor*, d. 155/1990, pp. 33–35; also Parchetul de pe lângă Înalta Curte de Casaţie şi Justiţie, Secţia Parchetelor Militare, 'Rechizitoriu, 27.07.2007, Dosar 74/P/1998', Section II. This document is extracted in 'Raport despre fratricidul din 13–15 iunie 1990' (2010 Edition), coordinated by Sorin Ilieşiu and Alin Rus, available at: http://mineriade.iiccmer.ro/pdf/dezbateri/raport_despre_fratricidul_din_13_15_iunie_1990.pdf, accessed 7 February 2011.

[18]Mihai Chiţac, testimony before the parliamentary commission, *Arhivele Camerei Deputaţilor*, d. 155/1990, pp. 20, 24; Parlamentul României (1991, p. 29).

[19]Ion Iliescu, testimony before the parliamentary commission, *Arhivele Camerei Deputaţilor*, d. 497/1990, p. 76; also cited in Ivan (1993, pp. 249–50).

[20]Parchetul de pe lângă Curtea Supremă de Justiţie, Secţia Parchetelor Militare, 'Rechizitoriu 18.05.2000, Dosar 74/P/1998', p. 8, author's personal archive.

[21]Ministerul de Interne, 'Raport privind acţiunile unităţilor Ministerului de Interne pe timpul desfăşurării evenimentelor din 13–15 iunie 1990', also available in Ursu (2008, p. 189).

demonstrate their support for the Front.[22] The workers' occupation of the square would advertise the people's supposed solidarity with the evacuation operation and, more broadly, their sympathy with the newly elected government. By generating a forum for public support of the Front, Chiţac stood to endear himself to the Front leadership—something that he needed to do, since Petre Roman was due to reshuffle the cabinet the following week and Chiţac's future in the government was rumoured to have been in doubt (Galloway & Wylie 1991, p. 250).

Evacuation and escalation. The evacuation operation in University Square began between 4:00 and 4:30 on 13 June 1990, under Diamandescu's command. From the outset, the police effort was characterised by unwarranted verbal and physical aggression, in a way that suggested the police commanders had little interest in minimising the gravity of the situation (Parlamentul României 1991, pp. 34, 110; Dumbrăveanu & Pîrvu 1992, pp. 153–56). Unsurprisingly, the police brutality soon prompted sympathy from some of those who had begun to arrive in the city centre for the work day.[23] Early objections came from students at the Institute of Architecture, which is located on University Square. Their protests were quickly muted, however, when police moved in and arrested them, along with other early objectors (Grupul pentru Dialog Social—Comitetul Helsinki 1990, pp. 30–37). By 7:00, 263 arrests had been made—most with no legal basis.[24] Rather than muting the situation in any way, the large-scale arrests simply intensified bystanders' objections to the police operation and prompted the objectors to gather in protest. Within a short time, members of Romania's small but active civil society began to make use of the dense communications structures that they had established during the seven-week-long opposition demonstration in University Square in order to spread word of the happenings in town.[25] Calls to action from civic leaders were met with a swift response and, by 10:00, up to 1,000 opposition protestors had gathered in the square, where they began to ask, 'Where are our colleagues?' (Grupul pentru Dialog Social—Comitetul Helsinki 1990, p. 39).

The early protestors remained peaceful. However, the situation tipped over into low-level violence when the 'pro-Front' factory workers ordered by the interior minister arrived. Although Chiţac had charged second-level Front leader, N. S. Dumitru, with recruiting some 5,000 workers, only 200 or so actually arrived from the 'IMGB' ('Heavy Machinery') and 'ICTB' ('Textile') factories because poor internal policing during the journey to the city centre had allowed reluctant recruits to simply

[22]The question of who exactly called for the workers' presence on 13 June was a point of much debate by the parliamentary commission investigating the violence. Amidst the inconsistency and ambiguity that characterised his responses, Mihai Chiţac acknowledged that it had been his initiative, *Arhivele Camerei Deputaţilor*, d. 155/1990, pp. 36–37, 45–51, 76–78; see also Parlamentul României (1991, p. 30).

[23]United States Embassy Bucharest, 'The Romanian Police Move against the Demonstrators in Bucharest's University Square', Department of State, Bucharest 06072 (June), 1990.

[24]Ministerul Public, Parchetul de pe lângă Înalta Curte de Casaţie şi Justiţie, Secţia Parchetelor Militare, 'Rechizitoriu, 27.07.2007, Dosar 74/P/1998', Section III.

[25]Based on comments made by a leader of the Students' League in 1990, interview with the author, 20 April 2005.

wander off on their way into town (Ivan 1996, p. 74; Parlamentul României 1991, pp. 34–35, 111–12). The workers who did make it, however, were a self-selecting group of belligerent agitators. Upon arrival, they made their way through to the front of the crowd and then aggressed the demonstration leaders, while chanting, 'The IMGB puts things in order!' and 'We work, we don't "think!"' (a protest against the supposedly 'intellectual' makeup of the original University Square demonstrators).[26] These verbal and physical attacks were both intimidating in themselves and also crucial to shifting the situation on the ground in University Square, in a way that created opportunities for the rapid escalation of violence and rioting that followed. Specifically, the workers' belligerence served to agitate the existing crowd and disturb the internal order that had characterised the demonstration until then. As agitation increased, University Square became a space of chaos and confusion that could, and would, offer anonymity to any opportunistic bystanders who were attracted by the idea of engaging in wanton violence without fear of sanction. Police passivity in the face of the factory workers' violence further confirmed to opportunists that University Square had become a space in which ordinarily criminal behaviour would go unpunished.

After the factory workers' intervention, violence escalated quickly. Much of that escalation was simply a product of the spontaneous exploitation of a crumbling security situation by a collection of actors who were described by officers from the United States Embassy (which sits on University Square) as 'marginalized and alienated elements of society'.[27] Early violence was restricted to the square, where youths threw rocks at the shield-bearing police, before the police responded by forcing the crowd to temporarily retreat from the square.[28] After some hours of these movements to and fro, the situation began to escalate more rapidly when a set of disaffected youths began to siphon petrol out of local cars, funnel it into bottles, and throw the resulting Molotov cocktails in the direction of the police (Parlamentul României 1991, pp. 36, 112). Opportunistic aggression then reached its first climax at around 15:00, when a small group of actors managed to break away from the crowd, move through the police cordon and set fire to the Interior Ministry buses that were serving as barriers to the arterial roads that fed into University Square. The identity of these arsonists has remained a point of controversy to this day because it has never been conclusively established, despite the existence of film footage which shows the perpetrators in action.[29] Regardless of who the arsonists were, however, their destructive acts were the catalyst for a fundamental change in the dynamics of the unfolding conflict—a change that can be best understood when seen through the lens of inter-agency competition.

Although the early, exaggerated actions of the police suggested that Interior Ministry leaders were willing to allow the situation on the ground to escalate beyond

[26]Testimony of eyewitness students given to Romanian state television reporters, *Arhivele Televiziunii Române*, unedited film footage, 13 June 1990; Parlamentul României (1991, p. 112); 'Rechizitoriu, 27.07.2007, Dosar 74/P/1998', Section III.

[27]United States Embassy Bucharest, 'Theories Regarding the Romanian Unrest—Factional Struggles, Plots, and Manipulation ... What Actually Happened in Bucharest?', Bucharest 06723 (June 1990).

[28]*Arhivele Televiziunii Române*, unedited film footage, 13 June 1990.

[29]*Arhivele Televiziunii Române*, unedited film footage, 13 June 1990.

its meek origins, there is no reason to think that Chiţac or Diamandescu wished to see the situation escalate completely out of hand. After all, if they had wanted to demonstrate the utility of the Interior Ministry as a provider of security in the new regime, then any threat—be it real or exaggerated—needed to be met with an effective response from the police. Problematically, however, after arson attacks had provoked an escalation of the situation at hand on the afternoon of 13 June, it became clear that the rioting was genuinely slipping out of the control of the police. Recordings of radio communications between Chiţac and Diamandescu on 13 June speak to that real sense of danger.[30] As conditions continued to deteriorate and the need for reinforcements became evident, provisional President Ion Iliescu took a decision to call for the intervention of the army,[31] rather than to mobilise any more of the 4,000 police that were on duty at the time in and around Bucharest.[32] In response to the call for security sector cooperation, however, both the Ministry of National Defence and the Ministry of the Interior showed reluctance. Specifically, the military initially refused to intervene in University Square and suggested, instead, that its forces be used to shore up strategic locations elsewhere in the city. Troops under the command of the Ministry of the Interior, meanwhile, simply withdrew from University Square altogether.

In deciding to withdraw, the Interior Ministry leaders took one of the two strategic paths that were arguably open to them as the security situation deteriorated. The first path was to remain in the square, wait upon the arrival of the two Interior Ministry garrisons that had been called in as backup, and then cooperate with the military brigades that Iliescu was requesting. However, there were two limits to the utility of this strategy. The first was that the police reserves might not arrive in time to provide the support that was needed. Second, by remaining in the square, Diamandescu might have been forced to subordinate control over the operation at hand to the Interior Ministry's institutional competitor—the Ministry of National Defence. Beyond the immediate ignominy of that step, such a subordination would have constituted a significant loss for the Interior Ministry in its informal competition with the military.

The second option for Chiţac and Diamandescu was to simply withdraw from the square. Not only would this strategy remove police brigades from the evident danger in which they found themselves, it would also transfer responsibility for the situation at hand to a military that may waver in its response to the president's call (because internal processes of depoliticisation in the army had seen low-ranking and mid-ranking officers insist that the military not be drawn into domestic conflicts). If the military did indeed waver, then the Ministry of National Defence would be shown as a poor replacement for the Interior Ministry and the latter would not, as such, suffer in its competition with the military for position in the new regime. Although there are no

[30]For extracts, see Ursu (2008, pp. 59–69).

[31]'Jurnalul activităţilor desfăşurate de unităţile Armatei, în garnizoana Bucureşti, în perioada 13–15.06.1990', cited in *Gardianul*, 16 June 2005; also cited in *Romania liberă*, 11 August 2005. This is a report by the army on actions that were taken by its Bucharest-based units between 13 and 15 June. It was seemingly leaked to newspapers in 2005, as it was extracted extensively in the cited newspapers on the cited dates.

[32]Corneliu Diamandescu, testimony before the parliamentary commission, *Arhivele Camerei Deputaţilor*, d. 162/1990, p. 86; also cited in Ivan (1993, p. 113). In his comments, Diamandescu told the parliament that he was only in a position to mobilise 1,000 of these troops.

records of the exact calculations of Chiţac and Diamandescu on the afternoon of 13 June, their actions can be seen to speak to their strategic thinking; at around 16:30, the police suddenly withdrew in an orderly fashion—a move that was described as a 'dangerous tactical error' by US Embassy officers who were reporting to Washington on the events as they unfolded.[33] As the police withdrew, Chiţac contacted the state major general and asked for the army to send troops into University Square.[34] Following that step, however, the Interior Ministry leaders then made no attempt to offer logistical or operational support to the military. Instead, by 17:30, Diamandescu had isolated himself in his office. When Chiţac joined him shortly thereafter, the Interior Minister found the police chief 'in a relaxed state "dressed casually, in slippers, with a bottle of whisky on the table and following the [World Cup football] match on television"'.[35] While following the football, the Interior Ministry leaders failed to maintain sufficient contact with government and state officials. Chiţac, in particular, remained absent and mute over the course of the two days of violence that followed.[36]

The diffusion of violence. The withdrawal of the police opened up space for a swift diffusion of violence beyond University Square. Two locations became central points of conflict and rioting on the afternoon of 13 June. The first was the area in and around the police headquarters and the Interior Ministry, where protestors moved after hearing rumours that those arrested earlier in the day were being housed there. Once the crowd had completed the short walk to the police station, patterns of violence mimicked those seen earlier in University Square. The vast majority of those present stood by passively, looking on with curiosity and perhaps throwing the odd stone, while between 50 and 60 belligerents—teenagers and youths—took advantage of the complete absence of state sanctioning mechanisms and continued their sport of throwing rocks and fire bombs.[37] Although severe material damage was incurred, primarily as a result of the fires that were started in the lower levels of the building (Parlamentul României 1991, pp. 114–18), no evidence has been produced to support Ion Iliescu's claim of the time that the attacks constituted a highly organised, fascist-inspired coup.[38] In fact, there is no reason to think that the

[33]United States Embassy Bucharest, 'Is Bucharest Burning? Depends Where You Are', Bucharest 06072 and 06090 (June 1990). There were other reports that the police withdrew as early as 15:30.

[34]See extracts from 'Jurnalul activităţilor desfăşurate de unităţile Armatei, în garnizoana Bucureşti, în perioada 13–15.06.1990', cited in *Gardianul*, 16 June 2005; also cited in *Romania liberă*, 11 August 2005.

[35]'Rechizitoriu 18.05.2000, Dosar 74/P/1998', p. 11. See also 'Raport-rechizitoriu despre fratricidul din 13–15 iunie 1990' (2009 edition), coordinated by Sorin Ilieşiu and Asociaţia 21 December 1989, p. 32, available at: http://mineriade.iiccmer.ro/pdf/dezbateri/raport_rechizitoriu_despre_fratricidul_din_13_15_iunie_1990.pdf, accessed 9 September 2010.

[36]Testimony of Ion Iliescu before the parliamentary commission, *Arhivele Camerei Deputaţilor*, d. 497/1990; testimony of Răzvan Theodorescu before the parliamentary commission, *Arhivele Camerei Deputaţilor*, d. 379/1990, p. 16.

[37]*Piaţa Universităţii—România* (V. Vasile, S. Gulea & S. Ilieşiu, directors [Film]), author's personal archive; Grupul pentru Dialog Social—Comitetul Helsinki (1990, p. 78).

[38]See comments from US Embassy officers made in: United States Embassy Bucharest, 'Letter from Prime Minister Roman to Secretary Baker on Events in Bucharest', Bucharest 06261 (June 1990).

perpetrators were anything other than disaffected youths; many, if not most, of those who were seen acting in and around the area were reported to be so young that they were 'almost children' (Grupul pentru Dialog Social—Comitetul Helsinki 1990, p. 76).[39]

The second focal point of violence on the evening of 13 June was the state television complex. Migration to the studios from the city centre began after Interior Ministry troops fired warning shots over the heads of the protestors (at around 18:30) and several bystanders were shot fatally in the back by ricocheting bullets.[40] Upon their arrival at the television studios, the protestors were met by army units that had been deployed there pre-emptively following the failure of the Interior Ministry to maintain control in the city centre. Although army conscripts were present in reasonable numbers, they initially seemed reluctant to commit themselves to defending the studios. Indeed, according to an eyewitness, 'The tanks . . . had their caps open and were deserted. The soldiers had been put at ease and were idling in small groups' (Berindei *et al.* 1990, p. 89). That initial passivity was, most likely, partly a function of reluctance from military commanders to further implicate the army in internal security matters, since lower-level army officers had previously made clear their objections to such a step. There was also a level of confusion in the military's command structures that evening, since Defence Minister Stănculescu had left Bucharest for Berlin in order to attend what would be the last Warsaw Pact summit. Regardless of the immediate cause, however, army conscript troops were slow to act when five or six youths charged through the army lines at around 19:45 (Grupul pentru Dialog Social—Comitetul Helsinki 1990, pp. 56–57). Once the army's passivity had been demonstrated, around a further 50 youths in the area then headed through the army lines and on into the television studios.

After forcing entry, most of the assailants simply engaged in wanton destruction of the valuable material goods that they found inside.[41] Some of the more determined violators, however, managed to make their way up to the 11th floor of the main building, where they confronted the heads of Romanian Television: Răzvan Theodorescu and Emanuel Valeriu.[42] The two television bosses were both harassed by a set of individuals that Valeriu described variously as 'youths', 'gypsies', 'French people' and 'supporters of Nica Leon' (an opposition civil society activist, who was known to be somewhat more radical than his fellow activists).[43] The inconsistency of these descriptions, and the incapacity of Valeriu and Theodorescu to offer any verifying evidence for their claims, has meant that the identity of the perpetrators has remained unclear until this day; but regardless of who they were, the assailants did not stay in the television bosses' offices for long. Instead, they fled after a few minutes,

[39]This is also evidenced in footage that appears in the film *Piața Universității* (1991).

[40]'Rechizitoriu 18.05.2000, Dosar 74/P/1998', pp. 15–17, author's personal archive.

[41]Around $1 million (in 1990 value) of damage was sustained at the television studios (Parlamentul României 1991, p. 48).

[42]Răzvan Theodorescu, testimony before the parliamentary commission, *Arhivele Camerei Deputaților*, d. 379/1990, p. 7; also cited in Ivan (1993, pp. 126–27).

[43]Emanuel Valeriu, testimony before the parliamentary commission, *Arhivele Camerei Deputaților*, d. 257/1990, pp. 2–3; also cited in Ivan (1993, p. 65).

because the military had been activated at around 20:15 and had begun a decisive effort to regain control of the complex. That task was completed swiftly and order was restored by 20:30.[44]

Despite the presence of the army, television bosses took the decision to cut transmission of the main television signal at around 20:20. The sudden severance was witnessed by viewers right across the country, because Romania's state broadcaster held a monopoly over television rights at the time. Coming as it did, without warning, the cut served to generate panic among the large national audience that was watching the World Cup. That panic laid the cognitive foundations for the message that President Iliescu went on to broadcast when the signal was re-established one hour later. In a prepared speech, Iliescu repeated the two main claims that he had initially diffused some hours earlier on state wire services. He first argued (without any corroborating evidence) that his government was facing an organised coup attempt—one that was led by 'anarchic' and 'legionnaire-type characters', who had 'systematically impeded' 'attempts by the fire brigade and security forces to intervene'. Furthermore, in what has since become the defining and most controversial moment of his presidency, Iliescu then called on 'all democratic forces in the country ... to support the quashing of this legionnaire rebellion, to work with the security forces and the army to re-establish order, [and to] isolate and arrest the extremist elements' (Parlamentul României 1991, pp. 126–27).

The rationale behind Iliescu's decision to dissolve the state monopoly on violence by calling for civilian support has been a point of constant speculation over the past 20 years. While various interpretations have been proposed on both sides of the political fence in Romania, the appeal may have simply been a short-sighted attempt from Iliescu to minimise the political damage that he and his government would incur as a result of the rioting. That is, if the chaos and violence could be blamed on the ineffectiveness of state institutions, rather than on the incapacity of the Front government to manage those institutions, and if civilians could be brought out onto the streets to demonstrate their support for the Front, then Iliescu and his associates would be well placed to come out of the affair without incurring major political costs. This line of thought may have had a political logic to it; however, it carried no practical logic in terms of consolidating order and security in Bucharest. Rather, by calling for civilians to act as vigilante law enforcers in the capital, the president actively dissolved the state's monopoly on violence and abrogated the rule of law in Romania. That top-down construction of functional anarchy immediately created an opportunity for the two secret services—UM 0215 and the SRI—to employ extra-constitutional, violent methods in support of their respective competitive efforts to win the favour of the governing Front elites. Those violent efforts saw officers from the secret services co-opt groups of belligerent civilians who mobilised in response to Iliescu's call, and then use those civilians as hired thugs in targeted attacks on political groups that had expressed their opposition to Iliescu and the Front.

[44]Col. Radu Cantuniari, testimony before the parliamentary commission, *Arhivele Camerei Deputaţilor*, d. 262/1990, p. 14; also cited in Ivan (1993, p. 74).

Phase II: civilian mobilisation and anti-opposition violence, 14–15 June 1990

The mechanisms of civilian mobilisation. Iliescu's calls for civilian vigilantism, which were relayed nationally and repeated in the form of government communiqués, were immediately met with intense efforts from local-level elites right across the country to mobilise civilian support for a descent on Bucharest. Those mobilisation efforts can be best understood when seen through the lenses of intra-state competition for power and resources in post-revolution Romania, at the local level.

Two sets of local actors were particularly responsible for driving the early mobilisation processes: regional political elites and the managers of local industrial plants. For regional and provincial leaders of the National Salvation Front, the president's call for civilian recruitment was an opportunity to demonstrate, and consolidate, the local power and influence that they had established for themselves since the revolution.[45] It also allowed them to demonstrate their commitment to Party elites in Bucharest—something that was important for local Front members and regional Party leaders, since most had simply joined the Party by default, when the Front had taken control of the organisational structures and patrimony of the Communist Party in early 1990. For local-level industrial elites such as factory managers, meanwhile, the incentives to initiate mobilisation efforts were filtered through the institutional interests of their national-level parent organisations, such as the Ministries of Industry, Mining and Transport. Since the president and his Party were set to hold discretionary control over the distribution of funding among these state organs for the indefinite future, each state institution had an interest in trying to curry Iliescu's favour, by attending immediately to his call for the mobilisation of civilians.

The most well-documented mobilisation processes took place in Transylvania's Jiu Valley mining region. Those processes seem to have been initiated by the Ministry of Mining, whose willingness to support civilian mobilisation efforts across the country was, most likely, rooted in the massive drop in productive output that the mining industry had suffered in 1990 (Comisia Naţională pentru Statistică 1994, p. 515), and the corresponding reliance of the moribund industry on the provision of government-allocated subsidies. That reliance meant that the Ministry of Mining had particular reason to try to seek the favour of the Front's governing elites by responding promptly and actively to Iliescu's call for mobilisation. As such, administrative officers in the ministry's Bucharest headquarters began to contact directors of mining plants in the Jiu Valley immediately after Iliescu's initial call for civilian assistance, in order to ask that workers be taken out of the mining shafts so that they could be organised for a trip to the capital. Those orders for mobilisation were then relayed onward by enterprise bosses to their foremen and, from there, down through the military-style hierarchy of the mines and onto the workers.[46] While many miners were immediately

[45]For examples of the implication of local Front leaders in the mobilisation process right across the country, see Parlamentul României (1991, p. 129).

[46]Testimony of Ion Albu (Ministry of Mining), Vasile Chirculescu (Director, Rovinari Mine) and Gheorghe Diaconescu (Engineer, Rovinari Mine) before the parliamentary commission (Ivan 1993, pp. 96–98).

compliant with the request for mobilisation, mine directors still chose to hold out threats of salary retention and redundancy, in order to ensure the participation of any workers who proved reluctant to join the movement. The process of coercive mobilisation was described in the following way by one mine foreman:

> I received a telephone call in the mine: 'Get people out, we're going to Bucharest'; but it wasn't explained why .... A mine is like the army, you have to obey .... There were 150 miners in my team, of which 90% came with me .... It was imposed on the miners who were worried about losing their jobs.[47]

Although some miners were reluctant to head to the capital, a sub-set of Jiu Valley workers actually celebrated the president's invitation to mobilise and showed themselves keen to volunteer for the trip at hand. Voluntary mobilisation was underwritten by four, quite diverse, sets of interests—some collective, others individual. On the collective side of the ledger, some miners were driven by a genuine, patriotic desire to respond to Iliescu's call for vigilante support and, in so doing, attend to what the president had described as a violent challenge for power by right-wing extremists.[48] Iliescu had produced no evidence to back up his claims of a fascist coup, but his call for assistance would have fallen on sympathetic ears in industrial regions such the Jiu Valley, since the president had built his electoral campaign around the idea that the Front was the defender of workers' interests against a host of right-wing opposition groups that were supposedly intent on destabilising the post-revolutionary order (Siani-Davies 2005, p. 257). The miners' collective willingness to answer Iliescu's call should also be seen in the context of the rich history of social activism in the Jiu Valley. The Valley had, for example, been home to the only public workers' strike during the Ceauşescu era (Mica 2008), and smaller groups of miners had already mobilised to move on Bucharest in January and February 1990, in order to express their support for Iliescu and the Front on the streets of the capital (Vasi 2004). Also, beyond collective will, three sets of 'selective incentives' (individual-level motives) would have rendered the movement to Bucharest an attractive prospect for miners in the Jiu Valley.[49] First, mobilisation offered all miners the opportunity to enjoy a free trip to the distant and exotic capital—a welcome relief from their gruelling work in the mines; second, miners who had headed to Bucharest in January and February had been hailed as heroes in the local press, and so those who mobilised in June faced the promise of an equally celebrated welcome upon their return;[50] and third, for the more belligerent and greedy miners in the Jiu Valley, mobilisation and movement to an apparently lawless Bucharest carried with it the possibility of engaging in looting, battery, material destruction and other ordinarily illegal activities without fear of state sanction.

As workers were being pulled out of the mines across the Jiu Valley, local political elites—both regional Front leaders and local union bosses—stepped in and

[47]'Doru Păunescu' (pseudonym), mine foreman, interview with the author, Vulcan, 10 June 2005.

[48]Comments made by a representative of the League of Mine Unions of the Jiu Valley, interview with the author, Vulcan, 10 June 2005.

[49]See the accounts in Uba (1990) and Rus (2007, p. 90).

[50]For examples of the local praise that miners received after their trip to Bucharest on 18–19 February 1990, see local Petroşani paper, *Zori noi*, 22 February 1990.

contributed to the recruitment effort by assuring the organisational resources that were needed for mobilisation. The president of the recently-formed League of Jiu Valley Miners' Unions (LJVMU, *Liga Sindicatelor Miniere Valea Jiului*), Miron Cozma, showed a particular willingness to demonstrate his newly won local power by implicating his organisation in the logistical side of the mobilisation effort (Uba 1990). Specifically, the LJVMU arranged for the collection of workers from mining plants around the Valley and their displacement to the central rail town of Petroşani (Rus 2007, p. 155). Once gathered, Cozma and other union leaders then took the lead in organising troops into detachments and readying them for the trip to Bucharest. The Petroşani train station chief, meanwhile, worked with local Front leader Wilhelm Kleibel to assure the provision of extra trains, which were used to transport some 6,000 Jiu Valley miners to Bucharest.[51]

The combined organisational input of local industrial, political and union elites on the evening of 13 June would have been sufficient to ensure the mobilisation of a large number of miners for the trip to Bucharest. Nevertheless, another set of actors chose to implicate themselves in the civilian recruitment efforts in order to guarantee that the Jiu Valley became a focal point for mobilisation. Specifically, officers from the two secret services allegedly contributed to the process of recruiting the Jiu Valley miners, some of whom would be used as shock troops after they arrived in Bucharest, in attacks that were coordinated by officers from UM 0215 and the SRI. While it remains unclear exactly when the two secret services took the decision to exploit the emerging situation in that way, there is evidence that senior secret police officers in Bucharest began to make contact with secret servicemen who were posted in the Jiu Valley on the evening of 13 June, in order to ask that local officers support the mobilisation processes that were unfolding there.[52] Specifically, it is alleged that Viorel Tache and Mugurel Florescu (associates of UM 0215 boss Voican Voiculescu) contacted Constantin Ilinescu and asked that the Aninoasa mine union leader put together a local mobilisation effort (Hihn 2007).[53] Contact was also made with Nicolae Cămărăşescu, a Jiu Valley-based former *Securitate* and SRI officer. Cămărăşescu then headed to Bucharest during the night of 13–14 June and, shortly after his arrival in the capital, he was seen leading a group of miners on violent raids about the city.

Arrival in Bucharest. The 6,000 miners who headed off from the Jiu Valley were among the first to arrive at Bucharest's Northern Station, at around 4:30 on 14 June 1990.[54] Despite the insistence of informal UM 0215 chief, Gelu Voican Voiculescu, that there

[51]Wilhelm Kleibel, testimony before the parliamentary commission (Ivan 1993, p. 93).

[52]There had been a disproportionately high number of *Securitate* officers deployed to the Jiu Valley after 1977, after local union leaders had organised a general strike.

[53]See interview between Petre Mihai Băcanu and Nicolae Cămărăşescu in *România liberă* (16 April 1993), in Ivan (1996, p. 135); also, Sabin Ivan's discussion of testimony given by Nicolae Cămărăşescu before the parliamentary commission (Ivan 1996, p. 87).

[54]A further 10,000 miners and factory workers would arrive in the capital from right across the country over the course of the day that followed. The total number of civilian vigilantes was, as such, 16,000 (author's estimate from details in Parlamentul României (1991, pp. 52–58 and 136–40).

was no question of any kind of organisational support being provided to the miners by the secret services or other state actors after their arrival in the capital,[55] participants have reported that they were greeted by a set of unidentified actors who had put together packed lunches for the incoming miners (Rus 2005, p. 340). The new arrivals were then organised into small groups before being led on to the nearby seat of the government in Victory Square where Ion Iliescu addressed them:

> Delegation of miners, led by Mr [Miron] Cozma, head towards University Square, which we want you to reclaim ... occupy it decisively, and then, working with the security forces, assure ... the necessary defence against all extremist elements that might appear in the area again. (Parlamentul României 1991, pp. 141–42)

Over the 48 hours that followed, that invitation for cooperation between civilians and state forces was acted upon by officers from Romania's two competing secret services, who worked with the most belligerent miners to terrorise the Bucharest-based opposition to the National Salvation Front.

The competing secret services take charge. Since the police operation on the morning of 13 June had been overt, the response of the street opposition to that operation had been public, and the subsequent introduction of the military had been transparent, there had been little scope for Romania's two covert security services—UM 0215 and the SRI—to implicate themselves in the events that unfolded on the streets of Bucharest on 13 June. By extension, there had been little scope for the secret services to use the unfolding situation as a basis for demonstrating the utility and loyalty of their respective institutions to the Front's governing elites, in a way that would have advanced their respective cases for institutional advancement in the new regime. However, Iliescu's announcement of the incapacity of the army and police to maintain order in Bucharest, and his subsequent call for civilian vigilante mobilisation, invited intervention from Romania's secret services. The president's dissolution of the rule of law in Bucharest also meant that there were few constraints on the form that the secret services' intervention could take. That is, within the context of a breakdown in the rule of law, both constitutional and extra-constitutional interventions were feasible. The constitutional course of action for UM 0215 and the SRI was to simply follow protocol and assist the military in maintaining order in the capital. An alternative, extra-constitutional course of action was to go beyond protocol, by responding to the president's call for cooperation between civilians and security forces in any way—legal or illegal—that might allow each of the services to demonstrate their particular loyalty, and potential utility, to the Front leadership. The co-optation of civilians who had mobilised at the president's request, and the use of those civilians in a violent repression of political groups that had expressed their opposition to Iliescu and the Front, was just such a way. Indeed, it was seemingly the way that was adopted by each of the secret services on 14 and 15 June 1990 (Oprea 2004, pp. 117–19; Deletant 2001, pp. 219–20).

[55]Gelu Voican Voiculescu, interview with *RIAS* radio, Berlin, reproduced in *Expres*, 27, July 1990.

Unsurprisingly, officers from both the SRI and UM 0215 initially denied their involvement in the violence of 14 and 15 June. Recently, however, the former heads of both organisations have publicly recognised that officers from their respective services did, in fact mobilise and/or lead groups of miners in attacks on political opposition groups in June 1990. Specifically, Doru Viorel Ursu, who inherited formal direction of UM 0215 on 14 June 1990 (when he replaced the missing Mihai Chiţac), has since written: 'A short time after I was appointed, I realised that the institution that I was leading had been implicated in the actions of the miners, after their arrival in the capital' (Ursu 2008, p. 145). Virgil Măgureanu, similarly, has recognized that some rogue SRI officers were involved in coordinating the events that unfolded in the wake of Iliescu's call for civilian support, although he maintains that those involved were not acting under orders to do so (Măgureanu & Stoenescu, pp. 9, 239). At the same time, a former senior actor from the SRI told the author that officers from UM 0215 received orders to implicate themselves in the events of 14–15 June.[56] The implication is that, by leading civilians in attacks on political opposition groups, UM 0215 was aiming to shore up the new, Front-led regime and, more particularly, UM 0215's position within that regime.

Miners, secret police, and the joint production of violence. If officers from each of the two secret services were to co-opt the newly arriving vigilantes for attacks on opposition groups, then they needed to resolve two logistical problems. First, a subset of the mobilised miners needed to be recruited for acts of violence. Second, the violent actions of those recruits needed to be focused on a finite set of political targets. Over the course of 14 and 15 June 1990, these two challenges were overcome through a simple device: as miners arrived in the city centre, guides indicated to the new arrivals where they could engage in ordinarily criminal activities without fear of state sanction. Although uncomplicated, this device was effective, on two counts. First, it served as an informal tool of thug recruitment because it invited those miners who had mobilised for the trip to Bucharest with the intent of engaging in looting and battery to step forward and register their willingness to engage in acts of violence. Second, it served as a tool for translating the violent, but essentially apolitical, interests of those belligerent miners into focused attacks on highly political targets. It did so by allowing the secret service officers to resolve an information problem that the miners faced. Specifically, since the army had taken control of parts of the city late on the night of 13 June and army battalions were guarding strategic locations,[57] miners who wished to engage in looting and battery needed to know where they could find targets that could be attacked without fear of state sanction. That information seems to have been provided by officers from the secret services, who guided belligerent miners to finite locations and then assured their recruits that acts of material destruction would be met with reward, not punishment. Those locations were almost exclusively the offices and residences of political organisations opposed to the Front.

[56]Interview with the author, Bucharest, 14 April 2009. He did not specify from whom the orders came, or if they were official.

[57]United States Embassy Bucharest, 'Romania's Miners: Here We Come to Save the Day', Bucharest 06093 and 06096 (June 1990).

While it remains unclear whether the officer guides were acting on formal orders and, if so, from where those orders were coming, it is clear that the involvement of the secret services was well prepared and organised. That organisation began with the preparation of 'costumes' for some of the guides, who were given mining-style overalls over the course of the night of 13 June. The secret service officers then donned their workers' outfits on 14 June, before heading out to direct the newly arrived miners around town (Grupul pentru Dialog Social—Comitetul Helsinki 1990, p. 157; Uba 1990)—presumably believing that their costumes would hide their identities and institutional affiliations from the Bucharest population. The miners themselves were under no such illusion, however. In fact, they were quite aware that the strangely well dressed 'miners' who were guiding them around the city were not from among their own stock: '[We knew] it was the old *Securitate* ... [they came] with clean overalls, new lamps and new little hats ... well, it's obvious that you're being led'.[58] Other secret service guides were less bothered about remaining covert and were, instead, quite happy to be seen leading their recruits across town while dressed in suits or brown leather jackets (informal uniforms of the secret services) (Grupul pentru Dialog Social—Comitetul Helsinki 1990, p. 157).

The guides led their miners to diverse institutional targets, which shared only one common trait: overt opposition to the retention of power by Ion Iliescu and the other second-level communist elites that constituted the Front leadership. Under that very broad umbrella, there were two sub-categories of targets. One set consisted of the informal, street-based opposition to the Front—civil society organisations that had participated in, or supported, the marathon anti-Front demonstrations that had taken place in University Square between late April and June. The first civil society actors attacked were those student leaders who had informally coordinated the University Square protests, including the president of the Students' League (*Liga Studenţilor*), Marian Munteanu. After arriving at the university's main building, the miners negotiated their way around the Byzantine interior of the building, 'with perhaps one or two persons guiding them' to the students' club room.[59] After the miners had turned the room over, looking for the US dollars that they had been told were there, they dealt out a severe beating to all present (Dumbrăveanu & Pîrvu 1992, p. 185). Munteanu and his brother received the most severe punishment and were beaten unconscious. As attacks continued at the university, further groups of aggressive miners were led to the headquarters of other organisations that had participated in the University Square demonstrations, including the December 21 Association (*Asociaţia 21 Decembrie*), the Romanian Writers' Association (*Societatea Scriitorilor Români*), the World Union of Free Romanians (*Uniunea Mondială a Românilor Liberi*), and the Association of Former Political Prisoners of Romania (*Asociaţiei Foştilor Deţinuţi Politici din România*) (Parlamentul României 1991, pp. 62–63, 149–50). Each site was trashed. The country's few independent publications were also singled out for attack—an indirect punishment for their willingness to act as the public voice of the anti-Front protestors. Specifically, a large group of miners was able to make its way out of the city centre to the complex in which the offices of the opposition newspaper, *România*

[58]'Doru Păunescu' (pseudonym), mine foreman, interview with the author, Vulcan, 10 June 2005.

[59]Marian Munteanu, interview with the author, Bucharest, 28 March 2005.

liberă, and independent publisher, *Humanitas*, were housed (Cosman 2005).[60] Both were ransacked.

The second sub-category of targets to which miners were led by their secret service guides was made up of the two main political parties that had run against the Front in the May elections: the National Liberal Party (*Partidul Național Liberal*) and the National Peasants' Party–Christian Democrat (NPP–CD, *Partidul Național Țărănesc–Creștin Democrat*). The scenario at the headquarters of both of these organisations played itself out similarly. After miners were directed toward the appropriate buildings, the offices were turned over, any valuable goods stolen, searches were carried out (to no avail) for the drugs and ammunition that were (falsely) rumoured to be concealed there and the headquarters were then occupied by the assailants (Parlamentul României 1991, pp. 148–49). Small group of miners were also guided to the personal residences of opposition leaders. At the home of NPP–CD leader, Corneliu Coposu, the miners managed to force entry by using pickaxes to smash their way through the front gate.[61] Under the guidance of UM 0215 officers, Ion Nicolae and Corneliu Dumitrescu, miners were able to break into the residence of NPP–CD presidential candidate, Ion Rațiu (Ursu 2008, p. 146). After a short chase, the septuagenarian Rațiu was cornered by miners and 'arrested' (Rațiu 1999, pp. 215–17).

The particular way in which the miners went about their destructive tasks at each of these institutional targets points to the fact that greed, rather than political grievance, was the main motive for the actions of the assailants. Before beating the student leaders, for example, the first priority of miners who forced their way into the university was to search out and loot anything of value (Grupul pentru Dialog Social—Comitetul Helsinki 1990, p. 118). Similarly, when attacks were made on the opposition Party headquarters and the homes of opposition Party leaders, the miners' first step was to seek out any cash or items of value that could be stolen. This seems to have been the case at the residence of Ion Rațiu, where assailants first went about gathering the $10,000 in cash that the NPP–CD presidential candidate had stored in various locations around the house, before chasing Rațiu himself (Oprea 2004, p. 118). While these efforts went some way to satisfying the interests of those who had come to Bucharest in the hope of filling their pockets, the miners' secret service guides did place limits on looting efforts in central Bucharest by only allowing the co-opted miners to realise their criminal preferences against selected political targets. To compensate for those limits, groups of miners were given free rein to loot as they wished in the peripheral, Roma-populated areas of Bucharest, such as the suburb of Ferentari (Helsinki Watch 1991). The particular choice of the Romani quarter is likely to have been made for two reasons. First, since the Romani population was socially marginalised and politically unorganised, it was unlikely that there would be popular backlash against the looting of 'gypsy' families and businesses. Second, since many in the Romani community were traders and entrepreneurs, their houses and businesses were sure to be stocked with rewarding goods. Those goods were systematically looted

[60] Also, Gabriel Liiceanu, director of *Humanitas*, interview with the author, Bucharest, 14 July 2005.

[61] Corneliu Coposu, testimony before the parliamentary commission, *Arhivele Camerei Deputaților*, d. 411/1990, p. 5; also cited in Ivan (1993, p. 119).

on 14 and 15 June, when buses of miners were given organised transport to, and from, the Ferentari area (Rus 2007, pp. 151–52).

Beyond attacks on institutional or collective targets, miners were also encouraged to 'arrest' any individuals who were suspected of opposing the incumbent political elites. Information problems meant that the coordination of these arrests was somewhat haphazard in comparison with the relatively ordered fashion in which attacks on institutional targets were implemented. Even if each of the two implicated secret services had managed to gather reliable intelligence on all of those who had opposed the Front over the preceding months, such information simply could not have been conveyed swiftly to the miners on 14 and 15 June. Instead, rough and rude means were used to identify supposed supporters of the opposition. For example, under the direction of their secret service guides, miners stopped random individuals and demanded to see their *buletine* (identity cards). Those whose cards suggested allegiance to the opposition (for example if their occupation was that of student or academic) were attacked and then taken into custody.[62] Evidently, this technique was inefficient, at best, but it proved to be far more effective than the miners' own method of identifying politically 'suspect' individuals, which was based on the application of crude visual indicators of a liberal political leaning, such as wearing glasses, having a beard or dressing in any unusual or challenging way (Grupul pentru Dialog Social—Comitetul Helsinki 1990, pp. 136–47). Unsurprisingly, almost all of those arrested on the basis of these criteria (around 1,000) were soon found to have engaged in no wrongdoing and were released. Of those that were detained for more than a few days, only a few were later found to have committed any infraction.[63]

Restoration of order and the movement home. By the morning of 15 June, officers from UM 0215 and the SRI had made their respective claims of loyalty to the leaders of the National Salvation Front by using the president's call for vigilante assistance as a basis for organising the violent repression of the Front's political opposition. The miners' basic interests had also been met; those who had come for personal profit had filled their pockets and those who had come to enjoy a day off work had already enjoyed two days liberty and had the prospect of a weekend at home awaiting them. At the same time, those miners who had come out of political conviction would have either felt that their job had been done or have recognised that their presence in the capital had only served to worsen the security situation there. Since the interests of each of the key actors had been met, both the participants and their guides were ready for the visitors to head home.

Gelu Voican Voiculescu took the initiative to bring the episode to a close, by calling for the miners to gather at a large exhibition hall, where they would be addressed by the president, before heading off to the station.[64] The evacuation plan was

[62]Based on comments made by Viorel Ene, president of the AVMR, interview with the author, Bucharest, 10 March 2005.

[63]Procuratura Municipiului Bucureşti, 'Informare privind temeinicia şi legalitatea măsurilor de arestare preventivă a inculpaţilor arestaţi în cursul evenimentelor din iunie 1990 faţă de care s-au dispus soluţii de netrimitere în judecată în anul 1991. Dosar Nr. S55/I/3/1992', author's personal archive.

implemented within hours and, by the afternoon of 15 June, groups of miners were flooding into the *Romexpo* centre. Once they had gathered, Iliescu came before the miners and spoke to the 'troops'. In what has become the most infamous speech of his political career, Iliescu refused to condemn the miners' actions. Instead, his tone suggested broad endorsement of actions that he may not have actually planned, but which did promise to strengthen his local grip on power. He stated:

> I thank you all again for what you have demonstrated during these days: that you are a powerful force, with a strong civic, workers' discipline; people to rely on in good times, but especially in hard times. On this occasion, you have demonstrated the importance of workers' solidarity .... You felt the difficult moment and with an exemplary [display of] self-sacrifice, you proved yourselves ready to show solidarity with the new regime. (Grupul pentru Dialog Social—Comitetul Helsinki 1990, p. 225)

Thus, with that stamp of presidential approval, the miners headed on their way, leaving behind a devastated capital and an equally devastated foundling democracy.

Phase III: articulating anarchy

Although the 13 June riots had broken out under the watch of the Front government, and the pogrom of 14 and 15 June had been directed against political groups opposed to the Front, public opinion polls taken in the months following the violence suggested that the public did not hold Iliescu or Front elites responsible for the collapse of security in Bucharest. In fact, more than 78% of respondents surveyed in July 1990 indicated that they trusted Iliescu and 67% supported his decision to call for vigilante assistance on 13 June (Datculescu 1992, pp. 132, 136–37). These views may appear surprising when seen from today's perspective, since the events of June 1990 and the role of Iliescu and senior Front elites in facilitating that violence are now both roundly condemned. However, these attitudes are more comprehensible when set within the context of the very limited information that existed at the time—one in which almost all media sources were state run and, therefore, under the control of the Front. That control afforded Front leaders and state elites a near-monopoly over the way in which the causes and dynamics of the 13–15 June violence were presented to the Romanian public in its immediate aftermath. Iliescu used that monopoly to publicly frame the violence in a way that would divorce him and his government from responsibility for the whole set of events.

Early articulation efforts took shape even as the violence was unfolding. They were addressed almost exclusively to the domestic audience and were designed to deflect responsibility away from the Front government by presenting the Party and its leaders as victims—rather than facilitators—of the violence. In support of that effort, Iliescu declared on national television that the assailants of 13 June were 'legionnaire-type extremists' (fascists), who were intent on leading a *coup d'etat* against the legitimate Front government (Parlamentul României 1991, pp. 126–27). Although the provisional president was unable to present any evidence in support of that claim

[64]Gelu Voican Voiculescu, testimony before parliamentary commission, *Arhivele Camerei Deputaţilor*, d. 423/1990, p. 16; also cited in Ivan (1993, p. 156).

(since there was none), the state-owned media immediately set about trumpeting his fascist-centred conspiracy theory in the days that followed Iliescu's initial claim. The main pro-Front newspaper, *Adevărul*, for example, ran a banner headline on 14 June which declared: 'Groups of Legionnaires Seen in Uniform'. Meanwhile, the Front-aligned newspapers *Azi* and *Dimineața* devoted much of their 15 and 16 June editions to an examination of the threat that legionnaires apparently presented to the Front government and to the installation and consolidation of democracy in Romania. Little coverage, however, was given to the actions of the miners against political opposition groups.

Although the local media minimised publicity of the miners' attacks, international reporters chose to focus almost exclusively on the miners' violence, partly because international media crews were not able to arrive in Bucharest until 14 June, and partly because the inter-personal violence seen that day was more sensational than the assaults on state buildings of the day before. As far as international journalists were concerned, the cause of the miners' violence was very simple: the Front had ordered and coordinated the miners' attacks on opposition groups. CBS News in the United States, for example, reported that 'the president of Romania, Ion Iliescu, has called these miners into Bucharest' (CBS 1990). French television reported similarly that 'the president-elect of Romania has made an appeal to miners to restore order ... and you get the feeling that you are seeing the *Securitate* operating through these black faces [of the miners]'.[65] These reports, although simplistic and arguably somewhat misleading in their understanding of the causes of the miners' attacks, gave those outside Romania a portrayal of the events that was more independent than the account offered to Romanians. Foreign governments were also able to access more objective (and more accurate) accounts of the situation on the ground in Romania through reports that they received from their Bucharest-based embassy staff. By combining the information and analysis coming from these two sources, the international community quickly came to a consensus on two broad points. First, there was agreement that Iliescu's claim of a fascist plot to overthrow his government was wholly unfounded. Second, there was agreement that state and political elites were somehow implicated in planning and implementing the miners' violence of 14–15 June, if not the violence of 13 June (Pick 1990).[66]

Since there was a swift hardening of international opinion around these views, Iliescu and the Front government needed to identify a new, internationally oriented articulation strategy if they were going to emerge from the June violence with any international legitimacy intact. Thus, from mid-June to late-June 1990, Iliescu and Roman began to shift the way in which they framed the violence when speaking to international audiences. Specifically, they began to make use of the commonly held assumption of the international community that chaos and violence are sometimes unavoidable within the institutionally ambiguous context of transition. The president

[65]French television news report (broadcast unidentified), June 1990, available at: http://www.youtube.com/watch?v=28frNfd9VNU&feature=mfu_in_order&list=UL, accessed 15 September 2011.

[66]United States Embassy Bucharest, 'Theories Regarding the Romanian Unrest—Factional Struggles, Plots, and Manipulation ... What Actually Happened in Bucharest?', Bucharest 06723 (June 1990); British Embassy Bucharest, 'From Bucharest to Immediate FCO, of 191340Z June 90'.

argued specifically that the capacity of Romania's state security forces had been weakened by the process of regime change, which had opened up opportunities for violence. He then claimed that those opportunities had been exploited on 13 June by small groups of 'fascist-type' belligerents. The miners' arrival on the following day, he suggested, had been a spontaneous and unstoppable, albeit regrettable, reaction from individuals who were shocked by the images of chaos that they had seen on television on 13 June.[67] Particular care was taken to emphasise the supposed structural unavoidability of the June violence within a transitional context, in an effort to deflect responsibility for the events away from the Front as an agent. To that end, Petre Roman made specific comparisons between the causes and dynamics of the violence at hand, which unfolded during the transition out of communism, and the causes and dynamics of violence that broke out in 1941, during Romania's protracted transition into totalitarian rule (Grupul pentru Dialog Social—Comitetul Helsinki 1990, pp. 237–39).

Despite the strategic logic that underwrote those claims, the international community proved less receptive to the Front's framing efforts than had the local population, and major Western governments quickly condemned the violence and the role of Romania's post-revolution elites in facilitating it. For example, the press secretary for US President George H. W. Bush stated plainly that the violence of 13–15 June had demonstrated that, although Romania had a 'democratically-elected government, they [were] not behaving in a democratic fashion' (Pick 1990). The British and French governments made similarly worded statements, as did the European Community (Champion & Crawshaw 1990). International condemnation did not stop at words, however. Much needed flows of international aid into Romania were suspended in the immediate wake of the violence. Such a suspension was felt intensely in a country that was already reeling after years of austerity measures under Ceauşescu. Beyond the short-term costs in terms of aid, the events of 13–15 June 1990 served to damage Romania's international reputation and initiate a period of international isolation which saw Romania fall significantly behind its transitional neighbours in attracting the foreign direct investments that helped drive post-communist economic development across the region.

Conclusion

Existing understandings of Romania's transitional violence tend to be based on over-simplified causal accounts of the so-called *mineriadă*. One set of arguments, which is usually proposed by former Front elite members, holds that the events of 13–15 June 1990 were an unavoidable, albeit regrettable, by-product of the transition process: state institutions weakened across the change in regime, fascist hooligans exploited the resulting opportunities for violence and civilian vigilantes acted spontaneously to defend the country against threats that the state was unable to manage. A second set of claims, most often articulated by those associated with the opposition groups that were attacked by miners in June 1990, hold that the whole set of events was planned

[67]United States Embassy Bucharest, 'Romania's President Tells His Side of the Story Regarding the June 13–15 Events', Bucharest 06497 (June 1990). This position was later articulated with clarity in Iliescu's memoirs; see Iliescu (1994, pp. 135–39).

and executed by Front elites in an effort to crush the opposition and reinstall a kind of crypto-communist regime in post-revolution Romania. In this essay, I have tried to show that these two polemical positions are both overly simplistic, and inaccurate in their own ways.

The transitional violence of June 1990 can be best understood as the partially unintended collective outcome of a series of intended, individual actions that were taken by state institutions and political elites in the context of inter-agency competition for prominence and resources in Romania's post-revolution regime. On 13 June 1990, that competition manifested itself in a significantly exaggerated police operation from the beleaguered Ministry of the Interior in response to a minor security threat—the presence of a handful of strikers in central Bucharest. That move served to spark rioting, which then escalated across the course of 13 June, after the Interior Ministry and Ministry of National Defence proved incapable of cooperating to secure the situation at hand. Provisional President Ion Iliescu then shifted the environment in which inter-agency competition could, and would, play itself out, by dissolving the state monopoly on violence in Bucharest and calling for vigilante support for the government. That call opened up space for provincial elites to demonstrate loyalty to their national-level superiors by answering the president's call with zeal and recruiting civilians for a move on Bucharest. As civilians mobilised, Romania's two main secret services availed themselves of the opportunity to demonstrate their loyalty to the new Front elites by co-opting belligerent miners and channelling their aggression into attacks on groups and individuals that had expressed opposition to the Front.

By way of conclusion, it is worth asking whether this reading of Romania's transitional violence offers a clear answer to what has arguably been the most politically sensitive question asked in Romania over the past 20 years: 'Who brought in the miners?' In short, it does not—at least not directly. Instead, the arguments offered suggest that such a narrow question simply invites simplistic and politicised responses. The posing of such a question, however, is understandable, since it is underwritten by an implicit wish to pin blame for an unfortunate, and painful, set of events on an individual or particular institution and, in so doing, take the first step towards putting the pain of those events to rest. This essay has tried to take that first step, by arguing that both the violence of 13 June and the miners' attacks of 14–15 June were products—albeit partially unintended—of deliberate actions that were taken by key state and political actors in June 1990. The fact that the collective outcome may not have been envisaged by the individuals and institutions that were implicated in the construction of that outcome does not diminish the individual responsibility of those who contributed to the explosion of rioting on 13 June, or the miners' attacks of 14 and 15 June. Rather, it invites recognition of the fact that a broad host of actors bear responsibility for Romania's transitional violence: political elites of the day, state institutions, individual perpetrators of violence, and those tens of thousands of civilians who stood by and watched—even cheered—as the miners went about their business of crushing Romania's chance to enjoy a swift and painless transition from communist rule to democracy.

University of Oxford

References

Almond, M. (1990) 'Romania since the Revolution', *Government and Opposition*, 25, 4, October, pp. 484–96.

Berindei, M., Combes, A. & Planche, A. (1990) *Roumanie, le livre blanc: la réalité d'un pouvoir néo-communiste* (Paris, La Découverte).

CBS News Transcripts (1990) 'Bucharest the Site of Violent Government Protest', *CBS News*, 14 June.

Cesereanu, R. (2003) *Imaginarul violent al românilor* (Bucharest, Humanitas).

Champion, M. & Crawshaw, S. (1990) 'EC Trade Deal with Romania under Threat; "Shocked" Brussels Puts Pressure on Bucharest as Ministers Try to Explain Away the Miners' Violence', *The Independent*, 16 June.

Comisia Naţională pentru Statistică (1994) *Anuarul statistic al României* (Bucharest).

Cosman, C. (2005) 'Cu bâtă şi lampaşul la batut intelectuali şi devastat redacţii', *România liberă*, 15 December.

Datculescu, P. (1992) 'Social Change and Changing Public Opinion in Romania after the 1990 Election', in Nelson, D. (ed.) (1992) *Romania After Tyranny* (Boulder, CO, Westview Press).

Deletant, D. (2001) 'The Successors to the Securitate: Old Habits Die Hard', in Williams, K. & Deletant, D. (2001) *Security Intelligence Services in New Democracies: The Czech Republic, Slovakia and Romania* (Houndmills, Palgrave).

Dumbrăveanu, G. & Pîrvu, E. (1992) *Piaţa Universităţii* (Bucharest, Imprimeria Coresi).

FBIS (1990) 'Daily Report, East Europe', *Foreign Broadcast Information Service*, FBIS-EEU-90-083, 30 April.

Gallagher, T. (2005) *Theft of a Nation: Romania since Communism* (London, Hurst & Co.).

Galloway, G. & Wylie, B. (1991) *Downfall: The Ceausescus and the Romanian Revolution* (London, Futura).

Grosescu, R. (2004) 'The Political Regrouping of the Romanian Nomenklatura during the 1989 Revolution', *Romanian Journal of Society and Politics*, 4, 1, May, pp. 97–123.

Grosescu, R. (2007) 'Traiectorii de conversie politică a nomenclaturii din România. Spre o taxonomie a partidelor create de fostele elite comuniste', in IICCR (ed.) (2007) *Elite comuniste înainte şi după 1989. Anuarul IICCR*, Vol. II (Iaşi, Polirom).

Grupul pentru Dialog Social, Asociaţia pentru Apărarea Drepturilor Omului în România—Comitetul Helsinki (1990) *Raport asupra evenimentelor din 13–15 iunie 1990, Bucureşti* (Bucharest, GDS).

Guvernul României (1989) *Monitorul oficial nr. 5/27 decembrie* 1989, Decret nr. 4/26-12-1989, available at: http://www.cdep.ro/pls/legis/legis_pck.htp_act?ida=14.

Guvernul României (1990a) *Monitorul oficial nr. 12/19 ianuarie 1990*, Decret-Lege nr.30/18-01-1990, available at: http://www.cdep.ro/pls/legis/legis_pck.htp_act?ida=78.

Guvernul României (1990b) *Monitorul oficial nr. 23/9 februarie 1990*, Decret-Lege nr. 65/08-02-1990, available at: http://www.cdep.ro/pls/legis/legis_pck.htp_act_text?idt=7477.

Helsinki Watch (1991) *Destroying Ethnic Identity: The Persecution of Gypsies in Romania* (New York, Human Rights Watch).

Hihn, M. (2007) 'Minerii au fost chemaţi la Bucureşti!', *Replica Hunedoara*, 240, 14–20 June.

Iliescu, I. (1994). *Revoluţie şi reformă* (Bucharest, Editura Enciclopedică).

Ionescu, D. (1994) 'UM 0215: A Controversial Intelligence Service in Romania', *RFE/RL Research Report*, 3, 30, July, pp. 27–30.

Ivan, S. (1993) *Anchetat, anchetator* (Bucharest, Editura Topaz).

Ivan, S. (1996) *Pe urmele adevărului* (Constanţa, Ex Ponto).

Măgureanu, V. & Stoenescu, A. M. (2008) *De la regimul comunist la regimul Iliescu* (Bucharest, Editura RAO).

Mica, A. (2008) 'Discussion on the 1977 Jiu Valley Strike as Scandal in Romania', *Sfera Politicii*, 129–30, pp. 31–42.

Niculae, C. (2004) *Schimbarea organizaţiei militare: o perspectivă (neo)instituţionalistă* (Bucharest, Tritonic).

Oprea, M. (2004) *Moştenitorii securităţii* (Bucharest, Humanitas).

Parlamentul României (1991) *Raportul comisiei parlamentare de anchetă instituită în vederea cercetării evenimentelor petrecute în zilele de 13–15 iunie 1990* (Bucharest, Guvernul României).

Pick, H. (1990) 'West Deplores Violence Used on Protesters', *The Guardian*, 15 June.

Pleşu, A., Roman, P. & Stefoi, E. (2002) *Transformări, inerţii, dezordini: 22 de luni după 22 decembrie 1989* (Iaşi, Polirom).

Raţiu, I. (1999) *În fine, acasă: note zilnice, decembrie 1989–decembrie 1990* (Bucharest, Editura Univers).

Rus, A. (2005) *Mentalităţi şi comportamente culturale în spaţiul Văii Jiului*, Unpublished Manuscript, Universitatea Babeş-Bolyai.

Rus, A. (2007) *Mineriadele: între manipulare politică şi solidaritate muncitorească* (Bucharest, Curtea Veche).

Shafir, M. (1990) 'The New Romanian Government', *RFE/RL Report on Eastern Europe*, 1, 2, 12 January, pp. 35–38.

Siani-Davies, P. (2005) *The Romanian Revolution of December 1989* (Ithaca, NY, Cornell University Press).

Smith, A. (2001) 'The Transition to a Market Economy in Romania and the Competitiveness of Exports', in Light, D. & Phinnemore, D. (eds) (2001) *Post-Communist Romania: Coming to Terms with Transition* (Houndmills, Palgrave).

Stănculescu, V. A. & Ursu, D. V. (1990) 'Comunicat din partea Ministerului Apărării Naţionale şi a Ministerului de Interne', *Armata poporului*, 27 June.

Tismaneanu, V. (2003) *Stalinism for All Seasons: A Political History of Romanian Communism* (Berkeley, CA, University of California Press).

Uba, T. C. (1990) 'Petroşani: acolo, sub pămînt, nu poţi face politică', *Expres*, 33/34, August.

Ursu, D. V. (2008) *Ministru de Interne (I)* (Bucharest, Editura CD Press).

Vasi, I. B. (2004) 'The Fist of the Working Class: The Social Movements of the Jiu Valley Miners in Post-Socialist Romania', *East European Politics and Societies*, 18, 1, February, pp. 132–57.

Verdery, K. (1996) *What Was Socialism, and What Comes Next?* (Princeton, NJ, Princeton University Press).

Watts, L. (2003) *Control and Oversight of Security Intelligence in Romania*, Working Paper No. 111 (Geneva, Geneva Centre for the Democratic Control of Armed Forces).

A Post-Socialist Capitalism

NIGEL SWAIN

IN THE TWO DECADES OR SO FOLLOWING 1989, the countries of East Central Europe[1] were transformed into market economies and liberal democracies, and became members of NATO and the European Union. Both the economic and the political transformations were radical; indeed the transition from socialism to capitalism was without precedent. Prior to the changes in East Central Europe, the (endogenous) development of capitalism in Europe has been much analysed by historians;[2] and political economists had investigated the externally driven integration of 'under-developed' and formerly colonial countries into global economic systems.[3] However, it was a step into the unknown to contemplate the creation of capitalism out of a developed, highly articulated socio-economic entity that had, with some success, been a significant challenger to the West for a number of decades. Based on central planning and with around 90% of the economy in state ownership of the means of production, distribution and exchange, East Central Europe under communist rule had been dominated by political structures that had rejected whole-heartedly both private ownership and the very logic of the market.

The following analysis seeks to identify the genesis and *differentia specie* of this post-socialist capitalism. It is empirical but not empiricist in conception. It is informed theoretically by the following scarcely contentious propositions: that what has emerged in post-socialist Eastern Europe is a form of capitalism; that it is a historically unique form of capitalism since, however the experience of the 1945–1989 period might be branded (for example as socialism, state socialism, state capitalism, or deformed workers' state), the transition from that socio-economic entity to capitalism had not happened before; and that it is therefore analytically useful to try to identify its specific characteristics.

Post-socialist capitalist democracy in Eastern Europe was fired in the crucible of four forces. The first of these was the socialist legacy, which left its imprint in the social, cultural and economic spheres. The second was equally an element of the

[1] This essay deals primarily with the six formerly communist-ruled countries that were neither parts of the former Soviet Union, nor the former Yugoslavia, and that have become EU members: Poland, the Czech Republic, Slovakia, Hungary, Romania and Bulgaria.

[2] See for example Hilton (1978), Thompson (1968), Landes (1966) and Holton (1985).

[3] See for example Amin (1977), Frank (1972) and Alavi (1972); also see the special issue on capitalism in Africa of *Review of African Political Economy*, 4, 8 (1977).

socialist past, but it operated against much of the legacy: the domestic political agents that emerged from late socialism to overthrow it and create the early post-socialist polity. The third force was the attitude of the major international political actors, to a lesser extent NATO, but in particular the European Union (EU); while the fourth also operated internationally, but was wholly economic: the transnational corporations (TNCs), which were mostly but, not uniquely, based in Western Europe. These four forces interacted in different ways in the creation of a post-socialist economy, society and polity, each of which is considered in turn in the following sections.

Market economies (with post-socialist characteristics)[4]

Three features of socialism's economic legacy were of determining importance for the manner in which the capitalist transformation, and privatisation as its *sine qua non*, took place after 1989. The first was the absence of a market to establish a universally recognised measure of value. The 40-year experiment to create an economy based on a calculus of socially necessary labour time left a legacy in which disputes of the overvaluation or undervaluation of assets would be unavoidable and irresoluble. The second was the low level of domestic personal savings with which assets might be purchased; and the third was the socialist economy's 'lack of international product competitiveness in quality rather than price' (Martin 1999, p. 86). Socialist economies were characterised by state-owned enterprises that were large (but not very large, and certainly not transnational), inefficient and organised for mass production. After 40 years of operating in an economic environment where prices did not reflect opportunity costs (Boltho 1971, p. 65); where 'total factor productivity' failed to improve (Swain 1998, pp. 202–4); where managers were motivated to continue with old technology, rather than risk innovation; such enterprises were of questionable viability by the last decade of the twentieth century.[5] These three features together created a context for privatisation which Mandelbaum characterised as 'selling assets with no value to people with no money' (1993, p. 6). There was, however, a fourth determining element in socialism's economic legacy: its disproportionate focus on industry. Sectors which dominated post-industrial, Western economies were weak or entirely absent. East Central European economies were economies with gaps that were ripe for exploitation, however unattractive their manufacturing industries. The focus on industry also meant that industrialisation had outstripped urbanisation, resulting in under-urbanisation and an unusually rural-based proletariat (Konrad & Szelenyi 1974; Kideckel 1993, pp. 63–64; Swain 1994, pp. 30–32).

Throughout the early-1990s there were heated debates between politicians and academics about the best mechanism for privatisation and the relative merits of 'shock therapy' and 'gradualism'. Radical reformers clustered around the former; managers and civil servants tended to favour the latter, but, from the perspective of two decades later, it was the common features of the socialist legacy, rather than the policies of the

[4]For a concise assessment of the first dozen or so years of the economic transition, see Dyker (2004, pp. 291–321); for an economic and social history of the region since 1973, see Berend (2009).

[5]See for example Hughes and Hare (1991, p. 80).

early post-socialist political actors, that counted.[6] 'Shock therapy' was quietly abandoned as soon as the 'shock' became politically unacceptable at home.[7] Furthermore, specific privatisation techniques did not affect the long-term outcome. The absence of domestic savings and the international unattractiveness of the assets on sale meant that most enterprises were sold off cheaply (by any measure of their value), mostly to their workforces and managers (because, these were the only people who had an interest in them).[8] International investors cherry-picked the few manufacturing 'crown jewels' which had an international reputation, such as Škoda or Tungsram, or companies which offered a virtual monopoly market share, such as tobacco or the food industry (Radice 1995, p. 296); and, later in the 1990s, they moved into utilities (which guaranteed a reasonable return) and banking and finance (which were essentially virgin territory).

The overwhelming unattractiveness of socialism's manufacturing legacy, and the exclusion from the realm of real-world possibilities of any 'East Asian' solution based on preserving a Comecon block that would be allowed temporarily to protect its own industries,[9] resulted in severe economic recession, a recession which lasted almost a decade in the more developed countries, and much more than a decade in the countries which had historically been less developed.

Nevertheless, the private sector grew rapidly in the first post-socialist decade, as Table 1 indicates, and the biggest engine behind the growing dominance of the private sector in the region was new company formation. As Estrin notes (1994, p. 13), 'The bulk of new firms everywhere, and of private sector jobs everywhere with the

TABLE 1
ECONOMIC PERFORMANCE 1989–2009

	Real GDP 1989 = 100			*Private Sector Share of GDP*		
	1995	*1998*	*2009**	*1995*	*1998*	*2009*
Bulgaria	76	66	108	45	65	75
Czech Republic	85	93	135	70	75	80
Hungary	86	95	127	60	80	80
Poland	99	117	181	60	65	75
Romania	84	78	117	55	60	70
Slovakia	84	99	156	60	75	80

Note: *denotes estimate.
Source: EBRD Economic Analyses and Forecasts, available at http://www.ebrd.com/pages/research/analysis/forecasts.shtml, accessed 18 February 2011.

[6]Dyker sees no clear-cut correlation between macroeconomic shock therapy and general success in transition in terms of rates of growth of GDP and productivity (2004, p. 349).

[7]It was abandoned except in the sense of opening up the Eastern economies to Western competition and prohibiting protecting domestic industries (Gowan 1995); for Gowan this is the essence of 'shock therapy' (1996, p. 130). For the abandonment of 'shock therapy' in Poland, see Myant (1993, p. 85).

[8]Earle and Estrin (1996, p. 29) give figures for the scale of employee (including management) companies. For comparative privatisation strategies, see Frydman *et al.* (1993).

[9]Amsden *et al.* (1994) make a powerful case for such policies, but no mainstream international organisation supported them.

possible exceptions of Czechoslovakia and Hungary, have emerged *de novo*, and primarily in small-scale service, construction, transport and retail firms'. The UN similarly noted a 'rapid expansion of new private businesses' in the mid-1990s (UN/ECE 1995, p. 72). Meanwhile, Johnson and Loveman attributed Poland's impressive early economic performance to its new private sector which had developed 'from scratch' (1995 pp. 8–9, 134–35), and Kostova noted the emergence of private companies 'from below' in Bulgaria (2000, p. 199). Moreover, Estrin's minor reservations about Hungary were not borne out by later figures: Laki reports individual proprietorships doubling between 1989 and 1993 to roughly seven million, while limited liability companies quadrupled to around 86,000. The latter almost tripled again by 2005, while the former rather stagnated (Laki 2008, pp. 124–25).

The reaction of most enterprises (whether state-owned or privatised) to the collapse of Comecon markets and trade liberalisation was to seek out new markets for existing products rather than develop new ones for which they lacked the necessary capital. They were trapped, selling products which lacked international competitiveness, and mired in inter-enterprise debt, which in 1991 represented around 50% of GDP (Martin 1999, pp. 84, 95). Moreover, with the encouragement of the EU, 'Western companies were attacking regional markets when indigenous firms were least capable of responding successfully' (Martin 1999, p. 134). The role of the EU, while it was most influential in the political sphere, also had an impact in the economic sector. EU accession negotiations proved to be a forum through which national governments of existing members could prosecute the interest of their national champions (Baun 2000, p. 213), while the Association Agreements, which were quickly introduced as part of the EU's aid package to the region, were criticised for favouring Western companies. While tariff adjustments favoured the applicant countries, the non-tariff barriers of the existing members were left in place, resulting in a tripling of EU exports to the region between 1989 and 1994 (Gowan 1995, pp. 25–28; Pollert 1999, p. 86; Martin 1999, p. 134).

It has been suggested that the interest of Western European TNCs in the region coincided with a period when North American companies were shifting production to their cheap-labour, less regulated 'back yard' in Latin America, and Japanese companies were doing likewise in East Asia (Berend 2009, p. 117; Kurz & Wittke 1998, pp. 63–64). Certainly labour costs at the beginning of the transformation were only 7% of those of the EU, and had only increased to 15% by 2001;[10] and socialist economies had been notoriously lax when it came to health and safety or environmental legislation. Western European companies, however, were equally concerned about markets. Dyker concludes that 'foreign investors have been more concerned to access markets than factors of production' (2004, p. 358); and Martin is persuaded that it was the region as a market that first attracted the interest of Western companies (1999, p. 142).[11] In the two post-socialist decades, China became the cheap, less-regulated workhouse of the whole world, not just of Japan; but East Central

[10]In Poland, Hungary, Slovakia, Slovenia and the Czech Republic labour costs in 2001 still stood at roughly a quarter, but in Romania and Bulgaria nearer a tenth of the European Union average, calculated at exchange rate parity. Even using the purchasing power parity measure, Eastern European wages only increased to between 30% and 35% of EU levels (Berend 2009, pp. 121–22).

[11]See also Pollert (1999, pp. 112–16) and Radice (1995, p. 294).

Europe's poorly developed consumer industries, its underdeveloped infrastructure, and its non-existent financial services industries offered market opportunities for Western European-based companies, and other TNCs, especially in the food and retail industries, the media, telecommunications and banking (Berend 2009, pp. 118–20).[12]

In the mid-1990s, in the view of the World Bank, the region had 'absorbed only a modest share of capital flows' (Martin 1999, p. 138), but, as the prospects of EU membership increased, so too did the likelihood that shortcomings with regard to clear ownership, transparency and uniform tax regulations would disappear. It was these shortcomings, along with the hesitancy to implement what Svejnar termed 'Type II' reforms—'the development and enforcement of laws, regulations and institutions that would ensure a successful market-oriented economy' (2002, p. 5)—that had put investors off. EU membership and the conditionality associated with it turned early 'low-commitment strategies' (simply marketing) into 'high commitment' strategies, such as joint ventures and wholly owned subsidiaries (Martin 1999, pp. 132–52). By the turn of the millennium, foreign companies in Poland and the Czech Republic accounted for at least 27% of employment, 53% of investment, 42% of sales and 59% of industrial exports, and the ratios were at least half as large again for Hungary (Berend 2009, p. 115). By 2008, between 76.5% (Poland) and 99.2% (Slovakia) of total banking assets of the six East Central European countries were in foreign hands.[13] Although some of this investment offered the possibility of 'complementary specialisation' and technological advance for Eastern European firms (Berend 2009, p. 124; Kurz & Wittke 1998, p. 65), Kurz and Wittke see the driving force to be structural adaptation by Western European companies (1998, pp. 77–78), and a study of the Central European automotive industry noted the region's 'heightened dependence on external forces' (Sadler 2003, p. 116). Dyker questioned the knock-on benefits of such investments, noting that 'even the most advanced transition economies have struggled to generate locally owned supply industries' (2004, p. 12). Both dependency and prospects are reflected in IBM's changing investment in Hungary. It invested in a hard-disk manufacturing plant employing 4,000 people in western Hungary in 1994, but closed it in 2002 and moved towards computer services. By 2008 it provided only 800 service jobs at the old location, but almost twice as many in new offices in Budapest.[14]

Turning to the domestic sector, small and medium-sized enterprises (SMEs), which are seen as central to transition success by supporting employment and introducing innovation and flexibility, moved into sectors where the socialist economy had been weak. However, according to Dallago and McIntyre, citing their own findings and the European Bank for Reconstruction and Development (EBRD)'s Transition Report

[12]Pollert paints a similar picture (1999, pp. 112–16), as does Martin (1999, p. 143). In the mid-1990s West European TNCs comprised some three quarters of FDI stock in Hungary and Bulgaria, and two thirds in the Czech Republic, Slovakia and Poland (Pollert 1999, p. 115).

[13]Taken from the EBRD's Structural Change Indicators available at: http://www.ebrd.com/pages/research/analysis/forecasts.shtml, accessed 18 February 2011.

[14]See also Pollert (1999, pp. 116–21) and Hardy (2009, pp. 87–90). For IBM, see Berend (2009, p. 129), and the following websites: http://www-05.ibm.com/employment/hu/idc/history.html; http://www-05.ibm.com/employment/hu/ibmissc/history.html; http://www.hartford-hwp.com/archives/63/143.html, all accessed 18 February 2011.

1999, their development was unsatisfactory. In some countries the sector remained small; in others, such as Poland and Hungary, it was more extensive but operated in niche markets and was not competitive. SMEs were concentrated in the personal services and construction, where returns were rapid and little investment was required (Dallago & McIntyre 2003, p. 210; EBRD 1999, pp. 150–59). Dallago and McIntyre also noted problems concerning 'concentration in trade (especially retailing), aversion to investment and growth, pursuit of rapid returns on investment, use of labour-intensive and traditional techniques, and involvement in the irregular economy' (2003, p. 214).[15] Making use of Richard Scase's distinction between 'entrepreneurship' and 'proprietorship', they considered post-socialist SMEs to be characterised by the latter: the pursuit of gain without long-term accumulation, using assets for personal consumption or trade (Scase 2003). Furthermore, the businesses themselves were very small. Between 90% and 96% of SMEs in transitional economies were in the 'micro-business' group (0–9 employees), and the levels of self-employment (around 20%) were twice the OECD average, although lower than Latin America and Asia (Glinkina 2003, p. 59). They also constituted a relatively small sector of the economy. Dyker reported that companies of up to 100 employees accounted for only 10% of employees in most countries in the region (20% in Poland and Hungary), compared with 50% for the EU as a whole (2004, p. 309).

It is perhaps in the agricultural sector that elements of a socialist legacy were most visible in post-socialist capitalism; yet it was also in agriculture that the EU exercised a profound and perverse influence. The dual structure of socialist agriculture, based on large-scale collectively worked farms and small-scale household plots, was maintained into the post-socialist era based on private ownership, as many studies have confirmed.[16] Non-land assets became concentrated within farms which, to varying degrees in different countries, were owned by private individuals, companies, or cooperatives; and they operated on a huge scale by Western European standards. Land ownership, however, remained in tiny (often notional) parcels, owned by countless individuals who received *de facto* as well as *de jure* ownership in 1992. Some of these small owners in rural communities attempted to farm for subsistence needs, along with many urban unemployed and commuting workers created by the region's under-urbanisation. Indeed those who owned land were effectively obliged to do so in Romania and Poland because they did not qualify for unemployment benefit (Swain & Vincze 2001, p. 176; Borowicz 1996, p. 20), but the bulk of the land was rented to the small number of large-scale farms that produced most of the food (Swain 2004, pp. 212–19); and producers seemed content with such land market 'imperfections', which were generally attributed to high transaction costs, including the persistence of co-ownership, asymmetrical knowledge and rights between owners and renters, and to imperfect competition (Ciaian & Swinnen 2006, pp. 799–802).[17] Some assume that a land market will spring into motion once the prohibitions on the purchase of land by

[15]See also Glinkina (2003, p. 62).

[16]See for example Swain (1999), Sarris *et al.* (1999), Pouliquen (2001), Ciaian and Swinnen (2006, p. 813) and Gorton *et al.* (2009).

[17]See also Lerman (2001, p. 100; 2004, p. 181).

non-resident foreigners are removed,[18] but this does not explain the failure of a domestic market to develop over the past 20 years; and the restrictions on land purchase did not keep foreigners out of Eastern European agriculture, certainly not out of Hungary where they operated with higher capital intensity than their domestic neighbours.[19]

This unusual structure of farming has accentuated the perversity of the EU's Common Agricultural Policy (CAP). The rule of thumb for critics of the CAP is that 80% of subsidies go to 20% of farmers (Grant 1997, p. 77). Recent research in Hungary revealed that some 70% of subsidies went to only 7% of farmers (Biró 2010, p. 77); data from Romania suggested an even starker imbalance (0.5% of farms eligible for 21% of support) (Gorton *et al.* 2009, p. 1313); while the organisation 'farmsubsidy.org' reported that the top 10% of recipients in 2008 received 75% of payments in the Czech Republic, 87% in Slovakia, but only 42% in Poland (similar to Denmark and midway between France and Germany).[20] At the same time, rural development lines of support, which might have benefited the rural poor, were not pursued (Gorton *et al.* 2009, p. 1310; Swain 2004, p. 211).

Capitalist society (with post-socialist characteristics)

In contrast to the economic structures, when considering the social structures created by post-socialist capitalism, socialism's social and cultural legacy played a more significant role. This section will first consider the social characteristics of the motor of a capitalist economy—capital and labour—before turning to social differentiation in terms of income, gender and race.

As far as capital and labour are concerned, two features of the socialist legacy were particularly significant. First, socialism created a 'service class' (Goldthorpe 1980, p. 40), rather than a 'bourgeoisie', a highly educated professional middle class, but without entrepreneurs. This service class shared a common, rather conventionally bourgeois culture, and developed personal ties both through general social contacts and, in particular, through Party membership.[21] It lacked economic capital, but it did not want for human and social capital. Second, economic performance required improvisation and innovation, but low levels of personal risk. Within socialism's large, inefficient, industrial and mass-production-based enterprises, neither management nor labour was encouraged to innovate according to their formal job descriptions. Management was motivated to defend its privileges, and labour to fulfil its norms; yet successful managers were those who could use informal channels to overcome endemic shortages of materials and supplies, while workers were also challenged by shortages and were obliged to innovate at the workface, in a way that was unknown amongst Western 'deskilled' labour. Outside the workplace, the tendency to retreat into the household and focus on consumption, that students of the GDR termed a 'niche society' (Gaus 1986), took place in the absence of large home-improvement stores:

[18]See Tesser (2004) for the security dimension to this issue.

[19]See figures provided by Biró (2010, pp. 29, 37).

[20]Available at: http://farmsubsidy.org/, accessed 18 February 2011.

[21]For the Party as a vector for networking, see Róna-Tas and Böröcz (2000, p. 218).

DIY also required improvisation, innovation and exploiting contacts.[22] In the interplay between the first and second economy, socialist sector jobs were secure; and workers used their innovation and improvisation in the 'second economy' in the knowledge that they could not lose their state sector jobs.[23]

It has become something of a commonplace to claim that the old political elites of late socialism converted their political capital into economic capital to become the economic elite of post-socialist capitalism; and there is a general truth to it, but it is a claim that lacks precision, as Eyal *et al.* have demonstrated in the case of the Czech Republic, Hungary and Poland at least (Eyal *et al.* 1998).[24] Their evidence is clear. Leading members of the '*nomenklatura*' were downwardly mobile; those who benefitted were the second rank, technocratic elite, and the less political elements of the socialist 'service class'. Such individuals were often members of the Party of course, and benefited from the social capital advantages that Party membership endowed, but they had not been members of the political apparatus (Eyal *et al.* 1998, pp. 117, 120). Słomczynski and Shabad reported produced broadly similar results: it was former middle managers, not the top managers who became entrepreneurs; and Party membership was not of itself an asset (1996, pp. 175–77). Róna-Tas and Böröcz found, for Bulgaria as well as the trinity of countries studied by Eyal *et al.,* that most of the new post-socialist economic elite had been socialist-era managers, that they were disproportionately likely to be Party members, and yet being a party functionary in itself gave no significant advantage (Róna-Tas & Böröcz 2000, p. 223).

Eyal *et al.* then claimed that what was developing in post-socialist Central Europe was 'capitalism without capitalists', that the new economic elites were not the owners of the resources that they controlled. The data that they collected in 1993 seemed to bear this out; but subsequent data, collected in the spring and autumn of 1996 in Hungary only, suggested two significant developments. First, analysis of the same firms as investigated in 1993 showed a sharp decline in public ownership at the expense of foreign ownership. Second, data from a different, smaller sample of enterprises revealed 'the Great Bank Robbery of 1993–96', that is to say a 'massive increase in the proportion of firms reporting ownership by domestic individuals' between 1993 and 1996 so that 'a fairly sizeable propertied bourgeoisie emerged between 1993 and 1996'. However, they were reluctant to accept that either development undermined their theory of post-communist managerialism (Eyal *et al.* 1998, pp. 116, 153–56), although what the evidence seemed to show was that while 'fuzzy' ownership had been maintained between 1989 and 1993, by the middle of the first post-socialist decade, private ownership by foreign and domestic owners was becoming ever more dominant, as Table 1 suggests. Certainly in the former collective farm sector, leading managers were attempting to establish ownership as well as control during this period (Kovács 1998). The evidence from Poland too suggests that, over a 10-year period, the

[22]For a Hungarian example, see Kenedi (1981).

[23]Likewise, for the most entrepreneurial private ventures of late socialism, the market was secure because they plugged the shortage gaps of the first economy; the key skill-set required was innovation in resourcing (because of shortage) rather than marketing. I am grateful to Bruno Dallago for this observation.

[24]Russia, Bulgaria and Slovakia were also included in the research, but not in the analysis presented in the book.

ownership of 'employee companies' (much more numerous in Poland than elsewhere) became concentrated in the hands of management, or outsiders, or both (Tittenbrun 2005),[25] even though, as Hanley argued, in 1993 workers' councils appeared to be successfully blocking the transfer of ownership rights to members of the communist-era elite (1999, p. 175).[26]

The data by Eyal *et al.* on the background of the new economic elite were confirmed in a Hungarian study published over a decade later, although not based on such a large and representative sample (Laki & Szalai 2006); and by this time it was clear that the elite consisted of business owners. Of the owner–managers that Laki and Szalai interviewed, all came from the service class in that all had spent some time employed in the state or cooperative sector of the socialist economy, and most had spent more than half of their working days in that sector (2006, p. 325). Laki and Szalai also noted distinct trajectories related to previous Party membership: 'Former Party members acquired property mainly by the privatisation of their working places', whereas, 'the majority of non-Party members were not involved in privatisation but founded new companies' (2006, p. 325).[27] Those who participated in privatisation were also more likely to have remained in the socialist sector right up to 1989, while those who established new businesses from scratch were more likely to have already left it by that date (2006, p. 326).[28] Johnson and Loveman's survey of new Polish entrepreneurs reported not dissimilar findings. Some 85% had worked previously in the state sector. Some left state employment before 1980, but more did so over the course of the 1980s and into the 1990s; and many had been involved in Solidarity (*Solidarność*) and were disillusioned by socialism (Johnson & Loveman 1995, pp. 108–9, 112). Cătălin Stoica's study of Romania also reveals both 'cadre' and 'from below' paths to employer status.[29]

Szelényi and his colleagues had investigated the role of pre-socialist family status on embourgeoisement even before communism collapsed (1988). In the post-socialist era, Róna-Tas and Böröcz found that the post-socialist economic elite of 1993 in Bulgaria,

[25]I know of no equivalent work for Romania where employee ownership was even more significant (see Earle & Estrin 1996, p. 29).

[26]The 'capitalism without capitalists' thesis was informed in part by an influential article by David Stark on recombitant forms of property, by which he meant a process whereby former managers were active in both the state and private sectors, but centralised their assets in the private sector and their liabilities in the socialist sector (1996). That manipulations of this type took place is not in doubt. It was one of the features of Hungarian 'spontaneous privatisation' and Polish '*nomenklatura* privatisation' that their early post-socialist governments tried to stamp out; it continued into the later 1990s in the Czech Republic where the term 'tunnelling' was invented to describe it; in Romania and Bulgaria the term 'parasitic privatisation', describing essentially the same process, was in use throughout the 1990s; for Bulgaria, see Kostova (2000, p. 199). The beneficent state, however, could not take over private liabilities forever, as the Czech government learnt to its cost in 1997.

[27]This is in line with the earlier findings of Böröcz and Róna-Tas, who found that the path from socialist-era to post-socialist entrepreneur was more common in Hungary than elsewhere (1995, pp. 772–74).

[28]Emblematic representatives of these trajectories in Hungary might be former socialist party Prime Minister Ferenc Gyurcsány on the one hand and *FIDESZ*-supporting, former boss of a small cooperative Gábor Széles on the other. (The term 'small cooperative' refers to a specific legal type covered by Hungarian legislation.)

[29]Because her definition of 'cadre' is rather broad, her findings do not significantly contradict the findings of Eyal *et al.* (Stoica 2004).

the Czech Republic, Hungary and Poland were likely to be descended from grandparents who owned a business in 1948 (2000, p. 221). Johnson and Loveman found that in Poland, while on average only 23.6% reported that their families had been in business before 1948, this proportion was 45% amongst those who founded their business before 1980, 15% for businesses founded in 1988–1989, rising to 22% for those founded in the 1990s (1995, p. 111). Laki and Szalai also addressed the issue. For them the key factors that gave the post-socialist entrepreneurs their advantage were an orientation to education (and in particular selection of secondary school by ambitious parents) and work learned in the socialist era (2006, pp. 330–34). However, the motivations behind these orientations were various; and pre-socialist familial status played a role in their genesis. They identified four life-history profiles:[30] the 'upwardly mobile', 'status convergers', 'status restorers' and 'self-made men' (and they are overwhelmingly men). The parents of 'status convergers' had lost their bourgeois status with the advent of socialism, retreated out of the limelight (into perhaps what Szelényi would term a 'parking orbit' (1988, pp. 61–76)), but instilled in their children bourgeois culture and life-skills such as languages as well as an antipathy to the Party; none of this group were Party members. Inherited elements of a bourgeois cultural capital, it would seem, were one of a number of factors which could implant in certain individuals the psychological orientation necessary to maximise the social and human capital resources that they had gained from their socialist education and membership of the service class to become post-socialist capitalists.[31]

Turning from capital to labour, in Poland, Hungary and Bulgaria, the demands for independent trade unions were integral to the 1989 revolution, and, in Poland in particular, *Solidarność* as a trade union pursued a political agenda (Ost 2001, p. 81), as in many ways did Bulgaria's *Podkrepa* (Gradev 2001, p. 126). Even where trade unions had not been political actors, laws were quickly passed in line with international labour standards, guaranteeing freedom of association, the right to strike and to free collective bargaining (Pollert 1999, pp. 136–39). Also, communist-era trade unions quickly democratised themselves and, in Romania, unusually, the unions became identified with post-socialist political parties (Kideckel 2001, p. 105). In the early post-socialist years, encouraged by the International Labour Organisation, tripartite industrial relations structures emerged (Pollert 1999, p. 141; Myant *et al.* 2000, p. 723; Martin 1999, pp. 109–13), but by the middle of the 1990s it was clear, certainly in Hungary, Poland and Czechoslovakia (and subsequently in the Czech Republic), that unions were weak, unequal partners (Pollert 1999, p. 144). Tripartitism operated as a medium for social consultation only (Myant *et al.* 2000, p. 736).[32] This was categorised by Ost as 'illusory corporatism ... neocorporatist forms are being used to generate neoliberal outcomes' (Ost 2000, p. 504).

At the local level, industrial relations were characterised by fragmentation, disorganisation and the absence of industry-level bargaining, the consequence of weak employers' associations and TNC disinterest in bargaining at this level; unions

[30]The 'self-made men' profile is discussed in footnote 12 (Laki & Szalai 2006, p. 330).

[31]Clearly there would be fewer 'status converger' entrepreneurs in countries where the bourgeoisie was less well developed prior to socialism.

[32]They give a much more nuanced account of Czech and Slovak tripartitism than is possible here.

faced the shrinking of their stronghold in the state sector and barriers to organisation in the private sector (Pollert 1999, pp. 146–47). In the first five years of transformation there were only two incidences of strike action being taken against a TNC, both of which were unsuccessful (Pollert 1999, pp. 124–28). Trade unions generally cooperated with restructuring plans and did not oppose labour-shedding, although Polish and Slovak trade unions defended working patterns more successfully than those of Hungary or the Czech Republic. They focused on communications and negotiating the annual collective agreement, not day-to-day issues of work organisation and increased flexibility (Pollert 1999, pp. 149–52), and Czech workers at least preferred to consult their first-line managers rather than their unions (Martin 1999, p. 116). Furthermore, workers' councils, which in Poland had enjoyed powers to veto privatisation, were lost when state enterprises were 'corporatised', as they were in Hungary; while the Czechoslovak equivalents, which had been dominated by the trade unions, were dissolved in April 1990 (Frydman *et al.* 1993, pp. 109, 141, 203–6; Pollert 1999, p. 135). In addition, demands for greater labour flexibility resulted in the use of self-employment contracts, the growth of employment agencies and in particular the spread of 'fractional contracts' for female supermarket workers, as Hardy reports for Poland (2009, pp. 123–24, 179). This decline in trade union power—'the dog that did not bark' (Martin 1999, p. 105)—cannot be divorced from the dramatic increases in unemployment (but to very different levels in each country) that accompanied the post-socialist recession and its aftermath, which are given in Table 2.

As market forces came to dominate post-socialist economies and the state's commitment to providing employment disappeared, options appeared to be stark: employment, entrepreneurship, casual employment, or surviving from benefits.[33] Entrepreneurs were, in the main, self-employed, force-of-circumstance entrepreneurs, accustomed to socialism's mutually supporting first and second economies, for whom Scase's 'proprietorship' was the norm. Juggling a multitude of income sources, including formal and informal economies, 'black', 'social' and 'household', remained central to post-socialist survival strategies (Wallace & Latcheva 2006). Wallace and

TABLE 2

UNEMPLOYMENT AS A SHARE OF LABOUR FORCE (%)

	1990	*1993*	*1996*	*1999*	*2002*	*2005*	*2008*
Bulgaria	1.6	16.3	13.0	17.0	16.8	10.1	5.1
Czech Republic	0.7	4.3	3.9	8.5	7.0	7.9	n/a
Hungary	1.4	11.9	9.9	7.0	5.8	7.3	7.8
Poland	6.5	16.4	13.2	15.1	20.0	16.9	6.7
Romania	n/a	10.4	6.6	6.8	8.4	5.9	4.4
Slovakia	1.2	14.4	11.3	16.2	18.5	16.2	9.6

Source: EBRD Economic Analyses and Forecasts, available at http://www.ebrd.com/pages/research/analysis/forecasts.shtml, accessed 18 February 2011.

[33]See Bodnár's article based on Budapest's Moscow Square's informal labour market (1998), which is also considered by Sik (2002, p. 12). Sik (1992) presents a more theoretical analysis.

Haerpfer used the New Democracies Barometer to trace the importance of formal and informal economies as sources of income for family survival in the 1990s. Although the formal economy was more important in Central Europe than in the Balkans, 90% of households were active in informal economies as either their first or second source of income, and even in Central Europe, one third of households were primarily dependent on the informal economy (household, social or cash) (Wallace & Haerpfer 2002, pp. 35–38). In Romania the informal economy increased from 33.6% of GDP in 1995 to 38.3% in 2000 (Ciupagea 2002, p. 191), while in Hungary the share of the 'hidden economy' peaked in 1993 at 33.1% of GDP, from 25.2% in 1989, and then fell in 1998 to 20.8% (Tóth & Sik 2002, p. 221).[34]

The introduction of market forces into formerly planned economies unsurprisingly also introduced market patterns of social inequality. Socialism had operated with a much narrower spread of social inequality than Western market economies, not least because there was no significant source of wealth other than income, and incomes were considerably controlled (Ferge 1979, pp. 168–70; Lane 1971, pp. 72–79; Lovenduski & Woodall 1987, p. 164). This legacy was undone in the first two post-socialist decades. The spread of inequality as measured by the Gini coefficient increased everywhere between the end of socialism and at least 2002, as Table 3 indicates.[35] Furthermore, Eurostat data from the new millennium cited by Hardy suggested that income inequality was still increasing and was approaching the EU25 average by 2005, and in Poland, income inequalities were considerably higher than the EU25 average (Hardy 2009, p. 132).[36]

As social inequality increased, so too did poverty. Table 3 reports the available 1990s data and suggests that absolute poverty was not insignificant everywhere, except in the Czech Republic, and relative poverty was significant everywhere. Also, as late as

TABLE 3
INDICES OF POVERTY AND INEQUALITY

	Poverty indicators %			*GINI* per capita *household income*		
	Date	*$4.30 per day*	*Relative poverty*	*1989–1990*	*1994–1995*	*2001–2002*
Bulgaria	1995*	18.2	13.3	23.3	38.4	37.0
Czech Republic	1996	0.8	5.0	19.8	21.6	23.4
Hungary	1997	15.4	7.9	22.5	24.2	26.7
Poland	1998	18.4	16.9	27.5	32.1	35.3
Romania	1998	44.5	12.6	23.7	30.6	35.3
Slovakia	1997	8.6	n/a	n/a	23.7	26.7

Note: *relative poverty figure is from 1997.
Sources: UN/ECE *Economic Survey of Europe*, 2004, No. 1, pp. 169–70; Heyns (2005, p. 174).

[34]For more qualitative accounts of informal economic activity, see Bridger and Pine (1998) and other contributions to Neef and Stănculescu (2002).

[35]Earlier data are given by Milanovic (1999, pp. 340–41) and Bunce (1999, p. 765). UN/ECE (2004, p. 167) gives GINI earnings figures until 2001.

[36]A more up-to-date table can be found at: http://epp.eurostat.ec.europa.eu/tgm/table.do?tab=table&init=1&language=en&pcode=tsdsc260&plugin=0, accessed 18 February 2011.

2002, the populations of Eastern Europe spent a much greater proportion of their household budgets on food (a standard proxy for poverty) than the old member states: ranging from 23.2% in the Czech Republic to 51.9% in Romania, compared to the EU15 figures which ranged from 10% to 19%; however, housing costs were much lower (ranging from 13% in Romania to 20% in Hungary, compared with the EU15 range of 20–30% (Heynes 2005, p. 179)). The percentage of the population at risk from poverty increased between 2000 and 2006 throughout Central and Eastern Europe (in countries where data were available) while the EU average remained constant at 16%, although in the two halves of the former Czechoslovakia it still remained below the EU average, while Hungary had reached the EU average by 2006 and Poland and Romania had exceeded it (Hardy 2009, p. 131).[37] The consequences of increasing poverty are illustrated by Hardy for Poland, who describes the case of the *nureks* who scavenge dustbins for paper and cans (Hardy 2009, pp. 129–300), while Smith *et al.* document the emergence of 'in-work' poverty in Bratislava and Kraków (Smith *et al.* 2008).

It has become one of the truisms of post-socialist capitalism that women lost out as a result of the transformation (Einhorn 1993). Even though 'actually existing socialism' lost contact early on with the emancipatory elements of socialism's 'woman question', it did need female labour and pulled women into the labour force, providing generous childcare provision in compensation.[38] In the post-socialist recession, when the logic of the 'cash-nexus' dominated political discourse, cash-strapped local authorities tasked with childcare provision cut back,[39] while enterprises reduced their employment of non-core labour. As a consequence, women were squeezed out of the labour market and back into their conventional roles of housewife and mother. This was most visible in Poland, where the Catholic Church returned to dominance and the ideological pressure on women to return to the household was considerable.[40] Domańsky found that women in Poland were disproportionately represented in the 'underclass', which in his analysis meant outside the labour market (2002), while the Polish state spent around half as much as its neighbours on family policies (Fodor 2005, pp. 18–19). Region-wide, Glass reported that, over time, motherhood had become a barrier to women holding down jobs (2008, p. 776).

In general, unemployment rates for women were higher than those for men (Fodor 2005, p. 7; Pollert 2003, pp. 338–39; 2005, pp. 215–16; Hardy 2009, p. 121), although this was not the case in Hungary (and Slovenia), a phenomenon generally explained by the fact that Hungary's still generous system of maternity benefits meant that a high proportion of women were not in the labour market. The decline in women's employment was much greater than that of men, especially in Hungary (Asztalos Morell 1999, pp. 203–5; Pollert 2003, pp. 338–39; 2005, pp. 215–16; Fodor 2005, p. 6).

[37]A more up-to-date table can be found at: http://epp.eurostat.ec.europa.eu/tgm/table.do?tab=table&init=1&language=en&pcode=tsdsc260&plugin=0, accessed 18 February 2011.

[38]For a good summary, see Pollert (2003, pp. 332–35), Fodor (2005, pp. 2–5) or Hardy (2009, p. 166). Provision was worse in Poland.

[39]Although Fodor (2005, pp. 15–16) reports a less unfavourable picture, partly because demand for childcare fell with a declining birth rate.

[40]See, for example, Hardy (2009, pp. 163, 170–73), Fodor (1997, pp. 471, 479–80), Glass (2008, p. 778) and Heinen and Portet (2009).

The UN's Gender Development Index fell consistently for the Central European countries under consideration here from 1990–1992 to 1998, increasing marginally in 1999 (Pollert 2003, p. 336; UNDP 1991, 1995, 1998, 2000, 2001), although Romanian data suggested a stronger socialist 'gender-equality' legacy in the Balkans (Pollert 2005, p. 215). The gender pay gap after a decade or so of post-socialism, at roughly 80% of comparable male earnings in 2001, was somewhat wider than the pre-accession EU norm, and women were disproportionately represented in the poorer-paying public sector (Pollert 2005, pp. 222–27).

Writing in the 1990s, Fodor argued that, all these negative features notwithstanding, a certain group of women had benefited from the re-evaluation of the financial sector and services generally during the transition (1997, pp. 472, 496). A standard characteristic of socialist enterprises was that finance was undervalued, and thus feminised (Swain 1992, p. 158; Fodor 2005, p. 10; Martin 1999, p. 90). The tertiary sector generally suffered similarly low prestige compared with mass-production-based industrial production (Asztalos Morell 1999, p. 205). With the 'world turned upside down', the services and financial management represented the future;[41] and women were disproportionately equipped with the necessary qualifications.[42] Unfortunately this period of post-socialist comparative advantage for women proved to be relatively short-lived. Fodor noted that by 2001 'women dominated the services to a lesser extent than they used to' (2005, p. 10), even though those women who remained in employment were increasingly concentrated in the service sector. More particularly, in the subsector of banking and financial services, she reported 'an increasing number of men started to claim jobs in financial mediation, and after the mid-1990s, parallel to this, we see an increase in the wage gap as well'.[43] She concluded that, 'not only are women being forced out; those who manage to stay are increasingly ghettoized in the lower paid end of the sector' (Fodor 2005, p. 11), a view confirmed by Glass (2008, p. 775).

For the Roma, there were not even sector-specific, short-term benefits from the transition. Under socialism, Roma had suffered from housing, educational and occupational segregation, and were given minimal opportunities to develop their cultural identity,[44] but socialism's shortage economy, including its labour shortage, had provided them with employment in the 'first economy', while their traditional skills suited them for success in the 'second' (Stewart 1997, pp. 123–24, 264). The security of 'first economy' employment evaporated as lower-grade, unskilled jobs

[41]Martin (1999, p. 89) describes management restructuring to reflect this.

[42]See also Pollert (2005, p. 220). Heynes (2005, p. 180) too reported broadly similar findings. Asztalos Morell (1999, pp. 205–9) provides analogous data for rural women in Hungary, citing figures which indicate that women who lost their jobs when agricultural cooperatives closed down were able to earn higher wages in their new employment than men, and that the proportion of women among managers increased in the post-socialist period. Lengyel and Barta (2000, p. 168) found women disproportionately represented in the banking elite—25% compared with 15% in the elite at large.

[43]The percentage of women employed in the sector fell by around 10 percentage points from the mid-1990s to 2001 in the Czech Republic and Poland, although by only two in Hungary; and their wages as a proportion of men's fell in all three countries, but by widely ranging amounts (14 percentage points in the Czech Republic, eight in Hungary but only one in Poland) (Fodor 2005, p. 11).

[44]See for example Stewart (1990, 1997, pp. 97–111), Guy (1998), Bárány (2002, pp. 112–53), McCagg (1991), Ladányi and Szelényi (2006, pp. 77, 85–87) and Crowe (1994, pp. 20–28, 54–64, 91–102, 135–43).

disappeared from the economy, and full-time survival from the informal economy proved precarious. The extent of the deprivation that this occasioned has been extensively documented (Bárány 2002, pp. 157–201; Stewart 2002, p. 136; Ladányi & Szelényi 2006), and its rural dimension, in part the consequence of under-urbanisation, should not be neglected. While between 75% and 80% of the rather smaller Roma populations of Poland and the Czech Republic were urban residents in the 1990s, in Bulgaria (with one of the biggest Roma populations) only 52% were, and in Hungary and Slovakia (both with large Roma populations) only 40% were (Bárány 2002, pp. 160, 163). Roma poverty was predominantly rural poverty. Ladányi and Szelényi further reported that while in Hungary economic advancement for Roma came from assimilation alone, in Romania and Bulgaria, partly because of their extreme exclusion, wealthy Roma remained in their segregated communities, such as abandoned Saxon villages in Transylvania or ghettoes in Bulgarian cities (Ladányi & Szelényi 2006, p. 19). Socialism had prevented the political exploitation of open anti-Roma sentiment (unlike anti-Semitic sentiment which it occasionally encouraged, such as in Poland in 1968),[45] but in the post-socialist era, violently expressed anti-Roma sentiment became commonplace,[46] and even mainstream politicians promoted anti-Roma rhetoric. The Czech Christian Democrat (*Křesťanská a demokratická unie—Československá strana lidová*) politician Jiří Čunek, for example, based his popularity on his tough policy towards the Roma.

Liberal democracy (with post-socialist characteristics)

In the political sphere, the political actors of late socialism, in particular the opposition movements which engineered revolution in 1989, together with their successors who consolidated democracy, set aside the one-party legacy and created hugely differing political systems which cannot be considered at length here. Indeed, by the imperfect standards of the real world, all of the countries under consideration here counted as democratic. Domestic critics might (and with reason) complain about the quality of democracy in their countries—the particular voting system, the nature of the choice, the extent of corruption, the absence of transparency, the independence (or lack of it) of the media, the state of civil society, and some worryingly extremist nationalist parties; but similar criticisms can be made of the political structures in countries long accepted into the family of Western democracies.[47]

Post-socialist democracies offered the electorate a choice; elections took place at regular intervals; power changed hands smoothly without recourse to violence or extra-parliamentary activities; and, in countries where the Party had had a strong reform wing, the 'return' to government of the former communists in the early 1990s did not diminish the commitment to market strategies. Regimes once dominated by unreformed communist elites took longer to conform to this pattern. In Romania, the

[45]For a recent gloss on these events, see Kunicki (2005).

[46]See the European Roma Right Centre website for up-to-date reports, available at: http://www.errc.org/index.php, accessed 18 February 2011.

[47]See Heywood (2002, p. 84) for a description of the real-world characteristics of a modern democracy.

continuity of the heirs of the Communist Party was broken in 1996; in Bulgaria, where the political power of unreformed communists was overcome by action on the streets as much as electoral change until 1997, the electoral process predominated thereafter; the increasingly authoritarian Vladimír Mečiar was voted out of Slovakian politics in 1998. The post-socialist recession left its mark on post-socialist politics in Hungary, Poland and Bulgaria in the form of pendulum politics: left and right, broadly defined, exchanged power alternately as the electorate despaired of whichever party was in power and voted in the opposition (Swain & Swain 2009, pp. 233–90). This ended in 2001 in Bulgaria (when the National Movement Simeon II [*Nacionalno Dviženie Simeon Vtori*] took over from the Union of Democratic Forces [*Sayuz na demokratichnite sili*]), in 2002 in Hungary (when the socialists were voted in for a second term), and in 2007 in Poland (when a more moderate right-of-centre government replaced its socially conservative and nationalist right-wing).

The main features of post-socialist democracy appear to be a left-of-centre social democratic space filled by former communist parties and a less stable political right where major new parties continue to be formed. The exception to the first of these was the former Czechoslovakia. In the Czech Republic, an unreformed Communist Party continued in existence and received a sizable share of the vote, although never sufficient to be a major party and social democracy was represented by the historic Social Democratic Party (*Česká strana sociálně demokratická*). In Slovakia, not only did the former communists disappear (although they were present in the early post-socialist years), but social democracy also seemed to be absent from the political palette until the victory of *Smer* in 2006. On the political right, in Hungary, *FIDESZ* took almost a decade to supplant the Hungarian Democratic Forum (*Magyar Demokrata Fórum*) and the Smallholders (*Független Kisgazda, Földmunkás és Polgári Párt*); in Poland, the Law and Justice Party (*Prawo i Sprawiedliwość*) and Civic Platform (*Platforma Obywatelska*) coalesced out of former Solidarity groupings; and in Bulgaria, the Union of Democratic Forces was eclipsed by the Simeon II Movement and then Citizens for the European Development of Bulgaria (*Grazhdani za evropeysko razvitie na Balgariya*). In Slovakia, the once-dominant Movement for a Democratic Slovakia (*Hnutie za demokratické Slovensko*) lost to the Slovak Democratic and Christian Union (Slovenská demokratická a kresťanská únia), and a new Freedom and Solidarity party (*Sloboda a Solidarita*) came third in the June 2010 elections; while in the Czech Republic the Greens (*Strana zelených*), Christian Democrats (*Křesťanská a demokratická unie—Československá strana lidová*), and latterly Public Affairs (*Věci veřejné*) and Karel Schwarzenberg's TOP09 (*Tradice Odpovednost Prosperita 09*) became more significant in the second post-socialist decade. Romania represented something of an exception in that the left transmogrified significantly too, and mergers and rebranding were more common than new party formation. The instability of the right reflects in part unresolved tensions in Eastern Europe's 'Janus-faced' nationalism, which feeds off senses of grievance towards historic persecutors (Swain & Swain 2009, p. 240). Nationalist tensions were to some extent neutralised around the turn of the millennium in advance of EU membership, but they reappeared in post-accession politics.

The first decade of post-socialism was an era of national paths to capitalist democracy during which the political forces that had overthrown socialism and their successors could pursue their own visions; but things changed as the century approached its end. 'By the end of 1995, EU policy had shifted firmly onto an irreversible path to enlargement' (Sedelmeier 2005, p. 83),[48] and the EU became a major actor in determining the complexion of post-socialist liberal democracy. Crucially it became increasingly prescriptive about what membership entailed, more prescriptive indeed than it was for existing members.[49] From 1997–1998 onwards, the path to 'Europe' was no longer one of demonstrating movement towards a nationally determined model of 'democratic institutions' and 'a functioning market economy', but of meeting the EU's strict conditionality criteria. Its *acquis communautaire* provided a concrete template for Svejnar's Type II reforms—laws, regulations and institutions that made a private-ownership-based market economy safe (see above). A Commission Opinion of more than 100 pages was published for each country in July 1997 covering political and economic criteria for membership, ability to assume the obligations of membership, and administrative capacity to apply the *acquis*; annual Regular Reports were published in October or November of each subsequent year; and from 2000 onwards these included all 29 chapters of the *acquis*.[50] All chapters had to be signed off, and only when the European Commission was satisfied. Eventually the 'laggards' of Romania and Bulgaria fell into line, although some felt reforms needed to be consolidated still 'from below' (Noutcheva & Bechev 2008, pp. 15–16). Occasionally EU conditionality intruded directly into national politics, such as its judgement on Mečiar (and more extensively on the politics of the former Yugoslavia), but its influence was most significant in the more mundane field of specifying and enforcing the legal and institutional norms of a market economy and democratic polity acceptable to Western European institutions.

It is not fanciful to interpret the post-socialist welfare systems in the region as resulting from EU influence. Given the strident calls for 'shock therapy' and neoliberal policies at the beginning of the 1990s, it is certainly surprising that, at the end of the first two post-socialist decades, they were still so mixed (Ferge 2001, p. 131). Tomasz Inglot's study of the former Czechoslovakia, Hungary and Poland stressed not only continuities from the socialist to the post-socialist periods, but also from the pre-socialist to the socialist: 'So far none of these new democracies decided to replace its original institutional blueprint that had served as the foundation of its social insurance systems throughout all of the twentieth century' (Inglot 2008, p. 297). It would seem to be the case that, as Deacon has argued (2000, p. 159), because EU conditionality was structured around European practice, extreme neoliberal models have been rejected.[51] Indeed, a survey conducted on behalf of the EU concluded that, 'all health care

[48]For a full account of the history of Europe's initial response to 1989 and the subsequent accession negotiations over agreements in Copenhagen, Madrid and Nice, see Sedelmeier (2005, pp. 52–100). For an account of Romania and Bulgaria's progress to membership, see Noutcheva and Bechev (2008).

[49]For increased EU prescriptiveness, see Grabbe (2003), Jacoby (1999) and Schimmelfennig and Sedelmeeier (2005). See also the *Europe-Asia Studies* special section on the 'European Union and Post-Communist Eastern Europe: Conditionality, Legacies and Europeanisation' (Cirtautas & Schimmelfennig 2010; Schimmelfennig & Scholtz 2010; Levitz & Pop-Eleches 2010; Bandelj 2010; Vermeersch 2010).

[50]The Opinions are available at: http://ec.europa.eu/enlargement/press_corner/key-documents/index_archive_en.htm;the Regular Reports available at:http://ec.europa.eu/enlargement/archives/key_documents/reports_1998_en.htm, both accessed 18 February 2011.

[51]Ferge (2001, p. 147) is sceptical, but questions outcomes rather than models.

financing reforms are in the mainstream of the Western European tradition' (Deacon 2000, p. 150). Deacon further noted that, 'The market for private pension schemes ... is small and the financial infrastructure undeveloped. This has meant that the main thrust of the World Bank's pension reform strategy in the region has only been positively responded to in a very limited number of countries such as Hungary [and] Poland since 1998', and that 'health-financing reforms have not been noteworthy for their emphasis on market competition or privatisation except in the fields of dentistry and pharmaceuticals' (Deacon 2000, pp. 154–55). The EU-inspired model nevertheless had some specific features. It has been suggested that means-tested social assistance, often the responsibility of underfunded local authorities, operated in a paternalistic fashion rather than the rights-based pattern of Western democracies (Deacon 2000, p. 154); and Ferge noted 'strong prejudices against the "undeserving poor"' (2001, p. 132).

It is almost universally acknowledged that, despite qualifying as democracies, the surveyed countries suffered from a political culture characterised by 'corruption', and that 'civil society' remained weak;[52] Rose-Ackerman saw Polish and Hungarian democracy as 'unconsolidated' because of the relative absence of civil society there (2007). Instrumental in the reputation for corruption was almost certainly a socialist legacy in which the boundaries between the public and the private had been unclear and conflict-of-interest legislation weak. Sajó also attributes significance to the high levels of clientelism in the emerging political systems, clientelism being, in his view, a central element in Eastern European corruption (1998).[53] Certainly East Central European countries consistently performed poorly (in comparison with Western Europe) in the perceptions of corruption indices produced by Transparency International[54] and the EBRD's and World Bank's Business Environment and Enterprise Performance Surveys, although by 2005 the latter was improving (Anderson & Gray 2006). Throughout the region corruption was sufficiently endemic for almost every regime in every country to have the corrupt practices of its ruling party politicians conveniently exposed in the run-up to elections. Furthermore, at the level of day-to-day 'bureaucratic encounters' between citizens and 'street-level bureaucrats', Miller *et al.* discovered a 'culture of corruption' where the passing over of gifts was perceived to be necessary, although people did not give willingly, nor to the same degree as they perceived it necessary, and did so because of the strong bargaining power of certain officials rather than cultural traditions (2001, pp. 73, 91, 131, 165, 277). Wallace and Latcheva have associated such perceptions of corruption strongly with declining trust in public institutions and in some countries to the South and East with participation in the black economy (2006, p. 99).

The weakness of post-socialist civil society in Hungary was noted by Cox and Vass in the mid-1990s (1994, pp. 161, 175), although they were somewhat more optimistic by the end of the decade (Cox & Vass 2000), while Miszlivetz and Jensen (1998, pp.

[52]Civil society figures as a crucial element in Heywood's definition of a real-world democracy (2002, p. 84).

[53]For corruption in the Czech Republic, see Appel (2001).

[54]Available at: http://www.transparency.org/policy_research/surveys_indices/cpi/2009, accessed 18 February 2011.

84–85) warned that despite an increase in numbers (a process also witnessed in Poland (Ekiert & Kubik 2001, pp. 101–7)), there was a problem of the 'pseudo existence' of many regional NGOs.[55] Rose-Ackerman noted, with particular reference to Hungary and Poland, the region's small number of weakly institutionalised civil society groups, but focused on their lack of funding, limited staffs and absence from policy advocacy (2005, p. 169), as was illustrated in the field of women's NGOs, for example, by Sloat (2005, pp. 439–41). Rose-Ackerman also produced evidence from the European Values Study indicating a much weaker propensity to engage in political activity other than voting and working with parties (2005, p. 10). Howard's analysis of membership in voluntary organisations in older democracies, post-authoritarian countries and post-communist countries found that the average number of memberships in the latter group was half that of the post-authoritarian countries and one third of that of the older democracies. Within the region, Romanians were more active generally, and Romanians and Slovakians were more active in church organisations; Bulgarians were active in only one tenth of the number of organisations that US citizens were (Howard 2003, pp. 62–66). Poland was not included in Howard's survey, but Barnes found that it had an unusually weak civil society (Barnes 1998, p. 127). Although Howard only attempted a causal analysis for Eastern Germany and Russia, the factors that he identified (mistrust of communist organisations, persistence of friendship networks and post-communist disappointment) (2003, pp. 105–9) almost certainly have a more general application.

Conclusion

This essay has identified four forces that influenced the framing of a distinctly post-socialist version of capitalism and liberal democracy that emerged in East Central Europe in the two decades following 1989. The socialist legacy operated in economic, social and cultural spheres. It left a weak economy, not well positioned to respond to the challenges of adjustment and competition, and an economy with gaps, in the services and finance in particular, that waited to be filled. As a consequence of the economic changes labour was very weak too, despite the early political salience in some countries of trade unions. Socialism also left a legacy of an agrarian sector in which medium-sized family farms, for which the EU's CAP had been designed, were absent.

Socialism's social legacy meant that the new capitalists came from a socialist service class (some from families that were originally bourgeois) which was poorly adjusted to a market economy. Meanwhile, workers and consumers were skilled in improvisation, but accustomed to the cushion of employment security. As a consequence, the SME sector was weak, and reliance on informal economic activity continued to be extensive. In the increasing social inequalities and poverty that accompanied market reform, a certain section of women benefited briefly, before motherhood became a barrier generally to retaining employment and competing with men. Under-urbanisation and the collapse of the symbiosis between the first and second economy came together to accentuate the deprivation of the rural Roma. Central features of socialism's cultural legacy were both a lack of clarity concerning the boundary between public and private,

[55]Myant (2005) demonstrates the ambiguity of the term at the highest level of Czech society.

and a withdrawal into the unambiguously private. These had impacts on degrees of corruption and commitment to civil society.

The political agents of late socialism and the transitional period created very different party political regimes which this essay could not study at length (although the importance of the strength of both socialist-era opposition groups and a reform wing within the Party has been noted). Reform communists became the bedrock of a social democratic left (although this did not take place within the old Communist Party in the former Czechoslovakia), while the political right proved less stable. Joining the European Union imposed the perverse arrangements of the Common Agricultural Policy on post-socialist agriculture and the rural economy, and also helped keep welfare systems within a European rather than a neoliberal model. More importantly, it exercised an early influence on the opening of East Central European markets to Western companies; and later on it imposed its *acquis* as a template for the laws, regulations and institutions required by a market economy, offering the promise of stability, security and transparency that attracted TNCs, particularly in conservative sectors such as banking. Although TNCs had immediately seen and acted on market opportunities in the region, and had quickly snapped up the 'crown jewels' of manufacturing, they were slower to develop 'high-commitment' strategies, until the clear prospect of EU membership rendered investment secure. Two decades after 1989 they had built East Central European manufacturing ventures into their wider European operations and dominated sectors such as banking, finance and telecommunications which had scarcely existed under socialism.

Poznanski (2001) has interpreted the high incidence of foreign ownership in the region *ipso facto* as evidence of 'deviant' capitalism. More prosaically, post-socialist capitalism might be seen to have forged a dependent zone within a Europeanised economy. Within this zone elements of the former socialist service class have dominated; Western European levels of inequality were partially mitigated by European welfare systems; women's careers were once again at risk if they opted for motherhood; deep poverty was countered by extensive activity in the informal economy; ethnic tensions (both within and across national borders) remained unresolved; and a weak civil society encountered persistent corruption.

The University of Liverpool

References

Alavi, H. (1972) 'The State in Post-Colonial Societies: Pakistan and Bangladesh', *New Left Review*, 74, July–August.

Amin, S. (1977) *Accumulation and Unequal Development* (Brighton, Harvester).

Amsden, A. H., Kochanowicz, J. & Taylor, L. (1994) *The Market Meets its Match: Restructuring the Economies of Eastern Europe* (Cambridge, MA & London, Harvard University Press).

Anderson, J. H. & Gray, C. W. (2006) *Anticorruption in Transition 3: Who is Succeeding, and Why?* (Washington, DC, World Bank).

Appel, H. (2001) 'Corruption and the Collapse of the Czech Transition Miracle', *East European Politics and Societies*, 15, 3, September.

Asztalos Morell, I. (1999) 'Rural Women and the Gender Division of Labour in the Post-communist Transition', in Starosta, P., Kovách, I. & Gorlach, K. (eds) (1999) *Rural Societies under Communism and Beyond: Hungarian and Polish Perspectives* (Łódź, Łódź University Press).

Bandelj, N. (2010) 'How EU Integration and Legacies Matter for Foreign Direct Investment into Central and Eastern Europe', *Europe-Asia Studies*, 63, 2, March.

Bárány, Z. (2002) *The East European Gypsies: Regime Change, Marginality, and Ethnopolitics* (Cambridge, Cambridge University Press).

Barnes, S. H. (1998) 'The Mobilization of Political Identity in New Democracies', in Barnes, S. H. & Simon, J. (eds) (1998) *The Postcommunist Citizen* (Budapest, Erasmus Foundation), p. 127.

Baun, M. J. (2000) *A Wider Europe: The Process and Politics of European Enlargement* (Lanham, MD & Oxford, Rowman & Littlefield).

Berend, I. T. (2009) *From the Soviet Bloc to the European Union: The Economic and Social Transformation of Central and Eastern Europe since 1973* (Cambridge, Cambridge University Press).

Biró, S. (2010) *A Hazai Birtokpolitika a Közvetlen Támogatási Rendszer Keretei Között* (Budapest, Agrárgazdasági Kutató Intézet).

Bodnár, J. (1998) 'Assembling the Square: Social Transformation in Public Space and the Broken Mirage of the Second Economy in Postsocialist Budapest', *Slavic Review*, 57, 3, Autumn.

Boltho, A. (1971) *Foreign Trade Criteria in Socialist Economies* (Cambridge, Cambridge University Press).

Böröcz, J. & Róna-Tas, Á. (1995) 'Small Leap Forward: Emergence of New Economic Elites', *Theory and Society*, 24, 5, October.

Borowicz, R. (1996) 'Rural Unemployment: Specific Traits', *Eastern European Countryside*, 2.

Bridger, S. & Pine, F. (1998) *Surviving Post-Socialism: Local Strategies and Regional Responses in Eastern Europe and the Former Soviet Union* (London & New York, Routledge).

Bunce, V. (1999) 'The Political Economy of Postsocialism', *Slavic Review*, 58, 4, Winter.

Ciaian, P. & Swinnen, J. F. M. (2006) 'Land Market Imperfections and Agricultural Policy Impacts in the New EU Member States: A Partial Equilibrium Analysis', *American Journal of Agricultural Economics*, 88, 4, November.

Cirtautas, A. M. & Schimmelfennig, F. (2010) 'Europeanisation Before and After Accession: Conditionality, Legacies and Compliance', *Europe-Asia Studies*, 63, 2, March.

Ciupagea, C. (2002) 'Economic Fluctuations of Informal Activities in Romania', in Neef, R. & Stănculescu, M. (eds) (2002).

Cox, T. & Vass, L. (1994) 'Civil Society and Interest Representation in Hungarian Political Development', *Journal of Communist Studies and Transition Politics*, 10, 3, September.

Cox, T. & Vass, L. (2000) 'Government–Interest Group Relations in Hungarian Politics since 1989', *Europe-Asia Studies*, 52, 6, September.

Crowe, D. M. (1994) *A History of the Gypsies of Eastern Europe* (New York, St. Martin's Griffin).

Crowley, S. & Ost, D. (eds) (2001) *Workers after Workers' States* (Lanham, MD & Oxford, Rowman & Littlefield).

Dallago, B. & McIntyre, R. J. (2003) 'Conclusions: The Role of Public Policy in SME Development', in McIntyre, R. J. & Dallago, B. (eds) (2003).

Deacon, B. (2000) 'Eastern European Welfare States: The Impact of the Politics of Globalization', *Journal of European Social Policy*, 10, 2, May.

Domański, H. (2002) 'Is the East European "Underclass" Feminized?', *Communist and Post-Communist Studies*, 35, 4, December.

Dyker, D. A. (2004) *Catching Up and Falling Behind: Post-Communist Transformation in Historical Perspective* (London, Imperial College Press).

Earle, J. S. & Estrin, S. (1996) 'Employee Ownership in Transition', in Frydman, R., Gray, C. W. & Rapaczynski, A. (eds) (1996) *Corporate Governance in Central Europe and Russia Volume 2: Insiders and the State* (Budapest, Central European University Press).

Einhorn, B. (1993) *Cinderella Goes to Market: Citizenship, Gender and Women's Movements in East Central Europe* (London & New York, Verso).

Ekiert, G. & Kubik, J. (2001) *Rebellious Civil Society: Popular Protest and Democratic Consolidation in Poland, 1989–1993* (Ann Arbor, MI, University of Michigan Press).

Estrin, S. (1994) 'Economic Transition and Privatization: The Issues', in Estrin, S. (ed.) (1994) *Privatization in Central and Eastern Europe* (London & New York, Longman).

European Bank for Reconstruction and Development (EBRD) (1999) *Transition Report 1999* (London, EBRD).

Eyal, G., Szelényi, I. & Townsley, E. (1998) *Making Capitalism without Capitalists: Class Formation and Elite Struggles in Post-Communist Central Europe* (London, Verso).

Ferge, Zs. (1979) *A Society in the Making: Hungarian Social and Societal Policy 1945–75* (Harmondsworth, Penguin).

Ferge, Zs. (2001) 'Welfare and "Ill-Fare" Systems in Central–Eastern Europe', in Sykes, R., Palier, B. & Prior, P. M. (eds) (2001) *Globalization and European Welfare States: Challenges and Change* (Basingstoke, Palgrave).

Fodor, É. (1997) 'Gender in Transition: Unemployment in Hungary, Poland, and Slovakia', *East European Politics and Societies*, 11, 3, September.
Fodor, É. (2005) *Women at Work: The Status of Women in the Labour Markets of the Czech Republic, Hungary and Poland*, Occasional Paper 3 (Geneva, United Nations Research Institute for Social Development).
Frank, A. G. (1972) *Lumpenbourgeoisie: Lumpendevelopment* (New York & London, Monthly Review Press).
Frydman, R., Rapaczynski, A. & Earle, J. S. (1993) *The Privatization Process in Central Europe* (Budapest, Central European University Press).
Gaus, G. (1986) *Wo Deutschland liegt: Eine Ortsbestimmung* (Munich, Deutscher Taschenbuch-Verlag).
Glass, C. M. (2008) 'Gender and Work during Transition: Job Loss in Bulgaria, Hungary, Poland, and Russia', *East European Politics and Societies*, 22, 4, November.
Glinkina, S. (2003) 'Small Business, Survival Strategies and the Shadow Economy', in McIntyre, R. J. & Dallago, B. (eds) (2003).
Goldthorpe, J. H. (1980) *Social Mobility and Class Structure in Modern Britain* (Oxford, Clarendon Press).
Gorton, M., Hubbard, C. & Hubbard, L. (2009) 'The Folly of European Union Policy Transfer: Why the Common Agricultural Policy (CAP) Does Not Fit Central and Eastern Europe', *Regional Studies*, 43, 10, January.
Gowan, P. (1995) 'Analysing Shock Therapy', *New Left Review*, 213, September/October.
Gowan, P. (1996) 'Eastern Europe, Western Power and Neo-Liberalism', *New Left Review*, 216, March/April.
Grabbe, H. (2003) 'Europeanisation Goes East: Power and Uncertainty in the EU Accession Process', in Featherstone, K. & Radaelli, C. (eds) (2003) *The Politics of Europeanisation* (Oxford, Oxford University Press).
Gradev, G. (2001) 'Bulgarian Trade Unions in Transition: The Taming of the Hedgehog', in Crowley, S. & Ost, D. (2001).
Grant, W. (1997) *The Common Agricultural Policy* (Basingstoke, Macmillan).
Guy, W. (1998) 'Ways of Looking at Roma: The Case of Czechoslovakia', in Tong, D. (ed.) (1998) *Gypsies: An Interdisciplinary Reader* (New York & London, Garland Publishing Inc.).
Hanley, E. (1999) 'Cadre Capitalism in Hungary and Poland: Property Accumulation among Communist-era Elites', *East European Politics and Societies*, 14, 1, December.
Hardy, J. (2009) *Poland's New Capitalism* (London, Pluto Press).
Heinen, J. & Portet, S. (2009) *Religion, Politics and Gender Equality in Poland* (Geneva, UN Research Institute for Social Development).
Heynes, B. (2005) 'Emerging Inequalities in Central and Eastern Europe', *Annual Review of Sociology*, 31.
Heywood, A. (2002) *Politics*, 2nd edn (Basingstoke, Palgrave Macmillan).
Higley, J. & Lengyel, G. (eds) (2000) *Elites after State Socialism: Theories and Analysis* (Lanham, MD & Oxford, Rowman & Littlefield).
Hilton, R. (ed.) (1978) *The Transition from Feudalism to Capitalism* (London, Verso).
Holton, R. J. (1985) *The Transition from Feudalism to Capitalism* (Basingstoke, Macmillan Education).
Howard, M. M. (2003) *The Weakness of Civil Society in Post-Communist Europe* (Cambridge, Cambridge University Press).
Hughes, G. & Hare, P. (1991) 'Competitiveness and Industrial Restructuring in Czechoslovakia, Hungary and Poland', *European Economy*, Special Edition 2.
Inglot, T. (2008) *Welfare States in East Central Europe, 1919–2004* (Cambridge, Cambridge University Press).
Jacoby, W. (1999) 'Priest and Penitent: The European Union as a Force in the Domestic Politics of Eastern Europe', *East European Constitutional Review*, 8, 1/2, Winter/Spring.
Johnson, S. & Loveman, G. (1995) *Starting Over in Eastern Europe: Entrepreneurship and Economic Renewal* (Boston, MA, Harvard Business School Press).
Kenedi, J. (1981) *Do it Yourself: Hungary's Hidden Economy* (London, Pluto Press).
Kideckel, D. A. (1993) *The Solitude of Collectivism: Romanian Villagers to the Revolution and Beyond* (Ithaca, NY & London, Cornell University Press).
Kideckel, D. A. (2001) 'Winning the Battles, Losing the War: Contradictions of Romanian Labor in the Postcommunist Transformation', in Crowley, S. & Ost, D. (eds) (2001).
Konrad, G. & Szelenyi, I. (1974) 'Social Conflicts of Under-Urbanisation', in Brown, A., Licari, J. A. & Neuberger, E. (1974) *Urban and Social Economics in Market and Planned Economies*, Vol. 1 (New York, Praeger).

Kostova, D. (2000) 'Bulgaria: Economic Elite Change During the 1990s', in Higley, J. & Lengyel, G. (eds) (2000).
Kovács, K. (1998) 'Elfújja a Szél? Esettanulmány a "Homokvár" Mgtsz Átalakulásáról', *Replika*, 33/34, December.
Kunicki, M. (2005) 'The Red and the Brown, Bolesław Piasecki, the Polish Communists and the anti-Zionist Campaign in Poland, 1967–1968', *Eastern European Politics and Societies*, 19, 2, May.
Kurz, C. & Wittke, V (1998) 'Using Industrial Capacities as a Way of Integrating the Central and East European Economies', in Zysman, J. & Schwartz, A. (eds) (1998) *Enlarging Europe: The Industrial Foundations of a New Political Reality* (Berkeley, CA, University of California, International and Area Studies).
Ladányi, J. & Szelényi, I. (2006) *Patterns of Exclusion: Constructing Gypsy Ethnicity and the Making of an Underclass in Transitional Societies of Europe* (Boulder, CO & New York, Columbia University Press).
Laki, M. (2008) 'The Strata of Young Entrepreneurs in Post-socialist Hungary: Chance or Illusion', in Blokker, P. & Dallago, B. (2008) *Youth Entrepreneurship and Local Development in Central and Eastern Europe* (Aldershot, Ashgate).
Laki, M. & Szalai, J. (2006) 'The Puzzle of Success: Hungarian Entrepreneurs at the Turn of the Millennium', *Europe-Asia Studies*, 58, 3, May.
Landes, D. S. (1966) *The Rise of Capitalism* (New York, Macmillan).
Lane, D. (1971) *The End of Inequality?* (Harmondsworth, Penguin).
Lengyel, G. & Barta, A. (2000) 'Hungary: Bankers and Managers after State Socialism', in Higley, J. & Lengyel, G. (eds) (2000).
Lerman, Z. (2001) 'Agriculture in Transition Economies: From Common Heritage to Divergence', *Agricultural Economics*, 26, 2, November.
Lerman, Z., Csaki, C. & Feder, G. (2004) *Agriculture in Transition: Land Policies and Evolving Farm Structures in Post-Soviet Countries* (Lanham, MD & Oxford, Lexington Books).
Levitz, P. & Pop-Eleches, G. (2010) 'Monitoring, Money, and Migrants: Countering Post-Accession Backsliding in Bulgaria and Romania', *Europe-Asia Studies*, 63, 2, March.
Lovenduski, J. & Woodall, J. (1987) *Politics and Society in Eastern Europe* (Basingstoke, Macmillan Education).
Mandelbaum, M. (1993) 'Introduction', in Islam, S. & Mandelbaum, M. (eds) (1993) *Making Markets: Economic Transformation in Eastern Europe and the Post-Soviet States* (New York, Council on Foreign Relations).
Martin, R (1999) *Transforming Management in Central and Eastern Europe* (Oxford, Oxford University Press).
McCagg, W. O. (1991) 'Gypsy Policy in Socialist Hungary and Czechoslovakia, 1945–1989', *Nationalities Papers*, 19, 3, Winter.
McIntyre, R. J. & Dallago, B. (eds) (2003) *Small and Medium Enterprises in Transitional Economies* (Basingstoke, Palgrave Macmillan).
Milanovic, B. (1999) 'Explaining the Increase in Inequality during Transition', *Economics of Transition*, 7, 2, July.
Miller, W. L., Grødeland, Å. B. & Koshechkina, T. Y. (2001) *A Culture of Corruption?: Coping with Government in Post-Communist Europe* (Budapest, Central European University Press).
Miszlivetz, F. & Jensen, J. (1998) 'An Emerging Paradox: Civil Society from Above?', in Rueschemeyer, D., Rueschemeyer, M. & Wittrock, B. (eds) (1998) *Participation and Democracy in East and West: Comparisons and Interpretations* (Armonk, NY, M.E. Sharpe).
Myant, M. (1993) *Transforming Socialist Economies: The Cases of Poland and Czechoslovakia* (Aldershot, Edward Elgar).
Myant, M. (2005) 'Klaus, Havel and the Debate over Civil Society in the Czech Republic', *Journal of Communist Studies and Transition Politics*, 21, 2, June.
Myant, M., Slocock, B. & Smith, S. (2000) 'Tripartism in the Czech and Slovak Republics', *Europe-Asia Studies*, 52, 4, June.
Neef, R. & Stănculescu, M. (eds) (2002) *The Social Impact of Informal Economies in Eastern Europe* (Aldershot, Ashgate).
Noutcheva, G. & Bechev, D. (2008) 'The Successful Laggards: Bulgaria and Romania's Accession to the EU', *East European Politics and Societies*, 22, 1, February.
Ost, D. (2000) 'Illusory Corporatism in Eastern Europe: Neoliberal Tripartism and Postcommunist Class Identities', *Politics and Society*, 28, 4, December.
Ost, D. (2001) 'The Weakness of Symbolic Strength: Labor and Union Identity in Poland, 1989–2000', in Crowley, S. & Ost, D. (eds) (2001).

Pollert, A. (1999) *Transformation at Work in the New Market Economies of Central and Eastern Europe* (London, Sage).
Pollert, A. (2003) 'Women, Work and Equal Opportunities in Post-Communist Transition', *Work, Employment and Society*, 17, 2, June.
Pollert, A. (2005) 'Gender, Transformation and Employment in Central Eastern Europe', *European Journal of Industrial Relations*, 11, 2, July.
Pouliquen, A. (2001) *Competitiveness and Farm Incomes in the CEEC Agri-Food Sectors* (Brussels, European Commission).
Poznanski, K. Z. (2001) 'Building Capitalism with Communist Tools: Eastern Europe's Defective Transition', *East European Politics and Societies*, 15, 2, March.
Radice, H. (1995) 'The Role of Foreign Direct Investment in the Transformation of Eastern Europe', in Chang, H.-J. & Noland, P. (eds) (1995) *The Transformation of Communist Economies: Against the Mainstream* (Basingstoke, Macmillan).
Róna-Tas, Á. & Böröcz, J. (2000) 'Bulgaria, the Czech Republic, Hungary, and Poland: Presocialist and Socialist Legacies among Business Elites', in Higley, J. & Lengyel, G. (eds) (2000).
Rose-Ackerman, S. (2005) *From Elections to Democracy: Building Accountable Government in Hungary and Poland* (Cambridge, Cambridge University Press).
Rose-Ackerman, S. (2007) 'From Elections to Democracy in Central Europe: Public Participation and the Role of Civil Society', *East European Politics and Societies*, 21, 1, February.
Sadler, D. (2003) 'Production Systems and Uneven Development in East Central Europe: The Limits to Regional Economic Management', in Keating, M. & Hughes, J. (eds) (2003) *The Regional Challenge in Central and Eastern Europe: Territorial Restructuring and European Integration* (Brussels, Berlin, Frankfurt am Main & Vienna, Peter Lang).
Sajó, A. (1998) 'Corruption, Clientalism, and the Future of the Constitutional State in Eastern Europe', *East European Constitutional Review*, 7, 2, Spring.
Sarris, A. H., Doucha, T. & Mathijs, E. (1999) 'Agricultural Restructuring in Central and Eastern Europe: Implications for Competitiveness and Rural Development', *European Review of Agricultural Economics*, 26, 3, September.
Scase, R. (2003) 'Entrepreneurship and Proprietorship in Transition: Policy Implications for the SME Sector', in McIntyre, R. J. & Dallago, B. (eds) (2003).
Schimmelfennig, F. & Scholtz, H. (2010) 'Legacies and Leverage: EU Political Conditionality and Democracy Promotion in Historical Perspective', *Europe-Asia Studies*, 63, 2, March.
Schimmelfennig, F. & Sedelmeier, U. (eds) (2005) *The Europeanization of Central and Eastern Europe* (Ithaca, NY & London, Cornell University Press).
Sedelmeier, U. (2005) *Constructing the Path to Eastern Enlargement: The Uneven Policy Impact of EU Identity* (Manchester, Manchester University Press).
Sik, E. (1992) 'From the Second to the Informal Economy', *Journal of Public Policy*, 12, 2, April.
Sik, E. (2002) 'Informal Labour Market-Place on the Moscow Square', in Neef, R. & Stănculescu, M. (eds) (2002).
Sloat, A. (2005) 'The Rebirth of Civil Society: The Growth of Women's NGOs in Central and Eastern Europe', *European Journal of Women's Studies*, 12, 4, November.
Slomczynski, K. M. & Shabad, G. (1996) 'Systemic Transformation and the Salience of Class Structure in East Central Europe', *East European Politics and Societies*, 11, 1, December.
Smith, A., Stenning, A., Rochovská, A. & Światek, D. (2008) 'The Emergence of a Working Poor: Labour Markets, Neoliberalisation and Diverse Economies in Post-Socialist Cities', *Antipode*, 40, 2, March.
Stark, D. (1996) 'Recombitant Property in East European Capitalism', *American Journal of Sociology*, 101, 4, January.
Stewart, M. (1990) 'Gypsies, Work and Civil Society', in Hann, C. M. (ed.) (1990) *Market Economy and Civil Society in Hungary* (London, Frank Cass).
Stewart, M. (1997) *The Time of the Gypsies* (Boulder, CO, Westview Press).
Stewart, M. (2002) 'Deprivation, the Roma and "the Underclass"', in Hann, C. M. (ed.) (2002) *Postsocialism: Ideals, Ideologies and Practices in Eurasia* (London & New York, Routledge).
Stoica, C. A. (2004) 'From Good Communists to Even Better Capitalists? Entrepreneurial Pathways in Post-Socialist Romania', *East European Politics and Societies*, 18, 2, May.
Svejnar, J. (2002) 'Transition Economies: Performance and Challenges', *Journal of Economic Perspectives*, 16, 1, Winter.
Swain, G. & Swain, N. (2009) *Eastern Europe Since 1945*, 4th edn (Basingstoke, Palgrave Macmillan).
Swain, N. (1992) *Hungary: The Rise and Fall of Feasible Socialism* (London, Verso).
Swain, N. (1994) *Collective Farms as Sources of Stability and Decay in Centrally Planned Economies of East Central Europe*, Working Paper 30 (Liverpool, University of Liverpool, Centre for Central and Eastern European Studies Rural Transition Series), pp. 30–32.

Swain, N. (1998) 'The Visegrad Countries of Eastern Europe', in Foley, B. J. (ed.) (1998) *European Economies since the Second World War* (Basingstoke, Macmillan).

Swain, N. (1999) 'Agricultural Restitution and Co-operative Transformation in the Czech Republic, Hungary and Slovakia', *Europe-Asia Studies*, 51, 7, November.

Swain, N. (2004) 'Saddling a Cow: The Acceding Countries and the Common Agricultural Policy', in Tabata, S. & Iwashita, A. (eds) (2004) *Slavic Eurasia's Integration into the World Economy and Community* (Hokkaido, Slavic Research Center Hokkaido University).

Swain, N. & Vincze, M. (2001) 'Agricultural Restructuring in Transylvania in the Post-Communist Period', in Light, D. & Phinnemore, D. (eds) (2001) *Post-Communist Romania: Coming to Terms with Transition* (Basingstoke, Palgrave).

Szelényi, I. (1988) *Socialist Entrepreneurs: Embourgeoisement in Rural Hungary* (Cambridge, Polity Press).

Tesser, L. M. (2004) 'East-Central Europe's New Security Concern: Foreign Land Ownership', *Communist and Post-Communist Studies*, 37, 2, June.

Thompson, E. P. (1968) *The Making of the English Working Class* (Harmondsworth, Penguin).

Tittenbrun, J. (2005) *Divide and Rule: Privatisation in Poland and the Working Class Economic Ownership*, paper presented at 37th World Congress of the International Institute of Sociology Stockholm, Sweden, July, available at: http://www.scasss.uu.se/IIS2005/total_webb/tot_html/papers/divide_and_rule.pdf,accessed 18 February 2011.

Tóth, J. I. & Sik, E. (2002) 'Hidden Economy in Hungary 1992–1999', in Neef, R. & Stănculescu, M. (eds) (2002).

United Nations Development Programme (UNDP) (1991) *Human Development Reports* (New York, Oxford University Press).

United Nations Development Programme (UNDP) (1995) *Human Development Reports* (New York, Oxford University Press).

United Nations Development Programme (UNDP) (1998) *Human Development Reports* (New York, Oxford University Press).

United Nations Development Programme (UNDP) (2000) *Human Development Reports* (New York, Oxford University Press).

United Nations Development Programme (UNDP) (2001) *Human Development Reports* (New York, Oxford University Press).

United Nations Economic Commission for Europe (UN/ECE) (1995) *Economic Survey of Europe in 1994–1995* (Geneva, United Nations).

United Nations Economic Commission for Europe (UN/ECE) (2004) *Economic Survey of Europe 2004, No. 1* (Geneva, United Nations).

Vermeersch, P. (2010) 'Contesting Europe: Strategies and Legacies in Polish Political Competition', *Europe-Asia Studies*, 63, 2, March.

Wallace, C. & Haerpfer, C. (2002) 'Patterns of Participation in the Informal Economy in East–Central Europe, 1991–1998', in Neef, R. & Stănculescu, M. (eds) (2002).

Wallace, C. & Latcheva, R. (2006) 'Economic Transformation Outside the Law: Corruption, Trust in Public Institutions and the Informal Economy in Transition Countries of Central and Eastern Europe', *Europe-Asia Studies*, 58, 1, January.

After the Party, the After-Parties? The Effects of Communist Successor Parties on Economic Reform in Central and Eastern Europe

ALEKSANDRA SZNAJDER LEE

WITH THE RISE OF GLOBALISATION AND THE DIFFUSION of neoliberal economic reform throughout the world, the relevance of partisanship for economic reform has become the subject of much controversy. Set against the existing scholarship on partisan effects in the OECD countries and Latin America, post-1989 Central and Eastern Europe presents an intriguing case for several reasons. As in the developed and developing countries alike, countries from Central and Eastern Europe also faced global economic pressures, but unlike them, they simultaneously needed to construct a market economy. Indeed, after the fall of communism in Central and Eastern Europe, the creation of a liberal capitalist system became one of the central goals proclaimed by the new democratic governments. This goal became reinforced by the desire for and the concrete steps taken towards rapid economic and political integration with the European Union (EU).[1]

Not only did the previously communist countries have to 'build capitalism without capitalists', but to the dismay of the former anti-communist opposition and numerous Western observers alike, the task of creating the new economic system paradoxically often rested with the re-elected members of ex-communist parties,[2] whose predecessors, only a few years earlier, had been in charge of running the centrally planned economies.[3]

I thank David R. Cameron, Geoffrey Garrett, Anna Grzymała-Busse, Shigeo Hirano, Chinyelu Lee, Ákos Róna-Tas, Kenneth Scheve, Roger Schoenman, David Stark, Iván Szelényi, Balazs Vedres, Gregory Wawro, Vineeta Yadav, participants of the Comparative Research Workshop at Yale University and of the seminar on Networks and Institutions in the Economic Transformation of Postsocialism at the Harriman Institute at Columbia University, as well as the anonymous reviewers, for their comments and suggestions. All remaining errors are my own. I gratefully acknowledge the financial support provided by the Postdoctoral Fellowship at the Harriman Institute at Columbia University.

[1]Romania, arguably the least reform-oriented country among the EU accession states, signed the Europe Agreement (EA), which set out the conditions of economic cooperation with the EU, in February 1993, only a little over a year after Hungary, Poland and Czechoslovakia, which signed the EAs in December 1991.

[2]For a discussion of 'making capitalism without capitalists', see Eyal *et al.* (1998).

[3]The terms post-communist, ex-communist and communist successor parties are used interchangeably.

The question of whether partisanship matters for the conduct of economic reform is therefore particularly salient in the case of the post-communist EU entrants.

Yet, the communist successor parties entered the transition period from different starting points. In countries where the anti-communist opposition rallied much popular support, such as Poland, Hungary, Czechoslovakia and Lithuania, the communist successor parties left office after being voted out in the first free elections. In many cases, they subsequently underwent profound internal restructuring in an effort to emerge victorious from the next electoral contest. Internal transformation in the social-democratic direction entailed a clear break with the past, substantial organisational overhaul and dramatic programmatic change (Grzymała-Busse 2002). In other countries, such as Bulgaria and Romania, the communist successor parties remained in power after the first post-1989 elections and faced limited domestic political pressure to change. They were effectively replaced by anti-communist coalitions running on a pro-reform platform as late as 1996–1997.[4] Only after eventual electoral defeat did these parties undergo substantial internal restructuring in the social-democratic direction.

This essay examines the impact of the communist successor parties on liberal economic reform in Central and Eastern Europe when they were in power. By economic reform I mean the structural change of the economy and the concomitant emulation of the basic institutions of the liberal capitalist system. When discussing the communist successor parties, I distinguish between those that underwent substantial internal restructuring in a social-democratic direction early in the transition period, and those that did not. I compare the effects on the level of economic reform exerted by governments formed by ex-communist parties that underwent social-democratic transformation, by ex-communist parties that did not undertake such a transformation early in the transition period, and by parties that were not communist successors. My analysis then turns to change over time and examines the effects of the timing of the communist successor parties' social-democratic transformation on economic reform proclivity.

The question of the impact of the two types of communist successor parties on economic reform relates to two distinct bodies of literature. The first deals with the issue of partisanship in the age of globalisation and the second with theories of post-communist transition and examines the composition, preferences and cultural capital endowment of the (post-)communist elites. So far, with the notable exception of Frye (2002), the question of partisan effects on economic reform in post-communist Europe has been the subject mostly of qualitative country case studies (Bartlett 1996; Blazyca & Rapacki 1996). However, while certainly informative, single-country studies make systematic comparisons across countries difficult. In this essay, I analyse partisan effects on economic reform in a quantitative manner over the years 1991–2007, using panel data for the entire sample of EU accession countries from Central and Eastern Europe which joined the EU in 2004 and 2007. The countries in the sample include

[4]In Bulgaria in 1992, the collapse of a new government formed earlier that year by the anti-communist coalition of the Union of Democratic Forces (*Suyuz na Demokratichnite Sili*) and the Movement for Rights and Freedoms (*Dvizhenie za Prava i Svobodi*) led to the formation of a government of the experts, which governed with the parliamentary support of the Bulgarian Socialist Party (*Balgarska Socialisticheska Partija*).

Bulgaria, the Czech Republic, Estonia, Hungary, Latvia, Lithuania, Poland, Romania, Slovakia and Slovenia.

Given the extraordinary impact of the EU accession process on the applicant countries, the choice of focusing solely on the EU accession states provides the greatest amount of control in terms of external pressures. This decision rule also happens to exclude countries that experienced war (countries of the former Yugoslavia, with the exception of Slovenia) or internal collapse (as did Albania in 1997). The post-Soviet states, with the exception of the Baltic countries, are excluded for several reasons. First, for an overwhelming majority of these countries, their democratic credentials have been questionable or outright lacking; they were considered 'partly free' or 'not free' by Freedom House throughout the transition period and, for the last decade, they have, at best, been included in the 'hybrid regime' category.[5] Second, in addition to non-democratic presidential regimes in the area, countries such as Ukraine (until 2006), Russia, Georgia and Armenia, have the president–parliamentary system, which limits the power of the parliamentary coalition by, among others, giving the president the discretion to dismiss the prime minister (Shugart 2005, pp. 337–38).

The essay proceeds as follows. The next section discusses various theoretical approaches to the performance of the two types of communist successor countries and derives testable hypotheses. This is followed by a presentation of the statistical model and the data used to test these hypotheses. The next section interprets and discusses the results while the final section concludes and draws out the implications of the findings.

Communist successor parties and theories of transition

In an era of globalisation, the effect of political parties on the conduct of economic reform and economic policy more generally has come under close scrutiny. Recognising the far-reaching convergence in areas such as privatisation and liberalisation, which may be surprising in view of traditional policy differences between left and right, some scholars have turned their attention to the more fine-tuned means through which partisanship is reflected in these policy outcomes (Murillo 2002; Murillo & Martínez-Gallardo 2007; Swank 2006; Simmons *et al.* 2006; Simmons & Elkins 2004). Others have examined the compatibility of the global economy with partisan preferences concerning social policy (Garrett 1998a, 1998b; Boix 1998; Swank 2006). Some scholars of post-communist transitions have carried out quantitative research in this vein by investigating social spending by right-of-centre and left-of-centre parties. Lipsmeyer (2002) argues that pension expenditures rise under right parties as a cushion to alleviate the effects of the liberalising economic policies these parties undertake. Her findings are corroborated by Tavits and Letki (2009), but their argument is different: left parties, whether communist successors or not, fear being associated with the communist-era left and thus demonstrate their commitment to market reform by supporting fiscal austerity measures and smaller social spending. However, neither Lipsmeyer nor Tavits and Letki distinguish between the types of communist successor parties in their quantitative analysis, although the latter indicate differences among communist successor parties in their qualitative studies. Also, all these authors examine

[5]Data available at: www.freedomhouse.org, accessed 15 June 2010.

social expenditure rather than the nuts and bolts of market institutions, which was the main structural challenge facing reformers in the post-1989 period.

The issue of partisanship in the context of fundamentals of economic reform would be expected to be particularly salient in post-communist Central and Eastern Europe. To begin with, most of these countries suffered from a 'regime divide' of varying intensity, which ran along the former regime–opposition fault line (Grzymała-Busse 2001; Kitschelt *et al.* 1999). Timothy Frye has argued that a high level of polarisation between the former communist and anti-communist factions had a detrimental effect on economic growth throughout the post-communist world (2002). Frye's influential quantitative analysis, however, focuses specifically on the partisan polarisation's implications for economic growth, rather than on the relative performance of each type of party while in power. Second, Frye is agnostic as to the distinction between the types of ex-communist parties. Third, the object of interest in Frye's piece is economic growth (reform outcome). In contrast this essay focuses specifically on the degree of structural change in the economy. It proposes that the direct effects on economic reform when either the post-communist left or its opponents were in power still needs to be explored. At first glance, if anywhere, the differences between the left and the right on economic reform would be expected to hold in Central and Eastern Europe.

The question concerning partisan effects is particularly relevant given the extensive presence of ex-communists in power in the post-1989 period. In seven out of the 10 countries considered, communist successor parties became part of the government (see Table 1). Over the 10-year period of 1991–2000, for nearly a third of the time, the communist successor parties held an average share of more than 20% of the governing

TABLE 1
YEARS COMMUNIST SUCCESSOR PARTIES HELD POWER IN CENTRAL AND EAST EUROPEAN COUNTRIES, 1991–2007

	Years communist successor parties held power	
	Social democratically transformed	*Transmuted*
Bulgaria	2005–2007	1991 1993–1997[a]
Czech Republic		
Estonia		
Hungary	1994–1998 2002–2007	
Latvia		
Lithuania	1992–1996 2001–2007	
Poland	1993–1997 2001–2005	
Romania	2000–2004	1991–1996
Slovakia	1994 1998–2002	
Slovenia	1993–1995 2000–2004	

Notes: for simplicity of presentation, the table includes election years. The Appendix lists the names of all of the elected communist successor parties.
[a]In 1993–1994, the Bulgarian Socialist Party lent its support to the government of the experts.

coalition votes. For 20% of the time, the former communists made up more than 50% of the governing coalition's voting power. Nor did the participation rate of ex-communists in government wane after 2000. In fact, from 2001 until 2007, more than 40% of the time communist successor parties held a share of at least 20% of the governing coalition's voting power. That share was equal to at least 50% of the coalition votes for a quarter of the time. In short, the communist successor parties seem to have been a remarkably enduring and frequent participant on the political scene.

Political rhetoric in the region has been very much concerned with party polarisation. Parties hailing from the former opposition circles have accused the communist successor parties of slow economic reform, particularly as far as privatisation is concerned, as well as of lingering central planning tendencies. However, in some ways the rhetoric is misleading. First, the economic reform record of centre-right governments often fell short of the expectations of both the electorate and the external observers (Bałtowski 2002). Second, while the persistence of polarisation suggests that the communist successor parties are a homogenous group, the theories of transition make it clear that the ex-communist parties should not be considered in a uniform fashion. These theories underscore that the communist parties entered the transition period under very different conditions. Shaped by the varying communist and even pre-communist-era legacies, these conditions affected the parties' resources and the potential for internal transformation in the social-democratic direction. This historically contingent transformation, in turn, both reflected and influenced the parties' willingness and ability to engage in economic reform during the transition period. In other words, party makeover was possible because there was sizeable internal support for both party transformation and economic reform. Through a feedback loop, party transformation further reinforced the pro-reform element.

Before exploring the argument in detail, it is worth noting that considerable research has been devoted to the internal transformation of the communist successor parties (Bozóki & Ishiyama 2002; Grzymała-Busse 2002; Ishiyama 1997; Ishiyama & Bozóki 2001; Orenstein 1998; Waller 1995; Ziblatt 1998) and to the implications of this transformation for democratic reforms and consolidation (Ishiyama 2009, 1999, 1995; Kuzio 2008). However, the implications of party transformation for the conduct of economic reform have not been explicitly analysed in a comparative fashion.

The ways in which communism fell throughout Central and Eastern Europe varied significantly, ranging from negotiated transition, to implosion, to pre-emptive reform (Linz & Stepan 1996, pp. 264, 295; Stark & Bruszt 1998, p. 18; Kitschelt *et al.* 1999, p. 39). The precise ways in which extrication from communist rule took place resulted both from differing balances of domestic political forces and from external demonstration effects exerted by neighbouring societies. Where system change was negotiated or where the regime imploded under the weight of popular opposition, the anti-communists emerged victorious in the first free elections. This happened in Czechoslovakia, Estonia, Hungary, Latvia, Lithuania, Poland and Slovenia. However, in Bulgaria and Romania, where the regime underwent pre-emptive reform in response to the crumbling of communism in the neighbouring countries, the communist party remained in power after the first elections. Thus, the results of the first free elections placed the communist parties under different kinds of electoral pressure. In the first set of countries, the communist parties needed to transform so they could gain the trust of the electorate in order to win the subsequent election. In the second set of countries, the objective of the freshly re-elected communist parties was to maintain power.

The past also endowed the communist parties with different types of resources that either facilitated or hindered their transformation in the social-democratic direction, critically affecting their future electoral fortunes. According to Grzymała-Busse, the 'portable skills' and 'usable pasts' of some of the communist parties later enabled them to undergo internal transformation in line with the social-democratic platform. These 'portable skills' in part developed out of frequent efforts to bring about economic reform in the past (Grzymała-Busse 2002, p. 5).

More specifically, transformation entailed a swift and radical disavowal of the communist legacy, the centralisation of power within the party and the reorganisation of party structure so as to enforce discipline and professionalism in parliamentary behaviour, as well as a marked effort to become identified with the social-democratic message that would appeal to broad sections of the electorate (Grzymała-Busse 2002, pp. 123–24). An indicator of transformation was the parties' eagerness to become identified with the Western social-democratic parties, not only using various public relations opportunities, but also by seeking the stamp of approval from the Socialist International (Waller 1995, p. 474). In those countries where such party transformation was successful, that is, in Hungary, Lithuania, Poland and Slovenia, and later Slovakia, the communist successors came back to power in the subsequent round of elections.

The same set of factors, especially the 'portable skills', that facilitated these parties' ability to transform under electoral pressure also conditioned their willingness and ability to engage in economic reform. In fact, we can take a step back and argue that the level of these 'portable skills' influenced the communist elites' preferences as far as transition itself was concerned. In his game-theoretic treatment of liberalisation and democratisation, Przeworski highlights the division between the reformers and the hardliners within the communist regime and the moderates and radicals in the opposition. The communist reformers, usually some of the politicians and economic managers, wanted to engage the opposition moderates in order to enhance their own power (Przeworski 1991, pp. 67–68).

The sociological literature on transition elaborates upon this particular aspect. There are two basic claims. On the one hand, the communist-era reformers and technocrats perceived an opportunity to convert political power into economic capital under the market system through extensive reliance on social networks, leading to the occurrence of 'political capitalism' (Hankiss 1990; Staniszkis 1990, 2001). According to the political capitalism thesis, formulated by Staniszkis (1990) in Poland and present in Hankiss' (1990) work on Hungary, the communist *nomenklatura*, using communist-era social networks, including informal ties and political connections, were able to gain access to attractive markets and to accumulate capital by often parasitic relations with state-owned enterprises. This, in turn, was expected to give rise to a nascent domestic capitalist class.

On the other hand, communist technocrats also possessed high levels of cultural capital and technocratic skills that would facilitate success under capitalism (Szalai 1994; Róna-Tas 1994; Eyal *et al.* 1998). Before transition, the technocrats often fought against the bureaucratic/hardliner faction of the communist *nomenklatura*, which lacked the requisite skills and an understanding of the principles of market economics.

As a result, the technocrats were potential allies of the anti-communist opposition. Moreover, some scholars claim that the skills of the technocratic faction of the communist party were superior to those of the anti-communist forces with primarily humanistic training that came to power in 1989 (Szalai 1994; Eyal *et al.* 1998). In any case, empirical research shows that the former communist-era managers are the social group that profited the most during the transition period as they became important members of the economic elite and were especially likely to hold managerial positions under the free market conditions (Szelényi & Szelényi 1995; Róna-Tas 1994; Böröcz & Róna-Tas 1995; Staniszkis 2001; Eyal *et al.* 1997).

Thus, the discussion so far suggests that the communist-era technocrats who prevailed over their communist bureaucratic/hardliner counterparts had both the skills and the personal connections and confidence that they would perform well under market conditions, be it by setting up their own businesses or by entering into partnerships with foreign corporations. This implies that the social-democratically transformed communist successor parties, relying on the expertise of communist-era technocrats, would be at least equally willing and perhaps better able to engage in economic reform than many of their former opposition counterparts. This leads to the first hypothesis (H_1), which holds that when the communist successor parties that initially transformed in a social-democratic direction were in power, they showed greater propensity to engage in liberal economic reform, compared to parties that were not communist successors.

The situation was vastly different in countries that had a more orthodox communist regime, namely Romania and Bulgaria, where pre-emptive reform was undertaken largely in response to external events. The communist parties in these countries recognised the need to emulate the changes elsewhere, seeing that if they did not do so, they would eventually be undermined by the growing opposition. In the extreme case of Romania, the sidelined elements of the Romanian Communist Party (*Partidul Comunist Român*) saw the opportunity of ousting Nicolae Ceauşescu as their chance to grab power. It is quite telling that Ion Iliescu, the single most influential figure of the Romanian transition, and the dictator's erstwhile close collaborator, claimed in his first post-revolution speech that Ceauşescu betrayed the ideals of communism (Pasti 1997, p. 270). Thus, the division between reformers and hardliners within the orthodox communist regimes was far less stark, if at all palpable. Consequently, the political will, as well as the preparation to embrace market principles was far smaller among the less variegated orthodox communist elites than it was among the technocrats of regimes that underwent partial liberalisation, such as Hungary, Poland and the Baltic states (as part of *perestroika*), let alone Slovenia.

The Slovak case is something of an outlier in this respect. While Czechoslovakia did not undergo either political or economic liberalisation, due to the history of Czech and Slovak relations during the post-1968 'normalisation', the Slovak Communist Party (*Komunistická Strana Slovenska*) was less orthodox and more flexible than its Czech counterpart (Grzymała-Busse 2002, pp. 36–37). During the transition period, the Slovak communist successor party (*Strana Demokratickej L'avice,* Party of the Democratic Left) underwent social-democratic transformation and was later able to participate in government. Its Czech counterpart, however, continued to maintain its orthodox communist approach, even retaining the word 'communist' in its name—*Komunistická Strana Čech a Moravy* (Communist Party of Bohemia and

Moravia)—and was never able to participate in a governing coalition (Grzymała-Busse 2002, pp. 36–37).

There is consensus in the literature that the Bulgarian and Romanian communist successor parties did not initially transform in a social-democratic direction. They shared a lack of clear dissociation from communism at the outset of the transition process, displayed organisational continuity and exhibited only gradual programmatic change. Moreover, there also occurred frequent struggles between the hardliners and the reformers, with the latter most often losing the fight. Rather than calling for integration with Western institutional structures, these parties often relied on populism, nationalism and clientelism (Grzymała-Busse 2002, p. 268; Ishiyama 1997; Linz & Stepan 1996; Crampton 1995).

In their comparative examination of the contents of the communist successor party programmes, Ishiyama and Bozóki (2001, p. 36) used the term 'transmutation' to refer to a situation in which the former communist parties adopted right-wing, nationalist rhetoric and advocated nationalist policies. According to the authors, both programmes indicated roughly equal levels of transmutation, 0.64 for Bulgaria and 0.67 for Romania, on a scale of zero to one, with one indicating the highest possible transmutation. At the same time, the Bulgarian Socialist Party's (*Balgarska Socialisticheska Partijia*) 1996 platform made far more references indicative of an attachment to communist ideals than the Romanian party's platform of 1997 (Ishiyama & Bozóki 2001, p. 39). Other scholars have examined the internal transformation of the party structures, with Grzymała-Busse arguing that while the Bulgarian Socialist Party displayed a higher level of internal transformation than its Romanian counterpart, it was not enough to place it in the social-democratic transformation category before 2000 (Grzymała-Busse 2002, pp. 267–69, 271).

Finally, as highlighted above, due to the relative weakness of the opposition, the partly transmuted communist successor parties also did not have a crucial electoral incentive to transform in a social-democratic direction. Their reliance on nationalist principles and limited desire for internal regeneration meant that they possessed a lower political will to transform the economy in a market-oriented direction than their non-ex-communist counterparts. Moreover, the dearth of technocratic skills within the transmuted communist successor parties meant that these parties had at most the same, but probably less ability to undertake economic reform than their non-ex-communist counterparts. The relatively low political will and ability to engage in economic reform by the partly transmuted parties result in the second hypothesis (H_2): in countries where the partly transmuted communist successor parties were in power, they showed less propensity to reform than parties that were not communist successors.

Until now, the discussion has not taken temporality into account (Pierson 2004). Nonetheless, there are three significant reasons to anticipate that the examined reform dynamic could change over time. These have to do with external and internal pressures for party transformation, path dependence and the effects of the timing of party transformation in the social-democratic direction, and the possibility of political capitalism or partial reform. Let us consider these in turn.

The first temporal dynamic has to do with the demands of EU accession. The transition countries found themselves under strong external pressure from the early days of reform, whether it was from the international financial institutions, such as the International Monetary Fund or the World Bank, foreign policy advisors, or the more diffuse pressures of the international financial markets (Epstein 2008; Linden 2002; Orenstein *et al.* 2008; Pop-Eleches 2009; Wedel 2001). However, Europeanisation, or the effort to transfer rules, policies and norms from the EU to the accession countries, attracted the bulk of scholarly attention (Ekiert & Zielonka 2003; Grabbe 2006; Grzymała-Busse 2006; Schimmelfennig & Sedelmeier 2005; Vachudova 2005). The EU's profound influence on the accession countries took place through the requirements of the *acquis communautaire*—or the body of EU laws, regulations and legal decisions—pertaining to domains such as economic policy (including central banking), minority rights, civil service, regional policy, social policy, agriculture, migration and environmental policy, among others (Grabbe 2006). The *acquis* needed to be adopted in full prior to accession. Its scope was so broad that the EU accession process even attracted criticism for reducing political competition to a contest over who was better able to implement the EU's rules and requirements (Grzymała-Busse & Innes 2003). Thus, one would expect the EU to have exerted very strong influence not only on the accession countries' conduct of economic reform, but also on their domestic political dynamic. Although Ishiyama (2006) suggests that it was domestic politics, rather than Europeanisation that was instrumental in shaping communist successor parties, it is plausible that the demands of EU accession altered the actual preferences of political parties, in addition to shaping the official reform agenda. The EU effect would most likely have strengthened as the accession negotiations got underway. Moreover, the levelling effect was expected to have been particularly striking in the case of the transmuted communist successor parties, where the initial programmatic polarisation was the greatest (Vachudova 2005).

There are also significant reasons to believe that the historically conditioned basis for the hypothesised effects of the two types of communist successor parties, those that initially underwent social-democratic transformation and those that partially transmuted, would have waned over time for purely domestic reasons. First, any advantage that the initially social-democratically transformed parties would have had would be expected to vanish over time, as the non-ex-communist parties gained technocratic skills. (This is suggested in hypothesis three (H_3)). Second, in the case of transmuted ex-communist parties, their eventual electoral loss led to internal party reorganisation and to an emulation of the process which the initial social-democratic transformers underwent at the outset of transition. Thus, after losing the 1997 elections, the Bulgarian Socialist Party underwent enough of a transformation to be placed in the social-democratic camp when it returned to power in 2005. Similarly, the Party of Social Democracy in Romania (PDSR, *Partidul Democrației Sociale din România*) underwent internal reform after being voted out of office in the December 1996 elections. In the November 2000 elections, the party ran on a reformist platform, complete with strong support for EU membership, much as its northern counterparts did. After it regrouped to form the Social Democratic Party (PSD, *Partidul Social Democrat*), in an effort to underscore its social-democratic credentials, the party's revamped logo brandished not one, but three red roses! One might expect that the freshly transformed communist successors in Romania and Bulgaria would have replaced more of the communist-era bureaucrats within their ranks with the newly trained technocrats, closing any potential gap with their non-communist successor counterparts.

Yet, the picture may be complicated by the second temporality-related concern, namely the path dependent effects of the timing of party transformation. Social democratic party transformation in the initial transition period, combined with the parties' electoral incentive to prove their ability to reform, may have led to increasing returns to the choice of the robust economic reform pathway. In the case of the second wave of social-democratic party transformation, the concomitant desire to engage in swift economic reform may have been weaker, due to continuing high returns to the slow economic reform pathway, driven by tight clientelistic ties originating in the non-technocratic communist-era social networks. Thus, for all the internal transformation, these second wave transformed parties would still be bound by the pre-existing clientelistic networks. The implications of this mechanism are captured by hypothesis four (H_4).

Communist-era social networks among the first wave transformers, however, raise the possibility of partial reform, which could represent yet another potential temporal effect. As the proponents of political capitalism and power conversion thesis have argued, communist-era social networks allowed for the conversion of political power into economic capital under the market system (Hankiss 1990; Staniszkis 1990). This could have led to 'partial reform', as formulated by Joel Hellman. In this scenario, well connected cadres would profit from various arbitrage opportunities made available by the initiated, yet unfinished reforms, such as trade liberalisation combined with continued government production subsidies. Afraid of losing these opportunities, they would seek to stall full reform (Hellman 1998, p. 204). However, in the initial phase, it would be in the cadres' interest to support economic reform measures, if for no other reason than to establish these arbitrage opportunities in the first place.

In other words, it is plausible that whereas the communist-era technocrats in the parties that underwent early social-democratic transformation had both the skills and the incentives to engage in reform due to their social and cultural capital early in the transition, over time, their reformist zeal may have diminished. They may simply have been unwilling to lose these initial advantages that would have disappeared with full reform. What follows is that the initial transformers would have been less avid market builders in the late transition period than their non-ex-communist counterparts. This notion is tested in hypothesis five (H_5).

When formulating hypotheses concerning temporal effects, I use the year 2000 as the demarcation point for two reasons. First, after 2000 the countries were increasingly stepping up their reform efforts as they were gearing up for the closure of the EU accession negotiations. Making progress on economic reform was very relevant in the case of the first wave (2004) of EU entrants. Romania and Bulgaria, the only countries in the sample that were not in the first wave of EU accession, were also very much under pressure to gain the status of market economies, a necessary, but not nearly sufficient condition for their EU entry in 2007. Second, 2000 was also the year when the newly social-democratised Romanian PDSR was re-elected (at the end of November that year). Therefore, this particular demarcation allows for the testing of the hypothesis concerning the timing of the party's social-democratic transformation (hypothesis four, H_4).

The following hypotheses summarise the discussion concerning the effects of the communist successor parties on liberal economic reform, taking into consideration change over time:

H_1: Communist successor parties that initially transformed in a social-democratic direction are more likely to engage in liberal economic reform during the early to mid-transition period (until 2000) than parties that are not communist successors.

H_2: Transmuted communist successor parties are less likely to engage in liberal economic reform than parties that are not communist successors.

H_3: In the later part of transition, the communist successor parties that initially transformed in a social-democratic direction are equally likely to engage in liberal economic reform as their non-communist successor counterparts.

H_4: The timing of party transformation in a social-democratic direction is significantly associated with liberal economic reform proclivity: communist successor parties that transform in a social-democratic direction in the second wave are less likely to engage in liberal economic reform than parties that transform in the first wave, compared to parties that are not communist successors.

H_5: In the later part of transition (post-2000), the communist successor parties that initially transformed in a social-democratic direction are less likely to engage in liberal economic reform than their non-ex-communist counterparts.

The following section discusses the model and the data used to test these hypotheses.

Data and methods

As is clear from the preceding discussion, liberal economic reform is the dependent variable. After the fall of communism, the creation of a liberal market system became the official goal, which was reinforced by the application for membership in the EU, submitted in the early 1990s by all countries considered in this essay. The creation of a functioning, liberal market system, congruent with the one in the EU member states, was one of the requirements for EU membership. Therefore, it makes sense to use the structure and institutions of advanced market economies as a benchmark against which to compare the countries in this sample.

It is difficult to operationalise indicators of liberal market reforms in a manner conducive to statistical analysis due to criticisms concerning data reliability. Recognising this criticism, this essay nonetheless relies on the standard means of comparing reform progress: transition indicators compiled by the European Bank for Reconstruction and Development (EBRD) for the period starting in 1991. The EBRD transition indicators represent the most comprehensive data on structural change since other datasets, such as the World Bank Liberalisation Index, are either more restricted in scope or represent cross-sectional data. Still, the existing measures of reform are highly correlated with each other (Frye 2010).

The EBRD transition indicators reflect reform progress on eight dimensions of the economy: large-scale privatisation, small-scale privatisation, governance and enterprise restructuring, price liberalisation, trade and foreign exchange systems, competition policy, banking reform and interest rate liberalisation, and the reform of securities markets and non-bank financial institutions. Thus, they cover key structural and institutional aspects of the economy, rather than simply measuring the effects of reform, such as economic growth, liberalisation and privatisation. Each country is assigned a grade annually ranging from 1 to 4+, with 1 indicating a complete lack of a given reform and 4+ demonstrating reform to the extent encountered in advanced market democracies. I transformed the '+' and '–' signs into 0.33 increments. For example, I coded grades of 3+ as 3.33 and grades of 4– as 3.67. For the purpose of operationalising a measure of capitalist reforms, I created an index averaging out the yearly scores obtained on each of the eight indicators.

The EBRD *Transition Reports* started to publish indicators in 1994, but the 2000 report ranked the countries' progress retrospectively since 1991. While the more recent versions of the report give rankings starting in 1989, it makes sense to use 1991 as the initial year of the analysis for several reasons. First, countries such as Estonia, Latvia, Lithuania and Slovenia became increasingly independent of the Soviet Union and Yugoslavia around 1990, which was the year when several of the first free elections were taking place. The first full year of economic reform for most countries was 1991.

The essay tests the following model:

$$\begin{aligned}
Economic\ Reform_{it} = {} & \beta_0 + \beta_1 Social\ Democratically\ Transformed\ Communist \\
& Successor\ Party\ in\ Coalition_{it} \\
& + \beta_2 Transmuted\ Communist\ Successor\ Party\ in\ Coalition_{it} \\
& + \beta_3 Economic\ Reform_{i(t-1)} + \beta_4 Wealth_{i(t-1)} + \beta_5 Growth_{i(t-1)} \\
& + \beta_6 FDI_{i(t-1)} + \sum(\beta_7 Country\ Dummy_{it}) \\
& + \beta_8 (91-92)\ Dummy_{it} + \beta_9 (98-00) Dummy_{it} \\
& + \beta_{10} (01-07) Dummy_{it} + \beta_{11} (01-07) Dummy * Social \\
& Democratically\ Transformed\ CSP_{it} + \beta_{12} (01-07) Dummy \\
& * Transmuted\ CSP_{it} + e_{it}
\end{aligned}$$

As far as the explanatory variables are concerned, I operationalised the participation of the communist successor parties in government as the share (%) of parliamentary seats the communist successors hold in the governing coalition in a given year.[6] I adjusted any year when the coalition make-up changed, either due to elections or to a coalition reshuffle, for the number of months the communist successor parties were actually part of the governing coalition.[7] In terms of the transformation

[6]I thank Ákos Róna-Tas for this suggestion.

[7]I compiled the dataset by corroborating the data from numerous sources, including *The Economist*, *Keesing's Contemporary Archives*, *Electoral Studies*, *Transitions*, as well as from various websites. Below are the source details for these references. For each country, I not only needed to gather the information on electoral results and eventual coalitions, but I also needed to account for any coalition reshuffles and their effects on seat distribution. Therefore, I often consulted more than one source to obtain the data to do the calculations.

Keesing's Record of World Events (1991–2007) (London, Longman);

The Economist (1991–2007) (London, The Economist Group);

of the ex-communist parties, the literature reflects a consensus regarding the classification of the Hungarian, Lithuanian, Polish, Slovak, as well as the Slovenian, communist successor parties as transformed in the social-democratic direction in the first wave, or early in the transition process. The pre-2000 Bulgarian and Romanian ex-communist parties were classified as not transformed in the social-democratic direction. Rather, the adoption by these parties of the anti-Western, nationalist rhetoric lent them the label of transmuted parties.[8] Following their eventual transformation in the social-democratic direction, the Romanian and Bulgarian ex-communist parties are considered to be second wave social-democratic transformers.

The model includes several standard control variables. The first control variable, wealth of the country (*Wealth*), was operationalised as GDP *per capita*, lagged by one year, and suggests that the wealth of a country may enhance its reform prospects.[9] Richer countries may find it politically more palatable to engage in structural reforms than the poorer ones since they are better able to cushion the deleterious effects of certain kinds of restructuring by means of a social safety net.

Similarly, I added the variable of economic growth (*Growth*), operationalised as the change in gross domestic product (GDP) over a given year, also lagged by one year.[10] As with wealth, it is plausible that a quickly growing economy would be more likely to have the economic resources necessary to cushion the negative effects of reforms. At the same time, it is also possible to argue the opposite: only when growth suffers will the politicians have a sufficiently strong incentive to engage in difficult reforms.

The third control variable (*FDI*) considers the effects of foreign direct investment (FDI) on economic reform, operationalised as FDI as a percentage of GDP, and also lagged by one year.[11] This choice is guided by the logic that FDI can often act as a

Transition (1995–1999) (Prague, Open Media Research Institute)—since 1999, available online as *Transitions Online: Regional Intelligence*, http://www.tol.org/;

Electoral Studies (1991–2003) (Elsevier Ltd);

Consortium for Elections and Political Process Strengthening. Election Guide, available at: http://www.electionguide.org/, last accessed 16 May 2008;

Election Resources on the Internet, available at: http://electionresources.org/eastern.europe.html, last accessed 10 May 2008.

In one case when a 'government of the experts', the Berov government in Bulgaria in 1993–1994, was acting with support in the assembly from the communist successor party, the latter was coded as participating in the governing coalition. The results do not change fundamentally when the Bulgarian Socialist Party was coded as not participating in that government, although the overall untransformed communist successor party effect on economic reform was weaker.

[8]For a discussion of Hungarian, Polish and Slovak communist successor parties, see Grzymała-Busse (2002). For the Slovak case, contrasted with that of the Czech Republic, see Grzymała-Busse (1998, 2002). For categorisation of all parties in this study, with the exception of Slovenia, see Ishiyama (1995). Linz and Stepan (1996) deal with the Hungarian, Lithuanian and Polish examples, while Dudek (1997) discusses the latter.

[9]Data on wealth were obtained from the World Bank's World Development Indicators database, available at: http://ddp-ext.worldbank.org/ext/DDPQQ/member.do?method=getMembers&userid=1&queryId=6, accessed 16 May 2008. Wealth is measured as GDP *per capita* in constant 2000 US dollars.

[10]Data on growth were obtained from the EBRD's *Transition Report* for the years 1999–2007, available at: http://transitionreport.co.uk/TRO/a/archives, accessed 19 May 2008.

[11]Data on FDI were obtained from the EBRD *Transition Reports* for various years (European Bank for Reconstruction and Development 1994–2007).

'carrot' for the government undertaking reforms. One may argue that the relationship is endogenous: that the higher the level of economic reform in the economy, the more FDI the country is capable of attracting. However, I suggest here that the presence of FDI, and more importantly, the fear of its loss or the failure to attract it in the future, may encourage the government to continue the reform process.

A statistically significant *F*-test result indicates that country fixed effects or dummies should be included in the model. In order to make sure that the outcomes are not overwhelmingly predicted by the historical legacies, it might be tempting to add legacy dummies to the model. Such an addition would be an effort to remove the potentially spurious association between party type and reform outcomes. The analysis by Kitschelt *et al.* (1999) presents a typology of communist legacies, dividing the countries in question into five categories: bureaucratic-authoritarian communism (the Czech Republic), national-accommodative communism (Hungary and Slovenia), patrimonial communism (Bulgaria and Romania), and two types of hybrid cases. These comprise a mix of bureaucratic-authoritarian and national accommodative communism (Poland) and a mix of national-accommodative and patrimonial communism (Slovakia, Estonia, Latvia and Lithuania) (Kitschelt *et al.* 1999, p. 39). However, introducing historical legacy dummies in the presence of country dummies is redundant, as one country in each legacy category is dropped from the model in order to prevent perfect multicollinearity. In the end, the regression results for a model with both country and legacy dummies and country dummies alone are the same for the variables of interest. Therefore, only the country dummies are included in the model.[12] These dummies should account for any additional country-specific factors, not captured by the variables in the model which might influence the outcome.

The model also includes a lagged dependent variable, $Economic\ Reform_{i(t-1)}$. The presence of the lagged dependent variable in the model is justified for both theoretical and econometric reasons. First, theoretically, the reform level at a given point in time is not independent of the reform level in the previous time period: the reform record is cumulative. In order to control for the impact of the previous reform level on the subsequent one, I include a lagged dependent variable in the model. Second, the inclusion of a lagged dependent variable solves the problem of serial correlation, which may seriously underestimate the true variance of the regression coefficients.[13]

In an effort to control for particular period effects, I introduce three period dummies.[14] A statistically significant *F*-test result indicates that these should be introduced into the equation. The first period dummy, (91–92)*Dummy*, pertains to the 1991–1992 time period and captures any upheavals and anomalies that may accompany the initial stages of transition, as well as the potential efforts to impress the international financial institutions in an effort to secure loans. The second period dummy, (98–00)*Dummy*, captures the 1998–2000 period, which was the time

[12]The results for the main variables of interest remain the same if the 'mode of exit from communism' dummies (implosion, negotiation or preemptive reform) are used instead of the communist system legacy variables.

[13]The Lagrange multiplier test confirmed the existence of serial correlation. After including the lagged dependent variable, I could not reject the null hypothesis of no serial correlation.

[14]I thank David Stark and Balazs Vedres for bringing the potential period effects to my attention.

immediately after the commencement of EU negotiations by the accession countries. During this time period, the homogenising effects of EU influence could conceivably become stronger. The final period dummy, (01–07)*Dummy*, pertains to the time when the formerly untransformed communist successor parties displayed their reformist credentials. It also marks the 'mature' period of the transformation process, with the end of the EU accession negotiations and eventual membership.

Finally, in order to test the hypotheses concerning temporal effects on partisan reform proclivities (H_3, H_4 and H_5), I account for the possibility of a structural break in the post-2000 period. I do so by including interaction terms of partisanship with a dummy variable for the years 2001–2007: (01–07)*Dummy**Social Democratically Transformed CSP* and (01–07)*Dummy**Transmuted CSP*.[15] Since I want to capture the effect of social-democratic party transformation on economic reform proclivity of the previously transmuted Romanian and Bulgarian ex-communist parties, in the post-2000 period, I continue to code these parties as transmuted. If these parties' nominal transformation in the social-democratic direction translated into improved economic reform performance, then we should observe a clear structural break in the post-2000 period (assuming that the parties' prior effect was negative). If the social-democratic transformation affects all ex-communist parties equally, regardless of its timing, then the second wave transformers' post-2000 economic reform proclivity should mirror that of the first wave of social-democratic transformers.

Given the relatively small sample size and in order to deal with the potential problems of non-spherical errors other than serial correlation, I use panel corrected standard errors (PCSE) to test the model (Beck & Katz 1995).[16]

Discussion of results

Table 2 summarises the results. Rejecting hypothesis one (H_1), the presence of the social-democratically transformed communist successor parties in power is not significantly associated with the level of economic reform in the early and mid-transition period. In other words, both the newly transformed social-democratic communist successor parties and the parties with non-communist roots were equally likely to engage in economic reform. This finding questions the arguments concerning the superiority of communist-era technocrats, and therefore of the communist successor parties, *vis-à-vis* their non-communist counterparts in the conduct of liberal economic reform in the relatively early stages of the transition process (Szalai 1994; Eyal *et al.* 1998).

Moreover, rejecting hypothesis five (H_5), the reform effect of the communist successor parties that transformed in a social-democratic direction in the first wave has been stable over time. There is no evidence that a structural break occurred in the post-2000 period; nor is there evidence to support the partial reform hypothesis,

[15] I thank Shigeo Hirano for a useful discussion and suggestion.

[16] To test for multicollinearity, I ran a variance inflation factor (VIF) test. The results returned two variables (lagged GDP *per capita* and a dummy for Slovenia), with values greater than 10, but less than 30, with the overall mean VIF average of 5.69. Since the more conservative threshold value for excluding variables is 30, I chose to leave both in the equation. An estimation of the model without these variables does not change the significance of the other variables and has a marginal effect on the main variables of interest. I thank one of the reviewers for this suggestion.

TABLE 2
EFFECTS OF COMMUNIST SUCCESSOR PARTIES ON ECONOMIC REFORM, 1991–2007

	Economic reform
Social-democratically transformed communist successor parties[a] (first wave transformers)	0.062 (0.062)
Transmuted communist successor parties	−0.248*** (0.052)
Social-democratically transformed communist successor party*post-2000 dummy (first wave transformers)	−0.061 (0.063)
Transmuted communist successor party*post-2000 dummy (second wave transformers)	0.160*** (0.056)
Economic reform$_{(t-1)}$	0.562*** (0.043)
Wealth[b]	0.002 (0.021)
Growth	−0.000 (0.003)
FDI	0.001 (0.004)
(91–92)*Dummy*	−0.332*** (0.054)
(98–00)*Dummy*	0.027 (0.038)
(01–07)*Dummy*	0.132** (0.055)
R^2	0.96
N	170
Regression	LSDV, PCSE

Notes: [a]coefficient indicates effect when all votes inside the governing coalition belong to ex-communist parties.
[b]Coefficient indicates change in \$1,000 *per capita* increments.
Standard errors in parentheses; * $= p < 0.10$, ** $= p < 0.05$, *** $= p < 0.01$.

whereby the well-connected first wave of social-democratically transformed communist successor parties would have been very willing to support reform in the earlier stages of transition, but less so later, when they would have a lot to lose from the completion of the reform process.[17] Rather, supporting hypothesis three (H_3), there seems to be a remarkable continuity in the support of the reform pathway by the social-democratic communist successor parties, on a par with parties that were not communist successors.

Turning to the transmuted communist successor parties, their presence in government is significantly and negatively associated with the level of economic reform, thereby confirming hypothesis two (H_2): transmuted ex-communists are indeed worse economic reformers than their non-ex-communist counterparts. Substantively, the magnitude of this negative effect is sizeable. Using the index created from EBRD indicators, a country at a given point in time could obtain a score ranging from 1 to 4+. Controlling for the previous reform level, country-specific effects (including historical effects) and other control variables, single-handed control

[17]While the coefficient signs are in the direction supporting hypotheses one and two, the significance level for both is far from being even marginally statistically significant.

by transmuted communist successor parties lowered the reform score for the given year by three quarters of a '+' or '–' sign.[18] Given that I created an index of EBRD scores by averaging eight separate indicators of market reform, this is equivalent to saying that single-handed control of the government by the transmuted communist successor parties lowered the reform score by a '+' or '–' sign on six out of eight reform indicators, compared with a situation when parties that were not ex-communist were in power. To illustrate, when parties that were not ex-communist were in power, a given country's reform score was a 3+ on all eight indicators used to create the index. If transmuted communist successor parties held power instead, the score would have fallen to 3 on six of the eight indicators.

What does this mean in terms of reform progress? If we take the institutional framework of advanced capitalist economies, reflected by the grade of 4+, as the desirable end-point of economic transition, and the grade of 1 as the starting point, three quarters of a '+' or '–' sign is equal to more than 7% of the total progress needed to create the institutional framework of advanced capitalist economies.[19] If, however, we control for the countries' different starting points in 1991 and the progress they made until 2007, the effect is actually greater and averages nearly 12% of the progress made by Bulgaria and about 14% of that made by Romania. Thus, the magnitude of the partisan effect is substantial.

Turning to the issue of temporality, there is a clear, statistically significant structural break in the post-2000 period as far as the transmuted ex-communist parties are concerned. After 2000 the transmuted parties underwent 'second wave' social-democratic transformation. However, the positive effect on reform (0.160) of the interactive term involving these second wave transformers does not completely offset the parties' overall negative effect coefficient. The total effect of the second wave transformers is mildly negative: –0.088. This is equivalent to a 'minus' sign on two out of the eight indicators and also means that the negative effect diminishes three-fold, compared to the 1991–2000 period. This leads us to accept hypothesis four (H_4) concerning the timing of the party's social-democratic transformation, albeit with a caveat. Whereas the results indicate that the second wave transformers are less successful in achieving liberal economic reform than the first wave transformers, this negative effect diminishes and it may well be a matter of time before the two equalise.

These findings suggest that in the case of the second wave transformers, the networks originating in the communist era have only limited success in halting economic reform. Differently put, there seems to be little evidence of path dependence as far as the pace of reform is concerned. While these networks may certainly determine who is able to start a business, and when and how they do it, the networks do not seem to be static entities that lock the countries into a permanently slower institutional development when the communist successor parties are in power. Rather,

[18]I also carried out the tests using dummy variables, with '1' indicating the presence of the communist successor party in the coalition equal to or greater than 19% of the coalition votes. The results were largely unchanged, though the magnitude of the negative effect of the untransformed party was smaller, as it dropped to –0.18, or more than half of a 'minus' sign.

[19]The calculation proceeds as follows: there are 10 '+' and '–' increments between 1 and 4+ (1+, 2–, 2, 2+, 3– and so on). Therefore, each increment represents 10% of total reform progress. Three quarters of a '+' or '–' sign, or of 10% of total reform progress, is equal to 7.5%.

the politically connected participants in these networks seem to respond and adapt to the changing circumstances and political opportunities, albeit slowly.

Finally, as far as the control variables are concerned, the effects of wealth, growth and FDI are negligible, most likely as a result of the inclusion of the lagged dependent variable, which absorbs the effects of these variables. As for the period dummies, only the 1991–1992 and 2001–2007 time periods are significant, suggesting that the period between the inception of the accession negotiations with the EU and the year 2000 did not differ in any special way from the previous transition experience. Instead, the post-2000 period of intensification of accession negotiations seems to have had greater positive effect on reform. This might be treated as supporting evidence for the value of EU conditionality across the board. The countries in question, irrespective of parties in power, would accelerate reform only when the EU deadline loomed, country and sectoral variation notwithstanding. At the same time, the initial (1991–1992) acceleration is consistent with initial efforts to impress international financial institutions in an attempt to secure loans.

Policy evidence from the region supports the statistical results as it shows that the transformed communist successor parties built upon the economic reform tasks started by their non-communist successor counterparts. In 1995 the Hungarian Socialist Party (*Magyar Szocialista Párt*), in coalition with the liberal junior coalition partner, the Alliance of Free Democrats (*Szabad Demokraták Szövetsége*), carried out the Hungarian 'shock therapy', with the introduction of the Bokros package. In Poland, the Democratic Left Alliance/Polish Peasants' Party (*Sojusz Lewicy Demokratycznej/Polskie Stronnictwo Ludowe*, SLD/PSL) coalition continued the reforms that started with the neoliberal Balcerowicz Plan. The SLD/PSL government passed and implemented reform initiatives that its right-of-centre predecessors had failed to implement, such as the long-announced (albeit modified) voucher privatisation programme in 1995, as well as bank restructuring and privatisation in 1996 (Bałtowski 2002; Blazyca & Rapacki 1996; King & Sznajder 2006). In 1998 in Slovakia, the Party of the Democratic Left (*Strana Demokratickej L'avice*, SDL') became an important member of the staunchly pro-reform coalition, which replaced the illiberal Mečiar regime. During the period 1998–2002, the SDL's Brigita Schmögnerová held the key post of Minister of Finance.

In those countries where the transmuted communist successor parties held power, namely Bulgaria and Romania, the government's resistance to economic reform was profound (Vachudova 2005). With much enthusiasm, the voters and external observers greeted the eventual alternation in power and the formation of the centre-right governments. However, these new governments' period in office turned out to be plagued by infighting and incompetence (EIU 2000). Nonetheless, in part under the pressure from the World Bank and the International Monetary Fund, they still managed to carry out reforms at a pace superior to their ex-communist counterparts (Negrescu 1999).

Conclusion

This essay has examined the effects of the communist successor parties on liberal economic reform in Central and Eastern Europe. The findings indicate that the influence of the communist successor parties in East–Central Europe is mediated by the countries' historical experience. The impact of the historical differences that shaped these countries' transition out of communism and the subsequent transformation of the communist successor parties, as well as their concomitant economic reform proclivities, has only recently begun to fade. In essence, there are two separate pathways through which the ex-communist parties affected the nascent market system.

Communist successor parties hindered the speed of the liberal market reform only where the transmuted communist successor parties were in power. However, the negative effect on reform of the transmuted communist successor parties diminished in the post-transformation period as they seemed to be converging with the communist successor parties that had transformed in the first wave. Thus, for all the initial differences between the two types of communist successor parties, there is no conclusive evidence to support path-dependent arguments.

The first wave transformers, on the other hand, displayed no difference in their economic reform record compared to parties with non-communist roots. These results are interesting for several reasons. First, they indicate no region-wide statistical support for transition theories that highlighted the technocratic superiority of the transformed left, a legacy of the cultural capital held by the reform-prone communist technocrats. Conversely, they also indicate no support for the outcomes one would expect to occur if the 'political capitalism' thesis held true, namely partial reform, where the politically connected communist-era technocrats would attempt to stall reform in its later stages, when the social-democratically transformed communist successor parties were in power, in an effort to continue seeking rent.

Finally, it is noteworthy that the first wave transformers displayed economic reform policy choices remarkably similar to the choices made by their leftist counterparts in areas of the world where market economy was more entrenched. Globalisation scholars have recognised the far-reaching convergence across the political spectrum as far as privatisation and liberalisation are concerned and have turned their attention to regulation or social policy (Murillo 2002; Murillo & Martínez-Gallardo 2007; Simmons *et al.* 2006; Simmons & Elkins 2004; Garrett 1998a; Boix 1998; Swank 2006).

The aim of this essay has been to investigate whether, and under what historical conditions, the erstwhile proponents of central planning and of state ownership of the means of production would be willing and able to embark on the project of 'building capitalism'. Thus the analysis did not conduct a comparative investigation of the ways in which party type might matter for the extent and type of regulation or, perhaps more importantly, redistributive policies. The question of the relevance of partisanship for social policy choice may be a promising avenue for future research.[20] The findings discussed in this essay have implications for such a research programme as they suggest that the timing of the social-democratic transformation of the communist successor left should be taken into account.

University of Richmond

[20]See, for example, Tavits and Letki (2009), Lipsmeyer (2002) and Cook *et al.* (1999).

References

Bałtowski, M. (2002) *Przekształcenia Własnościowe Przedsiębiorstw Państwowych* (Warsaw, Wydawnictwo Naukowe PWN).

Bartlett, D. L. (1996) 'Democracy, Institutional Change, and Stabilisation Policy in Hungary', *Europe-Asia Studies*, 48, 1, January.

Beck, N. & Katz, J. K. (1995) 'What to Do (and Not to Do) with Time-series Cross-sectional Data', *American Political Science Review*, 89, 3, September.

Blazyca, G. & Rapacki, R. (1996) 'Continuity and Change in Polish Economic Policy: The Impact of the 1993 Election', *Europe-Asia Studies*, 48, 1, January.

Boix, C. (1998) *Political Parties, Growth and Equality* (New York, Cambridge University Press).

Böröcz, J. & Róna-Tas, Á (1995) 'Small Leap Forward: Emergence of New Economic Elites', *Theory and Society*, 24, 5, October.

Bozóki, A. & Ishiyama, J. T. (2002) *The Communist Successor Parties of Central and Eastern Europe* (New York, M.E. Sharpe).

Cook, L., Orenstein, M. & Rueschemeyer, M. (eds) (1999) *Left Parties and Social Policy in Postcommunist Europe* (Boulder, CO, Westview Press).

Crampton, R. J. (1995) 'The Bulgarian Elections of December 1994', *Electoral Studies*, 14, 2, June.

Dudek, A. (1997) *Pierwsze Lata III Rzeczpospolitej, 1989–1995* (Kraków, Wydawnictwo Geo).

Economist Intelligence Unit (EIU) (2000) *Country Report. Romania* (New York, Economist Intelligence Unit).

Ekiert, G. & Kubik, J. (1998) 'Contentious Politics in New Democracies: East Germany, Hungary, Poland, and Slovakia, 1989–93', *World Politics*, 50, 4, July.

Ekiert, G. & Zielonka, J. (2003) 'The Next Great Transformation: The EU Eastward Enlargement', *East European Politics and Society*, 17, 1, April.

Epstein, R. (2008) *In Pursuit of Liberalism: International Institutions in Postcommunist Europe* (Baltimore, MD, The Johns Hopkins University Press).

European Bank for Reconstruction and Development (1994–2007) *Transition Report* (London, EBRD).

Eyal, G., Szelényi, I. & Townsley, E. (1997) 'The Theory of Post-Communist Managerialism', *New Left Review*, 222, March–April.

Eyal, G., Szelényi, I. & Townsley, E. (1998) *Making Capitalism without Capitalists: Class Formation and Elite Struggles in Post-Communist Central Europe* (New York, Verso).

Frye, T. (2002) 'The Perils of Polarization: Economic Performance in the Postcommunist World', *World Politics*, 54, 3, April.

Frye, T. (2010) *Building States and Markets After Communism: The Perils of Polarized Democracy* (Cambridge, Cambridge University Press).

Garrett, G. (1998a) *Partisan Politics in the Global Economy* (New York, Cambridge University Press).

Garrett, G. (1998b) 'Global Markets and National Politics: Collision Course or Virtuous Circle?', *International Organization*, 52, 4, October.

Grabbe, H. (2006) *The EU's Transformative Power: Europeanization through Conditionality in Central and Eastern Europe* (New York, Palgrave).

Grzymała-Busse, A. (1998) 'Reform Efforts in the Czech and Slovak Communist Parties and their Successors, 1988–1993', *East European Politics and Societies*, 12, 3, September.

Grzymała-Busse, A. (2001) 'Coalition Formation and the Regime Divide in East Central Europe', *Comparative Politics*, 34, 1, October.

Grzymała-Busse, A. (2002) *Redeeming the Communist Past: The Regeneration of Communist Successor Parties in East Central Europe* (Cambridge, Cambridge University Press).

Grzymała-Busse, A. (2006) 'The Discreet Charm of Formal Institutions', *Comparative Political Studies*, 39, 3, April.

Grzymała-Busse, A. & Innes, A. (2003) 'Great Expectations: The EU and Domestic Political Competition in East Central Europe', *East European Politics and Societies*, 17, 1, February.

Hankiss, E. (1990) *East European Alternatives* (Oxford, Clarendon Press).

Hellman, J. (1998) 'Winners Take All: The Politics of Partial Reform in Postcommunist Transitions', *World Politics*, 50, 2, January.

Ishiyama, J. (1995) 'Communist Parties in Transition: Structures, Leaders, and Processes of Democratization in Eastern Europe', *Comparative Politics*, 27, 2, January.

Ishiyama, J. (1997) 'The Sickle or the Rose?', *Comparative Political Studies*, 30, 3, June.

Ishiyama, J. (1999) 'Sickles into Roses: The Successor Parties and Democratic Consolidation in Post-Communist Politics', *Democratization*, 6, 4, Winter.

Ishiyama, J. (2006) 'Europeanization and the Communist Successor Parties in Post-Communist Politics', *Politics and Policy*, 34, 1, March.

Ishiyama, J. (2009) 'Historical Legacies and the Size of the Red Brown Vote in Post Communist Politics', *Communist and Post-Communist Studies*, 42, 4, December.

Ishiyama, J. & Bozóki, A. (2001) 'Adaptation and Change: Characterizing the Survival Strategies of the Communist Successor Parties', *Journal of Communist Studies and Transition Politics*, 17, 3.

King, L. & Sznajder, A. (2006) 'The State-led Transition to Liberal Capitalism: Neoclassical, Organizational, World Systems, and Social Structural Explanations of Poland's Economic Success', *American Journal of Sociology*, 112, 3, November.

Kitschelt, H., Mansfeldova, Z., Markowski, R. & Tóka, G. (1999) *Post-Communist Party Systems: Competition, Representation and Inter-Party Cooperation* (Cambridge, Cambridge University Press).

Kuzio, T. (2008) 'Comparative Perspectives on Communist Successor Parties in Central–Eastern Europe and Eurasia', *Communist and Post-Communist Studies*, 41, 4, December.

Linden, R. (ed.) (2002) *Norms and Nannies: The Impact of International Organizations on the Central and East European States* (Lanham, MD, Rowman and Littlefield Publishers, Inc.).

Linz, J. & Stepan, A. (1996) *Problems of Democratic Transition and Consolidation* (Baltimore, MD, The Johns Hopkins University Press).

Lipsmeyer, C. (2002) 'Parties and Policy: Evaluating Economic and Partisan Influences on Welfare Policy Spending during the European Post-Communist Transition', *British Journal of Political Science*, 32, 4, October.

Murillo, M. V. (2002) 'Political Bias in Policy Convergence', *World Politics*, 54, 4, July.

Murillo, M. V. & Martínez-Gallardo, C. (2007) 'Political Competition and Policy Adoption: Market Reforms in Latin American Public Utilities', *American Journal of Political Science*, 51, 1, January.

Negrescu, D. (1999) 'A Decade of Privatization in Romania', in Rühl, C. & Daianu, D. (eds) (1999). *Economic Transition in Romania – Past, Present and Future* (Washington D.C., Bucharest, The World Bank, Romanian Center for Economic Policies).

Orenstein, M. (1998) 'A Genealogy of Communist Successor Parties in East–Central Europe and the Determinants of their Success', *East European Politics and Societies*, 12, 3, September.

Orenstein, M., Bloom, S. & Lindstrom, N. (2008) *Transnational Actors in Central and East European Transitions* (Pittsburgh, PA, University of Pittsburgh Press).

Pasti, V. (1997) *The Challenges of Transition—Romania in Transition* (Boulder, CO, East European Monographs).

Pierson, P. (2004) *Politics in Time* (Princeton, NJ, Princeton University Press).

Pop-Eleches, G. (2009) *From Economic Crisis to Reform: IMF Programs in Latin America and Eastern Europe* (Princeton, NJ, Princeton University Press).

Przeworski, A. (1991) *Democracy and the Market: Political and Economic Reforms in Eastern Europe and Latin America* (New York, Cambridge University Press).

Róna-Tas, Á (1994) 'The First Shall Be Last? Entrepreneurship and Communist Cadres in the Transition from Socialism', *American Journal of Sociology*, 100, 1, July.

Schimmelfennig, F. & Sedelmeier, U. (eds) (2005) *The Europeanization of Central and Eastern Europe* (Ithaca, NY, Cornell Studies in Political Economy).

Shugart, M. S. (2005) 'Semi-Presidential Systems: Dual Executive and Mixed Authority Patterns', *French Politics*, 3, 3, December.

Simmons, B. A., Dobbin, F. & Garrett, G. (2006) 'Introduction: The International Diffusion of Liberalism', *International Organization*, 60, 4, October.

Simmons, B. A. & Elkins, Z. (2004) 'The Globalization of Liberalization: Policy Diffusion in the International Political Economy', *American Political Science Review*, 98, 1, February.

Staniszkis, J. (1990) 'Political Capitalism in Poland', *East European Politics and Societies*, 5, 1, December.

Staniszkis, J. (2001) *Postkomunizm—Próba Opisu* (Gdańsk, Wydawnictwo słowo/obraz terytoria).

Stark, D. & Bruszt, L. (1998) *Postsocialist Pathways: Transforming Politics and Property in East Central Europe* (Cambridge, Cambridge University Press).

Swank, D. (2006) 'Tax Policy in an Era of Internationalization: Explaining the Spread of Neoliberalism', *International Organization*, 60, 4, October.

Szalai, E. (1994) 'The Power Structure in Hungary after the Political Transition', in Bryant, C. & Mokrzycki, E. (eds) (1994). *The New Great Transformation: Change and Continuity in East-Central Europe* (London: Routledge).

Szelényi, I. & Szelényi, S. (1995) 'Circulation and Reproduction of Elites in Post-communist Transformation', *Theory and Society*, 24, 5, October.

Tavits, M. & Letki, N. (2009) 'When Left is Right: Party Ideology and Policy in Post-Communist Europe', *American Political Science Review*, 103, 4, November.

Vachudova, M. A. (2005) *Europe Undivided: Democracy, Leverage & Integration after Communism* (Oxford, Oxford University Press).
Waller, M. (1995) 'Adaptation of the Former Communist Parties of East–Central Europe', *Party Politics*, 1, 4, October.
Wedel, J. (2001) *Collision and Collusion: The Strange Case of Western Aid to Eastern Europe* (New York, Palgrave).
Ziblatt, D. (1998) 'The Adaptation of Ex-communist Parties to Post-communist East Central Europe: A Comparative Study of the East German and Hungarian Ex-communist Parties', *Communist and Post-Communist Studies*, 31, 2, June.

Appendix 1

TABLE A1
ELECTED COMMUNIST SUCCESSOR PARTIES, BY COUNTRY

Country	*Communist successor party*
Bulgaria	*Balgarska Socialisticheska Partija* (BSP) Bulgarian Socialist Party
Hungary	*Magyar Szocialista Párt* (MSzP) Hungarian Socialist Party
Lithuania	*Lietuvos Demokratinė Darbo Partija* (LDDP) Democratic Labour Party of Lithuania Since 2001: *Lietuvos Socialdemokratų Partija* (LSP) Social Democratic Party of Lithuania
Poland	*Socjaldemokracja Rzeczpospolitej Polskiej* (SdRP) Social Democracy of the Republic of Poland Since 1999: *Sojusz Lewicy Demokratycznej* (SLD) Democratic Left Alliance
Romania	*Partidul Democrației Sociale din România* (PDSR) Party of Social Democracy in Romania Since 2001: *Partidul Social Democrat* (PSD) Social Democratic Party
Slovakia	*Strana Demokratickej L'avice* (SDL') Slovak Party of the Democratic Left
Slovenia	*Združena Lista Socialnih Demokratov* (ZLSD) United List of Social Democrats Since 2005: *Socialni Demokrati* (SD) Social Democrats

Satisfied, Sceptical or Simply Indifferent? Current Public Opinion towards the Fall of Communism in the Czech Republic

PAT LYONS & ALŽBĚTA BERNARDYOVÁ

MOST RESEARCH ON CITIZENS' POLITICAL ATTITUDES IN post-communist states such as the Czech Republic has focused on the transition process. Much less is known about contemporary public opinion in former communist states toward the fall of communism. Although most citizens in Central and Eastern Europe have supported the new liberal democratic states and market economies, there is very little research on how today's citizens view the events of 1989. In relation to the Czech Republic for example, do Czech citizens see the Velvet Revolution as stemming from a groundswell of spontaneous public sentiment, or do they see it as the product of a small elite group of dissidents led by Václav Havel? The general question addressed in this essay is how citizens two decades after the Velvet Revolution perceive the events that led to the fall of communism in Czechoslovakia. In order to examine this issue a national survey undertaken in May 2008 is used to examine citizens' perceptions of the historical events of November 1989.

An important consideration in ascertaining citizens' opinions toward a key historical event is how to evaluate a process that was in essence unique. In practice, there is the difficulty of how to ask the public to evaluate an exceptional event in a manner that allows one to draw general conclusions about the fall of communism. Consequently, there is a need to outline some theoretical expectations as to why different segments of contemporary public opinion might exhibit varying attitudes toward the fall of communism.

A common approach within the social sciences to this type of research problem is to examine some general attributes of specific events. In the case of the Velvet Revolution of 1989, a sensible strategy is to evaluate current public opinion in terms of three fundamental questions. First, who do the Czech public think played the leading role in bringing about the Velvet Revolution—ordinary citizens or dissident counter-elites? Second, what were the primary motivations for change in 1989: was the Velvet

This research is part of a project entitled 'Citizens and the State in the Czech Republic: Influence and Legacy of the Prague Spring, 1968–2008' funded by the Czech Science Foundation (Grant No. GACR 407/08/1515).

Revolution primarily 'political' in espousing liberal democracy, or did it have a significant economic component in wanting the benefits of free market capitalism? Lastly, in the opinion of Czech citizens, why did the Velvet Revolution occur? Was the overriding goal reform of the system or a complete overthrow of the communist regime? By providing answers to these three questions it should be possible to map out the main contours of how contemporary Czech citizens view the fall of communism. The evidence presented in this essay reveals that contemporary Czech citizens do not have a single opinion toward the Velvet Revolution. Public sentiment is marked by satisfaction, scepticism and indifference which may be explained in terms of political, economic and informational factors.

A theory of public opinion toward the Velvet Revolution

Within public discussion of the events of late 1989, the Velvet Revolution is typically equated with the fall of communism in Czechoslovakia, and the peaceful mass demonstrations that occurred between 17 and 27 November are viewed as leading directly to the overthrow of the communist regime. The fact that the Velvet Revolution was 'gentle' or 'soft' was subsequently advocated as a template for the effective use of people power. Nonetheless, there has been a general recognition that the peaceful fall of communism in Czechoslovakia was in comparative terms exceptional.[1]

One suggested key reason for this Czechoslovak 'exceptionalism' was the existence of a well-developed civil society and a democratic tradition spanning back to 1918 (Huntington 1991, p. 270; Bradley 2000; Heimann 2009, pp. 48–86, 310).[2] This argument suggests that mass attitudes and behaviour are central to understanding the fall of communism in Czechoslovakia. If this is the case, this implies that the positive 'people power' legacy of the Velvet Revolution in the minds of citizens represents a central pillar of the legitimacy of the current political regime.

Given the rapid and extensive nature of the social, political and economic changes that occurred after 1990, it is not surprising to find that the positive symbolic meaning of the Velvet Revolution has changed over time. A key reason for changing public attitudes was the perceived shortcomings in the post-communist transition process. Consequently, the efforts expended to bring about the fall of communism were judged, in retrospect, not to have been sufficiently extensive to ensure a complete purging of the communist era legacy. Consequently, a negative facet of the legacy of the Velvet Revolution was the traditional tendency of Czech political leaders and a majority of citizens to avoid conflict as had been the case in 1938, 1948 and 1968 (Wydra 2007, p. 206).

Thus, the adoption of a 'velvet' approach towards ending communism and building a liberal democratic state with a market economy could also be interpreted as both a sign of weakness, in being unwilling to fight for real political and economic reforms, and a

[1]For details of the Velvet Revolution see: Bradley (1992), Wheaton and Kavan (1992), Kukral (1997), Vaněk and Otáhal (1999), Saxonberg (1999, 2001) and Suk (2003). For a global overview of the use of people power to instigate a transition from an authoritarian to a democratic regime, see Karatnycky and Ackerman (2005, p. 30).

[2]There is some debate on this point. For example, Kraus (2003, p. 53) contends that civil society had been 'decimated under communism' and did not effectively revive until the late 1990s.

sign of passivity in the face of all forms of corruption (Tucker 2000, pp. 209–41).[3] These positive and negative perspectives toward the legacy of the Velvet Revolution suggest that contemporary public opinion is likely to exhibit systematically different attitudes toward the goals, leadership and reasons used to explain the Velvet Revolution.

With the 10th, 15th and 20th anniversaries of the fall of communism, expert assessments of the popular mood toward the transition process of the 1990s emphasised the themes of citizens' 'disappointment' and 'disillusionment'. These attitudes were judged to have led to a 'crisis of expectations' and suggestions of a 'revolution betrayed' (Keller 2005, p. 471; Wydra 2007, p. 200; Rupnik 2010, p. 106).[4] Other evidence, based on Czech citizens' own evaluations given in mass survey interviews undertaken during the 1990s, reveals that feelings of disappointment with the post-communist system of governance and nostalgia for communism became more salient following a banking crisis, an economic downturn and a series of political corruption scandals during 1997–1998 (Kraus 2003, p. 56; Haerpfer 2002, pp. 6–20). This survey evidence suggests that political and economic factors shaped citizens' attitudes toward current and previous systems of governance. In this respect, Mischler and Rose (2002) found that citizen support for the new democracies of Central and Eastern Europe was primarily driven in the 1990s by political performance, and to a lesser degree by economic management and the legacy of communism. In short, evaluations of current regime performance influenced how citizens today viewed the communist system of governance and the fall of communism.

In order to limit the scope of research on Czech public opinion towards the Velvet Revolution to manageable limits, attitudes toward the events of late 1989 are restricted to the three central facets highlighted in the introduction. For each facet 11-point bipolar scales are used and details of the operationalisation of these scales are given in the next section and in Appendix 1. First, public perceptions of who provided leadership, whether dissident elites or participants in the mass demonstrations during November 1989, are assessed. Second, there is an exploration of the goals of the Velvet Revolution in terms of the extent to which this event aimed at reform or revolution. Lastly, the question of what were the key reasons for the Velvet Revolution, defined here in terms of political or economic change, is examined. Of course, examining current public opinion towards the fall of communism must take account of the possibility that some citizens have no strong opinions because of a lack of motivation or knowledge. Consequently, in the next subsection a simple model of public opinion towards the Velvet Revolution will be presented.

A simple model of public opinion toward the Velvet Revolution

Almost all accounts of the Velvet Revolution present what might be described as the 'dominant narrative' or '*status quo*' position. This may be summarised as follows.

[3]Rupnik (2010, p. 106) notes that 'nobody in Prague claims to own "copyright" on the term "velvet revolution" or can identify its author. Václav Havel ... attributes the name to a Western journalist. The term, like so much of what followed, seems to have originated in the West'.

[4]Kodýtek (1999) is an example of a different form of nostalgia evident among the core group of pro-communist citizens in the Czech Republic who assert that both the Prague Spring and the Velvet Revolution were betrayals of the workers revolution of February 1948 in Czechoslovakia. Members of this group constitute about one-in-20 of the Czech adult population (Haerpfer 2002, p. 16).

The fall of communism in Czechoslovakia was defined as being dominated by people power; it was primarily political in nature; and it was revolutionary. Within this essay this standard account will be used as the basis for exploring systematic differences within Czech public opinion. In the hypothesis testing undertaken, the central goal will be to identify and explain why specific subgroups express attitudes that are different from the general population. These statistically significant differences are identified using a difference of proportions test as shown in Tables 1–3.

Previous research on the fall of communism in Czechoslovakia, and elsewhere, emphasises the importance of two substantive explanations, based on politics and economics, in describing public attitudes toward the process of transition. Political explanations stress the importance of the relationship between the citizen and the state after the fall of communism. In this respect, different visions of democracy, such as liberal, republican, participatory and statist, have been used by intellectuals and citizens to evaluate the success of the transformation process. In contrast, the economic perspective is based on differences in attitudes among those who gained materially after the fall of communism (economic 'winners') and those who did not ('losers').[5]

The political and economic explanations represent two poles of the first substantive dimension of the public opinion analysis presented in this essay. The second dimension, as shown at the bottom of Figure 1, is the level of opinionation. Here, account is taken of the fact that citizens may not have strong opinions towards a political event that occurred two decades previously. Lack of opinionation is known from the public opinion literature to be strongly related to the level of mobilisation and political knowledge.

The simple model of public opinion toward the Velvet Revolution presented in Figure 1 aims to summarise the logic of the hypothesis testing reported in this essay. In essence, differences along the two (substantive and opinionation) dimensions represent variation in preferences among clearly identifiable subgroups within Czech public opinion. The statistical analysis does not aim to test causal relations, but is more modest in attempting to account for significant subgroup deviation from the pattern evident in total public opinion. It is appropriate at this point to explain in greater detail the two dimensions of analysis presented in Figure 1 and the subgroup bases for the hypotheses to be tested.

Economic calculations

One way in which current Czech citizens might evaluate the fall of communism is in terms of whether their lives have become materially better since 1990. In this respect, those who have been 'winners' in the free market reforms in post-communist states such as the Czech Republic are likely to have systematically different attitudes than those who have not made gains. It seems reasonable to argue that those who gained from the post-communist transition process are more likely to think the Velvet

[5]Tucker *et al.* (2002) use a similar argument to explain popular support for European Union membership in post-communist states.

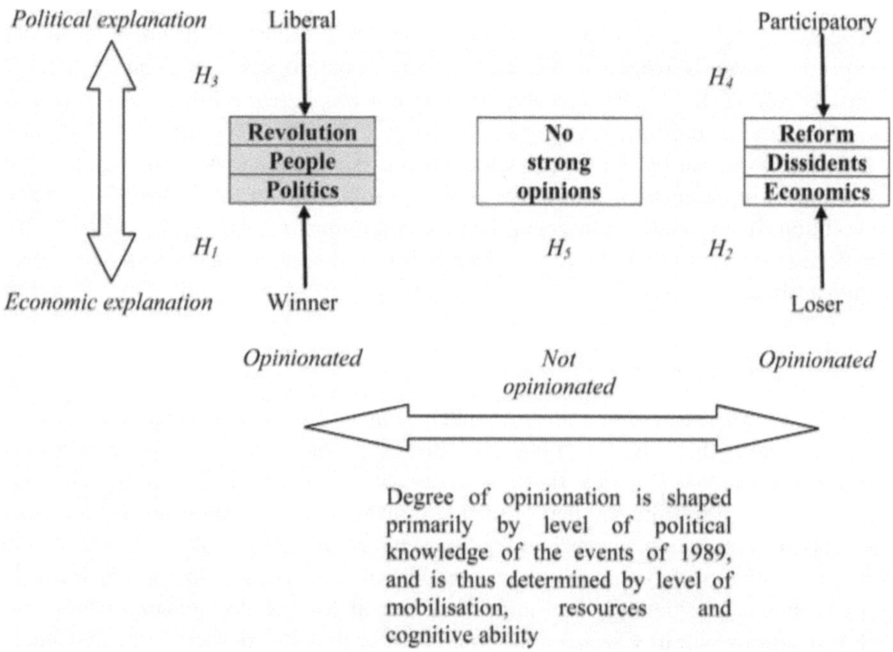

Note: this model of public opinion is based on two dimensions of analysis illustrated by the two large double-headed arrows: (a) substantive political and economic criteria, and (b) level of opinionation or willingness to express an opinion. The grey text box denotes the dominant '*status quo*' interpretation of the Velvet Revolution present in public discourse. The goal of this model is to explain significant statistical deviation from the dominant '*status quo*' interpretation by different subgroups.

FIGURE 1. MODEL OF PUBLIC OPINION TOWARD THE VELVET REVOLUTION

Revolution had positive effects consonant with the ideals of creating a functioning market economy.

In this research being a 'winner' or 'loser' is measured using a subjective evaluation of the respondent's standard of living in the household. In addition, position within the economy as defined by occupation is also an important indicator of success or failure. Those segments of public opinion not economically active—such as students, the unemployed and the retired—are likely to have different attitudes toward the Velvet Revolution than those who have been successful in the labour market, or in business. Using survey based income and occupational measures one may hypothesise the following differences between winners and losers.

Hypothesis 1 (H_1) Economic winners in the post-communist transition process will be significantly more likely to express the *status quo* interpretation of the Velvet Revolution, that the goal was revolution, based on political change, and it was led by a mass movement.

Hypothesis 2 (H_2) Economic losers are significantly less likely to adhere to the *status quo* interpretation and significantly more likely than the majority public opinion to state that the Velvet Revolution was about reform and economic change and that it was led by dissident elites.

The essential logic in these two hypotheses is that winners will adopt a positive perspective towards what the Velvet Revolution symbolises two decades after the event. Therefore, for them, the Velvet Revolution was a 'revolution' as it represented the end of the communist regime established in 1948. This revolution was primarily political and was led by the people rather than dissident elites. As a result, the fall of communism represents for economic winners a fulfilment of the ideals of the Velvet Revolution. In contrast, for losers in the post-communist transition process a negative perspective is more likely. Here the expectation is that economic losers will express significantly less support for the *status quo* interpretation of the fall of communism.

Political considerations

Apart from economic considerations, a likely source of difference within Czech public opinion towards the Velvet Revolution is citizens' political ideals. Dryzek and Holmes (2002, pp. 6–14, 268–71) argue that the process of democratisation in post-communist states is based on four key models of the relationship between the citizen and the state: the liberal, republican, participatory and statist models. Following the Velvet Revolution, two of these models, that is the liberal and the participatory perspectives, have been most influential. One important reason for the dominance of these two political visions within Czech public opinion was that the participatory and liberal models were promoted by the two most influential political actors in Czech politics since 1990: Václav Havel, the playwright, leading dissident and Czech President from 1993 to 2003; and Václav Klaus, the prime minister from 1993 to 1997, and president from 2003 until the time of writing.

It is important to keep in mind that these participatory and liberal strands within Czech politics have never been a key cleavage like the economic left–right orientation within party competition. Rather, these differing political visions formed a central theme of political discourse evident in the books and speeches of Havel and Klaus during inter-election periods. Within the media the competing political visions of Havel and Klaus have been represented as a conflict between 'idealist' and 'realist' views of citizen politics (Myant 2005). For this reason, many of the political supporters of Havel would not have necessarily adhered to his participatory non-partisan vision of political life.

For Václav Havel, citizenship is primarily a moral enterprise based on small group activities that have an educating and socialising function. Citizens should ideally act in a decentralised power system of 'non-political politics' or even 'anti-political politics'. This is a position that comes close to rejecting a role for political parties (Masaryk 1927, p. 47; Havel 1988, pp. 391–98; 1990; Keane 1999, p. 464; Pontuso 2004 pp. 123–51). In essence, citizen politics is conceptualised as a communal, rather than individual endeavour with a strong Tocquevillean flavour (Putnam 2000). Therefore, for Havel, citizenship is primarily associated with participation through a community rather than through political party organisations.

In contrast, Klaus (1992, 2002) conceptualises citizenship in terms of a central role for political parties. Adopting a neoliberal economic perspective based on the ideas of Schumpeter (1943), Hayek (1944) and Friedman (1962), Klaus sees citizens' political activity playing its most important role in the form of participation during elections.

During inter-election periods citizens delegate power to politicians. As a result, citizens inhabit a 'centralised' political state where mass political activity is circumscribed to short periods of time. For Klaus, democratic politics is mainly about citizens acting as individuals expressing self-interest in their choice of parties during regular, free and fair elections.

In general terms, adherents to Klaus's liberal view of politics are likely to be more satisfied with the Velvet Revolution as an event associated with political change and as a genuine project of the people. Conversely, those supportive of Havel's participatory vision are more likely to view the Velvet Revolution more sceptically in terms of its outcome, and see its legacy as being more reform-oriented, focusing on economic change and having evolved into an elite-led rather than a truly citizen-led process. Within the dataset examined there are, unfortunately, no direct measures of the participatory and liberal political orientations. Therefore, these political positions are inferred using a number of indicators suggested within the literature on political attitudes. In this respect, supporters of the participatory model of citizenship are more likely to be left wing and liberal adherents are expected to be right wing.[6]

Hypothesis 3 (H_3) Citizens adhering to a liberal political vision often associated with a right-wing orientation will be more likely to think the Velvet Revolution had the goal of revolution, and that leadership for political change was provided by the people.

Hypothesis 4 (H_4) Individuals with a participatory view of citizen politics, typically identified by those on the left, will be significantly more likely than total public opinion to say the Velvet Revolution was about reform, was led by dissident elites and had an economic component.

Moreover, partisanship is also likely to be important where supporters of Klaus' Civic Democratic Party (ODS, *Občanská demokratická strana*) adopt a more (liberal) positive view of the Velvet Revolution, while voters for the Social Democrats (ČSSD, *Česká strana sociálně demokratická*) and the Communist Party (KŠC, *Komunistická strana Československa*) are expected to be more sceptical, or negative, than overall public opinion.

Political knowledge and level of opinionation

A final consideration in modelling contemporary Czech public opinion towards the events of late 1989 is to take account of different levels of opinion. Here it is argued that citizens with lower levels of political knowledge are less likely to express definite opinions. A more detailed discussion of this argument is given in the next section. Previous research demonstrates that there are systematic differences in levels of political knowledge among citizens, and these differences are often identifiable with

[6]This linking of liberal with right wing and participatory with left wing is a simplification where alternative visions associated with stances such as left-wing authoritarianism are not explored directly in order to keep the data analysis tractable.

specific subgroups (Delli Carpini & Keeter 1996; Althaus 2003; Grönlund & Milner 2006; Lyons 2008).

One explanation of differences in citizens' level of political knowledge is the 'mobilisation–resources–cognitive ability' model. This model asserts that one would expect systematic variation on the basis of motivation to learn about political affairs; possession of the requisite resources to efficiently gather information about politics; and the capacity to understand and comprehend political information (Hyman & Sheatsley 1947; Converse 1974, p. 730; 1975, pp. 96–97; Zaller 1992, pp. 21, 42–43, 331ff.). In this research, the respondents' levels of political knowledge was measured using a political quiz technique (see Appendix 2 for details).

Political mobilisation is measured in this research using four indicators: electoral participation, level of party attachment, degree of trust in political institutions and possession of an ideological orientation (left or right wing). Citizen resources are operationalised in terms of material wealth, subjective household standard of living and occupation, where those who are in positions of economic dependency—such as the unemployed, retired or students—are judged to have fewer resources. It is important to note here that citizen resources also form part of the economic 'winners and losers' model. This duplication demonstrates the difficulty of evaluating independent explanations of public attitudes toward the Velvet Revolution due to complex causal relationships and observational equivalence. These thorny methodological issues are not directly addressed here as the goal is to map out the profile of Czech citizens' attitudes.[7]

In addition, position in society is also seen as reflecting differential access to resources where women are expected to encounter greater obstacles through their lower positions, skill sets and salaries in the labour market. Age is conceptualised here as a rough proxy measure of political experience while being married is used as an indicator of social integration. Finally, cognitive ability is typically measured in terms of level of education. This ability is a key resource for converting interest in politics and access to information carried typically through the media into long-term information about political life. On the basis of these considerations the following hypothesis regarding level of opinionation may be expressed.

Hypothesis 5 (H_5) Citizens with higher levels of opinionation as indicated by degree of political knowledge will be more likely than total public opinion to express definite opinions toward the Velvet Revolution in terms of its goals, leadership and reasons for change. The opposite pattern should be evident for those with low levels of political knowledge or opinionation.

This section has provided a brief theoretical overview of the factors that previous scholarly work suggests are likely to explain differences among contemporary Czech citizens toward the Velvet Revolution. Prior to testing these hypotheses with reference to our national survey dataset of May 2008, it is necessary first to describe the methodology and data used in the empirical analyses reported in the following section.

[7]This work forms the foundations for testing rival causal models in future research work.

Methodology and data

The methodological approach adopted in this essay is to explore contemporary Czech public opinion employing a national survey of political attitudes. Using a standard methodology for this type of empirical research, survey questions relating to the Velvet Revolution were asked in a specially designed module within an omnibus monthly (quota sample) survey of citizens' political attitudes. Here standard questions dealing with political satisfaction ratings, voter intentions in a future election, left–right orientation and trust in political institutions were implemented. The survey module relating to contemporary attitudes towards the immediate reasons for the fall of communism in Czechoslovakia in late 1989 was, for methodological reasons, divided into three parts.

Survey response effects and use of open-ended questions

In the first part an open-ended question probed respondents about what words came to mind when the term 'Velvet Revolution' was mentioned. Interviewers recorded these verbatim responses. The main reason for asking this question was to elicit any unprompted considerations that Czech citizens had concerning the Velvet Revolution. Such an approach is based on Zaller and Feldman's (1992) theory of survey response which emphasises the importance that priming, framing and other questionnaire effects may have on the nature and stability of attitudes measured. The key insight here is that for most Czech citizens, thoughts about political issues, and more especially past political events, are not something that occur on a regular basis. Therefore, when respondents are spontaneously asked their attitudes about something they have not considered recently (or may never have contemplated) they are compelled to create and report an opinion in a short period of time. One efficient way of making a response in this situation is to use recently encountered information as the basis for providing an answer.

Unsurprisingly, this process of survey response may result in bias stemming from cues provided by prior items in a survey questionnaire yielding question ordering, priming, framing and social desirability effects (Schuman & Presser 1996, pp. 23–78, 68, 99, 100, 110; Zaller 1992, pp. 42, 44, 48–49; Tourangeau *et al.* 2000, pp. 197–229). For these methodological reasons it is sensible to measure what immediate considerations respondents bring to their answers when asked about the Velvet Revolution.

Attitude scales

The second part of the module presented respondents with a set of bipolar scales that were intended to capture three central facets of the Velvet Revolution. The reasoning behind each of these scales has been outlined earlier. However, it is important here to describe how these scales were implemented. Respondents were given a show card for each item that graphically illustrated the bipolar nature of the scale and its 11-point structure ranging from zero to 10, where point '5' is the mid-point (see Appendix 1 for details of these scales). In order to encourage those interviewed to provide answers, non-committal responses (such as 'don't know', no answer, or answer refused) were not presented on the show card, but were recorded if the respondent failed to indicate a point on the scale. An odd-numbered scale (in this case 11-point) was used in order to capture the well-known tendency of respondents with weak or no opinions to select the 'centre point' in attitude scales rather than admit to the interviewer that they 'don't know' (Schuman & Presser 1996; Tourangeau *et al.* 2000). Moreover, using scales with a large range, that is point scales of 11 rather than nine, seven, five or three, allows respondents to make nuanced answers and facilitates post-survey aggregation of these scales for subgroup analyses.

Assessing citizens' level of political knowledge

The final part of the survey module evaluated how much information each respondent had about politics using a series of seven quiz items where a simple true or false answer was requested. Most of these items referred to political history dealing with the Prague Spring (1968), Velvet Revolution (1989) and the first democratic elections of 1990. As the survey work was undertaken during the 40th anniversary of the events of 1968, there was much media discussion and public commentary on these political topics (see Appendix 2 for details of the political knowledge questions). This methodology replicates standard approaches used in academic surveys such as successive waves of the American National Election Survey.[8]

The central reason for exploring citizen's level of informedness is that citizens' ability to provide answers to survey questions and exhibit consistency across different attitude scales depends on level of political knowledge (Zaller 1992; Alvarez 1997; Converse 2000). One might argue that level of education might be a more useful measure of informedness about public affairs; however, previous research reveals that education level is not a good predictor of political knowledge (Galston 2001, p. 226). In short, differences in level of political knowledge are expected to be an important explanation of willingness to express an opinion or level of opinionation and type of attitude reported.

In this research, simple summated rating scales were constructed from the seven political quiz items where a correct answer was scored as a '1' and all other answers (incorrect, don't know or no answer) were coded as zero. It should be noted that there is no consensus within the survey design literature as to how best to measure level of political knowledge, and more specifically how to correctly analyse and interpret 'don't know' and incorrect responses (Mondak 2001; Mondak & Davis 2001; Mondak & Anderson 2004). Most previous research simply divides respondents into those who give correct answers to quiz items and those who give uncommitted or incorrect answers. Consequently, a majority of the political knowledge literature reports the use of simple summated rating scales, or in the absence of suitable political quiz items, researchers use interviewer's subjective evaluations of respondents' general level of

[8]The American National Election Survey (ANES) is a long-term project in existence since 1948. It consists of an archive of hundreds of surveys dealing with elections and political attitudes based at the Institute for Social Research, University of Michigan at Ann Arbor. More information about this academic survey methodology is available from the following website: http://www.electionstudies.org/OurStudies/OurStudies.htm, last accessed 14 July 2011.

familiarity with current affairs as evident in the survey interview (Zaller 1992, p. 333ff; Delli Carpini & Keeter 1996; Althaus 2003).

Survey data

The analysis of public attitudes toward the Velvet Revolution in the Czech Republic is based on a mass survey fielded during the period of 12–19 May 2008. This survey was implemented by the 'Centre for Public Opinion Research' (CVVM, *Centra pro výzkum veřejného mínění*).[9] This survey has a typical methodology for this series of opinion polls. This national face-to-face survey interviewed 1,066 adults aged 15 years and older using quota sampling on the basis of region, size of community, sex, age and education. There were almost 270 interviewers ($n = 267$) who undertook an average of four interviews each.

The sample is representative of the entire territory of the Czech Republic with a mean of 15 interviews being undertaken in each Primary Sampling Unit ($n = 71$).[10] The response rate for this survey is unknown as this information is not recorded by interviewers, although they were asked to record other details such as their evaluations of respondent cooperation, the interviewees' level of political knowledge and the households' income level. Moreover, no weighting variables were produced to reflect the size of the household from which a respondent was selected, thereby reflecting the different probability of being selected for interview. (Summary statistics for all explanatory variables are given in Appendix 3.)

Having described the methodology and data used in the analyses presented in this essay, the next section will focus on mapping public opinion towards the Velvet Revolution and on differences between subgroups of citizens on the basis of structural and attitudinal criteria.

Analysis of the opinion poll data

The analysis will focus first on the ideas that the Czech public has towards the Velvet Revolution when unprompted by other sources of information. These survey data are invaluable in assessing the extent to which the events of 1989 are salient in the minds of contemporary citizens, and what considerations are cognitively most accessible when respondents hear the term 'Velvet Revolution'. Thereafter, the examination of Czech public opinion will shift towards a study of the closed-ended questions. It is expected that citizens' attitudes toward the Velvet Revolution are likely to vary among different segments of the Czech adult population, and a central goal of this research was to investigate systematic differences among subgroups in terms of the theoretical expectations outlined earlier in the first section.

[9]This is a specialised section within the Institute of Sociology of the Czech Republic's Academy of Sciences.

[10]The Primary Sampling Unit is based on the local government district or county (Czech: *okres*, plural *okresy*). These administrative units are the basis for aggregated census statistics and are thus used for survey sampling purposes because socio-demographic data are readily available.

Unprompted ideas relating to the Velvet Revolution

When those interviewed were asked what words came to mind when the term 'Velvet Revolution' was mentioned, one of the strongest abiding memories in the Czech public's consciousness regarding 1989 was the ringing or tinkling of keys (*'zvonění klíčema'*, *'cinkání klíčí'*, *'zvonění a cinkání klíčí'*) during the mass demonstrations in Wenceslas Square, Prague. It seems that this inspired act of political symbolism, aimed at creating a common bond among the demonstrators on Wenceslas Square, was more important to the participants of the Velvet Revolution than its cursory mention in the history books suggests.[11]

Two substantive themes also emerged from verbatim responses. The first was Czech citizens' emphasis on the fact that the Velvet Revolution was a peaceful 'political overthrow' ('political upheaval' (*'politický převrat'*), 'We had our bare hands! putsch politics' (*'Máme holé ruce! převrat politiky'*), 'peaceful transfer of power' (*'klidné předání moci'*)). The fact that respondents used the term 'overthrow' (*'převrat'*) is significant as it underscores the theme of regime change completed in an open manner where the public rose suddenly against the communist government (Pithart 2009, pp. 17–23, 55). Significantly, very few respondents explicitly linked the legacy of the Prague Spring with the Velvet Revolution—although this is a common subject within the scholarly literature (Wydra 2007, pp. 325, 327, 342).

The second theme noted by respondents was their sense of disappointment in the failure of the Velvet Revolution to meet its own ideals. A typical unprompted response in this respect was 'great frustration, I too believed Havel, but he disappointed the entire nation' (*'těžká blamáž, moc jsem věřila Havlovi, ale zklamal celý národ'*). Consequently, current public opinion toward the Velvet Revolution exhibits a certain pride in bringing about a political 'overthrow' without violence; however, there is also a sense of betrayal in not achieving the ideals expressed during November 1989. Ironically, this negative perspective is likely to be strongest among contemporary Communist Party (KSČM, *Komunistická strana Čech a Moravy*) voters, who are typically of retirement age and believe that the abandonment of socialism after the fall of communism was a mistake (Kodýtek 1999).

In summary, the responses to open-ended questions in the survey data demonstrate the distinct positive and negative facets of public opinion towards the Velvet Revolution outlined earlier in the theory section. Before exploring in greater detail the nature of these positive and negative facets, and their structural and attitudinal foundations, it is important first to outline the overall contours of Czech public opinion towards the events of November 1989.

[11]In the absence of unprompted open-ended survey questions towards the events of late 1989, polling companies would most likely not capture this important facet of the public's memory of the fall of communism. More generally this evidence suggests the need to undertake more research which deals more comprehensively with citizens', rather than academics' and commentators', evaluations of events such as the Velvet Revolution.

Overall public attitudes toward the Velvet Revolution

A central assumption behind the attitude scales used to examine key features of the Velvet Revolution is that they represent different facets of public opinion. This implies that the attitudes expressed on each of the scales are not strongly correlated, and hence may be considered independent of each other. A simple test of the statistical association, shown at the end of Appendix 1, between each of the 11-point scales examined reveals that there was not a strong relationship between any of the scales (Spearman rho estimates range from -0.02 to -0.25[12]), confirming that this assumption is a valid one.

Turning now to an examination of public opinion for the three bipolar scales relating to attitudes toward the goals, leadership and reasons for the Velvet Revolution, these demonstrate the following main features. First, a majority of the Czech public (59%) believed that the goal of the events of late 1989 was revolution rather than reform (15%). Second, a majority of the respondents (58%) felt that the main reasons for the Velvet Revolution were political change, rather than economic considerations (10%). Third, public opinion was divided in May 2008 over who provided the main leadership during the Velvet Revolution: 37% of those interviewed thought it was citizens acting through a mass movement, while 26% believed it was counter-elite dissidents such as Václav Havel; and the remainder (37%) expressed no strong opinions on this issue. Fourth, a number of respondents ranging between 26% and 37% did not express definite opinions on the three facets of the Velvet Revolution examined. This evidence underscores the view, outlined earlier, that citizens may not always have strong opinions about events that academics and media commentators consider to be very important. Since the numbers of respondents who did not express strong opinions on the three Velvet Revolution scales are not trivial, this may be evidence of a lack of consensus within Czech public opinion on this issue.

Is there a consensus within Czech public opinion?

An examination of the Czech public's perception of the Velvet Revolution reveals that there is not a strong consensus on the historical meaning of the events of 1989. It seems more correct to speak of distinct facets of public opinion towards the fall of communism. Estimation of Perceptual Agreement statistics for all three ordinal rating scales supports this finding (van der Eijk 2001) (see Appendix 1 for details). Overall, there is no strong consensus within current public opinion towards the Velvet Revolution. There is least consensus (0.15) on the question of whether the Velvet Revolution was led by an elite group of dissidents rather than being seen as a mass movement.[13]

[12]Spearman rho is a measure of statistical association between two variables that are at the ordinal level of measurement (i.e. an ordinal scale ranges from low to high where the differences between each point on the scale may not be equal).

[13]One might reasonably criticise using a scale based on an 'elite–people' dichotomy to measure public attitudes toward the Velvet Revolution. However, in defence of this question, the results in Table 2 demonstrate that current perceptions of who led the Velvet Revolution splits a majority of the Czech public into supporters of the 'elite' (26%), 'people' (37%) interpretations. The remaining

This survey evidence is important as it demonstrates that different groups within Czech society hold different perceptions of the nature and consequences of the reforms associated with 1989. This topic will be examined more systematically in the next subsection. However, it is possible to divide the May 2008 opinion poll into three age groups or generations—Prague Spring, Velvet Revolution and post-communist—and to examine if these cohorts of citizens have different political attitudes. The presence of generational differences in attitudes toward the Velvet Revolution and the Czechoslovak communist regime (1948–1989) has been a central element in contemporary debates on the legacy of communism.

The opinion poll results shown in Figure 2 demonstrate that, in general, there are few large differences between the three cohorts identified, but closer inspection reveals two noteworthy patterns. First, the older generations were more likely to think that the Velvet Revolution had a strong economic aspect than the younger cohorts. Second, the younger post-communist generation was more likely to think that the Velvet Revolution was more strongly influenced by citizens rather than dissident elites than those actually present at the events of late 1989. These inter-generational differences make considerable sense and appear to lend support to the opinions expressed during the 'Kundera Affair' that age and experience do matter when Czech citizens come to interpret key events in their recent past.[14]

Nonetheless, while these cohort effects are interesting they should be treated with caution as the differences observed are not large. In fact, from a surveying point of view it seems fairer to conclude that there are, in reality, few differences in opinion across the generations. This evidence suggests that age, taken here as a proxy for political experience, is not a central determinant of differences between Czech citizens in their attitudes towards the fall of communism. This being the case, it is important to see if other factors such as level of political knowledge, ideological orientation or other political attitudes may help explain the differences in opinions observed in the survey data.

Differences within Czech public opinion towards the Velvet Revolution

Examination of variation in the level of public opinion towards the three facets of Czech citizens' attitudes toward the Velvet Revolution is based on a series of cross tabulations presented in Tables 1, 2 and 3. The subgroups chosen for analysis were selected on the basis, first, of the five hypotheses outlined in the second section, and

'middle' group (37%) appears from the evidence in Table 2 to be composed of those who lacked sufficient knowledge to express a definite opinion. Consequently, the lack of consensus observed is due to ambivalence or equivocation for a majority of opinionated respondents (63%), and uncertainty for a minority (Alvarez & Brehm 2002, p. 11; Martinez *et al.* 2005). In short, respondents interpreted the 'elite–people' dichotomy as intended and this item provided valuable information on the nature of public opinion toward the fall of communism.

[14]On 13 October 2008, *Respekt*, an influential weekly Czech current affairs magazine, published an article claiming that the influential Czech novelist Milan Kundera had cooperated with the authorities in April 1950 in capturing a 'western spy' of Czech origin (Hradílek & Třešňák 2008, pp. 38–44). During this affair, commentary by figures such as former Czech President Václav Havel suggested that 'young historians' may not have sufficient understanding and experience to interpret documents from the communist era (Havel 2008, p. 15).

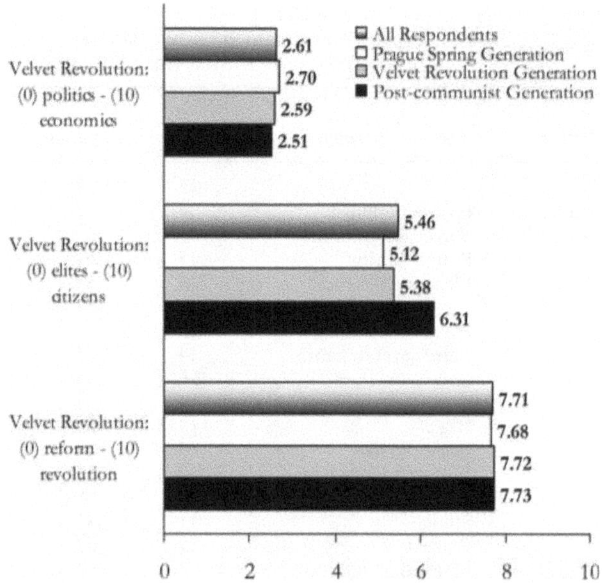

Note: all scales are 11 point (0–10) and include all respondents aged 15 years or more. Note the 'Prague Spring Generation' refers to respondents who were 15 years or older in 1968 and similarly for the 'Velvet Revolution Generation' in 1989. The 'Post-communist Generation' refers to all those born after 1974 who only came to early adulthood (i.e. 15 years) after 1990. The interpolated median scores reported in this figure are used because finite ordered rating scales often have biased measures of central tendency and dispersion if mean and standard deviation estimates are used. For this reason an interpolated median measure is employed, which locates the median by linear interpolation between respective category boundaries (see van der Eijk 2001). For the sake of clear presentation confidence estimates for these data points are not shown.
Source: CVVM 12–19 May 2008, questions 27–30.

FIGURE 2. COMPARISON OF ATTITUDES TOWARD THE MEANING OF THE VELVET REVOLUTION 1989 BY AGE COHORT (INTERPOLATED MEDIAN SCORES)

second, on having a sufficient number of cases ($n \geq 70$) to determine significant statistical differences using a series of difference of proportions tests. Here the goal is to see if subgroup opinion differs significantly from the pattern evident in the total sample.

Reform or revolution? A subgroup analysis of the first 11-point bipolar scale inquiring into the goals of the Velvet Revolution is presented in Table 1. This empirical evidence regarding H_2 reveals limited support for the idea that losers in the transition process exhibited above-average support (15%) for the idea that reform was the main goal of the Velvet Revolution. This is evident in the pattern of opinion supportive of reform for those with the lowest subjective standard of living (24%). In contrast, as H_1 asserts, economic winners illustrated some of the highest level of support for the interpretation of the goals of the events of 1989 as a revolution.

It should also be noted that support for the interpretation of 1989 as a revolution was also high among the self-employed (70%), those with high levels of political knowledge (69%) and education (65–66%), and respondents exhibiting a right-wing

TABLE 1
PROFILE OF CITIZENS' ATTITUDES TOWARD THE PERCEIVED GOALS OF THE VELVET REVOLUTION—REFORM OR REVOLUTION (%)

Explanatory variable	*Subgroups*	*Reform*	*Revolution*	*Middle, Don't know*	*N*
All respondents		15	59	26	1,066
Age cohort generation	Post-communist	14	**52**	**35**	347
	Velvet Revolution	15	63	22	358
	Prague Spring	17	61	**21**	328
Level of education	Elementary or less	14	**52**	**34**	220
	Lower secondary	17	57	26	412
	Higher secondary	13	**66**	**21**	303
	Third level or more	14	65	21	131
Subjective standard of living	Low	**24**	**48**	29	195
	Average	14	59	28	480
	High	12	**66**	22	391
Occupational status	Unemployed	**3**	46	**51**	33
	Full time employee	17	57	26	289
	Self-employed	10	**70**	20	94
	Student	11	**47**	**42**	107
	Retired	17	61	22	247
Marital status	Married, cohabiting	14	62	24	658
	Single	14	**50**	**36**	266
Sex	Male	16	59	25	522
	Female	14	59	26	544
Level of political knowledge	Very low	11	**43**	**45**	211
	Low	18	**53**	29	297
	High	15	**69**	**16**	356
	Very high	14	**69**	**17**	202
Interested in politics	No	15	57	28	784
	Yes	16	**66**	**18**	282
Ideology	Left wing (0–3)	15	62	23	162
	Right wing (7–10)	14	**66**	**20**	341
Vote in Chamber elections	Would not vote	17	**51**	**32**	456
	Would vote	13	**65**	**22**	610
Vote intention	Civic Democrats (R)	14	**68**	**18**	186
	Social Democrats (L)	16	63	21	265
	Communists (L)	13	57	29	112
	Christian Democrats (R)	18	61	22	51
	Green Party (R)	15	68	18	62
Level of party attachment	Very close	16	63	21	75
	Fairly close	15	**65**	**21**	361
	Sympathiser	16	61	23	155
	Close to no party	15	**54**	**31**	475
Trust in political institutions	Very low	17	57	26	207
	Low	14	59	27	393
	High	14	61	25	287
	Very high	15	60	25	179
Current political situation	Not satisfied	15	59	26	924
	Satisfied	12	62	26	142
TOTAL (N)		*159*	*632*	*275*	*1,066*

Notes: for vote intention 'L' and 'R' in parentheses refer to left and right wing parties. The 'post-communist' generation are 15–33 years, 'Velvet Revolution' generation 34–54 years, and the 'Prague Spring' generation 55–74 years. Rows sum to 100% subject to rounding error. Responses denoting 'Reform' (0–3), 'Revolution' (7–10) and 'Middle, Don't know' (4–6 and 'don't know') refer to a recoding of the 11-point scale in question 27. Figures in bold and grey shading are significantly higher ($p \leq 0.01$) than the estimate for all respondents, while the bold underlined estimates are significantly lower than the national average.
Source: CVVM 12–19 May 2008, question 27 (see Appendix 1).

TABLE 2

PROFILE OF CITIZENS' ATTITUDES TOWARD THE PERCEIVED LEADERS OF THE VELVET REVOLUTION—DISSIDENTS OR THE PEOPLE (%)

Explanatory variable	*Subgroups*	*Dissidents*	*People*	*Middle, Don't know*	*N*
All respondents		26	37	37	1,066
Age cohort generation	Post-communist	**18**	36	**46**	347
	Velvet Revolution	28	40	**32**	358
	Prague Spring	**32**	34	34	328
Level of education	Elementary or less	21	32	**47**	220
	Lower secondary	28	33	39	412
	Higher secondary	26	**43**	**31**	303
	Third level or more	27	44	**29**	131
Subjective standard of living	Low	29	**30**	41	195
	Average	27	35	38	480
	High	24	**43**	34	391
Occupational status	Unemployed	27	36	37	33
	Full time employee	27	36	37	289
	Self-employed	25	42	33	94
	Student	**9**	37	**54**	107
	Retired	**32**	34	34	247
Marital status	Married, cohabiting	29	39	**32**	658
	Single	**17**	35	**48**	266
Sex	Male	27	37	36	522
	Female	25	37	38	544
Level of political knowledge	Very low	**17**	**29**	**54**	211
	Low	26	35	39	297
	High	**31**	38	**31**	356
	Very high	27	**46**	**27**	202
Interested in politics	No	25	35	40	784
	Yes	29	42	**29**	282
Ideology	Left wing (0–3)	**41**	33	**26**	162
	Right wing (7–10)	22	**45**	33	341
Vote in Chamber elections	Would not vote	**21**	34	45	456
	Would vote	30	40	**30**	610
Vote intention	Civic Democrats (R)	21	**44**	35	186
	Social Democrats (L)	28	**43**	**29**	265
	Communists (L)	**49**	**22**	**29**	112
	Christian Democrats (R)	27	45	27	51
	Green Party (R)	31	40	29	62
Level of party attachment	Very close	**43**	36	**21**	75
	Fairly close	29	41	**30**	361
	Sympathiser	25	36	39	155
	Close to no party	**21**	34	44	475
Trust in political institutions	Very low	32	**28**	41	207
	Low	28	38	34	393
	High	24	39	37	287
	Very high	**18**	42	39	179
Current political situation	Not satisfied	27	36	37	924
	Satisfied	20	44	36	142
TOTAL (N)		*278*	*394*	*394*	*1,066*

Notes: rows sum to 100% subject to rounding error. Responses denoting 'Dissident' elites (0–3), 'People' or a mass movement (7–10) and 'Middle, Don't know' (4–6 and 'don't know') refer to a recoding of the 11-point scale in question 28. Figures in bold and grey shading are significantly higher ($p \leq 0.01$) than the estimate for all respondents, while the bold underlined estimates are significantly lower than the national average.
Source: CVVM 12–19 May 2008, question 28 (see Appendix 1).

TABLE 3
PROFILE OF CITIZENS' ATTITUDES TOWARD THE PERCEIVED REASONS FOR THE VELVET REVOLUTION—POLITICAL OR ECONOMIC (%)

Explanatory variable	*Subgroups*	*Political*	*Economic*	*Middle, Don't know*	*N*
All respondents		58	10	32	1,066
Age cohort generation	Post-communist	53	8	**39**	347
	Velvet Revolution	61	11	**27**	358
	Prague Spring	60	11	29	328
Level of education	Elementary or less	**51**	**6**	**43**	220
	Lower secondary	57	12	31	412
	Higher secondary	62	9	29	303
	Third level or more	**66**	**15**	**19**	131
Subjective standard of living	Low	57	13	30	195
	Average	57	10	33	480
	High	60	10	30	391
Occupational status	Unemployed	58	6	36	33
	Full time employee	60	10	30	289
	Self-employed	60	11	29	94
	Student	**45**	7	**48**	107
	Retired	58	12	30	247
Marital status	Married, cohabiting	61	11	**28**	658
	Single	**50**	8	**42**	266
Sex	Male	57	11	32	522
	Female	59	9	32	544
Level of political knowledge	Very low	**42**	9	**48**	211
	Low	62	8	29	297
	High	**65**	10	**25**	356
	Very high	56	**15**	29	202
Interested in politics	No	**62**	10	**28**	784
	Yes	62	12	**26**	282
Ideology	Left wing (0–3)	62	10	28	162
	Right wing (7–10)	**64**	12	**24**	341
Vote in Chamber elections	Would not vote	55	9	36	456
	Would vote	61	11	**28**	610
Vote intention	Civic Democrats (R)	**65**	11	**24**	186
	Social Democrats (L)	63	11	**26**	265
	Communists (L)	63	10	27	112
	Christian Democrats (R)	63	10	27	51
	Green Party (R)	58	15	27	62
Level of party attachment	Very close	**69**	**5**	25	75
	Fairly close	60	12	**27**	361
	Sympathiser	59	9	32	155
	Close to no party	54	10	36	475
Trust in political institutions	Very low	**50**	**14**	36	207
	Low	59	9	31	393
	High	58	10	32	287
	Very high	**65**	8	26	179
Current political situation	Not satisfied	57	11	32	924
	Satisfied	**64**	9	27	142
TOTAL (N)		620	110	336	*1,066*

Notes: rows sum to 100% subject to rounding error. Responses denoting 'Political' change (0–3), 'Economic' change (7–10) and 'Middle, Don't know' (4–6 and 'don't know') refer to a recoding of the 11-point scale in question 29. Figures in bold and grey shading are significantly higher ($p \leq 0.01$) than the estimate for all respondents, while the bold underlined estimates are significantly lower than the national average.
Source: CVVM 12–19 May 2008, question 29 (see Appendix 1).

orientation (66%) and a vote intention for the rightist Civic Democrats (68%). The evidence regarding political orientation (liberal or participatory) is supportive of H_3, but is less compelling in terms of H_4. With regard to opinionation, the data in Table 1 are supportive of the expectations outlined in H_5 that mobilisation, resources and cognitive ability do indeed help shape expression of a definite opinion on the goals of the Velvet Revolution.

Leadership by dissident elites or by the people? Turning now to public opinion towards perceived leadership of the Velvet Revolution, the expectations expressed in H_1 and H_2 are largely confirmed in Table 2. In accordance with the expectations expressed in H_4 there were higher than average levels of support from those with a left-wing orientation (41%) that dissident elites provided leadership for the Velvet Revolution. However, it is important to note that particular segments of Czech public opinion have a greater than average belief that the Velvet Revolution was a dissident counter-elite project. This pattern is evident among Communist Party voters (49%), those who were adults during the Prague Spring of 1968 (32%), the retired (32%) and those who know most about politics (31%).

From such evidence it appears that some older Czech citizens who support the current Czech Communist Party have a negative view of the Velvet Revolution typified by comments such as 'the end of socialist development in our country' ('*ukončení socialistického vývoje u nás*') and a 'grandiose manipulation of the people' ('*grandiózní manipulace s lidmi*'). In contrast, a more positive interpretation of the Velvet Revolution as being a project of the people was held by those with a liberal vision of politics as postulated in H_3. Evidence supportive of this hypothesis is given by the fact that the highest level of support for this opinion came from those with a right-wing orientation (45%) and Civic Democrat voters (44%).

Finally, it is important to note that a (joint) plurality of respondents (37%) in May 2008 did not express strong opinions on the leadership of the Velvet Revolution. In general, the evidence presented in Table 2 reveals that those who were least politically mobilised had the lowest levels of resources such as political experience as indicated by age, and cognitive ability as measured by level of education, and were thus most likely not to express definite opinions about the events of 1989. This general pattern in the survey data is consonant with the expectations expressed in H_5.

Political or economic origins of 1989? As noted earlier in this section, only a minority of one in 10 respondents agreed that the origins of the Velvet Revolution were primarily economic in nature. Contrary to the theoretical expectations outlined in the first section, the subgroups showing higher than average support for an economic interpretation of the Velvet Revolution were those with the highest levels of education and political knowledge, and those who expressed least trust in contemporary political institutions (14–15%). These respondents would appear to be among the most 'critical' groups of Czech citizens; and this pattern underscores the expectations expressed in H_5 rather than the predictions made in the other four hypotheses. In this respect, one might argue that this well informed but sceptical minority interpreted the fall of communism more as an embracing of free market capitalism, rather than as a desire to create a liberal representative multiparty democracy.

As noted earlier, a majority of Czech citizens (58%) believe that the Velvet Revolution occurred primarily for political reasons. Moreover, this opinion appears to be strongest among those with a liberal view of politics as suggested in H_3. This pattern is also evident among those who are right wing (64%) and Civic Democrat voters (65%) and have the greatest informational resources denoted by level of education and political knowledge.

Moreover, popular support for the dominant narrative of the end of communism appears also to be associated with this political interpretation of the reasons for the Velvet Revolution. In this respect, those with the highest levels of party attachment, trust in political institutions and satisfaction with political institutions think the events of late 1989 had political rather than economic origins. This survey evidence is supportive of the general predictions expressed in H_1 and H_3. As with the other two Velvet Revolution scales, higher than average levels of opinionation are positively associated with being politically mobilised, having membership of a high resource subgroup and possessing higher cognitive abilities. Such a profile fits with the predictions of H_5. Significantly, Table 3 illustrates no evidence in favour of H_4.

In summary, a subgroup analysis of Czech public attitudes toward the Velvet Revolution in terms of its origins, goals and leadership reveals that citizens' evaluations are shaped, as hypothesised, by level of opinionation, and economic and political considerations. Economic winners in the post-communist transition process tend to have a 'positive' view of the Velvet Revolution believing it was revolutionary in scope, led by the people and was primarily concerned with political change. In contrast, economic losers in the post-communist transition process tend to believe that the Velvet Revolution is best characterised as a process limited to reform rather than real change, and that it was led by an elite primarily motivated by economic considerations. In political terms, adherents to a liberal view of politics tend to exhibit a more positive view of the Velvet Revolution than those with a participatory perspective.

Conclusion

This study of contemporary citizens' attitudes toward the fall of communism in Czechoslovakia in late 1989 contrasts different subgroups' responses to the 'dominant narrative' where a majority are said to believe that the Velvet Revolution was led by the people, that it was political in nature and that its goals were revolutionary. On the basis of political, economic and knowledge (level of opinionation) criteria this research developed five hypotheses. The first two hypotheses outlined expectations regarding two economic subgroups. Economic 'winners' (H_1) were expected *ceteris paribus* to be more supportive of the dominant narrative than economic 'losers' (H_2). The second pair of hypotheses suggested that political liberals (H_3) will be more supportive of the dominant narrative than those who support a civic participatory view of politics (H_4). The final hypothesis asserted that citizens with higher levels of political knowledge and mobilisation would be least likely not to express opinions regarding the dominant narrative.

The survey evidence presented in this essay has shown that contemporary Czech public opinion towards the fall of communism exhibits facets of satisfaction, scepticism and indifference. In short, there is no single public attitude towards the Velvet Revolution of 1989. Specifically, a majority of Czechs believe that the goal of the events of late 1989 was revolution rather than reform, and the main reasons for the Velvet Revolution were political rather than economic. More than a third think that the fall of communism was led by the people, one in four assert it was counter-elite dissidents such as Václav Havel, and the remainder (37%) have no strong opinions because they lack sufficient knowledge or motivation to take an interest in political issues. Overall, public indifference towards the Velvet Revolution constitutes at least a quarter of the Czech adult population. By virtue of its size this segment of public opinion cannot be considered a marginal group. Not having an opinion about the fall of communism is undoubtedly related to the transition process and the current political situation.

In this essay, five hypotheses were used to examine three key questions. For the 'who' question, which explored which actor (dissident elite or the people) provided the primary leadership for the Velvet Revolution, all five hypotheses were confirmed. With the 'what' question there was an investigation of Czech citizens' retrospective perceptions of the essential nature of the Velvet Revolution: three hypotheses were confirmed (H_1, H_3 and H_5) and two were rejected (H_2 and H_4). In the final 'why' question, the central motivation for the events of late 1989 was examined in terms of reform or revolution and the evidence was again mixed. Here, three hypotheses were accepted (H_1, H_3 and H_5), H_2 was partially accepted, and there was no strong evidence for H_4. Overall, these results demonstrate that contemporary citizens' adherence to the dominant narrative of the Velvet Revolution is most strongly associated with being an economic winner (H_1), having liberal political orientation (H_3), and possessing knowledge or being politically mobilised (H_5). However, being an economic loser in the post-communist transition process (H_2) or adopting a civic participation political stance is not consistently associated with rejecting the dominant narrative's explanation of the Velvet Revolution.

These empirical results are important because they qualify the assumption that there is a single dominant narrative of the fall of communism in Czechoslovakia in late 1989. It is true that there are not two competing narratives as there is little statistical evidence at the subgroup level indicating popular support for an alternative narrative of the Velvet Revolution that is essentially negative. However, the survey evidence shows that citizens who do not embrace the dominant narrative are best described as being either sceptical or indifferent. This case study of current public opinion in the Czech Republic on the fall of communism in Czechoslovakia has five general implications for future research in the domains of methodology, theory, explanatory power, cross-time and cross-national analyses, and consequences for contemporary political life.

First, the model of public opinion concerning the Velvet Revolution presented in this article may be sufficiently general to facilitate undertaking similar studies in other post-communist states, thereby creating the foundations for evaluating the legacy of the fall of communism. Second, Wydra's (2007) basic thesis may be summarised as follows: citizens' experience of communism is fundamental to understanding how they evaluate both the fall of communism and the subsequent transition process. The research presented here shows that while there may be a dominant narrative regarding the Velvet Revolution, this does not mean that all citizens accept this account. Third, future research should determine whether the economic or political interpretation has greatest power in explaining opinions toward the Velvet Revolution using individual level models. Fourth, the explanatory model presented in this research may have application to citizens' evaluations of other historical events. In the Czech case the legacy of the Prague Spring of 1968, or in Poland the Solidarity strikes of 1980–1981, represent cogent case studies for this type of research. Fifth, the question of whether citizens' evaluations of events such as the Velvet Revolution have any measurable consequence on contemporary politics provides a direct indicator of the importance of the legacy of communism. Here, research using survey data could examine electoral behaviour, trust in public institutions and satisfaction with politics.

The use of survey methods to elicit contemporary popular perceptions of key historical events has not been a common research strategy within the social sciences. This is because it is difficult to interpret what popular attitudes to the past mean when measured in mass surveys, and to derive general theoretically grounded conclusions from such research. It is hoped the straightforward approach presented in this study will encourage more survey research on how citizens perceive their own past, and thus increase scholarly understanding of the importance and legacy of the fall of communism for citizens.

Czech Academy of Sciences
Radio Free Europe/Radio Liberty (RFE/RL)

References

Althaus, S. (2003) *Collective Preferences in Democratic Politics: Opinion Surveys and the Will of the People* (New York, Cambridge University Press).

Alvarez, M. R. (1997) *Information and Elections* (Ann Arbor, MI, University of Michigan Press).

Alvarez, M. R. & Brehm, J. (2002) *Hard Choices, Easy Answers. Values, Information, and American Public Opinion* (Princeton, NJ, Princeton University Press).

Bradley, J. F. N. (1992) *Czechoslovakia's Velvet Revolution: A Political Analysis* (Boulder, CO & New York, East European Monographs, Columbia University Press).

Bradley, J. F. N. (2000) 'Czechoslovakia: External Crises and Internal Compromise', in Berg-Schlosser, D. & Mitchell, J. (eds) (2000) *Conditions of Democracy in Europe 1919–39. Systematic Case Studies* (Houndsmills, Basingstoke, Macmillan).

Converse, P. E. (1974) 'Some Priority Variables in Comparative Electoral Research', in Rose, R. (ed.) (1974) *Electoral Behavior: A Comparative Handbook* (New York, Free Press).

Converse, P. E. (1975) 'Public Opinion and Voting Behavior', in Greenstein, F. I. & Polsby, N. W. (eds) (1975) *Handbook of Political Science* (Reading, MA, Addison-Wesley).

Converse, P. E. (2000) 'Assessing the Capacity of Mass Electorates', *Annual Review of Political Science*, 3, June.

Delli Carpini, M. X. & Keeter, S. (1996) *What Americans Know about Democracy and Why it Matters* (New Haven, CT, Yale University Press).

Dryzek, J. & Holmes, L. (2002) *Post-Communist Democratization* (Cambridge, Cambridge University Press).

Eijk, van der, C. (2001) 'Measuring Agreement in Ordered Rating Scales', *Quality and Quantity*, 35, 3, August.

Friedman, M. (1962) *Capitalism and Freedom* (Chicago, IL, University of Chicago Press).

Galston, W. A. (2001) 'Political Knowledge, Political Engagement, and Civic Education', *Annual Review of Political Science*, 4, June.

Grönlund, K. & Milner, H. (2006) 'The Determinants of Political Knowledge in Comparative Perspective', *Scandinavian Political Studies*, 29, 4, November.

Haerpfer, C. W. (2002) *Democracy and Enlargement in Post-Communist Europe. The Democratisation of the General Public in Fifteen Central and East European Countries, 1991–1998* (London, Routledge).

Havel, V. (1988) 'Anti-political Parties', in Keane, J. (ed.) (1988) *Civil Society and the State: New European Perspectives* (London, Verso).
Havel, V. (1990) *O lidskou identitu* (Prague, Rozmluvy).
Havel, V. (2008) 'Dva vzkazy', *Respekt*, 43, 20–26 October.
Hayek, F. (1944) *The Road to Serfdom* (London, Routledge).
Heimann, M. (2009) *Czechoslovakia: The State that Failed* (New Haven, CT, Yale University Press).
Hradilek, A. & Třešňák, P. (2008) 'Udaní Milana Kundery', *Respekt*, 42, 13–19 October.
Huntington, S. (1991) *The Third Wave: Democratization in the Late Twentieth Century* (Norman, OK, University of Oklahoma Press).
Hyman, H. H. & Sheatsley, P. B. (1947) 'Some Reasons Why Information Campaigns Fail', *Public Opinion Quarterly*, 11, 3, Autumn.
Karatnycky, A. & Ackerman, P. (2005) *How Freedom is Won. From Civic Resistance to Durable Democracy* (New York, NY, Freedom House).
Keane, J. (1999) *Václav Havel: A Political Tragedy in Six Acts* (London, Bloomsbury).
Keller, J. (2005) 'The Czech Republic: Fifteen Years Later', *European Journal of Social Theory*, 8, 4, November.
Klaus, V. (1992) *Proč jsem konzervativcem?* (Prague, TOP Agency).
Klaus, V. (2002) *Občan a obrana jeho státu* (Prague, Centrum pro ekonomiku a politiku).
Kodýtek, Z. (1999) *'Pražské jaro' a 'sametová revoluce' ve světle dneška* (Prague, JUDr. Jaroslav Weber).
Kraus, M. (2003) 'The Czech Republic's First Decade', *Journal of Democracy*, 14, 2, April.
Kukral, M. A. (1997) *Prague 1989: Theatre of Revolution* (New York, Columbia University Press).
Lyons, P. (2008) 'Co občané České republiky vědí o politice a proč je to důležité', in Mansfeldová, Z. & Kroupa, A. (eds) (2008) *Proměny reprezentace zájmů po vstupu do Evropské unie* (Prague, Sociologické Nakladatelství, SLON edice studie).
Martinez, M. D., Craig, S. C. & Kane, J. G. (2005) 'Pros and Cons: Ambivalence and Public Opinion', in Craig, S. C. & Martinez, M. D. (eds) (2005) *Ambivalence and the Structure of Political Opinion* (New York, McMillan).
Masaryk, T. G. (1927) *The Making of a State: Memories and Observations, 1914–1918* (London, Allen and Unwin).
Mischler, W. & Rose, R. (2002) 'Learning and Re-learning Regime Support: The Dynamics of Post-communist Regimes', *European Journal of Political Research*, 41, 1, January.
Mondak, J. J. (2001) 'Developing Valid Knowledge Scales', *American Journal of Political Science*, 45, 1, January.
Mondak, J. J. & Anderson, M. R. (2004) 'The Knowledge Gap: A Re-examination of Gender Based Differences in Political Knowledge', *Journal of Politics*, 66, 2, May.
Mondak, J. J. & Davis, B. (2001) 'Asked and Answered: Knowledge Levels When We Will Not Take "Don't Know" for an Answer', *Political Behavior*, 23, 3, September.
Myant, M. (2005) 'Klaus, Havel and the Debate Over Civil Society in the Czech Republic', *Journal of Communist and Transition Politics*, 21, 2, June.
Pithart, P. (2009) *Devětaosmdesátý. Vzpomínky a přemýšlení. Krédo* (Prague, Academia).
Pontuso, J. F. (2004) *Václav Havel: Civic Responsibility in the Postmodern Age* (Blue Ridge Summit, PA, Rowman and Littlefield).
Putnam, R. D. (2000) *Bowling Alone: The Collapse and Revival of American Community* (New York, Simon and Schuster).
Rupnik, J. (2010) 'Twenty Years of Postcommunism. In Search of a New Model', *Journal of Democracy*, 21, 1, January.
Saxonberg, S. (1999) 'The "Velvet Revolution" and the Limits of Rational Choice Models', *Czech Sociological Review*, 7, 1, Spring.
Saxonberg, S. (2001) *The Fall: A Comparative Study of the End of Communism in Czechoslovakia, East Germany, Hungary and Poland* (Reading, MA, Gordon & Breach).
Schuman, H. & Presser, S. (1996) *Questions and Answers in Attitude Surveys: Experiments on Question Form, Wording and Context* (Thousand Oaks, CA, Sage).
Schumpeter, J. (1943) *Capitalism, Socialism and Democracy* (London, Allen and Unwin).
Suk, J. (2003) *Labyrintem revoluce* (Praha, Prostor).
Tourangeau, L., Rips, L. J. & Rasinski, K. (2000) *The Psychology of Survey Response* (Cambridge, Cambridge University Press).
Tucker, A. (2000) *The Philosophy and Politics of Czech Dissidence from Patočka to Havel* (Pittsburg, PA, University of Pittsburg Press).
Tucker, J., Pacek, A. & Berinsky, A. (2002) 'Transitional Winners and Losers: Attitudes toward EU Membership in Post-communist Countries', *American Journal of Political Science*, 46, 3, July.

Vaněk, M. & Otáhal, M. (1999) *Sto studentských revolucí: Studentí v období pádu komunismu—životopisná vyprávení* (Prague, Lidové noviny).
Wheaton, B. & Kavan, Z. (1992) *The Velvet Revolution: Czechoslovakia in Transition, 1988–1991* (Boulder, CO, Westview Press).
Wydra, H. (2007) *Communism and the Emergence of Democracy* (Cambridge, Cambridge University Press).
Zaller, J. (1992) *The Nature and Origins of Mass Opinion* (Cambridge, Cambridge University Press).
Zaller, J. & Feldman, S. (1992) 'A Simple Theory of Survey Response: Answering Questions versus Revealing Preferences', *American Journal of Political Science*, 36, 3, August.

Appendix 1: Velvet Revolution attitude scales

Q.27: In the context of the Velvet Revolution there are often different views as to what was its principal goal. On a scale from 0–10, where (0) means that the main purpose of the Velvet Revolution was reform of the (communist) system and (10) indicates that its purpose was a revolutionary change, please indicate on this scale your own opinion.

Q.28: There is also a disagreement over whether the Velvet Revolution was a reform movement led by dissidents, or was a mass movement. On a scale from 0–10, where (0) means that the Velvet Revolution was a reform movement led by dissidents and (10) indicates that the Velvet Revolution was a mass movement, please indicate on this scale your own opinion.

Q.29: What do you think was the primary objective of the Velvet Revolution? On a scale from 0–10, where (0) stands for the argument that the primary objective of the Velvet Revolution was political change and (10) maintains that the primary objective of the Velvet Revolution was economic change, please indicate on this scale your own opinion.

Appendix 2: Measurement of political knowledge

Instructions read by the interviewer to all respondents: 'For the following questions (Q.31–37) please answer if the statement is true, if you are not sure about the right answer please go ahead and choose the "don't know, I am not sure" option. This answer is more valuable to us than guessing'.

The response options were 1 'Yes', 2 'No' or 3 'Don't know, not sure'. The correct answers are given in parentheses and were coded as '1' in the dataset, while incorrect answers and non-committal responses were coded as '0'.

Q.31: The political leader during the Prague Spring was Alexander Dubček? (Yes, true)

Q.32: The Prague Spring came after Charter 77? (No, false)

Q.33: Troops from the Warsaw Pact entered Czechoslovakia in the summer of 1968 and left at the start of the 'Normalisation Period' in early 1969? (No, false)

Q.34: The 'Normalisation Period' represented the end of the reform movement begun in 1968? (Yes, true)

Q.35: The phrase 'socialism with a human face' was a theme promoted by Alexander Dubček during 1968? (Yes, true)

Q.36: During the Velvet Revolution the Warsaw Pact threatened to invade Czechoslovakia? (No, false)

Q.37: ODS under the leadership of Václav Klaus won the first democratic elections after the fall of communism in 1990? (No, false)

TABLE A1
ATTITUDE SCALES SUMMARY STATISTICS FOR MAY 2008 SURVEY

Items	*Mean*	*Median*	*Standard deviation*	*Interquartile range*	*Skewness*	*Kurtosis*	*Perceptual agreement**	*N*
Q.27	7	7	3	4	−0.81	−0.34	0.36	969
Q.28	6	6	3	5	−0.15	−1.02	0.15	945
Q.29	3	3	3	4	0.08	7.47	0.38	867

Notes: *see Appendix 3 for details. Total number of cases in the sample is 1,066.
The Perceptual Agreement statistic indicates the degree to which there is public consensus on the opinions expressed, e.g. optimism or pessimism. The scale ranges from +1 to −1 where +1 indicates complete public consensus, −1 denotes complete disagreement, and zero indicates a uniform distribution where all points on the scale were chosen by equal numbers of respondents. See van der Eijk (2001) for details of how this statistic is estimated.

TABLE A2
CORRELATION BETWEEN THE VELVET REVOLUTION SCALES, MAY 2008

Items	*Q.27: Revolution*	*Q.28: Masses*	*Q.29: Economic*
Q.27: Revolution	1.00	–	–
Q.28: Masses	0.19	1.00	–
Q.29: Economic	−0.25	−0.02	1.00

Note: estimates of association are Spearman rho as all the scales are ordinal. Similar results are obtained with a Pearson correlation estimator. All estimates have a $p \leq 0.001$ and are derived from analyses of between 854 and 969 cases due to differential item non-response.

TABLE A3
POLITICAL KNOWLEDGE QUESTIONS RESULTS (%)

Item	*Yes*	*No*	*Don't know*	*Total*
Q.31	**70**	4	27	101
Q.32	16	**42**	42	100
Q.33	32	**44**	23	99
Q.34	**47**	15	39	101
Q.35	**63**	3	34	100
Q.36	17	**49**	34	101
Q.37	38	**36**	26	102

Note: estimates in bold and underlined represent correct answers. The mean percent of 'correct' answers for all seven questions is 50%, 'incorrect' is 18%, and for 'don't know' it is 32%. Row totals do not always sum to 100% due to rounding errors.

Appendix 3: Summary statistics for all explanatory variables

TABLE A4
SUMMARY STATISTICS FOR ALL EXPLANATORY VARIABLES

Explanatory variable	*Subgroups*	*Mean*	*Standard deviation*	*Minimum*	*Maximum*
Age	Age in years	44.410	17.384	15	89
Level of education	Elementary or less	0.206	0.405	0	1
	Lower secondary	0.386	0.487	0	1
	Higher secondary	0.284	0.451	0	1
	Third level or more	0.123	0.328	0	1
Subjective standard of living	Low to high	2.184	0.719	1	3
Occupational status	Unemployed	0.031	0.173	0	1
	Full time employee	0.271	0.445	0	1
	Self-employed	0.088	0.284	0	1
	Student	0.100	0.301	0	1
	Retired	0.232	0.422	0	1
Marital status	Married, cohabiting	0.617	0.486	0	1
	Single	0.250	0.433	0	1
Sex	Male = 1, female = 2	1.510	0.500	1	2
Level of political knowledge	Low to high	2.515	1.013	1	4
Interested in politics	Yes (1) or no (0)	0.265	0.441	0	1
Ideology	Left wing (0–3)	0.152	0.359	0	1
	Right wing (7–10)	0.320	0.467	0	1
Vote in Chamber elections	Yes (1) or no (0)	0.572	0.495	0	1
Vote intention	Civic Democrats (R)	0.174	0.380	0	1
	Social Democrats (L)	0.249	0.432	0	1
	Communists (L)	0.105	0.307	0	1
	Christian Democrats (R)	0.048	0.214	0	1
	Green Party (R)	0.058	0.234	0	1
Level of party attachment	Not close to very close	2.966	1.032	1	4
Trust in political institutions	Low to high	2.411	0.983	1	4
Current political situation	Satisfied, dissatisfied	0.133	0.340	0	1

Source: CVVM 12–19 May 2008, $N = 1,066$.

Evaluating Transitions: Human Rights and Qualitative Democracy in Central and Eastern Europe

BRAD K. BLITZ

THE POLITICAL RESTRUCTURING OF THE FORMER socialist states since 1989 has transformed Central and Eastern Europe into a region which scores particularly well when evaluated against political procedural criteria of democratic consolidation: elections are contested peacefully and fairly; there is an active civil society and an autonomous economic sector; and the rule of law is generally respected. Nonetheless, there are several areas where the legacies of former ideologies, policies and governmental structures continue to undermine the substance and quality of democracy enjoyed in these states. In particular, procedural accounts of democratic consolidation can underestimate the degree to which normative developments are institutionalised in domestic human-rights enforcing bodies, including courts and police. Focusing on two cases, those of Slovakia and Slovenia, this essay introduces the notion of 'qualitative democracy'. This is examined in the context of the judiciary's capacity to address complaints in Slovenia and the degree to which Slovak authorities have been able to protect the rights of Roma minorities. The central premise of this essay is that the state's capacity to guarantee the protection of human rights to all is an essential indicator of democratic success. The extent to which there is an observed lack of effective enforcement of human rights is explored, and claims of consolidation are therefore called into question.

The idea of 'quality' as a measure of democracy is particularly relevant both to new EU member states and Central and East European countries undergoing pre-accession reforms. It is explicitly recorded in the European Union's social policy agenda and has been part of the Lisbon strategy (European Commission 2005), but it also finds expression in earlier studies of political transition where it serves as an indicator of internal change and consolidation (O'Donnell *et al.* 1986; Linz & Stepan 1996). 'Qualitative democracy' emphasises democratic maturity as a guide to consolidation. It exposes both the operations of the state and its normative character and supplements procedural accounts of democracy which prioritise the conduct of elections and the smooth functioning of the rule of law for effective transition and the consolidation of liberal practices. It develops O'Donnell's critique of procedural biases as indicators of consolidation (1996), and instead suggests that by comparing formal institutional rules (constitutional provisions, laws and administrative orders) and operational practices, one may arrive at a deeper understanding of political change. Evidence for qualitative democracy may be found both at the attitudinal level and by examining the degree to which states have the capacity to enforce reforms that address particularly vulnerable sectors of the population, including those hard to reach and on the fringes of the polity.

Qualitative democracy is rights-reinforcing; it assumes that people can access their rights and that the state or relevant authority is competent to enforce these rights through domestic institutions. While European citizens have recourse to the European Court of Human Rights, a further premise of this study is that the reliance on external arbiters to enforce their rights exposes weaknesses within the state to resolve disputes and hence undermines claims of democratic maturity. Indicators of qualitative democracy include respect for the principle of non-discrimination; the effective operation of the judiciary as a guarantor of rights and freedoms to all; the development of shared social values; and the internalisation of democracy as an expression of state actions and public attitudes. In the context of the European Union, qualitative democracy also relates to the delivery of universalist social policy goals and the expansion of real opportunities and the guarantee of fundamental and social rights to all.[1]

This essay evaluates the qualitative dimension of the transitions in two states since 1989. The first part of this essay makes the case for a qualitative approach to democratisation. It reviews the literature on the effectiveness of conditionality and role of external actors as indicators of reform and democratic maturity. The second part evaluates some key developments in the area of human rights in Central and Eastern Europe. The third part examines the political transition of Slovenia and Slovakia by scrutinising how the introduction of new laws and accession to international instruments has been accompanied by operational developments in the justice sector. These countries were selected because, although they acceded to the European Union in the same year, they followed different trajectories and yet both have recently been condemned for their human rights record on specific issues. Slovenia, which was identified early on as a post-communist success story, was condemned by the European Court of Human Rights for failing to address the problem of 'the erased', the non-Slovene former Yugoslav nationals who did not take up Slovenian citizenship in 1991 and then saw their rights to residency revoked and acquired rights destroyed (European Court of Human Rights 2010). Slovakia, which began as a less promising reformer, was the target of much criticism, most recently by Amnesty International over its treatment of the Roma minority.[2]

[1]'Qualitative measures' include the delivery of social policy goals and are evidenced in the areas of: 'quality of work', 'quality in industrial relations' and 'quality of social policy' (Eurofound 2011). The way in which qualitative democracy is measured by the European Commission includes a range of criteria that reflect both materialist and post-materialist concerns such as better jobs and more balanced ways of combining working life with personal life; high levels of social protection; good social services which are universally available; and the capacity to build consensus between workers and employers.

[2]See 'Slovak Republic' in Amnesty International (2010).

In Slovenia, the focus is on the effectiveness of the justice sector and in particular the right to an effective judicial remedy. In Slovakia the focus is on the state's ability to protect the rights of minorities. In both cases, the emphasis is on the state's ability to protect and uphold the rights of citizens through the courts and law enforcement bodies. The final part of this essay concludes with an evaluation of the concept of 'qualitative democracy' as it applies to the selected states.

Quality, conditionality and the substance of democracy

Qualitative assessments of political transition emphasise domestic-level developments where reform is suggestive of internalised change. This is particularly relevant for the European Union whose influence over the region has grown as a result of the disbursement of structural funds and other monies, and above all by holding out the prospect of accession. Arguably, the developmental paths taken by the former socialist states of Central and Eastern Europe have been affected by the application of 'conditionality'—a concept usually linked with areas of the *acquis* and understood in terms of the incentives and sanctions applied in response to state compliance or non-compliance with EU norms and rules.

In terms of political requirements imposed by the European Union in its dealings with applicant states, conditionality includes the provisions that states adhere to the 'Copenhagen Criteria' and transpose the *acquis communautaire* into domestic law. In practice, it also entails adherence to parallel systems of human rights law since the European Union frequently invokes the growing body of international and regional human rights jurisprudence as a condition for participation in EU activities. For example, the various United Nations and especially the European conventions are now crucial anchors for transitional states seeking EU support.[3] It should be noted that the parallel systems of international law are important, not least because they contain specific monitoring and reporting requirements by international bodies, including the Council of Europe.

The European Union's influence as both a broker and political monitor in the former socialist bloc took on greater significance following the 2003 European Council in Thessaloniki, which set an important agenda for the inclusion of the Western Balkans in the European Union's sphere which seeks to close a large, illiberal, hole in the map of Europe (Council of the European Union 2003). Since Thessaloniki, the EU has spent millions of Euros on programmes carried out through Community Assistance for Reconstruction, Development and Stabilisation (CARDS)[4] and has simultaneously taken over activities that were formerly conducted by the Organization for Security and Cooperation in Europe (OSCE). It has also explicitly linked human rights issues with the accession process, for example in the case of Croatia where it made cooperation with the International Criminal Tribunal for the former Yugoslavia (ICTY) and improved relations with the Serbian minority a condition for membership

[3]Especially, the UN Convention Against Torture, the European Convention on Human Rights and the European Convention for the Prevention of Torture and Inhuman or Degrading Treatment or Punishment.

[4]CARDS was adopted with the Council Regulation (EC) No. 2666/2000 of 5 December 2000.

(Blitz 2007). The same applies in the case of Serbia where cooperation with the ICTY has been a condition for accession (Council of the European Union 2010).

In a less direct way, the European Union has also been able to exercise its soft power to cement its normative agenda in the area of human rights. This has gained greater prominence as a result of the signing of the 2007 Charter of Fundamental Rights and the completion of the Lisbon process. The Charter and Lisbon Treaty attempt to bring the European Union in line with the European Convention on Human Rights and have allowed institutions in Brussels and Strasbourg to draw upon provisions contained in both European Commission (EC) law and European human rights jurisprudence. For example, the European Court of Human Rights ruled in *D.H. and Others v. Czech Republic* that the Czech Republic's failure to transpose the EU Race Equality Directive into law prevented the establishment of anti-discriminatory measures to protect Roma in Czech schools.[5] This brought the Czech government into conflict with the European Court of Human Rights which in turn cited provisions on non-discrimination contained in EC law in its decision (European Court of Human Rights 2006). Such developments have strengthened the supranational character of the European Union and given it greater scope to intervene in states on matters of human rights.

For political scientists the sustained involvement of the European Union in the reconfiguration of Central and Eastern Europe, and the use of conditionality and soft power as potential levers for reform, introduce several challenges to our understanding of political transition. First, the involvement by the European Union complicates causal explanations for behavioural change at the level of the state and potentially undervalues the role of domestic interest groups in setting reformist agendas. This is significant because within the literature on political transition far greater weight has historically been given to internal forces rather than external actors or transnational influences as explanations for both regime change and ultimately democratic consolidation (O'Donnell *et al.* 1986). Indeed, one unifying factor in contemporary studies on transition is the emphasis placed on domestic politics and the need to examine change in relation to the state itself. Moreover, the application of conditionality and the extension of soft power support claims of relative democratic immaturity and suggest the possible co-existence of non-democratic alternative modes of governance which necessarily undermine the goal of consolidation and the integration of European norms and value systems (Przeworski 1986).

Recent research on the 2004 enlargement has called into question the application of conditionality for the successful transition to democracy and installation of the rule of law (Brusis 2005; Hughes *et al.* 2007; Kochenov 2008; Raik 2004). One unintended consequence in the elitist approach taken by the European Union has been the non-transposition of EC directives and the failure to achieve comprehensive reforms (Raik 2004). Some scholars question governmental willingness to promote substantive political change, charging that once the incentives had been met for EU membership and countries had acceded to the European Union, momentum for reform was lost (Blitz 2006; Pridham 2008). Rather, conditionality was arguably seen as a short-term

[5]D.H. and Others *v.* Czech Republic, 57325/00, Council of Europe: European Court of Human Rights, 7 February 2006, available at: http://www.unhcr.org/refworld/docid/469e020e2.html, accessed 22 July 2011.

approach which became less effective once the accession date was set and the EU accepted the candidate's state of reforms as sufficient (Steunenberg & Dimitrova 2007). The act of EU membership has also been associated with a decline in the number of civil society actors, including human rights monitors, which ironically has allowed some pre-accession abuses to continue, often with little censure from Brussels (but occasionally from the European Court of Justice) (Blitz 2006). An additional body of criticism claims that the influence of EU conditionality upon accession states has been quite exaggerated and has varied from one policy area to another (Haughton 2007). This may partly be explained by the diversification of external checks and balances and the creation of new policy goals.

While political conditionality has grown in importance with every round of enlargements, the goalposts have also shifted (Hughes *et al.* 2007), as have the levers for change, with the Commission becoming relatively less demanding than other European institutions (Pridham 2007). As Heather Grabbe notes in her discussion of the 2004 enlargement process, while the European Union primarily relied on soft power in its attempts to bring candidate countries to accept its norms and methods, the European Council also used its considerable bargaining power in a coercive manner at key points during the membership preparations (Grabbe 2006). Moreover, scholars have suggested elsewhere that the application of conditionality by the European Union and Euro-Atlantic institutions has not resulted in normative integration, as required for a truly consolidated state of democracy. Rather, they argue there remain measurable differences in the levels of political development achieved by the former socialist states of Central and Eastern Europe: while the promise of accession and NATO membership appealed to 'norm-violating' but reform-minded states, the European Union enjoyed less success with authoritarian governments where the costs of compliance were considered too high (Schimmelfennig 2007). For example, Estonia and Latvia, both reformer states, managed to accede to the European Union while only partially addressing their nationality problems which have left half a million stateless.[6] Equally, Slovenia was admitted to the European Union while the issue of the 'erased' was left unresolved (Blitz 2006; Zorn 2009; Zorn & Lipovec Čebron 2008). By contrast, Croatia has been held to a high level of accountability while it remains on the slow track to EU accession (Blitz 2007).

A further challenge to the conditionality literature may be found in the sociological scholarship on networks and regime change. Like the literature on transition, this body of writing places emphasis on the domestic dimension and has generated several evaluations of the process of political change which raise the bar further in their analyses of democratic alternatives (Stepan 1996). Notably, a collection of East European sociologists has drawn upon empirical evidence of corruption and state capture in the former Eastern bloc to call attention to earlier classical theories of oligarchies and the role of elites in the development of anti-democratic political networks (Shlapentokh *et al.* 1999). Furthermore, some of the critical literature on the nature of social capital records that networks may not simply facilitate international

[6]Regarding Latvia see Hughes (2005) and Council of Europe (2006c); on Estonia see Kionka and Vetik (1996) and Vetik (1993, 2001, 2002, 2008).

exchanges but also frustrate the creation of open systems and hence prevent sustained democratic reform (Gargiulo & Benassi 1999; Portes 1998; Putzel 1997).

A brief survey of human rights reforms

Universal human rights provisions

One of the major tests of democracy in Central and Eastern Europe has been universal application of human rights, irrespective of one's national or ethnic status. Human rights are covered by both international and European regional instruments including European Union level legislation, which has a direct effect, and the 1950 European Convention on Human Rights (ECHR) which is the only international human rights agreement providing such a high degree of individual protection.[7] In terms of international law, there is also a significant body of law that has elaborated the principle of non-discrimination as a non-derogable norm that prohibits discrimination on the basis of race, ethnicity and related criteria.[8] One of the most significant human rights instruments is the 1965 Convention on the Elimination of All Forms of Racial Discrimination (CEFoRD), which provides a precise definition of racial discrimination. This also highlights the consequences of states creating conditions which exacerbate the vulnerability of minority populations and which make the state liable.[9] Some of the key elements of this Convention include a universal provision under Article 5 that state parties are obliged to guarantee equality for all in the enjoyment of civil, political, economic, social and cultural rights, to the extent that they are recognised under international law (Weissbrodt 2008).

Within the European systems, there is an important body of European law that reinforces the principle of non-discrimination as set out in the 1950 European Convention on Human Rights (ECHR), its five protocols, corresponding rulings from the European Court of Human Rights, and the Consolidated Treaties of the European Union. Under Article 14, the Convention sets out a universal prohibition against discrimination, including against national minorities. In addition, the European Convention on Nationality (ECN) reaffirms the principle of non-discrimination in questions of nationality, sex, religion, race, colour, and national or ethnic origin. The above human rights instruments complement the prohibition of discrimination on the basis of nationality which is at the heart of the European Union where it is set out as a general principle under Article 12 of the EC Treaty, and in other provisions of the Treaty framework in respect of specific

[7]It should be remembered that state parties can also take cases against other state parties to the Court, although this power is rarely used.

[8]The principle is enshrined in key instruments including the 1965 Convention on the Elimination of All Forms of Racial Discrimination; the 1979 Convention on the Elimination of Discrimination Against Women (CEDAW); the 1992 Declaration on the Rights of Persons Belonging to National or Ethnic, Religious and Linguistic Minorities; and the 2003 Migrant Rights Convention, as well as in significant bodies of case law (UN General Assembly 1965, 1979, 1992, 1990). UN General Assembly (1990) came into force in 2003 but was drafted in 1990.

[9]The text states that 'racial discrimination' shall mean any distinction, exclusion, restriction or preference based on race, colour, descent or national or ethnic origin which has the purpose or effect of nullifying or impairing the recognition, enjoyment or exercise, on an equal footing, of human rights and fundamental freedoms in the political, economic, social, cultural or any other field of public life (UN General Assembly 1965).

situations regarding the free movement of workers (Article 39), the right of establishment (Article 43) and the freedom to provide services (Article 50). More recently, the introduction of the Race Equality Directive has sought to extend the European Union's enforcement of non-discrimination to issues of race and ethnicity.

Minority rights

A major dividing line in the classification of minorities in Central and Eastern Europe is whether or not people were considered habitually resident before 1989 (and in some cases much earlier): 'autochthonous minorities' are those which are formally considered to have greater historical claim and often receive constitutional protection while 'non-autochthonous minorities' are those who are considered newcomers or occupiers. This definition is not absolute and neither is the point of cut off. For example, in the case of Russian-speakers in Estonia the date of arrival tends to be the 1940s, not 1989. However, the distinction between the two categories of minority is nonetheless important because it has led to differentiated treatment of people not simply on the basis of ethno-national origin but also on the basis of length of residency. As a result some 'newer' minorities, including groups of Roma, have been more vulnerable to removal and the withdrawal of rights (Boucková 2007, p. 1). For example, by the first half of 1997, local Czech courts and police had expelled 851 Roma to Slovakia on the grounds that they were Slovak, even though this was undocumented and some had never lived in Slovakia (US Department of State 2000).

In terms of formal mechanisms for protection, all of the constitutions of East-Central and South-Eastern European states include elaborate human rights provisions which are further reinforced by the European Convention on Human Rights. Minority rights are frequently covered in specific articles on cultural rights, although there are considerable collective political rights afforded to most minorities in several states. Autochthonous populations are also often protected under specific laws that guarantee institutional representation (including reserved seats in the legislature) and provide communal channels for dialogue with state agencies through national councils. These 'historic minorities' may also benefit from affirmative action or equal opportunity programmes regarding participation in civil, military and police services. Nominally, autochthonous and non-autochthonous minorities should enjoy greater protection from non-state actors since the new European states have also introduced laws prohibiting incitement to racial hatred, and many have signed onto key international legal instruments, including the 1992 European Charter for Regional or Minority Languages (ECRML) (Council of Europe 1992) and the 1995 Framework Convention for the Protection of National Minorities (FCNM) (Council of Europe 1995). It should be noted, however, that not all states have acceded to these conventions; for example, while all the new EU member states are parties to the FCNM, Bulgaria, Estonia, Latvia and Lithuania have not ratified the ECRML.[10]

[10]See *European Charter for Regional or Minority Languages, CETS No.: 148, Treaty Open for Signature by the Member States and for Accession by Non-member States. Status as of 28/10/2010*, available at: http://conventions.coe.int/Treaty/Commun/ChercheSig.asp?NT=148&CM=8&DF=&CL=ENG, accessed 27 July 2011.

At the constitutional level, however, there are still considerable differences in terms of the political accommodation of minorities as described in Table 1.

Finally, it is important to note the massive investment across the justice sectors in East-Central and South-Eastern European states. This includes the construction of

TABLE 1
MINORITY RIGHTS AND REPRESENTATION: SELECTED EXAMPLES

Country	*Examples*
Albania	There are no special bodies or seats reserved in parliament; minority rights treated as human rights but the constitution distinguishes between national (Greek, Macedonian) and linguistic minorities (Vlach).[a]
Croatia	Serbs, Czechs, Slovaks, Italians, Hungarians, Jews, Germans, Austrians, Ukrainians, Ruthenians and others are protected under the Constitutional Law on the Rights of National Minorities (155/22) 13 December 2002, which determines the organisation of local minorities councils in communities, cities and counties.[b]
Czech Republic	The Act on Rights of Members of National Minorities and Government Council for National Minorities (Act 273/2001Sb) guarantees members of national minorities the right to effective participation in cultural, social and economic life and in public matters. It also guarantees the right to the name and surname in the language of the national minority in question, the right to multi-linguistic names and signs, the right to use the language of the national minority during official contacts with offices and courts, the right to use the language of the national minority in elections, the right to training in the language of the minority, the right to the development of the culture of the minority, and the right to the expansion and acceptance of information in the language of the minority.[c]
Slovakia	Though minorities are represented by political parties, there are no specific constitutional provisions apart from the right to use minority languages. The Language Act of 30 June 2009, however, has been seen as a restrictive law which only allows citizens who are members of a national minority to use their native language in official communications if the law explicitly allows it.[d]
Slovenia	Italians and Hungarians are protected under the constitution, each having a representative in the National Assembly. In ethnically mixed areas, bilingualism is guaranteed, nurseries and schools are provided for minority children, and minority languages are used by the local media.[e]
Serbia	A Charter of Human and Minority Rights and Civil Liberties was adopted on 26 February 2003 and presides over several minority councils.[f] Article 19 provides for the election of national councils exercising rights of self-government regarding the use of language and script, education, information and culture. The councils represent the national minority in respect of official use of language, education, information in the language of the minority, culture, and participate in decision making or decide on issues in these fields, as well as establishing institutions in these fields.

Notes: [a]Albanian constitution, Approved by the Albanian parliament on 21 October 1998, available at: http://www.president.al/english/pub/doc/Albanian%20Constitution.pdf, accessed 27 July 2011.
[b]Constitutional Law on the Rights of National Minorities, *Official Gazette*, 155/22, 13 December 2002, available at: http://www.vsrh.hr/CustomPages/Static/HRV/Files/Legislation__Constitutional-Law-on-the-Rights-NM.pdf, accessed 27 July 2011.
[c]The Charter of the Council of the Government for National Minorities, published by the Government of the Czech Republic, Supplement to the Government Resolution Nr. 1034 from 10 October 2001, available at: http://www.vlada.cz/assets/ppov/rnm/statut-rnm-en.pdf, accessed 27 July 2011.
[d]Opinion on the Act on the State Language of the Slovak Republic, adopted by the Venice Commission at its 84th Plenary Session (Venice, 15–16 October 2010), available at: http://www.venice.coe.int/docs/2010/CDL-AD(2010)035-e.asp, accessed 27 July 2011.
[e]*Constitution of the Republic of Slovenia*, available at: http://www.dz-rs.si/index.php?id=351&docid=25&showdoc=1, accessed 27 July 2011.
[f]Republic of Serbia (2003).

new courts, the introduction of case management systems to reduce delays, and the provision of wide-ranging technical assistance and training. Some states have particularly benefited. For example, 40% of CARDS funding in Albania from 2002 to 2006 went to justice sector development projects (€104.8 million) (Blitz 2008). Such investment is unprecedented since the EU has even directed funds at capital programmes to build prisons in Albania.[11]

Practical realities

In spite of the above-mentioned human rights architecture, the extension of greater political rights to minorities and the development of institutional structures to improve the functioning of the justice sector, several loopholes have not been closed over the past two decades. Many states have struggled to protect minorities against violence from non-state parties as skinheads and other organised groups have attacked minorities on a regular basis. Though racist attacks are not limited to Central and Eastern Europe, violence directed against Roma minorities generated a significant number of asylum applications to Western Europe over the past two decades. Ill-treatment in prisons was a characteristic of the justice sector throughout the 1990s and, even recently, states such as Albania (European Committee for the Prevention of Torture 2009a), Latvia (European Committee for the Prevention of Torture 2009b) and Lithuania (European Committee for the Prevention of Torture 2009c) have been condemned by the Council of Europe's Committee for the Prevention of Torture (CPT) which has identified the lack of medical provision, the poor food regime, the use of solitary confinement, and the lack of air and exercise among its criticisms. Some of the most disturbing abuses carried out by European Union member states from 2005 to 2009 include forced sterilisations, segregationist policies regarding the housing and education of certain minority groups, *refoulement* of refugees and the repossession of property by the state.[12] More generally, there is also discrimination throughout educational systems, in the media, in the provision of housing, and in many practical barriers that prevent minorities from accessing essential services. Such practices were especially noted in the former Yugoslavia where returning minorities refugees and displaced people encountered multiple barriers from corrupt housing commissions which prevented the repossession of homes (Blitz 2007). In the Czech Republic, discrimination against minorities has proved particularly problematic both in the application and design of laws (Boucková 2007), as noted in the above-mentioned case of *D.H. and Others v. the Czech Republic*.

[11]See: 2006/54/EC: Council Decision of 30 January 2006 on the principles, priorities and conditions contained in the European Partnership with Albania and repealing Decision 2004/519/EC, available at: http://eur-lex.europa.eu/LexUriServ/LexUriServ.do?uri=OJ:L:2008:080:0001:01:EN:HTML, accessed 27 July 2011.

[12]According to the US Committee for Refugees and Immigrations (USCRI), in 2006, Slovakia reportedly returned Chechen asylum seekers to Ukraine with Ukraine returning them to the Russian Federation. Slovakia granted asylum to only eight of the nearly 2,900 persons who applied during the year and none the year before (United States Committee for Refugees and Immigrants (USCRI) (2007).

The right to a fair trial is also a concern for states which have struggled to manage the large number of applications and resources required, including sufficiently trained judicial staff. Croatia, Lithuania and Poland have all been condemned by the European Court for Human Rights (ECtHR) for the excessive length of time required to conduct court proceedings. In some states, the use of sentencing also provoked significant criticism from international monitors, for example, in both Albania and Latvia where there was, until recently, an estimated 90% conviction rate and where irregularities exist concerning trials *in absentia* (Commission of the European Union 2009). In the case of the former Yugoslavia, there have been repeated claims of insufficient judicial independence and impartiality. This point was raised in some of the most notable war crimes cases in Croatia and Serbia (Human Rights Watch 2004; OSCE 2005, 2006). The Council of Europe has also acknowledged concerns that intimidation of judges is a problem in Serbia. Finally, there is the issue of non-enforcement of court orders and non-execution of court judgments.

Media reporting during the past two decades has also revealed examples of illiberal elements in many states of Central and Eastern Europe. One important consequence is that some chauvinistic media reporting in these countries has activated racial hatred to encourage minority flight. For example, in the Czech Republic in the late 1990s large numbers of individuals were involved in a mass emigration of more than 1,200 Roma to Canada. The context for this flight was most controversial and appeared to have been influenced by a television documentary about life in Canada. The European Roma Rights Center noted that several Czech officials had exploited the broadcast with a view to encouraging the mass departure of Roma populations. Liana Janáčková, Mayor of the Marianské Hory district in the northern Moravian town of Ostrava, reportedly suggested that Roma who moved to Canada would receive payment for two thirds of the cost of their flights, on the condition that they abandoned their flats and returned their licenses of tenancy. The mayor described this suggestion as 'a friendly gesture' to 'help' Roma who 'don't want to live here' (European Roma Rights Center 2007).

An additional problem facing those who seek access to the justice system is the lack of documentation. This has principally affected Roma across the region but has been most problematic in the Czech and Slovak Republics and in the case of the 'erased' in Slovenia. In one particular instance, it has been caused by the use of interim legislation by an inexperienced state. In Macedonia, a 2004 transitory clause (under Article 26 (US Department of State 2007)) which temporarily eased naturalisation requirements for foreigners married to Macedonian citizens, persons without citizenship and persons with refugee status, expired in March 2006 leaving many vulnerable to denial and deprivation of citizenship.

Methods

In order to explore the concept of 'qualitative democracy', Slovenia and the Slovak Republic were selected as suitable case studies where systemic problems had been identified. Both the Slovak Republic and Slovenia also introduced interesting points of contrast: both had seceded from larger former socialist political units yet, while Slovenia spent much of the 1990s as a leading example of democratic transition,

Slovakia was mired by accounts of political corruption during the authoritarian rule of Vladimir Mečiar. Moreover, in spite of considerable investment and technical assistance from the European Union, both countries had been criticised for their ineffective justice systems, which raised questions over the protection and enforcement of human rights. In the context of Slovenia, uncertainty over its ability to protect the rights of its citizens was made public by a 2005 'pilot judgment' issued by the European Court of Human Rights in the case of *Lukenda v. Slovenia* (European Court of Human Rights 2005). This case centred on excessively long domestic court proceedings in Slovenia—the result of some 500 Slovenian 'length of proceedings' cases which had been referred up to the Strasbourg Court. The problems in Slovakia, by contrast, pointed to wider issues of governance and targeted discrimination. The state had repeatedly been condemned for police mistreatment of Romani suspects and lengthy pre-trial detention, while the integrity of the judiciary had been called into question, as had national and local governments, which had been described as corrupt. Further, societal discrimination and violence against Roma and other minorities had been frequently cited as major problems (US Department of State 2010).

Measuring substantive change or quality issues in the process of democratic transition and consolidation introduces a number of practical and methodological challenges. Although, the European Convention on Human Rights (ECHR) provides one mechanism to gauge the enforcement of human right norms, the operation of the justice sector is addressed by different articles, for example Article 3 on the Prohibition Against Torture which covers a wide range of abuses, both pre- and post-trial; Article 6 on the right to a Fair Trial; and Article 8 on the Right to Respect for Private and Family Life (Council of Europe 2010). The ECHR is not sector specific and while it covers much similar territory to say, the Charter on Fundamental Rights, is not as far-reaching. For this reason, the research introduced broader qualitative measures which were not tied to specific articles of the ECHR or similar legal instruments, but were rather informed by the operation of justice-sector institutions. Specifically, the research sought to examine how three sets of indicators informed the nature of democracy in Slovenia and Slovakia: the extent to which people are able to access their rights through the court system; state capacity to enforce rights through domestic bodies, including protective agencies of law enforcement; and the degree to which political reform is internally located, as opposed to being promoted by external arbiters.

Research on Slovenia was informed by documentary analysis, interviews and focus groups with human rights experts, civil servants based in the Ministry of Justice, and lawmakers and lawyers ($n = 20$) in Ljubljana in Spring 2009.[13] Research on Slovakia

[13]Focus groups (three) and interviews ($n = 14$) were held with government officials, members of parliament, legal experts and human rights advocates in Ljubljana between 1 and 4 June 2009. One further interview was conducted with two experts in London. Full interview details are as follows—Aldo Mihlonić, Peace Institute, Ljubljana, 3 June 2009; Boštjan and Mateja Verstovšek, Ljubljana, 17 June 2009; Darja Lavtižar Bebler, National Assembly, Ljubljana, 2 June 2009; Dean Zagorac, Editor, *Pravna Praksa*, Ljubljana, 3 June 2009; Ivan Šelih and Jiri Rovšek, Ombudsman's Office, Ljubljana, 2 June 2009; Judge Urška Klakočar of the Supreme Court, Ljubljana, 1 June 2009; Judge Krisper Kramberger, Constitutional Court, Ljubljana, 3 June 2009; Neža Kogovšek, Peace Institute, Ljubljana, 1 June 2009; Peter Pavlin and Zoran Skubic, Ministry of Justice, Ljubljana, 1 June 2009;

was carried out by means of documentary analysis of human rights reports from the US Department of State, Amnesty International and Human Rights Watch since 1991. The interview data and documentary findings were then analysed to assess how legal provisions and operational practices matched up. The aim was to ascertain the degree to which the judiciary in both states could guarantee rights and freedoms to all, including respect for the principle of non-discrimination, and to identify the locus of political reform.

The case of Slovenia

As it prepared for accession to the European Union, Slovenia was heralded as a European success story (Bebler 2002; Ramet 1998; Schopflin 2002; Vucetic 2004); however, two issues in particular undermined this reputation. First, there is the unresolved matter of the 'erased', the former residents of the Yugoslav republic who saw their residency rights withdrawn along with their social and economic entitlements following the introduction of new nationality legislation in 1992. The 'erasure' of their rights affected some 25,000 people, many of whom had settled in Slovenia and married Slovenes. It rendered them effectively stateless (Blitz 2006; Dedić *et al.* 2003; Zorn 2009; Zorn & Lipovec Čebron 2008). Second, there were problems concerning the constitutional rights of individuals to access courts and receive timely judgments. This section will focus on the latter issue, the enforcement of human rights provisions and the performance of the Slovene judiciary more broadly.

The issue of access to effective judicial remedies is an important marker of qualitative democracy. In the case of Slovenia, in spite of extensive constitutional provisions, the lack of legal remedies remains a major challenge to the functioning of the justice sector. The problem is essentially two-fold: in addition to an ineffective judiciary, there is an overwhelming demand made on courts. Slovenia is a highly litigious nation with an estimated 500,000 suits filed per year. In 2004, there were 566,588 cases pending, not including misdemeanours (Ministry of Justice of Slovenia 2005). In interviews, Slovenian legal experts offered several explanations for the backlog of cases which call into question the state's capacity to protect the rights of its citizens. During one focus group meeting, participants drew attention to the large proportion of young and inexperienced judges and uninformed court registrars; and the lack of alternative dispute mechanisms.[14] In addition, some interviewees noted that legislative incompatibilities in the civil procedures act, and the occasional industrial dispute including the 'White Strike' of 2008 (a form of industrial action when judges refused to take on new cases), allowed a culture of litigation to flourish at the expense of swift judicial remedies. Bureaucratic explanations for the lack of judicial capacity contrast with the considerable ease of access to bring cases to court, including the right of Slovenes to appeal directly to the Constitutional Court. While the great access enjoyed by Slovenes suggests a high degree of freedom, the Ministry of Justice pointed

Vita Habjan, Pravno-informacijeskega centra nevladnih organizacij (PIC, Legal Information Centre for NGOs), Ljubljana, 3 June 2009; interview with Zinka Strašek, President of the Celje High Court and President of the Supreme Court Celje, 1 June 2009.

[14]Focus group B with the author, Ljubljana, 2 June 2009.

out that the net result was many frivolous suits.[15] Slovenian legal expert Rok Lampe offers the following opinion:

> … the major factor [preventing the courts from operating effectively] can be traced to the complaint procedure and even broadly, to the role of attorneys in litigation. The Civil Procedure Act namely foresees complaints against the first instance judgments in a very liberal way which is connected to the entrepreneurial logic of attorneys. There is probably not even one civil litigation action in which parties are represented by attorneys that is not 'tested' at the appellate court. Most complaints are basically 'shots in the dark' because the appellate courts are obliged to test the first instance judgment ex officio (of course if a complaint was brought). Logically an attorney has consequently nothing to lose by bringing a complaint—either way he is going to 'win' and clients (who lost in the first instance) are keen on complaints. Therefore extremely long and ineffective civil litigations do not result just from vague civil procedure rules, but from deeper practical relations in our legal system. (Lampe 2008, p. 417)

The process of justice may be compromised by a combination of inexperienced staff, and the fact that cases may be referred from lower courts to high courts and back down. Further, it is important to note that the Supreme Court had been flooded with supervisory appeals where it had been called upon to question the decisions of lower courts.[16]

The significant delays in the handling of mostly civil cases were recognised in 2005 by the Constitutional Court of Slovenia which decided that the Administrative Dispute Act of 1997, a piece of legislation regarding civil dispute procedures which fall under administrative law, was 'unconstitutional in respect of some of its provisions which did not contain an effective legal remedy against the right to a trial within reasonable time' (Pavlin 2006, p. 6). The above-mentioned problems with the Slovenian justice system were considered endemic by the European Court of Human Rights (ECtHR) which issued a pilot judgment against the state—a form of judgment which is intended to help the national authorities to eliminate the systemic or structural problems highlighted by the Court as giving rise to repetitive cases (European Court of Human Rights 2009). In the case of *Lukenda v. Slovenia*, the first pilot judgment case which involved Slovenia, the Court found that Slovenia was guilty of systemic violations of the right to a fair trial without undue delay (European Court of Human Rights 2009).

The *Lukenda* judgment prompted the Slovenian government to initiate a series of reforms, characterised by the introduction of new laws and an action programme that aimed to accelerate concrete cases for legal remedy. This programme included: the appointment of an extra 140 judges, 650 judiciary personnel and 175 administrative staff; simplified legislation; and ensured that all courts were to be fully computerised and that judges and prosecutors were trained. Courts too were to be reorganised and

[15]Interview with Peter Pavlin and Zoran Skubic, Ministry of Justice, Ljubljana, 1 June 2009.

[16]A supervisory appeal is 'an appeal by a party or his drawing to the attention of supervisory authority (president of the same or a superior state body) that he should take measures under the right of supervision against the activity of his/her subordinates or subordinate or lower state body' (Pavlin 2006, p. 4). Supervisory appeals, however, do not constitute a legal remedy, even though the Supreme Court may act as the final arbiter.

the Act on Judicial Service amended to give incentives to judges and court staff. The Code of Civil Procedure and the Code of Criminal Procedure were also subject to extensive amendments to ensure that legislation was consistent.

While the ECtHR was identified by interviewees as the driver of reform, interviews with officials revealed that the pilot judgment provided the state with opportunities and set in place reforms that, although desired, had been impeded by the court system.[17] Two laws in particular characterised the *Lukenda* project—the plan of action which was put in place by the Slovenian Ministry of Justice following the European Court of Justice's decision—the Ministerial Law on the Protection of the Right to a Trial Without Undue Delay of 2005, known as ZVPSBNO, and the amended Novella ZVPSBNO A introduced in summer 2009.[18] The first law, arguably the most important, attempted to redistribute the burden that had fallen on the Supreme Court and, indeed, higher level courts. The central features of this law were the introduction of binding criteria for decision making in procedures of supervisory appeal, motions for a deadline and just satisfaction and the imposition of a time line requiring all parties to file claims for compensation within 18 months. The second law sought to complement the first by strengthening the role of the court president and preventing fragmentation where cases could be referred from one court to another. It placed a greater burden on first instance courts to resolve disputes.

Initial assessments by the Ministry of Justice of the *Lukenda* project which resulted from the ECtHR decision were positive.[19] The most recent data from the Ministry of Justice point to a small decline in the backlog, with a reduction of 3% of cases before district (*okružni*) courts and a 3.5% reduction at the local (*okrajni*) courts.[20] However, it was also noted that legislative, judicial and organisational developments that were primarily directed at courts could only offer partial reform. It was recognised by two interviewees that the shortened response time would restrict access to courts and might strengthen attempts to institute subsidiarity, so that cases do not simply move and up and down the judicial ladder.[21] However, it was equally noted that the increased number of judges and staff has not, in itself, addressed the way in which courts

[17]Interview with Peter Pavlin and Zoran Skubic, Ministry of Justice, Ljubljana, 1 June 2009.

[18]Zakon o varstvu pravice do sojenja brez nepotrebnega odlašanja (ZVPSBNO) 12 May 2006, Act on the Protection of the Right to a Trial Without Undue Delay, available at: http://www.mp.gov.si/fileadmin/mp.gov.si/pageuploads/2005/PDF/zakonodaja/23.08.06-Act_on_the_protection_of_the_right_to_trial_without_undue_delay_of_Slovenia_eng.pdf, accessed 27 July 2011. The 'novella' is the Act Amending the Act on the Protection of the Right to a Trial Without Undue Delay (ZVPSBNO-A) No: 003-02-7/2009-10, issued in Ljubljana, 23 July 2009, available at: http://www.mp.gov.si/fileadmin/mp.gov.si/pageuploads/2005/PDF/zakonodaja/090918_Amended_ZVPSBNO_2009_eng.pdf, accessed 27 July 2011.

[19]Interview with Peter Pavlin and Zoran Skubic, Ministry of Justice, Ljubljana, 1 June 2009.

[20]Focus group A with the author, 1 June 2009. As of 31 December 2007, there were 287,175 cases (excluding minor offences and cases before the Supreme Court) pending before courts in Slovenia. On 31 December 2008, there were 276,332 cases pending (excluding minor offences and cases before the Supreme Court). As of 31 December 2007, at the higher courts (of which in Slovenia there are four higher courts and one special court) there were 1,898 cases pending. As of 31 December 2008, at the higher courts there were just 853 cases pending (interview with Peter Pavlin and Zoran Skubic, Ministry of Justice, Ljubljana, 1 June 2009).

[21]Interview with Peter Pavlin and Zoran Skubic, Ministry of Justice, Ljubljana, 1 June 2009.

function nor the hours judicial staff keep.[22] Further, the lowering of the age limit for judges was met with claims of inexperience and also accusations that there is still a high turnover of personnel, including judges. Partially this is a result of the increasingly feminised sector and also the age at which staff are appointed.[23] One frequent remark was that there were now many young female judges and more judges away on maternity leave.[24]

There are also particular problems in certain courts, above all Celje municipal court. While ZVPSBNO A offers greater power to court presidents, for some interviewees there is still a sense that some cases will be not heard, including those that relate to the hundreds of cases filed in the local court in Celje.[25] Rather, officials described these multiple suits as 'spam' or nuisance complaints.[26] There remains potential for conflict at lower level courts, in spite of the introduction of new laws. Finally, interviews and focus groups with legal experts suggested that, in general, there is a lack of understanding about human rights in Slovenia and how they are covered in the constitution (through international and European case law). There is also a lack of appreciation for the importance of EU law—for example, Article 236 which permits cases to be referred to the European Court of Justice (ECJ) is never applied and rarely do judges seek additional information.[27]

The reforms in Slovenia raise interesting conclusions regarding the democratic maturation of the country. Whereas the Constitutional Court had been under constant pressure, the burden has now shifted to lower courts indicating that caseloads have been redistributed. There are, nonetheless, many problems that need to be addressed regarding the management of large caseloads in lower courts. Equally, there is a need to explain how cases may be referred to European courts and how the court system may be better managed to address the expectations of Slovene complainants to ensure that human rights apply across the judicial and related sectors. The challenge for Slovenia is to establish a mature culture of rights, as opposed to a culture of complaint.

The case of Slovakia

The democratic challenges for Slovakia were more complex and could not solely be attributed to immature institutions and inexperienced public servants. Rather, the problems in Slovakia lay in broader problems of governance and societal discrimination. Slovakia joined the European Union in May 2004 having already set in place substantial human rights protections.[28] The rights of national minorities were also covered under Articles 33–34 of the constitution which provides for cultural

[22]Interview with Aldo Mihlonić, Peace Institute, Ljubljana, 3 June 2009.

[23]Interview with Zinka Strašek, President of the Celje High Court, 1 June 2009.

[24]Interview with Zinka Strašek, President of the Celje High Court, 1 June 2009.

[25]Interview with Boštjan and Mateja Verstovšek, 17 June 2009.

[26]Interview with Zinka Strašek, President of the Celje High Court, 1 June 2009.

[27]Interview with Neža Kogovšek, Peace Institute, Ljubljana, 1 June 2009.

[28]See, under Human Rights and Equality (in Part 1, Articles 11–12; more specifically in Part 2, Articles 14–25 of the 1992 constitution), *The Constitution of The Slovak Republic*, available at: http://www.vop.gov.sk/constitution-of-the-slovak-republic, accessed 27 July 2011.

rights.[29] Torture was covered under Article 16(2) of the constitution and is included in the Penal Code but racially motivated crimes, including murder, are not specifically mentioned.[30] In addition to the above-mentioned domestic legislation, Slovakia is a signatory to a wide body of international legal instruments,[31] yet the management of minority relations, above all with the Roma communities, has proved especially troubling.

The situation of the Roma in Slovakia

According to the 2001 Census, the population of Roma was 89,920 or 1.7% of the total population.[32] This statistic, however masks the large number of Roma who were not registered and, arguably, the total number of Roma may be many times greater than officially recorded (International Helsinki Federation 2004). Roma are considered autochthonous minorities who have inhabited the area for hundreds of years and are today spread across 600 settlements in Slovakia. During the communist period, several laws were introduced in Czechoslovakia (in both the Czech and Slovak Socialist Republics) aimed at assimilating Roma, either directly or indirectly, and included programmes of dispersal and resettlement in urban dwellings (UNHCR 1998). The promise of democracy in the late 1980s raised the prospect that the assimilationist policies would be shelved following the introduction of new provisions that recognised the Roma population's education, social and cultural rights. The 'Declaration of Basic Human Rights and Freedoms' accepted by the Federal Assembly of Czechoslovakia on 9 January 1991, also gave Roma the right to freely decide their own ethnic affiliation. However, the first few decades of Slovakia's independence also saw increasing levels of racially motivated violence from nationalist and skinhead groups which forced the state to increase levels of policing in areas where disturbances had occurred (European Roma Rights Center 1998, 1999a, 1999b, 2000a, 2000b, 2000c, 2001a, 2001b, 2002a, 2002b).

From 1993 onwards, there was a marked backlash against Roma communities by non-state actors and local officials. One result of the increased police activity in

[29] *The Constitution of The Slovak Republic*, available at: http://www.vop.gov.sk/constitution-of-the-slovak-republic, accessed 27 July 2011.

[30] *Consideration of Reports Submitted by States Parties Under Article 19 Of The Convention, Second Periodic Reports of States Parties due in 1998, Addendum, SLOVAK REPUBLIC**, 1 February 2007, available at: http://www2.ohchr.org/english/bodies/cat/docs/AdvanceVersions/CAT-C-SVK2.pdf, accessed 27 July 2011.

[31] These include: Council of Europe Convention for the Protection of Human Rights and Fundamental Freedoms (18 March 1992); International Convention on the Elimination of All Forms of Racial Discrimination (28 May 1993); International Covenant on Civil and Political Rights (28 May 1993); International Covenant on Economic, Social and Cultural Rights (28 May 1993); Convention on the Elimination of All Forms of Discrimination against Women (28 May 1993); Optional Protocol to the Convention on the Elimination of Discrimination against Women (17 November 2000); Convention against Torture and Other Cruel, Inhuman or Degrading Treatment or Punishment (28 May 1993); Convention on the Rights of the Child (28 May 1993) (Council of Europe 1950; UN General Assembly 1965, 1966, 1979, 1989, 1990, 1992, 1999; International Covenant 1966).

[32] Štatistického úradu Slovenskej republiky (Statistical Office of the Slovak Republic), *Population by Nationality—2001, 1991*, available at: http://portal.statistics.sk/showdoc.do?docid=7611, accessed 27 July 2011.

Eastern Slovakia was reported incidences of police abuse of Roma and of attacks taking place under the watchful eye of permissive and complicit police officials (US Department of State 1995). Some police made counter charges to pressure Romani victims of police brutality to drop their complaints and medical doctors and investigators were accused of cooperating with police by refusing to describe accurately the injuries involved; lawyers were often reluctant to represent Roma in such situations for fear this would have a negative effect on their practice (US Department of State 1996). In less than a decade, attacks by skinheads were commonplace and human rights groups noted the lack of police protection. Human rights monitors even suggested that the failure to protect Roma against racially motivated attacks was largely due to governmental complicity and institutionalised racism, with many police officers sympathising with the extremists who carried out the violence (Amnesty International 2002).

An additional source of concern was the way in which acts against Roma were described by law enforcement officials, who often dismissed the gravity of physical attacks and failed to recognise the racial motivation behind them (UNHCR 1998). Throughout 1999, the European Roma Rights Center published reports on police abuse in eastern Slovakia, including beatings, verbal attacks, and the shooting of Roma following police raids (European Roma Rights Center 1999a, 1999b). Their accounts were supported by human rights monitors that noted the deterioration of human rights over the following five years. Recorded abuses included: police brutality and lack of protection from racist violence (Amnesty International 1999; Human Rights Watch 2000); the illegal sterilisation of Roma women (European Roma Rights Center 2005); and discrimination against Roma in the fields of education, employment, housing, health, social care and access to services (US Department of State 2002, 2003).

Abuses during the acquis *process*

In December 1999, just as Slovakia was formally invited to begin accession talks with the European Council, human rights monitors reported on the rise in xenophobia (International Helsinki Federation 2004). The European Roma Rights Center (ERRC) documented many claims and noted three important trends in cases of police abuse. First, there was a disturbing rise in the nature of physical attacks, especially while victims were detained in police cells. Roma reported that they were slapped across the face and beaten with truncheons on the arms, legs and back, and were sprayed with tear gas before money was extorted; others noted that pistols were put into the mouths of children and witnesses during raids on Roma homes (European Roma Rights Center 2000c). Second, victims were forced to sign documents which have served as confessions and statements, often incriminating other Roma (European Roma Rights Center 2000c). Third, international monitors noted that doctors and lawyers for Roma victims were harassed and threatened; some anti-racist organisations were targeted with arson (Amnesty International 2002).

In 2001, there was another report of Slovak police officers killing a Roma while in detention. The account of Karol Sendrei, who died in a police station in Revuca, drew the attention of international monitors, not least because the local mayor was also accused of participating in the beating of the victim (European Roma Rights Center 2001b). By 2002, the numbers of reported racially motivated crimes had increased to 109 (US Department of State 2003). Similar accounts of abuse against Roma were described by international monitors. Moreover, the Slovak government was accused of consistent stonewalling (Amnesty International 2002, 2004a, 2004b; US Department of State 2002, 2003, 2004).

From 2002 onwards, police abuse was finally described in terms of torture. Amnesty International charged that the Slovak government permitted torture and ill-treatment of Roma by law enforcement agencies and that victims were not allowed to contact family members, lawyers or doctors of their choice, thus violating key international human rights provisions to which the state was a signatory (Amnesty International 2004). Following a visit to Slovakia, the Committee for the Prevention of Torture (CPT) found evidence of ill-treatment at the pre-trial phase.

The types of ill-treatment alleged consisted mostly of slaps, punches and kicks, or blows with hard objects such as batons; further, certain persons claimed that they had been struck with pistol-butts, flashlights or plastic bottles filled with water. In a notable proportion of the cases which came to the attention of the CPT's delegation, the alleged victims of ill-treatment were Roma. In a number of cases, the delegation gathered medical evidence consistent with the person's accounts of ill-treatment (Council of Europe 2006a, p. 51).

Post-accession developments up to the present

Since accession, successive Slovak governments have recognised the importance of addressing the Roma question but many illiberal practices have continued. For example, there have been repeated reports of sterilisation campaigns, which have drawn the attention of international monitors (Committee on the Elimination of Racial Discrimination 2010). Some reforms have been initiated, including creating a cabinet position for a representative of the Roma communities and a 10-year action plan for Roma inclusion, yet these have not fully addressed the scope of the problem. Moreover, official responses to human rights abuses have been met with stonewalling, denial, and in the case of illegal sterilisations of Roma women, outright duplicity (European Roma Rights Centre 2005). The government's reluctance to address the substantive criticisms made by international monitors is noted in the tone of reports that relate to the post-accession period including the most recent report by the US Department of State which identified extensive government and societal discrimination against Roma (US Department of State 2010). While noting reports of police mistreatment of Roma, the most disturbing feature of the Department of State report is that few racially motivated acts have resulted in prosecutions.

> Racially motivated attacks on minorities (Roma and others) were widely reported throughout the year, but investigation of attacks and law enforcement varied by jurisdiction. Of the 213 cases of racially motivated crimes during 2008, two cases of racially motivated assault involving serious injury resulted in convictions; 33 cases of violence against a racial or ethnic group resulted in convictions; and 178 cases of promoting and supporting extremist groups resulted in convictions. There were no prosecutions for racially motivated murder in 2008. (US Department of State 2010)

Since 2008 Slovakia has made some measurable progress, in spite of the criticism of the Council of Europe and other monitoring bodies. In 2009, Amnesty International reported that the Supreme Court confirmed the sentences of six former police officers who were convicted of ill-treatment and the unlawful death of Karol Sendrei, a 51-year-old Romani man who died in police custody in 2001. Further, in response to the outcome of the 2010 UN Human Rights Council's Universal Periodic Review, which had condemned Slovakia over the forced sterilisation of Romani women, Slovakia announced that it had adopted legislative measures, including requiring health workers to seek informed consent for sterilisation and the definition of a new criminal offence of 'illegal sterilisation', though it had not introduced guidelines for the implementation of these measures.

Analysis

The above case studies, though substantively different, provide two illustrations of the challenges of institutionalising reforms that can reach down to individuals and guarantee their protection, which are the first and second indicators of qualitative democracy. In the case of Slovenia, the ineffective workings of the judiciary prevented citizens, without distinction, from accessing their rights; the state was found to be ill-equipped to ensure that complaints could be dealt with in a timely manner. Individuals seeking legal remedies had to navigate through the complex and uncoordinated public administration and judicial bodies. The fluid structures within the judiciary, which permitted judges to refer cases to higher level courts, and back down again, further complicated the delivery of justice. The problems within the Slovenian justice sector are system-wide, as found by the European Court of Human Rights, yet the proposed remedies have only offered a partial solution to an immature judiciary which remains overburdened by complaints.

In the case of Slovakia, historical patterns of segregation and forced assimilation of Roma have contributed to the exclusion of this minority which remains vulnerable to abuse. Entrenched traditions of intolerance have been given new expression by far right-wing groups which have tested the state's recent commitments to protect the rights of the Roma and other minorities; yet, in spite of the introduction of international and European human rights instruments in domestic law, the police and court system have failed to uphold the rights of Roma in a consistent manner and, in some documented situations, there is evidence of police misconduct and ill-treatment of Roma. Though human rights monitors correctly distinguish between direct abuse by state agencies (such as the police) and violence perpetrated by non-state actors (such as skinheads), Slovakia's record in both preventing and prosecuting abuse against the Roma minority points to a central failure of democratic reform.

The third indicator of qualitative democracy, namely the degree to which political change is internally located, highlights the shallowness of reform in both Slovenia and Slovakia, which appears to have been provoked from outside. The lure of EU accession forced Slovakia to introduce action plans for the Roma minority, especially programmes aimed to address their social exclusion. These plans however, have neither been able to provide effective protection nor address deeper causes of violence and discrimination against Roma (US Department of State 2010). In the case of

Slovenia, although the Constitutional Court had ruled on the problems of undue delay, it was, primarily, the threat of a further ECtHR judgment from Strasbourg that precipitated the *Lukenda* programme of reforms.

While Slovenia and Slovakia represent two particular Central and East European states, the relevance of the above case studies for other instances of political transition is further borne out by the assessments of the European Union and the Council of Europe. The above findings also affirm the claims made by Pridham (2007) and Steunenberg and Dimitrova (2007) regarding the limited power of conditionality to instil normative change. This is particularly evident in Slovakia which has proved unable to constrain non-state parties which have abused Roma. Slovakia's human rights record has been further tarnished by evidence of ill-treatment and collusion by police in anti-Roma violence. Thus the reactive and short-term political reforms in Slovakia in particular have not created conditions for rights-reinforcing behaviour, as required for qualitative democratic change.

Conclusion

This essay claims that by comparing formal provisions and laws aimed at protecting human rights and comparing them against operational practices, one may arrive at a deeper understanding of political change. The concept of 'qualitative democracy' is introduced here to inform our understanding of democratic consolidation which is examined in rights-enforcing sectors, for example in the court system and police. The main findings of this essay are that two European Union states failed to ensure that the rights of significant sections of their public were enforceable through the courts and respected by law enforcement bodies. These findings therefore call into question claims of democratic consolidation in Slovenia and Slovakia. While most European states have struggled to prevent racist abuse against Roma populations within their borders, none have been identified for the degree of complicity and complacency shown by Slovak authorities over the past two decades. Equally, it should be recognised that while the justice sector is often among the last and most complicated sectors in which one may identify evidence of institutional reform, the number of unresolved cases in Slovenia is staggering for a country with such a small population.

By introducing the concept of qualitative democracy, and highlighting areas where reform has yet to reach down to individuals and guarantee their protection, this essay seeks to add to the literature on democratic change and political transition. Although Slovenia and Slovakia have distinct histories, the above study of qualitative democracy has greater regional relevance: Slovakia's challenges with its Roma population are not unrelated to those experienced by the governments of the Czech Republic or Romania; and Slovenia's huge backlog of cases and lack of administrative capacity are not dissimilar to some of the problems confronting Croatia and other neighbouring states which are seeking membership of the European Union (Blitz 2007). There is a need therefore for further qualitative assessments, including examinations of the justice sector, to evaluate the degree to which norms of behaviour and state practices are substantively transformed and embedded in Central and East European states.

Kingston University London

References

Amnesty International (1999) *Slovak Republic: Reported Ill-treatment of Roma by Police Officers*, Document Number EUR 72/01/99, 9 March, available at: http://web.amnesty.org/library/pdf/EUR720011999ENGLISH/$File/EUR7200199.pdf, accessed 31 January 2010.

Amnesty International (2002) 'Slovakia', in *Amnesty International Report 2002* (covering the period January–December 2001), available at: http://web.amnesty.org/web/ar2002.nsf/4e9e3156549cbcae80256a4e00588885/a81fdd95f7f5b26280256bc0003b391f/$FILE/slovakia.pdf, accessed 31 January 2010.

Amnesty International (2009) *Belarus: Ending Executions in Europe: Towards Abolition of the Death Penalty in Belarus*, Document Number EUR 49/001/2009, 24 March, available at: http://www.amnesty.org/en/library/asset/EUR49/001/2009/en/d3b9c42d-a356-4dee-ad16-5b05842ba01a/eur490012009en.pdf, accessed 1 November 2010.

Amnesty International (2010) *Amnesty International Report 2010—The State of the Worlds Human Rights*, pp. 287–98, available at: http://thereport.amnesty.org/sites/default/files/AIR2010_AZ_EN.pdf#page=234, accessed 27 July 2011.

Bebler, A. (2002) 'Slovenia's Smooth Transition', *Journal of Democracy*, 13, 1, pp. 127–40.

Blitz, B. K. (2006) 'Statelessness and the Social (De)Construction of Citizenship: Political Restructuring and Ethnic Discrimination in Slovenia', *Journal of Human Rights*, 5, 4, pp. 1–27.

Blitz, B. K. (2007) 'Democratic Development, Judicial Reform and the Serbian Question in Croatia', *Human Rights Review*, 9, 1, pp. 123–35.

Blitz, B. K. (2008) 'Post-Socialist Transformation, Penal Reform and Justice Sector Transition in Albania', *Journal of South East European and Black Sea Studies*, 8, 4, pp. 345–64.

Boucková, P. (2007) *Executive Summary—Czech Republic Country Report on Measures to Combat Discrimination* (European Network of Legal Experts in the Non-discrimination Field), available at: http://www.migpolgroup.com/public/docs/125.CzechRepublic_DiscriminationCountryReport_EN_01.07.pdf, accessed 31 January 2010.

Brusis, M. (2005) 'The Instrumental Use of European Union Conditionality: Regionalization in the Czech Republic and Slovakia', *East European Politics & Societies*, 19, 2, pp. 291–316.

Commission of the European Union (2009) *Albania 2009 Progress Report Accompanying the Communication from the Commission to the European Parliament and the Council Enlargement Strategy and Main Challenges 2009–2010* [COM(2009) 533] (Brussels, European Commission).

Committee on the Elimination of Racial Discrimination (2010) *Consideration of Reports Submitted by States Parties under Article 9 of the Convention Concluding Observations of the Committee on the Elimination of Racial Discrimination—Slovak Republic*, 15 February–12 March, available at: www2.ohchr.org/english/bodies/cerd/docs/co/CERD.C.SVK.CO.6-8.doc, accessed 8 November 2010.

Council of Europe (1950) *Convention for the Protection of Human Rights and Fundamental Freedoms as Amended by Protocols No. 11 and No. 14*, available at: http://conventions.coe.int/treaty/en/treaties/html/005.htm, accessed 27 July 2011.

Council of Europe (1992) *European Charter for Regional or Minority Languages*, Council of Europe, Strasbourg, 5.XI.1992, available at: http://conventions.coe.int/treaty/en/Treaties/Html/148.htm, accessed 1 November 2010.

Council of Europe (1995) *Framework Convention for the Protection of National Minorities*, Council of Europe, Strasbourg, 1.II.1995, available at: http://conventions.coe.int/Treaty/en/Treaties/Html/157.htm, accessed 1 November 2010.

Council of Europe (2006a) *Report to the Government of the Slovak Republic on the Visit to Slovakia Carried Out by the European Committee for the Prevention of Torture and Inhuman or Degrading Treatment or Punishment (CPT) from 22 February to 3 March 2005*, Document Number CPT/Inf (2006) 5 (Strasbourg, Council of Europe), available at: http://www.cpt.coe.int/documents/svk/2006-05-inf-eng.pdf, accessed 31 January 2010.

Council of Europe (2006b) *Response of the Government of the Slovak Republic to the Report of the European Committee for the Prevention of Torture and Inhuman or Degrading Treatment or Punishment (CPT) on its Visit to Slovakia from 22 February to 3 March 2005*, Document Number CPT/Inf (2006) 6 (Strasbourg, Council of Europe), available at: http://www.cpt.coe.int/documents/svk/2006-06-inf-eng.pdf, accessed 31 January 2010.

Council of Europe (2006c) *Rights of National Minorities in Latvia*, Council of Europe, Parliamentary Assembly, 8 November, Doc. 11094, available at: http://www.unhcr.org/refworld/docid/45659bf54.html, accessed 1 November 2010.

Council of Europe (2010) *Convention for the Protection of Human Rights and Fundamental Freedoms as Amended by Protocols Nos. 11 and 14* (Strasbourg, Council of Europe), available at: http://www.echr.coe.int/NR/rdonlyres/D5CC24A7-DC13-4318-B457-5C9014916D7A/0/ENG_CONV.pdf, accessed 27 July 2011.

Council of the European Union (2003) *Thessaloniki European Council 19 and 20 June 2003: Presidency Conclusions. Council of the European Union*, Brussels, 1 October, 11638/03 (POLGEN 55) (Brussels, European Council), available at: http://www.consilium.europa.eu/ueDocs/cms_Data/docs/pressdata/en/ec/76279.pdf, accessed 31 January 2010.

Council of the European Union (2006) *2006/54/EC: Council Decision of 30 January 2006 on the Principles, Priorities and Conditions Contained in the European Partnership with Albania and Repealing Decision 2004/519/EC* (Brussels, European Council).

Council of the European Union (2010) *Conclusions on Serbia 3040th GENERAL AFFAIRS Council Meeting Luxembourg, 25 October 2010*, available at: http://www.europa.rs/upload/documents/documents/news/GAC%20Conclusions%20-%20Serbian%20membership%20application.doc, accessed 8 November 2010.

Crowe, D. (1996) *History of the Gypsies of Eastern Europe and Russia* (New York, St Martin's Press).

Dedić, J., Jalušič, V. & Zorn, J. (2003) *The Erased: Organized Violence and the Politics of Exclusion* (Ljubljana, Mirovni Institut).

Eurofound (2011) *Quality of Work*, available at: http://www.eurofound.europa.eu/areas/industrial relations/dictionary/definitions/qualityofwork.htm, accessed 27 July 2011

European Commission (2005) 'Working Together for Growth and Jobs. A New Start for the Lisbon Strategy', *Communication from President Barroso in Agreement with Vice-President Verheugen, Brussels, 2.2.2005* [COM(2005) 24 final] (Brussels, European Council), available at: http://eur-lex.europa.eu/LexUriServ/LexUriServ.do?uri=COM:2005:0024:FIN:EN:PDF, accessed 30 January 2010.

European Committee for the Prevention of Torture (2009a) *Report to the Albanian Government on the Visit to Albania Carried Out by the European Committee for the Prevention of Torture and Inhuman or Degrading Treatment or Punishment (CPT) from 16 to 20 June 2008 Strasbourg, 21 January 2009*, available at: http://www.cpt.coe.int/documents/alb/2009-06-inf-eng.pdf, accessed 1 November 2010.

European Committee for the Prevention of Torture (2009b) *Report to the Latvian Government on the Visit to Latvia Carried Out by the European Committee for the Prevention of Torture and Inhuman or Degrading Treatment or Punishment (CPT) from 27 November to 7 December 2007*, Strasbourg, 15 December, available at: http://www.cpt.coe.int/documents/lva/2009-35-inf-eng.pdf, accessed 1 November 2010.

European Committee for the Prevention of Torture (2009c) *Report to the Lithuanian Government on the Visit to Lithuania Carried Out by the European Committee for the Prevention of Torture and Inhuman or Degrading Treatment or Punishment (CPT) from 21 to 30 April 2008*, Strasbourg, 25 June, available at: http://www.cpt.coe.int/documents/ltu/2009-22-inf-eng.pdf, accessed 1 November 2010.

European Court of Human Rights (ECtHR) (2005) *Lukenda v. Slovenija* (Application No. 23032/02), Judgment of the European Court of Human Rights from 6 October (Strasbourg, European Court of Human Rights).

European Court of Human Rights (ECtHR) (2006) *D.H. and Others v. Czech Republic*, 57325/00, Council of Europe: European Court of Human Rights, 7 February, available at: http://www.unhcr.org/refworld/docid/469e020e2.html, accessed 31 January 2010.

European Court of Human Rights (ECtHR) (2007) *Grand Chamber Case of D.H. and Others v. the Czech Republic* (Application No. 57325/00), Judgment of the European Court of Human Rights from 13 November (Strasbourg, European Court of Human Rights).

European Court of Human Rights (ECtHR) (2009) *The Pilot-Judgment Procedure: Information Note Issued by the Registrar* (Strasbourg, European Court of Human Rights), available at: http://www.echr.coe.int/NR/rdonlyres/DF4E8456-77B3-4E67-8944-B908143A7E2C/0/Information_Note_on_the_PJP_for_Website.pdf, accessed 31 January 2010.

European Court of Human Rights (ECtHR) (2010) *Case of Kurić and Others v. Slovenia*, 13 July, available at: http://cmiskp.echr.coe.int/tkp197/view.asp?action=html&documentId=871256&portal=hbkm&source=externalbydocnumber&table=F69A27FD8FB86142BF01C1166DEA398649, accessed 1 November 2010.

European Roma Rights Center (ERRC) (1998) *ERRC Calls for Investigation of Police Assault on Roma Settlement in Slovakia*, 2 November, available at: http://www.errc.org/cikk.php?cikk=168&archiv=1, accessed 31 January 2010.

European Roma Rights Center (ERRC) (1999a) *Abuse of Roma by Officials in Slovakia*, available at: http://www.errc.org/cikk.php?cikk=555&archiv=1, accessed 31 January 2010.

European Roma Rights Center (ERRC) (1999b) *Romani Man Shot in Police Custody in Slovakia*, available at: http://www.errc.org/cikk.php?cikk=968&archiv=1, accessed 31 January 2010.

European Roma Rights Center (ERRC) (2000a) *Police Abuse in Slovakia*, available at: http://www.errc.org/cikk.php?cikk=646&archiv=1, accessed 31 January 2010.

European Roma Rights Center (ERRC) (2000b) *More Disturbing Events in Slovak Police Custody*, available at: http://www.errc.org/cikk.php?cikk=1043&archiv=1, accessed 31 January 2010.

European Roma Rights Center (ERRC) (2000c) *More Police Abuse of Roma in Slovakia; Slovak Courts Don't Mind*, available at: http://www.errc.org/cikk.php?cikk=1228&archiv=1, accessed 31 January 2010.

European Roma Rights Center (ERRC) (2001a) *Legal Action in Slovak Police Killing*, available at: http://www.errc.org/cikk.php?cikk=1249&archiv=1, accessed 31 January 2010.

European Roma Rights Center (ERRC) (2001b) *Slovak Officials Kill Another Rom*, available at: http://www.errc.org/cikk.php?cikk=1707&archiv=1, accessed 31 January 2010.

European Roma Rights Center (ERRC) (2002a) *Police Brutality in Slovakia*, available at: http://www.errc.org/cikk.php?cikk=943&archiv=1, accessed 31 January 2010.

European Roma Rights Center (ERRC) (2002b) *Police Violence against Roma in Slovakia*, available at: http://www.errc.org/cikk.php?cikk=1636&archiv=1, accessed 31 January 2010.

European Roma Rights Center (ERRC) (2004) *Urgent Measures Needed to Address Deep-Seated Racism Issues in Slovakia*, 26 February, available at: http://www.errc.org/cikk.php?cikk=341, accessed 31 January 2010.

European Roma Rights Center (ERRC) (2005) *Helsinki Commission Statement Against Sterilisation without Consent*, available at: http://www.errc.org/cikk.php?cikk=2579, accessed 31 January 2010.

European Roma Rights Center (ERRC) (2007) *Mass Exodus of Roma to Canada, 15 August 1997*, available at: http://www.errc.org/cikk.php?cikk=139, accessed 27 July 2011.

Fribergh, E. (2008) *Pilot Judgments from the Court's Perspective*, Stockholm Colloquy, 9–10 June (Strasbourg, European Court of Human Rights), available at: http://www.echr.coe.int/NR/rdonlyres/43C75D00-0F57-4176-8A7C-0AE28DBD4EE8/0/StockholmdiscoursFribergh0910062008.pdf, accessed 31 January 2010.

Gargiulo, M. & Benassi, M. (1999) 'The Dark Side of Social Capital', in Leenders, R. & Gabbay, S. (eds) (1999) *Social Capital and Liability* (Dordrecht, Kluwer).

Government of the Czech Republic (2001) *The Charter of the Council of the Government for National Minorities, Published by the Government of the Czech Republic, Supplement to the Government Resolution Nr. 1034 from 10 October 2001*, available at: http://www.vlada.cz/assets/ppov/rnm/statut-rnm-en.pdf, accessed 1 November 2010.

Grabbe, H. (2006) *The EU's Transformative Power: Europeanization Through Conditionality in Central and Eastern Europe* (London, Palgrave Macmillan).

Haughton, T. (2007) 'When Does the EU Make a Difference? Conditionality and the Accession Process in Central and Eastern Europe', *Political Studies Review*, 5, 2, pp. 233–46.

Hughes, J. (2005) 'Exit in Deeply Divided Societies: Regimes of Discrimination in Estonia and Latvia and the Potential for Russophone Migration', *Journal of Common Market Studies*, 43, 4, pp. 739–62.

Hughes, J., Sasse, G. & Gordon, C. (2007) 'Europeanization and Regionalization in the EU's Enlargement to Central and Eastern Europe: The Myth of Conditionality', *Journal of Common Market Studies*, 45, 2, pp. 525–27.

Human Rights Watch (2000) 'Slovakia—"Human Rights Developments"', in *World Report 2000*, available at: http://www.hrw.org/wr2k1/europe/slovakia.html, accessed 31 January 2010.

Human Rights Watch (2004) *ICTY Justice at Risk: War Crimes Trials in Croatia, Bosnia and Herzegovina, and Serbia and Montenegro*, 14 October, pp. 12–13, available at: http://hrw.org/reports/2004/icty1004/, accessed 31 January 2010.

International Covenant (1966) *International Covenant on Civil and Political Rights Adopted and Opened for Signature, Ratification and Accession by General Assembly Resolution 2200A (XXI) of 16 December 1966*, available at: http://www2.ohchr.org/english/law/ccpr.htm, accessed 27 July 2011.

International Helsinki Federation (2004) 'Slovakia', in *Human Rights in the OSCE Region: Europe, Central Asia and North America, Report 2004 (Events of 2003)*, available at: http://www.ihf-hr.org/viewbinary/viewdocument.php?download=1&doc_id=5536, accessed 31 January 2010.

Kionka, R. & Vetik, R. (1996) 'Estonia and the Estonians', in Smith, G. (ed.) (1996) *The Nationalities Question in the Post-Soviet States* (London & New York, Longman), pp. 129–46.

Kochenov, D. (2008) *EU Enlargement and the Failure of Conditionality: Pre-Accession Conditionality in the Fields of Democracy and the Rule of Law* (Alphen aan den Rijn, Kluwer Law International).

Lampe, R. (2008) 'Slovenia', in Koziol, H. & Steininger, B. C. (eds) (2008) *European Tort Law 2006* (Vienna, Springer), pp. 417–28.

Linz, J. & Stepan, A. (1996) *Problems of Democratic Transition and Consolidation* (Baltimore, MD, Johns Hopkins University Press).

Ministry of Justice of Slovenia (2005) *Joint State Project—The Elimination of Court Backlogs: The Lukenda Project Operational Action Plan. Ljubljana, 12 December*, available at: http://www.mp.gov.si/fileadmin/mp.gov.si/pageuploads/2005/PDF/zakonodaja/The_Lukanda_Project-_v_ANGLESCINI.pdf, accessed 31 January 2010.

O'Donnell, G. A. (1996) 'Illusions About Consolidation', *Journal of Democracy*, 7, 2, pp. 34–51.

O'Donnell, G. A., Schmitter, P. C. & Whitehead, L. (eds) (1986) *Transitions from Authoritarian Rule: Southern Europe* (Baltimore, MD, Johns Hopkins University Press).

Office of the President of Albania (1998) *Albanian Constitution Approved by the Albanian Parliament on 21 October 1998*, available at: http://www.president.al/english/pub/doc/Albanian%20Constitution.pdf, accessed 1 November 2010.

Organization for Security and Cooperation in Europe (OSCE) (2005) *Organization for Security and Cooperation in Europe Mission to Croatia Status Report No. 17 On Croatia's Progress In Meeting International Commitments Since July 2005*, Report Issued 10 November, pp. 3–4, available at: http://www.osce.org/documents/mc/2005/11/17011_en.pdf, accessed 31 January 2010.

Organization for Security and Cooperation in Europe (OSCE) Mission to Croatia (2006) *2006 Review—Report On Croatia's Progress In Meeting International Commitments Since 2001*, Document Number C.FR/13/06, 9 June, available at: http://www.osce.org/documents/mc/2006/06/19522_en.pdf, accessed 31 January 2010.

Pavlin, P. (2006) 'Overview of the Contents of the Protection of the Right to a Trial without Undue Delay Act of the Republic of Slovenia of 2006', 4 December, unpublished manuscript.

Portes, A. (1998) 'Social Capital: Its Origins and Applications in Modern Sociology', *Annual Review of Sociology*, 24, pp. 1–24.

Pridham, G. (2007) 'Change and Continuity in the European Union's Political Conditionality: Aims, Approach, and Priorities', *Democratization*, 14, 3, pp. 446–71.

Pridham, G. (2008) 'The EU's Political Conditionality and Post-Accession Tendencies: Comparisons from Slovakia and Latvia', *Journal of Common Market Studies*, 46, 2, pp. 365–87.

Przeworski, A. (1986) 'Some Problems in the Study of the Transition to Democracy', in O'Donnell, G. A., Schmitter, P. C. & Whitehead, L. (eds) (1986).

Putzel, J. (1997) 'Accounting for the "Dark Side" of Social Capital: Reading Robert Putnam on Democracy', *Journal of International Development*, 9, 7, pp. 939–49.

Raik, K. (2004) 'EU Accession of Central and Eastern European Countries: Democracy and Integration as Conflicting Logics', *East European Politics & Societies*, 18, 4, pp. 567–94.

Ramet, S. P. (1998) 'The Slovenian Success Story', *Current History*, 97, 617, March, p. 113.

Republic of Croatia (2002) *Constitutional Law on the Rights of National Minorities*, Official Gazette, 155/22, 13 December, available at: http://www.vsrh.hr/CustomPages/Static/HRV/Files/Legislation__Constitutional-Law-on-the-Rights-NM.pdf, accessed 1 November 2010.

Republic of Serbia (2003) *Charter of Human and Minority Rights and Civil Liberties*, available at: http://www.mfa.gov.rs/Facts/charter_min.pdf, accessed 27 July 2011.

Republic of Slovenia (2006) *Constitution of the Republic of Slovenia*, available at: http://www.dz-rs.si/index.php?id=351&docid=25&showdoc=1, accessed 1 November 2010.

Schimmelfennig, F. (2007) 'European Regional Organizations, Political Conditionality, and Democratic Transformation in Eastern Europe', *East European Politics & Societies*, 21, 1, pp. 126–41.

Schopflin, G. (2002) *Nation, Identity, Power: The New Politics of Europe* (London, Hurst and Company).

Shlapentokh, V., Vanderpool, C. & Doktorov, B. (eds) (1999) *The New Elite in Post-Communist Eastern Europe* (College Station, TX, Texas A & M University Press).

Stepan, A. (1996) 'On the Tasks of a Democratic Opposition', in Diamond, L. & Plattner, M. F. (eds) (1996) *The Global Resurgence of Democracy* (Baltimore, MD, John Hopkins University Press).

Steunenberg, B. & Dimitrova, A. (2007) 'Compliance in the EU Enlargement Process: Institutional Reform and the Limits of Conditionality', in Josselin, J.-M. & Marciano, A. (eds) (2007) *Democracy, Freedom and Coercion: A Law and Economics Approach* (Cheltenham, Edward Elgar).

United Nations General Assembly (1965) *International Convention on the Elimination of All Forms of Racial Discrimination*, 21 December, United Nations, Treaty Series, vol. 660, p. 195, available at: http://www.unhcr.org/refworld/docid/3ae6b3940.html, accessed 22 July 2011.

United Nations General Assembly (1966) *International Covenant on Economic, Social and Cultural Rights*, Adopted and opened for signature, ratification and accession by General Assembly resolution 2200A (XXI) of 16 December 1966, available at http://www2.ohchr.org/english/law/cescr.htm, accessed 28 July 2011.

United Nations General Assembly (1979) *Convention on the Elimination of All Forms of Discrimination Against Women*, 18 December, United Nations, Treaty Series, vol. 1249, p. 13, available at: http://www.unhcr.org/refworld/docid/3ae6b3970.html, accessed 22 July 2011.

United Nations General Assembly (1984) *Convention against Torture and Other Cruel, Inhuman or Degrading Treatment or Punishment*, available at: http://www2.ohchr.org/english/law/pdf/cat.pdf, accessed 28 July 2011.

United Nations General Assembly (1989) *Convention on the Rights of the Child*, Adopted and opened for signature, ratification and accession by General Assembly resolution 44/25 of 20 November.

United Nations General Assembly (1990) *International Convention on the Protection of the Rights of All Migrant Workers and Members of their Families*, 18 December, A/RES/45/158, available at: http://www.unhcr.org/refworld/docid/3ae6b3980.html, accessed 22 July 2011.

United Nations General Assembly (1992) *Declaration on the Rights of Persons Belonging to National or Ethnic, Religious and Linguistic Minorities*, 18 December, A/RES/47/135, available at: http://www.unhcr.org/refworld/docid/3ae6b38d0.html, accessed 22 July 2011.

United Nations General Assembly (1999) *Optional Protocol to the Convention on the Elimination of All Forms of Discrimination against Women*, available at: http://www.un.org/womenwatch/daw/cedaw/protocol/text.htm, accessed 28 July 2011.

United Nations High Commissioner for Refugees (UNHCR) (1998) *Guidelines Relating to the Eligibility of Slovak Roma Asylum Seekers*, 10 February, available at: http://www.unhcr.org/refworld/docid/3ae6b31c54.html, accessed 31 January 2010.

United States Committee for Refugees and Immigrants (USCRI) (2007) *US Committee for Refugees and Immigrants World Refugee Survey 200—Europe*, 11 July, available at: http://www.unhcr.org/refworld/docid/469638801e.html, accessed 31 January 2010.

United States Department of State (1995) *Slovak Republic—Country Reports on Human Rights Practices for 1994*, released by the Bureau of Democracy, Human Rights, and Labor, February, available at: http://dosfan.lib.uic.edu/ERC/democracy/1994_hrp_report/94hrp_report_eur/SlovakRepublic.html, accessed 31 January 2010.

United States Department of State (1996) *Slovak Republic—Country Reports on Human Rights Practices for 1995*, released by the Bureau of Democracy, Human Rights, and Labor, March, available at: http://dosfan.lib.uic.edu/ERC/democracy/1995_hrp_report/95hrp_report_eur/SlovakRepublic.html, accessed 31 January 2010.

United States Department of State (2000) *Czech Republic—Country Reports on Human Rights Practices 1999*, released by the Bureau of Democracy, Human Rights, and Labor, 23 February, available at: http://www.state.gov/g/drl/rls/hrrpt/1999/325.htm, accessed 31 January 2010.

United States Department of State (2002) *Slovak Republic—Country Reports on Human Rights Practices—2001*, released by the Bureau of Democracy, Human Rights, and Labor, 4 March, available at: http://www.state.gov/g/drl/rls/hrrpt/2001/eur/8338.htm, accessed 31 January 2010.

United States Department of State (2003) *Slovak Republic—Country Reports on Human Rights Practices—2002*, released by the Bureau of Democracy, Human Rights, and Labor, 31 March, available at: http://www.state.gov/g/drl/rls/hrrpt/2002/18390.htm, accessed 31 January 2010.

United States Department of State (2004) *Human Rights Report on Country Practices-Slovak Republic*, released by the Bureau of Democracy, Human Rights, and Labour, 25 February, available at: http://www.state.gov/g/drl/rls/hrrpt/2003/27863.htm

United States Department of State (2006) *Slovak Republic—Country Reports on Human Rights Practices—2005*, released by the Bureau of Democracy, Human Rights, and Labor, 8 March, available at: http://www.state.gov/g/drl/rls/hrrpt/2005/61674.htm, accessed 31 January 2010.

United States Department of State (2007) *Macedonia—Country Reports on Human Rights Practices*, released by the Bureau of Democracy, Human Rights, and Labor, 6 March, available at: http://www.state.gov/g/drl/rls/hrrpt/2006/78826.htm, accessed 27 July 2011.

United States Department of State (2008) *Macedonia—2007 Country Reports on Human Rights Practices*, released by the Bureau of Democracy, Human Rights, and Labor, 11 March, available at: http://www.state.gov/g/drl/rls/hrrpt/2007/100571.htm, accessed 27 July 2011.

United States Department of State (2010) *Slovakia—2009 Country Reports on Human Rights Practices*, released by the Bureau of Democracy, Human Rights, and Labor, 11 March, available at: http://www.state.gov/g/drl/rls/hrrpt/2009/eur/136057.htm, accessed 1 November 2010.

Venice Commission (2010) *Opinion on the Act on the State Language of the Slovak Republic, Adopted by the Venice Commission at its 84th Plenary Session (Venice, 15–16 October 2010)*, available at: http://www.venice.coe.int/docs/2010/CDL-AD(2010)035-e.asp, accessed 1 November 2010.

Vetik, R. (1993) 'Ethnic Conflict and Accommodation in Post-Communist Estonia', *Journal of Peace Research*, 30, 3, pp. 271–80.

Vetik, R. (2001) *Democratic Multiculturalism: A New Model of National Integration* (Mariehamn, Åland Islands Peace Institute).

Vetik, R. (2002) 'The Cultural and Social Makeup of Estonia', in Kolstø, P. (ed.) (2002) *National Integration and Violent Conflict in Post-Soviet Societies* (Lanham, MD, Rowman & Littlefield), pp. 71–105.

Vetik, R. (2008) 'State Identity and the Cohesiveness of the Society's Public Sphere', in *Integration Monitoring of the Estonian Society 2008* (Tallinn, Integration Foundation and Bureau of Population Minister), pp. 164–79.
Vucetic, S. (2004) 'From Southern to Southeastern Europe: Any Lessons for Democratization Theory?', *Southeast European Politics*, V, 2–3, pp. 15–141.
Weissbrodt, D. (2008) *The Human Rights of Non-Citizens* (Oxford, Oxford University Press).
Zorn, J. (2009) 'A Case for Slovene Nationalism: Initial Citizenship Rules and the Erasure', *Nations and Nationalism*, 15, 2, pp. 280–98.
Zorn, J. & Lipovec Čebron, U. (2008) *Once Upon an Erasure: From Citizens to Illegal Residents in the Republic of Slovenia* (Ljubljana, Študentska založba).

Index

Page numbers in **bold** represent figures and tables